Limited Classical Reprint Library

# HEROES OF ISRAEL

BY

W. GARDEN BLAIKIE, D.D., LL.D.,

Foreword by
Dr. Cyril J. Barber

*Klock & Klock Christian Publishers, Inc.*
*2527 Girard Avenue North*
*Minneapolis, Minnesota 55411*

Originally published by
Thomas Nelson and Sons
London, 1894

40229

ISBN:  0-86524-082-5

Printed by Klock & Klock in the U.S.A.
1981 Reprint

# FOREWORD

One writer whose books I have always enjoyed reading is William Garden Blaikie (1820-1899), for many years a minister of the Free Church of Scotland and later Professor of Apologetics and Pastoral Theology, New College, Edinburgh. During his long and fruitful life, Dr. Blaikie authored his widely acclaimed *Bible History* (1859), *For the Work of the Ministry* (1873), *Glimpses of the Inner Life of Our Lord* (1876), *The Personal Life of David Livingstone* (1880), *The Public Ministry and Pastoral Methods of Our Lord* (1883), other important biographies of notable leaders in the Christian church, expositions in the *Pulpit Commentary* and *Expositor's Bible*, and numerous other works including his famous *David, King of Israel* (1861).

A graduate of the universities of Edinburgh and Aberdeen, Professor Blaikie later received an *honoris causa* D.D. from Edinburgh (1864) and was also the receipient of a Doctor of Laws degree from Aberdeen.

In his present work, *Heroes of Israel*, Dr. Blaikie briefly surveys the history of the Bible from Adam to Abraham. Then, beginning his character studies with the Patriarch, he discusses God's dealings with him and his successors, Isaac, Jacob and Joseph. This work is not brought to a close, however, until this revered author has also provided some excellent insights into the character and contribution of Moses. The excellent discussions deal with such varied themes as the domestic life of the people, the covenant, the principles of intercession, human vices as well as virtues, the providence of God in His dealings with His own, and the qualities of leadership which are so clearly portrayed in Moses, a person whom the writer of Hebrews describes as a "servant" who was faithful in all God's house.

These challenging chapters provide good models of the art of preaching on Bible characters. They also demonstrate how this kind of ministry lends itself to the application of truth to all of life. These features alone will make Dr. Blaikie's work one which pastors and lay Bible students will want to read again and again.

Cyril J. Barber, D. Lit.
Author, *The Minister's Library*

# PREFACE.

THIS volume was written at the suggestion of the late Mr. Thomas Nelson, among whose latest projects the issue of a series of Bible biographies, illustrated from the historical and topographical materials which modern research has supplied, had a prominent place.

The field has already been traversed in some degree by the present writer in his "Manual of Bible History in Connection with the General History of the World." But the limits of that book afforded little opportunity of doing what has been attempted here—to draw full-size portraits of some of the great men of the Bible, and to place them as living characters before the eye of the reader. The author is deeply sensible that while it is possible to throw no little light from modern sources on the Scripture narrative, it will ever retain, in its brevity, simplicity, and graphic power, that incomparable character which in all ages has been felt to be so emphatic an evidence of the divinity of its origin.

W. G. B.

# CONTENTS.

## PART I.

### Abraham and Isaac.

## PART II.

### Jacob and Joseph.

# PART III.

## Life of Moses.

# INTRODUCTORY.

I T is very remarkable that so large a portion of Scripture, and especially of the earlier part of it, should consist of biography. The circumstance is unique, for we find nothing of the kind in what are called the sacred books of other religions, and not much in books of history. It is easily explained when we consider that the great purpose of God in the Scriptures is to throw light, and to effect a change, on the relation between God and man —to picture that relation as it was originally, as it is now, and as, by God's grace, it may become. While God has revealed his will to us "at sundry times and in divers manners," he has not done so in the early books in systematic form. Instead of that, he has placed himself alongside of men as they trudged along the common paths of life ; he has taught us what he is himself by showing us how he dealt with them ; he has revealed his purpose somewhat after the manner of the philanthropist when he shows us pictures of his rescued children, first as they were, and then as they have become.

Now, biography is obviously well suited to this method of God's manifestation. It shows us God and man in actual contact ; it shows us the clay in the hands of the potter, the scholar in the hands of the teacher, the patient under the treatment of the physician. It is what may be called the clinical method. It takes us into the great hospital of the world, and, selecting certain individuals from the mass of patients, it shows us what was wrong

A

with them, and how it was put right. In carrying out such a plan, it is necessary to have a large number of cases, and to dwell on some more fully than on the rest. Hence the circumstance we have adverted to—the large portion of Scripture devoted to biography. And hence also the differences in the length of the biographies. We may have a biography in a single verse : " Enoch walked with God : and he was not; for God took him ;" or we may find, as in the case of Joseph, the biographer going elaborately into the details of his life. We may have lives of men in high positions, like David and Solomon ; or we may have biographies of shepherds—of men who in secular life were never more than shepherds —like Abraham, Isaac, and Jacob.

But in all, the supreme point of interest is—their relation to God. We see that men of all ranks and of all varieties of character are capable of being brought into a very close and blessed relation to him. They are capable of a vital connection whereby certain qualities of the divine Being flow into them under the modifications necessary to finite creatures. We call this the divine life in man. It is the glory of Scripture that it represents God as aiming at nothing short of this. It is the very opposite of the process, familiar to us in nature, whereby trees or animals are turned into fossils. In that case, stony matter takes the place of organic tissue ; in this, divine life penetrates and quickens inert souls. And when the change has been accomplished in the case of individuals, the way is prepared for a corresponding process in the case of communities. In the case of the individual, God first brings him near, allays his fears, pacifies his conscience, assures him of his good-will, and of forgiveness and acceptance when he repents and believes. Then he proceeds to assimilate him, to purge away his dross, to gain his will and his heart, to renovate his whole nature, with a result like that of the gilder when his earthen vessel shines in gold. And having by such means won individuals, he proceeds to win communities ; first, to place them under wholesome laws, and then to foster the love of what the laws require ; to awaken and diffuse a spirit of brotherhood, by making each interested in the welfare of all, and all in the welfare

of each; thus carrying out the favourite image of Scripture—
" The wilderness shall rejoice and blossom as the rose."

It is as bearing on this great object that the prominence of
biography in Scripture, and especially in the historical part of the
Old Testament, is to be vindicated. But there are likewise subordinate benefits of this method. The prevalence of biography
brightens the sacred page, and affords the opportunity for many a
vivid picture, many a striking anecdote, many a thrilling scene,
that touch the most sensitive parts of our being. Strip Old Testament history of its biography, and what would it be? Certainly
not the captivating record it often is to children, and hardly, we
think, the instructive book it is to the spiritual Christian. It is
because at every other page we make a new acquaintance, and a
remarkable acquaintance, that the Old Testament is so interesting
to most of us, and especially to children. It may be that at first a
child apprehends but little of what bears on the great point—man's
relation to God; but the foundation is admirably laid for insight
into that great subject in after years.

And, indeed, it is one of the objects of the New Testament to
help us to make the transition from the literal to the spiritual
aspect of Old Testament lives. How often does our Lord refer to
them! The days of Noah and the flood (Matt. xxiv. 37); the
Messianic hope of Abraham (John viii. 56); the awful effects of
worldliness in the case of Lot's wife (Luke xvii. 32); the angels of
God ascending and descending on the Son of man, as in Jacob's
ladder (John i. 51); the use made by Moses of the brazen serpent
(John iii. 14); David and his men eating the shewbread (Matt. xii.
4); the Queen of Sheba coming to hear the wisdom of Solomon
(Matt. xii. 42); the relation of Elijah to John the Baptist (Matt.
xvii. 12); the symbolic purport of the strange history of Jonah
(Matt. xii. 40)—are samples of our Lord's use of Old Testament
biography, and the enlivenment which it contributed to his dis-
courses. Then, besides the references in the epistles of St. Paul,
have we not, in the eleventh chapter of Hebrews, the choicest of
portrait galleries, all devoted to Old Testament biography? It is
a constellation of holy examples unrivalled in all literature—a

collection of brilliant pictures, remarkable in themselves, and remarkable for the setting in which they are there placed, followed by an appeal so thrilling that it would be a stolid heart that did not receive an impulse from the cloud of witnesses that are thus calling us to follow in their honoured footsteps.

We have said that the biographical character of the Old Testament narrative makes it more picturesque. Men's lives are spent in particular localities, and the life and the locality bear much upon each other. If we would thoroughly understand the life, we must have a vivid idea of the locality. The time was when in reading the Bible narrative men took little notice of place ; they connected the events with no locality in particular, but thought of them as occurring just in some indefinite portion of space—it hardly mattered where. That time has quite passed away. The last half-century has added immensely to our knowledge of Bible lands, and puts it in our power to fill in the local colouring, to picture out the surroundings of every incident, and thus greatly increase the vividness of the story. Even a sceptical writer like Renan can bear his testimony that a personal visit to Palestine is like a fifth Gospel for the life of Jesus. What new touches of reality and interest can be given to the Bible narrative by familiarity with the scenery could not be shown better than in the late Dean Stanley's " History of the Jewish Church." Under the graphic pen of that brilliant writer, events that used to loom vaguely in the distance are placed in the vivid form and colouring of a close inspection. The present writer would be gratified if, following in his footsteps in that respect, *sed longo intervallo,* he could do for the mass of readers what Dean Stanley has done for the learned. In several respects, however, the plan of this book is different, especially as being more biographical, and as keeping prominently in view the purpose of the Old Testament as a progressive revelation of the grace of God.

It is only when we come to Abraham that the characteristic biography of the Old Testament begins. The present work therefore starts with him. The preceding part of Scripture contains the history of at least two thousand years within the compass of eight or ten pages, and it could not be expected that much of that space would be devoted to biographical details. Yet the biographical tendency shows itself even there. It shows itself, however, under two peculiar conditions : in the first place, it does not introduce biographies, but only biographical fragments ; and in the second place, it is very sparing of topographical details. It is tolerably minute indeed in defining the locality of Paradise ; but somehow geographers have never been able to follow its delimitation, and except that the garden was somewhere in the neighbourhood of the river Euphrates, we have no certain knowledge of the spot where the history of our race began. In what precise spot Adam fixed his dwelling when expelled from Paradise ; where the tragedy of Cain and Abel occurred ; where Jabal set up his tents, and Tubal-cain had his forge, and Jubal gave his concerts ; where Noah had his great ship-building yard, or what parts of the earth had come to be inhabited before the flood—are all questions which we cannot answer. No more can we find a locality for Noah when he left the ark, except that it was somewhere in the region of Ararat ; and although the parts occupied by his sons and their descendants are carefully specified, there are none of the details that serve to vivify individual lives. Even tradition has failed to mark out spots to which pilgrims might direct their steps. But when we come to the history of the tower of Babel, we find the locality carefully described.

All this shows that the plan of narrative which is developed so fully from the time of Abraham was in the mind of the writer from the very first, although it could not be given full effect to, owing to the necessary brevity of the record. And it serves to show that there must be more in this biographical and geographical way of bringing out God's revelation to man than we have been accustomed to think. The first aspect which the biblical record presents to us is that of history. But when we examine it in detail, when we resolve the historical web into its component filaments, we find biography and geography very conspicuous. To these, therefore, we must give special attention, if we would thoroughly comprehend the biblical narrative. The object of the following work is to bring out their significance and value in this point of view.

Having made our beginning with Abraham, it will be useful here, by way of introduction, to glance briefly at the pre-Abrahamic period, and trace the narrow stream that begins there to expand into a copious river.

1. The case of Adam and Eve is so peculiar that the ordinary laws of biography cannot be applied to it. As individuals they do not impress us favourably. Adam in particular is wanting in manliness, throwing the blame of his transgression on the woman, whom, instead of following in her temptation, it was his part to direct and fortify towards higher things. It is strange indeed how little we see to admire and love in these the founders of our race, of whom it would be so natural to think as possessed of qualities that even in their wreck were noble and beautiful. But they are introduced to us for one purpose only, and all that is said of them bears on that. Their story shows us the nature of the relation there was originally between God and man ; it shows us also how that relation was wrecked ; and it gives us a hint as to how it is to be restored.

We see that as man was created in God's image, so he was privileged at first to enjoy his fellowship. God directs his life, furnishes him with employment, brings him his helpmeet, and comes into the garden in visible form to hold communion with him. The supreme condition of man's being is realized : he is in vital contact with his Maker, and in a position to receive all those influences whereby the divine life is sustained and advanced in him. For man even in his original state is not a self-contained creature capable of all growth, intellectual, moral, and spiritual, through forces inherent in him. He is no more independent of God than the globe which he dwells on is independent of the sun. Without the sun the earth would soon become a hard, dark, lifeless ball, "where all life dies, death lives," an abortion in the universe of God. It is the sun that brings it light and heat and genial influence ; that gives colour and brightness to earth and sea and sky ; that ripens the grain, and gives bloom and fragrance to flower and fruit, filling all with life and beauty. So a divine influence, of which the sun is the best emblem, must operate on man if he is to reach his prime—if his intellect is to become as rich, manifold, and commanding as it is capable of being, and if his moral and spiritual nature, kept steady and harmonious in every part, is to develop according to the highest standard.

In this happy relation to God man stood at first. This benign process of development he would have undergone, had he remained in that relation. The Bible record shows us how the relation was disturbed by man's sin ; how at one and the same time he lost God's favour and his fellowship ; how the force that had kept his nature in integrity and harmony was withdrawn, and a process of disorder and dissolution began, which was really death. At the same time God shows his interest in him by clothing him with skins—possibly a symbolical indication of another covering. And when uttering doom on the serpent, he announces that one day the woman's seed will gain a greater victory over him than he has now gained over her. The woman's seed will bruise the head of the serpent, and thus become a great deliverer. Man will rise above the cause of his ruin ; the Son of the woman will crush her seducer.

This is the great lesson from that earliest biographical fragment of Scripture, the history of Adam and Eve. It is the fundamental truth of all Bible history, the starting-point of all God's further dealings with man. For as the whole race of man shares the degradation which our first parents caused, so every member of it comes into the world under a changed relation to God. God retains his warm love for man ; but, being a sinner, man has forfeited his favour, and there is not now that communication of his highest influences on which man's welfare depends. The more man sins the greater is the gulf between him and God. But there is a provision for restoring the original relation ; and when it is restored, the result is truly blessed. Thus mankind come to be divided between those in whom the relation is restored, and those in whom it is not. The great current of humanity is seen flowing apart from God, and disorder and violence are the results. Only a portion of the race attain to the restored relation ; and even they are compassed with many infirmities. And thus mankind presents a conflicting aspect, for the two sections cannot agree ; and the collisions that occur between them are not trifling disturbances, but often fierce and fiery conflicts ending in death.

2. Of this we have a painful proof in the next fragment of biography with which Scripture presents us—that of Cain and Abel. Agriculture was at first man's only occupation, and the brothers were divided between its two departments—tilling the ground and tending flocks. Abel is presented to us as one in whom the normal relation to God was restored, and Cain as one in whom it was not. Both are worshippers of God, but in a different spirit ; the offering of the one is accepted, that of the other is rejected. Jealousy and envy rage in the bosom of Cain. He cannot rest till he gets rid of the brother whose very presence makes him uncomfortable, because it reminds him that he is doing wrong, and that God is at strife with him. When they are together in the field, Cain rises up against Abel and slays him. For this he is taken to task : the earth which has opened her mouth to receive his brother's blood seems to reproach him, his parents whose son he has slain cannot have him beside them, God cannot put up with him, and he becomes a fugitive and vagabond in the earth. He is the type of the godless seed, for he has shown in an awful manner to what depths of wrong and violence the God-forsaken spirit of man can go. He represents sin in its wildest form, overleaping every restraint, not recking even of a brother's life if that brother stands in its way. He typifies the men of violence and blood that have ravaged the earth from generation to generation, and proved the scourge and terror of their race. We note especially in him the selfishness that refuses to own any claim of his fellows—"Am I my brother's keeper?" Let every man look after himself, and, as far as he can, carry out his own projects, no matter what becomes of his brother !

Thus at the very threshold of Scripture we find God's anathema pronounced against that selfishness which has been the prolific mother of so much wrong and misery in the world. Whether it be the great soldier sacrificing thousands of lives to his ambition, or the lawless adventurer hunting down his fellow-men to make them slaves; whether it be the trader exercising all his craft and ingenuity to cheat his customer, or the master-workman making the cry of his defrauded labourers rise to heaven; whether it be might trampling on right, or cunning overreaching simplicity, or hypocrisy jilting truth, or wealth sucking the blood of poverty—everything of the kind, every unbrotherly transaction or habit, is placed under God's ban before we have turned the second page of the Bible.

3. The next fragment of biography gives a glimpse of a family history. Lamech is of the line of Cain—an independent, wilful, self-pleasing man. He violates the law which God virtually made when he joined one man and one woman, for it is his pleasure to have two wives—Adah and Zillah; he makes short work of a young man who, according to the Revised Version, has wounded him, for he takes his life; he disposes of the fears of his wives, who are alarmed at the blood-stain on his hands, by a confident assurance that he is more than safe; and he defies public opinion by composing and publishing a ditty in which he seems to glory in his deed,—

" Adah and Zillah, hear my voice ;
Ye wives of Lamech, hearken unto my speech :
For I have slain a man for wounding me,
And a young man for bruising me.
If Cain shall be avenged sevenfold,
Truly Lamech seventy and sevenfold."

Strong, fearless, determined, and selfish, he is manifestly the leading man of his time, and a very dangerous leader he is ; and as for his sons, whether or not they share his spirit, they certainly inherit his ability. Jabal invents tents or movable dwellings, making the business of the shepherd, the herdsman, the traveller, and the warrior much easier; Jubal is a great musician, "father of all such as handle the harp and pipe;" and Tubal-cain is a great mechanist, "the forger of every cutting instrument of brass and iron."

Thus from the members of this single family comes a great advance in civilization, a great progress both in the mechanical and the fine arts—in all, in short, that ministers to the usefulness and the pleasantness of life. The ungodly seed naturally bestow much pains on promoting the enjoyment of life, that being the object which commends itself to them most; and in this they are often successful. No blame is insinuated against them for their improvements; but there is always a risk that when civilization advances rapidly, without the regulating or moderating influence that comes from the fear of God, it will breed corruption and hasten dissolution. It puts enormous power into the hands of individuals that is often used to the hurt of the race; it facilitates the creation of weapons of destruction that may be brought to bear with terrific effect on all who stand in their way; and it encourages a listless, luxurious, voluptuous style of living which saps the virtue and energy of the community. These results seem to have flowed from this early development of civilization, and to have contributed to the result when all flesh having corrupted its way, and the earth being filled with violence, it became necessary to destroy it by the flood.

4. A biographical glimpse of a very different kind is given us in connection with the family of Seth, the son of Adam who represented the godly seed. It was many generations after Seth when Enoch was born, and we have no information whatever of the circumstances or conditions of his life. But what little is said of him shows that, amid the growing corruption of the times, he realized in the highest and fullest sense the divine life in the soul of man. "Enoch walked with God." The spiritual thermometer has never marked a higher point than this, nor can we well conceive how a higher point could be reached by men breathing the atmosphere of this world.

Our reverence for this saintly man is greatly increased when we learn that almost alone of mankind he left this world by another gate than that of death: "He was not; for God took him." He was evidently a bright and shining light, and the impression of his life and character must have been all the greater from the comparatively early period of life at which he was lost to his race; for the whole term of his life was not much more than one-third of the period then common, so that he must have left behind him the fresh and fragrant memory which a young man prematurely cut off leaves among us.

No more impressive picture could have been found of the right relation between God and man. Athwart the growing gloom of the sky his light shone with a steady lustre, and bore a testimony which no sophistry could dim. In the age when he lived it is probable that unbelief was loud and contemptuous, deriding all pretence to real religion, and practically denying the existence of God and of a life to come. Like a rock in the ocean over which the surf breaks in vain, Enoch stood forth a witness for God that could not be gainsaid. His life spent visibly among men testified to the divine fellowship that purified and elevated it, and his departure by a translation bore conclusive witness to the life to come. The exceeding quietness with which both his life and his translation are recorded increases the effect. It is not in this way that men are accustomed to deal with legends. If we take the legendary translation of the Virgin as a sample, represented in paintings without number with all the attractions of the highest art, we see the kind of commotion and embellishment with which an event of this sort is set forth by men. The very calmness and simplicity of the narrative of Enoch has something awful about it. As we read it, we are like Moses at the burning bush—our very instincts tell us that the place whereon we stand is holy ground. His history must have been a great encouragement to the faithful few found among the faithless in an age of growing corruption and forgetfulness of God. How far it served, directly and indirectly, to arrest the growing corruption and delay the judgment of the flood we cannot tell. But if one sinner destroyeth much good, one righteous man is not less efficient in his way. One Enoch, one Abraham, one Elijah, one Paul, one Luther, one Wesley—what marvellous good has been done by individual men!

5. The last of our biographical fragments concerns the life of Noah. It is not easy for us to understand all the statements we

find of the growing corruption of the times. Much of it is ascribed to the promiscuous intercourse of beings of a higher order with the daughters of men. It is certain that the case had become very desperate when, speaking of the race of man, God said to Noah, " The end of all flesh is come before me ; for the earth is filled with violence through them ; and, behold, I will destroy them with the earth." Noah was the great-grandson of Enoch, and knew like him the life of divine fellowship. " Noah walked with God." On his birth, a prophetic indication seems to have come to his father of the beneficent character of his life—" This same shall comfort us for our work, and for the toil of our hands, because of the ground which the Lord hath cursed."

That his piety began in youth seems to be implied in the statement, " Noah was a righteous man, and perfect [or blame-less—*marg.*] in his generations." Such a record would not have been written of one who began life recklessly, and, like a prodigal son, was not recovered to godliness till an ugly and evil history had gathered on his youth. However brilliant service men recovered from vice may render to God, with whatever intensity they may throw their souls into his service, as if to make up for talents squandered and much mischief done in early life, there is something in the calm, steady tread of one who has never wandered far from the narrow path, but has consistently and uniformly served God, that fits him better than the other for a course of long, patient, persevering testimony against the evil of the world and of resistance to its ways.

It was work of this kind that was appointed to Noah. For six hundred long years he had to stand against the world, and testify, always by his life and often with his voice, against its ungodly ways. No man could have done this that did not walk with God. The divine communion which he enjoyed replenished and invigorated his springs of activity and resistance, and kept him from yielding to the feeling of weariness and discouragement which cannot but come to all who have little success in trying and arduous work. Noah's duty seems to have been somewhat like that of Elijah in the days of Ahab and Jezebel, when iniquity had come in like a flood. New forms of wickedness were constantly coming into practice, against which it was necessary for him to raise his voice. Often, like Jeremiah, he may have cried out, " Woe is me, my mother, that thou hast borne me a man of strife!" Like Elijah, he may have known temptations that would have driven him into the wilderness had he yielded to their power. All men claim our respect and honour who abide patiently at an irksome post. The garrison that will not surrender, though wounds and death and sickness have deprived it of half its number ; the martyr who will not give in, though day by day he gets a fresh turn of the rack, and every hour in his dreary cell brings its new instalment of pain and misery ; the maiden that will not give up her betrothed for all the taunts and arguments of worldly parents intent on a high connection—all command our approval. And so surely must this man of God, when he abode so long and so faithfully at the unpopular task of condemning the world and warning it of coming destruction.

We have a better knowledge of Noah from the brief memoir of Scripture than of any other man before Abraham. We readily realize the ridicule he must have encountered all the time the ark was preparing, which one passage seems to indicate was a hundred and twenty years (Gen. vi. 3). We are interested to find that all his family went with him into the ark, which seems to imply that he had that union of geniality and earnestness which in matters of religion usually draws children to follow in their father's steps. Even Ham was induced to take this step, though so undutiful afterwards. It seems certain that Noah was a man of substance, and that in entering the ark he had to abandon lands and houses and flocks. We can hardly think of him but as an adept in the mechanical arts when he undertook the construction of such a fabric. As little can we suppose him not to have had a full knowledge of natural history when he could superintend the gathering of all the living creatures that were collected there. For it is a principle of God's government not to bring in the supernatural till the natural is exhausted ; so that whatever exercise of supernatural power there may have been in connection with these things, it could only have been as supplementing, not superseding, the exertions of Noah.

But what shines in Noah above all other features is his faith. All that he does and endures, he does and endures in the belief that it is the will of God. Whatever is God's will must be right, and whoever does God's will must prosper in the end. No amount of ridicule can disturb a man who has these convictions. He is in partnership with God, and what he cannot do God will.

The strength of Noah's domestic affection is apparent from a statement in Hebrews (xi. 7) that he prepared the ark " to the saving of his house." Here is the touch of nature that makes us kin. This great spiritual giant can feel his soul thrilled by the thought of danger to wife and children, and is impelled to bestir himself for their protection. Amid the vast bearings of an event that affects the wide earth, and that threatens destruction to untold millions, he can be specially moved by imagining the terror-stricken faces of his children, and from their cries derive an impulse to the tremendous enterprise which will secure their safety. It is an interesting illustration of the manner in which a supreme regard to the will of God may be buttressed and strengthened by inferior and yet very genuine considerations. All depends on the relative place which they occupy : if God's will be first, the other will come in as it should ; if even family affection be before God's will, there is a reversal of the true order, from which evil must ensue.

Many a writer has employed his genius in imagining Noah entering the ark, and has given expression to his probable feelings as the waters gradually rose and submerged the earth. Of this experience of the patriarch we do not attempt any lengthened delineation. The prevailing feeling in his mind at first, beyond all doubt, was thankfulness for the safety of himself and his family. This, too, is the first and strongest feeling of every believing father who, besides being saved himself, finds his children saved around him. But it is not a feeling that lasts for ever. In the case of Noah other experiences would soon arise. Anxiety for the safety of the ark itself might sometimes flit across him ; and after the flood had attained its height, he might wonder whether the waters would ever abate, and whether a home on dry land would be found anywhere for him and his family.  Again and again we think of him rallying his faith by recalling God's promise and remembering his faithfulness.  His sending forth the raven and the dove in order to ascertain whether the waters had yet abated, showed that light on that subject was only to be obtained by natural means.  How gladly he welcomed the dove when she returned with the olive leaf—what a flood of emotion rushed over him at this token that nature was returning to itself, that the old aspect of things was coming round, that he might look soon for release from the ark, with all its strange and bewildering associations—we can hardly conceive.

But now another consideration must have taken a deep hold of his mind.  Here was he, the only survivor of the old race, and the head of the new.  What a responsibility !  The old race had been destroyed for sins which had become unbearable ; how might a new race be reared free from the wickedness of the old ?  What a charge was laid on him, to give such a start to the new generation that they should not relapse into the old ways, but serve God better than their fathers !

The great lesson of the flood to Noah was, that separation from God meant destruction.  Sooner or later it must come to this.  Just as there are some trees which, after they are cut down, send out buds and leaves for a time, but must ultimately lose every trace of life, so there are some men that may for a time evince no little of virtuous habit ; but unless their roots are in God, they must wither in the end.  The destruction of the whole race of man showed the result of unchecked sin.  When sin is finished, it bringeth forth death.  That submerged world had deliberately cut the roots of connection with God, and there it was.  Only by close fellowship with God had Noah himself been preserved from perishing with the rest.  How shall the vital connection with God be preserved for the generations that are to come ?  Of course Noah was not bound to answer this question for all time.  He was responsible only for himself and his family.  But it was a solemn question, and to one about to launch the human family on a new career it must have been profoundly impressive.

At last Noah leaves the ark on the mountains of Ararat, and descends to some part of the Armenian plains, to begin life anew with his sons. But before he quits the ark he has a solemn service. He builds an altar, and he takes of every clean beast and every clean fowl and offers a burnt-offering to the Lord. Here is the fullest account of ancient worship in pre-Abrahamic times. It was followed by the expression of the divine satisfaction and blessing, and by the assurance that never again should the ground be cursed for man's sake, nor every living thing destroyed. And inasmuch as the destruction of the race might have seemed to imply that human life was of no great value in God's sight, it was required of Noah that when animals were used as food, their blood, the token of their life, should not be eaten; and that whoever shed the blood of his brother should thereby forfeit his own. To confirm his promise, God was pleased to throw it into the form of a covenant, and the rainbow was made the token or sign of it. As often as men looked on the " immortal arch " they were to regard it as a sign that however deep men might sink in wickedness, they would never again undergo such a punishment. This covenant was a foreshadow of the covenant with Abraham, and, later, of God's covenant dealings with the nation of Israel.

Thus, for the second time, the human race is started on its career. And it seems started now under more hopeful auspices than before; for the head of it is a man whose relation to God has been tested and secured in an unprecedented way, and whose family, having also come through an extraordinary ordeal, may be reasonably expected to follow in his steps. The great lesson of early history has been written with a pen of iron; the difference between a right and a wrong relation to God has been proclaimed as with a voice of thunder. To break away from God has been shown to be ruin; to wait on him in faith and filial trust, life and salvation.

But a dark cloud, rather two dark clouds—one springing out of the other—rise on the fair prospect. " Noah began to be an husbandman, and he planted a vineyard : and he drank of the wine, and was drunken ; and he was uncovered within his tent." We find in this statement something more serious than those persons suppose who think that this was merely the result of the accidental discovery of the intoxicating quality of the fermented grape. It is so solemnly put as to denote something far more serious. Through what cause Noah thus fell we cannot tell. Whether, after passing through the tremendous ordeal of the flood, he fell . into the snare of self-confidence, and ceased to watch and pray ; or whether his case was that of many who, feeling their weakness in great trials, cast themselves at such times on God, but thinking nothing of little trials go carelessly into them ; or whether, depressed by the sad catastrophe which he had witnessed, he found in the intoxicating influence of the vine a soothing balm, like the waters of Lethe, which for the moment set him free from his sadness,—the distressing truth which the historian makes no effort to conceal is, that he drank to excess, and lay uncovered in his tent.

Is all his past life hereby vitiated ? Has he been a hypocrite all the time ? That is a supposition which cannot in any fairness be entertained. But most certainly the integrity of his character is broken, and in his old age he is found guilty of a sin which would have horrified him in his youth. And it bodes ill for the new race of which he is to be the father. When Noah falls, notwithstanding all his past fellowship with God, notwithstanding the awful lesson on sin which the flood had taught him, and notwithstanding the high responsibility under which he lay as father of the new race, what may we expect of his descendants ? How can the stream rise above its source ? Already we begin to fear that the new departure for the human race is to end no better than the old ; for the man that of all others might have been expected to stand the test most firmly has been weighed in the balances, and found wanting.

And this fear grows more and more when we see the behaviour of his son Ham. There is no filial piety in his soul. And the man who has no piety towards his father can have no reverence for God. From Ham's side of the house we can look for nothing good or great. The lessons of the flood have been lost on him, and the old corruption may be expected to burst forth unchecked among his descendants. Thus one-third of the human family is already shut out from all our hopes of reformation ; and with regard to the other two-thirds, when we see such traces of disease lingering in Noah, the root, we cannot look for perfect soundness in the branches. Our hopes of a great improvement in the new race are greatly damped, and our anticipations of the future are bathed in gloom.

It is difficult to say with accuracy how long time elapsed between the flood and the call of Abraham. The chronology of the period is briefly adverted to in the following treatise (pp. 11, 12), and a leaning expressed towards the system of the Septuagint, which gives an interval of about twelve hundred years between these events. Whatever the interval may have been, its history is almost entirely a blank. The tenth chapter of Genesis is a very important and valuable document, as giving the genealogy of the sons of Noah, and the probable origin of many of the great nations of antiquity. But it gives no hint of the moral or spiritual history of our race. A few glimpses may be got from some of the recently disinterred monuments of antiquity, but they are so fragmentary and incomplete that no systematic history can be constructed from them.

In the Bible record, the only specific event recorded of that period is the building of the tower of Babel. In a biographical point of view, it is remarkable that this part of the record is wholly anonymous—no man's name is given in connection with it. To some degree this want of information is compensated by the geographical details connected with the tower. It is said that the idea of building it occurred as men were travelling from the east—or in the east, as the Revised Version has it ; the point of view being Canaan, with reference to which Babylonia was in the east, or north-east. They reached the plain of Shinar, a plain where there was no building-stone, but an inexhaustible supply of clay, and of slime or bitumen, which served for mortar. The enormous remains of brick buildings in that quarter abundantly attest this statement as to the facilities and materials for building.

The project proposed was a vast tower, whose top should reach
to heaven—an exaggeration, no doubt, but manifestly denoting a
height that in that level plain would make the tower conspicuous
in every direction. The tower was designed to serve as a bond
of union. It was to be a rallying-point for all the surrounding
population, who were naturally tending to separation and dispersion, and liable to gather round little centres and to form new
communities apart from the rest. The nameless leaders of the
movement deemed this an evil tendency. They desired to concentrate the united energies of the whole race in one spot, and to
constitute one vast dominion, that should be able to command the
services and direct the energies of the most distant portions. Out
of the entire mass of humanity they wished to construct one vast
engine, which should be worked from the city conspicuous for its
colossal tower. The danger was, that should the design succeed,
and should the engine fall into bad hands, it would be used as an
instrument of oppression and tyranny, and become the scourge of
the race. The after-history of mankind showed too plainly that
concentration of great power in one centre and in one ruler was
no benefit but a great evil. It was a plan for magnifying and
glorifying man—for taking the destinies of the world into his own
hands, and counteracting the great law of dispersion and de-
centralization. It seems to have been chiefly for this reason that
the plan met with the opposition of God. It is remarkable that
one of the favourite maxims of modern political wisdom favours
the distribution, not the concentration, of power. Distribution is
favourable to liberty, concentration to despotism. By the confusion of tongues the Lord defeated the plan, vindicated national
liberty, laid the foundation for a wide dispersion of men, and likewise for the gathering of them into distinct nations and social
bodies—a process which seems hitherto to have hardly begun.

Some of the corresponding legends—for instance, the classical
fable of the Titans piling Mount Ossa upon Pelion in order to
reach Olympus—ascribed to their project a purpose resembling that
of Satan and his angels in their rebellion against God. The spirit
of the undertaking, as a man-glorifying project, was certainly very

ungodly, but its avowed object does not seem to have been of this sort. Indeed, if the existing ruin at Borsippa be the remains of the tower of Babel, it was a building with a religious basis, its seven stories or stages bearing the names of the seven planets, and being apparently designed to subserve the worship of the gods. But the main reason why the building of the tower of Babel and the dispersion which followed it are introduced in this part of the Bible record seems to be, not so much to exemplify the wickedness of man, as to show how the way was prepared for the new departure which God was about to make in his mode of dealing with mankind. As distinct nations had hardly existed hitherto, specific dealings with particular peoples could not have taken place. The dealings of God were mainly with the human race as a whole ; and being thus diffused, were of little avail. The development of nations, however, altered the state of things, and made it possible for God to adopt a new method, whereby for two thousand years to come his express revelations should be made to one family and one nation.

The period between the flood and the call of Abraham seems to have been much quieter than the previous age, when "the earth was filled with violence." The evolution of evil seems to have been more in the direction of idolatry allied to sensuality. But this evolution of idolatry was very disastrous, and threatened the extinction of the light and the destruction of the worship which had come down from Noah. A great risk arose that the knowledge of the true God would be entirely lost, and as men could not come into a right relation to a God whom they did not know, that the whole race would fall into that state of ruin which is involved in entire separation from him.

It pleased God, therefore, to adopt a new method of revealing himself to men, and promoting a right relation between them and himself. It pleased him to select a particular nation with whom he was to come into the closest national relation, and to whom he was to make such communications and revelations of his will as were needful from time to time. The greater concentration which God's dealings might in this way have was not the only advantage of this method. It admitted of the social principle in religion being brought much more fully into play. It admitted of a social community being formed, all the parts of which should be related to each other, so that by mutual action and reaction the religious influence and impression might become stronger and more general. It admitted of a thorough system of laws being prescribed favourable to the great object of the movement, and having a wholesome restraining effect even on those who were out of sympathy with their spirit. It admitted, moreover, of a system of worship directed in all its parts to the great end, and administered by a body of priests who might be expected to enter sympathetically into the divine plan. It admitted of the whole affairs of the nation being carried on with an immediate reference to the will of God, so that the nation should become a theocracy, guided throughout by divine rules and principles, which should be seen resulting in remarkable order, prosperity, and happiness. The plan was well fitted to correct that great abuse in religion, the parent of unnumbered evils, that the service of God is but a department in human life, to be carefully attended to by mechanical observances, leaving all the rest of life to be regulated by other considerations. According to the new method, the divine will was to be the grand pervading rule for every action of every life. Thus the kingdom of God was to be built up on earth, and, not the professional priesthood only, but the whole nation was to be a kingdom of priests.

This new departure began with the call of Abraham. Before the coming of Christ, that was the most important event in the spiritual history of the world.

---

*NOTE ON THE PROPOSED RECONSTRUCTION*
*OF HEBREW HISTORY.*

In present circumstances it would hardly be right to present a connected view of Old Testament biographies, mainly on the old lines, without some reference to the new theory of Hebrew literature and history—a theory that calls for a reconstruction of the early history of Israel, and the abandonment of what is called the old or traditional view. It is true that the department of biography is not directly affected by the proposed change—at least as it is put by believing critics; but even biography would need to be looked at from a new point of view if the reconstruction contended for should be accepted.

We say "as put by believing critics," for there is another class of scholars, chiefly foreign, who throw overboard, not only the inspiration of Scripture, but the entire supernatural basis of Scripture history. It is by these critics that the new view of Hebrew literature and history has been originated and worked out; and worked out, we must say, with extraordinary industry and ingenuity. But there is another class of critics, chiefly English, to whom the researches of the unbelieving scholars have so far commended themselves that they accept their view of the origin of the Hebrew books and history, while still holding the inspiration of the one and the supernatural basis of the other. It is with this class of theologians alone that we can discuss the question, Is the traditional view to be retained, or must it be abandoned in favour of the new? We should be sorry to follow the example of some who have disregarded the distinction between the two classes of scholars, and have ascribed to the one all the offensive and pernicious views which are chargeable against the other. Whatever may be thought of the drift and tendency of the views of the more believing section, full credit ought to be given for their earnest desire to conserve the inspiration of the books and the supernatural basis of the history.

So far as the Book of Genesis is concerned, the views of the critics have met with very general acceptance. According to them, Genesis is not a single narrative, but a compound of two or rather three or more narratives, that are not always fused into each other so as to present a united whole, but run parallel, the various narratives supplementing each other. The first distinction observed between different parts of Genesis lay in the systematic use of the name Jehovah (LORD) in some parts, and in other parts Elohim (God). Afterwards it was contended that there must have been two Elohist writers, for though both used the name Elohim, their style otherwise was not similar.  The present contention is, that one of these Elohist writers (sometimes known as the second Elohist, and more frequently as the author of "the priestly code") laid down the framework of the book, and made use of the two other documents, which had been written previously, in filling up details.  This theory of different documents having been used in the composition of Genesis commends itself as explaining little discrepancies in the narrative not otherwise to be accounted for.  We may understand, for example, how it should be said in one place that Noah took two of every clean beast into the ark, and in another seven.  The divine guidance under which the compiler of the book constructed it did not require him to correct every slight discrepancy there might be between the several narratives.  In composing the book he acted under the inspiration of God ; but it was not necessarily implied that every word in the narratives of which he made use was written under divine inspiration.  In some cases that might be, but for the most part all that was guaranteed was their accuracy as vehicles of historical information —as the setting or framework of God's supernatural revelation of himself in connection with the history of Israel.

No one has assigned the composition of Genesis to an earlier author than Moses, and as the events recorded took place hundreds and even thousands of years before his day, it was indispensable that the author, whoever he was, should have made use of earlier materials.  As to the age of the various narratives, opinions have differed greatly, and some critics contend that even the oldest of them was much later than Moses.  For this, however, there is no real authority, and the theory of various documents is quite compatible with the Mosaic authorship of the book.

It is probable that some of the other historical books of Scripture are constructed on a similar plan, and that more than one earlier document was used by their authors.  Sometimes reference is expressly made to some of these sources, as for instance in the Books of Kings and Chronicles.  According to the critics, the same writers are to be traced from Exodus to Joshua, and the hand of the author of "the priestly code" may be seen clearly in much that was written after the return from the captivity.

But this contention of the critics has by no means met with the same acceptance as the other. It is frankly acknowledged by Driver and others that even in Exodus, and still more in later books, the traces of the earlier writers are by no means so clear as in Genesis. In fact, the weakest position of the critics is their claim to be able to separate not only paragraph by paragraph but line by line of the Pentateuch and the historical books, and assign each fragment to a separate author. In reality there is no sufficient ground for believing that all that falls under "the priestly code" was written by the same author. Nothing is more natural than that the style of writers of the same school, continuing the same work from age to age, should have a resemblance to that of their predecessors. This is really all that can be reasonably alleged.

It used to be said that among the Jews the art of writing was unknown till a late period, and that there could be no written records so early as Moses. But the Tell-el-Amarna tablets recently discovered in Egypt show that in that country, as well as in Canaan and adjacent lands, writing was long before a familiar art ; and can it be supposed that one educated as Moses was in Egypt should not be familiar with it? It is admitted that some parts of the Pentateuch and the early historical books, such as the song of Moses, the song of Deborah, and the like, are of very early date, and this is ascribed to the practice of committing such pieces to memory ; but it is just as easy to believe that they were committed to writing. And as for the allegation that the Jews were not a literary people till about the eighth century before Christ, it can be shown that even the Canaanites, who were before them, had cities—like Kirjath-sepher ("city of books")—whose very names were derived from their literature ; and the day may come when from the ruins of these cities there shall be disinterred substantial evidence of this, perhaps in the form of clay tablets like those in the British Museum that give us so vivid an impression of early Assyrian literature.

But a far more serious position is that which has been taken up by the critics in connection with the origin of the books of the law, and the manner in which the law itself was developed in the history of the people. It is admitted on all hands that what is generally known as the law of Moses does not consist of one uniform, harmonious code, but that in point of fact we have various codes in various parts of the Pentateuch, and that in some of these we find enactments not in very strict accord with other passages, as if the various codes had not been given at the same time.

According to the modern view, the Pentateuch contains at least three codes. The earliest in date is that of Ex. xx.–xxiii., containing the ten commandments, certain "judgments," mostly in the line of the commandments, bearing on moral and social interests, and a few instructions on sacrifices, festivals, and other religious observances. This code is commonly called "the Book of the Covenant" (Ex. xxiv. 7), and it is held to have been the chief written or prescribed directory for religious duty and service during the whole period extending from the exodus to the reign of King Josiah.

The second code is that contained in the Book of Deuteronomy. One of the chief features in which this differs from the Book of the Covenant is its strict injunction to the people to regard "the place that the Lord shall choose to cause his name to dwell there" as the only legitimate sanctuary—the only place where they were to bring their burnt-offerings, sacrifices, tithes, heave-offerings, and vows unto the Lord. This injunction is regarded as a proof of the late date of the book. According to the view of the critics, Deuteronomy must have been written before the eighteenth year of King Josiah. It was the book which Hilkiah the priest found in the temple and brought to the king. This Deuteronomic code was the outcome of the great lessons that had been urged on the nation by the prophets, and of a desire to preserve the nation from the contaminating influence of their idolatrous neighbours by making Jerusalem the one seat of the national worship.

The third code is that which is found mainly in Leviticus. It was not in use till after the return from the captivity in Babylon. It was shadowed forth by Ezekiel some fourteen years after the destruction of Jerusalem in his vision of the restored city, the restored temple, and the reoccupation of the country, but was not formulated till the days of Ezra and his companions, more than a century later. This was the full development of the ritual system of which the germs had long existed. It could be carried into effect only now when Israel was no longer a nation but a church. The supporters of this theory argue strongly that while neither the Deuteronomic nor the Levitical code was given by Moses, both might legitimately be ascribed to him, as being in harmony with many traditional practices derived from him, and likewise as being the development of the system of law and mode of worship which he began.

In support of this theory the chief argument is derived from the notices in the historical books of the religious observances prevalent in the earlier periods of Hebrew history. It is contended that not only do we find no evidence of the observance of the elaborate ritual of Leviticus for several centuries, but we have reason to believe that it was not known at all. So far from the sacrifices being confined to a single sanctuary, we find Gideon building an altar and sacrificing at Abiezer, Manoah near his private dwelling, Saul at Gilgal, Samuel at Bethlehem, Solomon at Gibeon, and so forth. And it is not careless and ignorant men that act thus, but often the best men of the nation, acting apparently under God's directions, if not by his express instructions. The whole religious observances of the time correspond to the first or earliest code, and are suitable to the circumstances of a simple, primitive community before minute regulations began to be prescribed. Much liberty was allowed as to places of sacrifice, and, while there was a priesthood, laymen were not excluded from the right of officiating. Before the days of Solomon there was no restriction either as to the place or manner of sacrificing to God. Many shrines were freely made use of.

But in the course of time it was found that the use of many shrines had pernicious effects. From the practice of erecting "high places" in honour of false gods, similar high places came to be erected to Jehovah, the tendency of which was to assimilate the worship of Jehovah to that of the pagan deities. The prophets were particularly strong in denouncing all high places. Hezekiah had tried in vain to do away with them. Stronger measures needed to be taken. Hence, in the days of Josiah, the Book of Deuteronomy was written, enunciating, among other things, the law that Jerusalem was to be the only place of sacrifice. The Deuteronomic code was ascribed to Moses, because it was substantially a development of his legislation, and because it was believed that the authority of Moses might succeed in this most vital matter where other authority had failed.

During the captivity in Babylon the law was much in the thoughts of the devout, and the desire arose that when the people returned to their land it should be fenced about with such a complete and elaborate ritual as would effectually put a stop to the idolatrous tendencies that had ever been manifesting themselves during all the past history of the nation. While Ezekiel foreshadowed this process, the system that finally commended itself was that elaborated in the Book of Leviticus in the days of Ezra. This, too, was ascribed to Moses, for the same reasons as before ; and the wisdom of the course thus adopted was manifest from the fact that from that time all idolatry was suppressed, and Jehovah alone was worshipped as the God of the nation.

Here, it is argued, was an intelligible and self-consistent process. It is of the nature of all law to develop itself from simple beginnings onward to an elaborate system. No cast-iron system of law, complete from the beginning, would be found workable, because new conditions require new provisions, while old enactments necessarily become obsolete with the state of things for which they were designed.

Such, stated as fully as our space allows, is the new view of Hebrew history and the development of Hebrew law. Its advocates admit that much is still uncertain, and that on some points difference of opinion prevails among themselves ; but they declare with great confidence that the main positions are thoroughly established. And so strong does the current run in this direction that it is not without long and careful consideration that the present writer has come to the conclusion that the verdict regarding the theory ought to be at least "not proven." He is deeply impressed with some of the difficulties of the traditional view, and holds that much patience should be shown by all interested in the discussion, as it is only by careful and diligent inquiry that the truth can be expiscated. The following are the chief reasons why the biographical sketches that follow have been accommodated to the old and not to the modern view :—

1. Some of the chief difficulties ascribed to the old view may be quite satisfactorily explained. For instance, the sacrifices of Gideon, Manoah, and others were offered in the places specified because *God had of his own accord appeared to them there*, and by his personal presence superseded the rule that required them, *if they desired to meet him*, to resort to the national sanctuary. Moreover, this direct contact with God gave them the privilege of priests—that is, of direct access to him—and therefore it entitled them to offer sacrifice. Again, the apparently irregular worship of which we read (for example) in the days of Samuel was offered at a time when there was *no national sanctuary*—no recognized place of meeting with God. The sacred ark, the symbol of God's presence, was at Kirjath-jearim. In fact, during the whole period between the fall of Shiloh and David's placing the ark on Mount Zion, or rather perhaps God's acceptance of Solomon's temple as his shrine—that is, for more than a century—there was no place recognized as the national sanctuary (1 Kings iii. 2). Apart from this period, the recognition of one great sanctuary may be clearly traced throughout all Hebrew history. To sacrifice there was the rule of the nation, but subject to exceptions. Shiloh was consecrated in the days of Joshua. But there is no command, save in the Deuteronomic and Levitical codes, out of which the separation of Shiloh as the national sanctuary could have arisen.

2. In explanation of the early neglect of the Levitical worship, too little account has been taken of the temper and spirit of the nation when they entered Canaan. We are apt to think that under Moses in the wilderness the people became perfectly docile, and that they accepted his instructions as enthusiastically as the

disciples of Socrates and Plato accepted theirs in a subsequent age. We fail to make allowance for the strong prejudices and perversions that were grained into their very nature during their long residence in Egypt. It is true that "they were all *baptized* unto Moses in the cloud and in the sea;" but baptism is only the beginning, and far from the completion, of a process. The golden calf is a clear proof that they were to a large degree penetrated with the idolatry of Egypt. Amos tells us (v. 26) that in the wilderness they carried about "the tabernacle of their Moloch and Chiun their images, the star of their god" (*R.V.*) Their frequent murmurings and rebellions against Moses, and even against God, were proofs that neither the one nor the other was regarded with much honour. It was, indeed, after his death that Moses gained such exalted consideration. It is true that under Joshua the people were in a better spirit; but Joshua felt that this was but a temporary impulse, and in his dying charge he expressed his conviction that, owing no doubt to their carnal spirit, they "could not serve the Lord" (Josh. xxiv. 19). It need be no surprise to us that such a people were little disposed to carry out all the Mosaic ordinances, which even the apostle Peter described as "a yoke which neither our fathers nor we were able to bear" (Acts xv. 10).

3. It is often forgotten that in the wilderness the observance of the ceremonial law was in the main suspended. After the rebellion of the spies, if not sooner, circumcision itself, the ancient seal of the covenant, dating from the days of Abraham, was discontinued. Once only after the exodus does the passover seem to have been observed. We err greatly if we suppose that during the forty years' wandering the people were carefully trained in all the institutions of their religion. From Jer. vii. 22 and Amos v. 25 some have indeed inferred that even sacrifice was not required in the wilderness; but this cannot have been, because the very plea on which Moses and Aaron demanded leave of Pharaoh for their departure was that they might sacrifice to their God. But evidently there was great laxity in the wilderness, for in Deut. xii. 8 it is enjoined, "Ye shall not do after all the things

that we do here this day, every man whatsoever is right in his own eyes." In the wilderness Moses found it beyond his power to train them to observe his laws. It was when they should be settled in the land that they were expected to do full justice to them (Deut. xii. 10).

4. It is also overlooked that for many generations they never were completely settled in the land. Most of the tribes failed to implement one of the conditions on which the prosperity of religion and the welfare of the nation at large depended—they failed to drive out the old inhabitants. Whether in peace or in war, the presence of Canaanites in their midst hindered them from complying with the enactments of their law. The new-comers necessarily depended on the old inhabitants for information as to the culture of their fields and vineyards; and inclined as the Israelites were to superstition, they would be ready enough to accept the nostrums of the Canaanites as to the best way of securing the favour of local deities. Thus they were seduced to idolatry. In times of war, again, as in the days of Shamgar and Jael, when "the highways were unoccupied, when the inhabitants of the villages ceased in Israel," it was simply impossible to go up to Shiloh to the sacrifices. Moses and Aaron were now dead, and their successors did not enjoy the same influence as they did, and were not able to enforce the Mosaic system with the necessary vigour. It is hardly wonderful that, between the idolatrous tendencies of the people, the disturbed condition of the country, and, we may probably add, the inadequate provision made by the people for the Levites, the full scope of the Mosaic ritual ceased to be remembered.

5. The new view proceeds on a disregard of all the external evidence applicable to the subject. It affirms, in fact, that there is no external evidence, because the Jews of later times knew just as little of the origin of their books as we do, and it rests the whole question on internal probabilities. Now, if we mistake not, those whose business is to study evidence are of opinion that it is neither satisfactory nor safe to depend on internal evidence alone; and it used to be a canon of criticism that we are to give due respect to what a writer says of himself, and to what his earliest

followers say of him. It is certain that the earliest followers of the writers of the Old Testament books of whom we have any knowledge accepted the traditional view ; and although they may have been wrong, the fact that they did so is not to be dismissed as of no importance whatever. And as for statements in the books themselves, we hold the treatment of these by the critics to be sometimes wholly unwarrantable. If a book affirms that a certain tabernacle was constructed in the wilderness, and gives the names of the constructors, and describes minutely how the cost of it was provided for, some weight ought surely to be attached to these statements. The common-sense of mankind will not allow all this to go for nothing simply because we do not hear of this structure in the future history where we might expect to hear of it ; nor will it be satisfied with the explanation that it was only an ideal structure, a sort of shadow of the temple of Solomon or of that of the restoration.

6. The new view conspicuously fails in accounting for the place uniformly ascribed in Scripture to Moses as the author of the Jewish law. What is said is, that Deuteronomy and Leviticus are developments of the code which Moses gave ; and that as we continue to call Watt the inventor of the steam-engine, although the modern steam-engine is very different from Watt's, so the Levitical system may fairly be ascribed to Moses, although the greater part of it is of more recent origin. But are the critics here consistent with themselves ? Dr. Robertson Smith contends strongly that the early religion of Israel was constructed on a theory "diametrically opposite" to the later ; the difference between them was "essential ;" they early "departed from the first axioms of the Levitical service." * How then could the one be a development of the other ? But even granting development, will any man who can estimate the force of language say that this fairly represents all that is ascribed to Moses ? When it is said, in Deuteronomy, that "these be the words which Moses spake to all Israel" (i. 1), or that "Moses wrote this law, and delivered it unto the priests," can it be said that nothing more is implied

---

* "Old Testament in Jewish Church," pages 235, 238, 240.

than that, long ages before, the germs of these laws were pro-
mulgated by him? Or what are we to make of the thirty-three
places in Leviticus and the fifty-one in Numbers where the formula
is used, "God spake unto Moses, saying." We are perfectly open
to believe that both Deuteronomy and Leviticus may to a large
extent present us with the full text of what Moses gave only in
outline; but it is hard to believe that the laws therein contained
were merely the development of Mosaic germs or the embodi-
ment of Mosaic traditions. Can it be fairly said that our Lord
and his apostles claimed no more for Moses than this? On the
new hypothesis, our Lord and his apostles were either ignorant
of the real state of the case, or accepted the traditional view,
knowing it to be erroneous.

7. Another vital point in which the new theory fails is in
doing away with the odour and the odium of *pious fraud.* For
the people's book this is a serious blemish. Granting that it
is unfair to call Deuteronomy and Leviticus forgeries, still it is
plain that, according to the new theory, their authors were not
straightforward men. They could not trust to the goodness of
their cause or to the essential force of truth; they had to resort
to artificial methods, and to conjure with the name of Moses, in
order to commend their laws to general acceptance. Now this is
what plain men cannot understand. In military tactics it is poor
strategy to leave a strong fortress unreduced, and in Biblical
discussion it is ruinous to leave a charge of pious fraud behind.
Until it is thoroughly disposed of, the new theory cannot recommend itself to the mass of plain, honest people. We do not say
that no better explanation can be found, but certainly it is wanting at the present date.

These substantially are our reasons for not constructing our
chain of biographies from the standpoint of the modern theory.
We again say we are well aware of the difficulties of the traditional
view; but in the new view there are difficulties of another kind,
affecting the most vital interests. What we contend for is, that
we are warranted to hold by the old so long as a verdict of "not
proven" must be returned in the case of the new.

# HEROES OF ISRAEL.

## PART I.
### Abraham and Isaac.

## CHAPTER I.

### EARLY LIFE OF ABRAHAM.

ABRAHAM is by far the most commanding figure in history from Adam to Moses. His life was so quiet and so simple that it is only when we think carefully what he was and what he did that we apprehend his true greatness. God chose him to be the father of a great nation and the founder of a great religion—two very lofty functions in connection with his great scheme for the redemption of the human race. When all the world was rushing after idols and worshipping other gods, the majestic figure of Abraham stood apart; one God alone existed in all the universe for him; and his life was spent in such communion with him as to show what nobility and blessedness that fellowship brings. It was to his seed that all future revelations and communications from God were to be made, until at last there should arise that seed of the woman who was to bruise the head of the serpent, and in whom, as it was more explicitly put to him, " all the families of the earth were to be blessed."

All this was connected with a new page of history which God had just turned over. Men had been showing such disregard of the divine light and such love of darkness, that, leaving the world to its cherished ways, God had resolved to concentrate the light on a single family and a single race, and thus preserve the truth till

(393)                    1

the world should become ripe for a fuller revelation. Abraham was the man chosen to receive this light and found this race. It seems as if we might hear him saluted, as was one of his descendants afterwards, " Hail, thou that art highly favoured among men!" Of such a man every scrap of biography is of profoundest interest.

The biography of a great man usually begins with his family. It is not mere curiosity that desires to know from what sort of people he sprang; for if his forefathers were in any way remarkable, it is useful to see how they influenced their son. Even in the case of Jesus himself, it is significant, from the human point of view, that he was the son of Mary and the son of David.

But in the case of Abraham such inquiries come to very little. Of his forefathers we know hardly more than the names. Even of Shem, the son of Noah, we know nothing but that, like his brother Japheth, he was a more dutiful son than Ham. *Ex ungue leonem* fails us here : we cannot construct the lion from his claw. We must believe that Abraham's fathers followed the mode of life that we know to have been common in the Semitic race, and that in the main they were as such men generally have been. They were stock-farmers—perhaps we should now say ranchmen—and that on a large scale. Terah, Abraham's father, appears to have been a farmer; his three sons certainly were. Of his mother neither Scripture nor tradition gives the faintest hint, although to her he may have owed some of his most notable features both of body and mind. As women were not placed in the genealogical records, so they were little considered as influencing the family history. Haran, one of Terah's sons, perhaps the eldest, died before his father; but the possessions of his son Lot in flocks and herds seem to have been not much, if at all, inferior to those of Abraham (Gen. xiii. 7). Nahor, Abraham's other brother, likewise became the head of a great establishment of flocks and herds (Gen. xxiv.). Abraham himself was equally prosperous, and at least equally rich in this wealth of the time. The fact of interest here is, that unlike other great religious leaders, Abraham was a layman, and engaged very fully during his whole active life in business pursuits. It seems to have been God's purpose to show through him not only that honest secular business does not disqualify for high service and divine communion, but that it may be followed even by those chosen servants of God who, as great religious reformers, confer the highest blessings on the world.

But Abraham's early life must have been moulded by influences far above those of his earthly calling. However useful and honourable the life of a stock-farmer may be, it is not very elevating; the thoughts do not rise very high when they are much with cattle. Nor is it an advantage when all the family are of the same calling. When the pursuits of one are different from those of the others, new ideas and associations are thrown into the circle, and there is some chance of the freshness that is bred of variety. But when all are working among cattle, thinking of cattle, talking of cattle, a bucolic dulness and low level of life are apt to ensue. Influences from other quarters are needed—from religion, from education, from public life—to prevent the character from becoming stunted and the life wasted. It must have been some of these influences, working too with extraordinary intensity, that raised Abraham so high above the common level, and turned the Chaldæan farmer into a great hero, to be honoured to the end of time.

The chronology of Abraham's life is not very clear. If we add up the intervals between father and son as given in Gen. xi. 10–26, in "the generations of Shem," the whole period from the Flood to the birth of Terah's eldest son is only two hundred and ninety-two years. If we consider that Shem lived after the Flood five hundred years, this reckoning would make his life extend over the greater part of Abraham's, even supposing Abraham to have been a younger son of Terah, and born long after his eldest brother. So Milton seems to have thought, when Michael expresses his wonder that men should have been idolaters while

"The patriarch lived that 'scaped the flood."

But we can hardly conceive the interval so short as this. We are thrown back on the chronology of the Septuagint, which adds a

hundred years to the life of each of five patriarchs before the birth
of their eldest sons; also adds fifty years to the life of Nahor (in
one version a hundred and fifty), and interposes a Cainan between
Arphaxad and Salah, making at this point a difference of a hundred and thirty years. The whole period between the Flood and
the call of Abraham would thus be extended to eleven hundred
and forty-seven or twelve hundred and forty-seven years. The
tendency of modern opinion is strongly in the direction of the
longer chronology, in favour of which it is urged that according to
the Hebrew method of noting numbers, mistakes in transcription
might occur very readily, and that the Septuagint followed much
older Hebrew manuscripts than any that are extant now. Moreover, the memorials of transactions of great magnitude, and stretching over long periods, which have come down to us in the recently
deciphered monuments of Egypt and Assyria, create a strong
feeling in favour of the more extended period. The birth of
Abraham has been placed approximately by some recent writers at
B.C. 2150.

We get into a region of more promise and productiveness when
we inquire as to Abraham's native country and native city. The
country was Chaldæa, and the city with which his family was
connected was "Ur of the Chaldees."

Next to Egypt, if not on a level with it, Chaldæa was the most
interesting, the most remarkable, and the most civilized country
of those distant times. The two countries were alike in this, that
both were reclaimed from the desert; not indeed by the hand of
man, but by an agency of nature's own. From near the west
coast of Africa to near the east coast of Asia there stretches a
gigantic wilderness, the western part mostly of level sand, the
eastern of barren mountains. It is a strip of the African desert
that has been turned into a garden by the river Nile, the overflow
of whose waters has been at once the cause and the symbol of
fertility and abundance from the earliest ages of human history.
A portion of the Asiatic desert has in like manner been fertilized
by the two great rivers, the Euphrates and the Tigris. Both are
streams of imperial rank, having their origin in snow-clad moun-

tains, from which they have carried down into the plain of Chaldæa a mass of alluvial soil that makes it one of the richest countries in the world. It is nearly agreed among geographers, ancient and modern, that the name Chaldæa is not given to the whole of the plain watered by the two rivers, but only to the lower part of it, the part formed by the deposits. Part of this is also called in Scripture the land of Shinar (Gen. xi. 2). In this restricted sense, Chaldæa was a small country, of only about twenty-three thousand square miles. It was rather larger than Greece, less than Scotland, about equal to Holland (which in some respects it resembled), and almost exactly the same size as Denmark.\* It was not in consequence of its size, therefore, that it became a great country, but for causes similar to those which have given to Egypt, Palestine, Phœnicia, Greece, Venice, Holland, and Scotland their remarkable place in the history of the globe.

On the west, Chaldæa was bounded by the Arabian desert, consisting, in its first reach, of sand and gravel, and further west becoming more stony—a region where no settled population can at any time have found a subsistence, and where the occasional inhabitants are subject to sand-storms, and to the destructive simoom, whose deadly blast, sweeping across the entire tract, proves fatal alike to man and beast. On the north-west of Chaldæa lay Mesopotamia, which on its northern and north-eastern boundary touched Assyria. The plain of Assyria embraced the country between the Tigris and Media, and differed from that of Chaldæa in being less flat and of higher elevation. To the south-east of Chaldæa was the country known to the Jews as Elam, and to the Greeks as Susis or Susiana. Chaldæa at its southern corner touched the sea. This was one of the causes of its early pre-eminence, for, excepting Elam, the countries adjacent to it enjoyed no such advantage. The Indian Ocean invited to commerce, and gave easy communication with India, Arabia, Egypt, and Ethiopia. The trade of Chaldæa with other countries not only enlarged its resources, but quickened the energies and stimulated the intellect of its people. It was not among a sluggish

\* See Rawlinson's "Five Great Monarchies," i. 1-5.

race that Abraham was born, but one that knew how to use the advantages that nature had given them, and enrich their life by the material products and mental attainments of other lands.

The city in or near which Abraham was born was called Ur— "Ur of the Chaldees," to distinguish it probably from other Urs, of which there seem to have been several. For many ages tradition assigned his birthplace to a town now called Urfah or Orfah, known also in classical history as Edessa, the capital of the kingdom of that King Agbarus who is said in an old but unauthentic tradition to have received a letter from our Lord, along with his portrait. Some authorities still hold by Orfah, and Dean Stanley, in his "Lectures on the Jewish Church," has given it the high sanction of his name. But it seems a fatal objection to Orfah that it was situated, not in what was known as Chaldæa proper, but in what was afterwards known by the Hebrews as Aram-Naharaim (Syria of the two rivers) or Padan-Aram (the plain of Syria), and by the Greeks as Mesopotamia.* Besides, Orfah is but some twenty miles from Haran, and the removal of Abraham, with his father and nephew, from Ur to Haran, would not have had the importance which it bears if the two places had been so near.

In quite recent years it has been discovered from inscriptions on disinterred cylinders that a town now called Mugeyer, or Mugheir, near the right bank of the Euphrates, was formerly called Ur, or Hûr, and was in all probability "Ur of the Chaldees." † It was in many ways a notable place. Its history, as recently brought to light from the monuments, carries us far back, and indicates a progress reached at that time in many of the arts of civilized life for which we were not prepared.

From these monuments it appears that the Chaldæan plain was in early times possessed by a people known as the Accadians, who

---

* See Smith's "Dictionary of the Bible," article *Ur*, by Professor Rawlinson. In Stephen's account of the call of Abraham, he says it took place "while he dwelt in Mesopotamia, before he came to Haran." But it is plain that he uses Mesopotamia in a very wide sense, for he adds that "Abraham came out of the land of the Chaldæans, and dwelt in Haran." This seems to show that Ur of the Chaldees could not have been Orfah, for in that case Abraham would not have come "out of the land of the Chaldæans" to dwell in Haran.

† See Rawlinson's "Five Great Empires," and other writings.

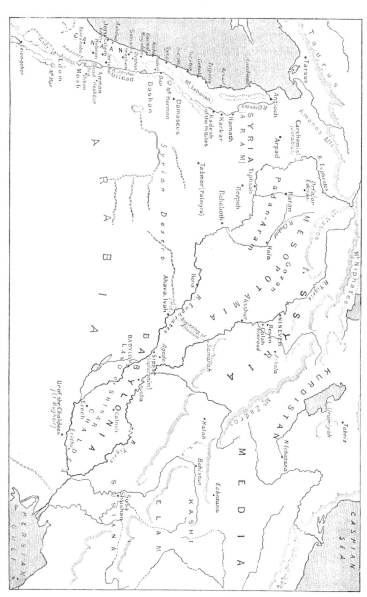

MAP OF BABYLONIA AND ASSYRIA.

Page 5.

seem to have come down from an earlier settlement among the hills, and founded two kingdoms, a northern and a southern, the capital cities of which were Accad and Ur respectively. The language of this people was of the Turanian family.* They were probably not of Semitic but of Cushite origin ; and their civilization appears to have been of a high order, and their literature extensive and varied. The towns Accad and Ur contained large libraries, with as many as ten thousand volumes, carefully arranged and numbered, and there are still found among the ruins remains of clay tickets, with the names and numbers of the books which readers desired to get from the librarian. Many of these tickets appear to have been written while the Accadian was yet a spoken language, probably before the time of Abraham. It is held by most British scholars, but not by all those of the Continent, that the Accadian civilization was the parent of the Chaldæan. †

After being settled in the Chaldæan plains, the Accadians appear to have been attacked and conquered by a people from Elam of Semitic origin, who adopted the civilization of the conquered race, their religion, art, literature, customs of various kinds—everything except their language. This conquest is believed to have taken place considerably before the time of Abraham. Abraham's family was Semitic, and would seem to have been long settled in Ur of the Chaldees before he was called to leave it. The new conquerors appear to have been active and aggressive, extending the confines of their empire wherever they had a chance. In Abraham's time a body of confederate kings from Elam, Shinar, and other places in the neighbourhood, invaded the country round Sodom and Gomorrah, and carried off his nephew Lot, but were pursued and defeated by him. Some of this aggressive army, though probably not all, were of Abraham's own race, and they would not have been attacked by him but for the necessity of rescuing one who was still nearer to him than they.

* The three great families of languages, according to Max Müller, are the Aryan, the Semitic, and the Turanian, corresponding vaguely to the three sons of Noah—Japheth, Shem, and Ham respectively.
† Sayce's "Babylonian Literature."

It is an interesting fact which the Assyrian monuments have brought to light, that the Accadian people who played so important a part in the early history of Chaldæa were of Turanian or Cushite origin. This agrees with what used to be a perplexing statement of Scripture, that Cush begat Nimrod, "the beginning of whose kingdom was Babel, and Erech, and Accad, and Calneh, in the land of Shinar." Besides the Cushites and Semites thus accounted for, there seem to have been two other nationalities among the early Chaldæans; for we find the early kings constantly designated in the inscription as *Kiprat-arbat*, "the four nations," or *arba lisun*, "the four tongues." "It would result from this review of the linguistic facts and other ethnic indications," says Canon Rawlinson, "that the Chaldæans were not a pure but a very mixed people. Like the Romans in ancient, and the English in modern Europe, they were a *colluvio gentium omnium*, a union of various races between which there was marked and violent contrast. It is now generally admitted that such races are among those which play the most distinguished part in the world's history, and most vitally affect its progress." * Among such races, therefore, we are to class the Hebrew.

Though Ur is now situated five or six miles back from the Euphrates, and a hundred and twenty-five miles from the Persian Gulf, it was formerly on the banks of the river, and not far from the sea; for the soil borne down by the river has encroached so continually on the sea that places formerly seaports are now considerably inland. In former times it was practically the seaport of Babylon. The inscriptions constantly speak of the ships of Ur, and of the brisk commerce carried on by its inhabitants. The ruins of Ur cover an oval space, a thousand yards long by eight hundred broad, and consist mostly of low mounds. Near the northern end are still to be seen the remains of a remarkable building. "It is a temple of the true Chaldæan type, built in stages, of which two remain, and composed of brick, partly sunburnt, and partly baked, laid chiefly in a cement of bitumen." It was dedicated to the moon-god, Hurki, from whom

* "Five Ancient Monarchies," i. 55, 56.

the town itself seems to have derived its name. " Ur retained its metropolitan character for above two centuries, and even after it became second to Babylon, was a great city, with an especially sacred character. The notions entertained of its superior sanctity led to its being used as a cemetery city, not only during the time of the early Chaldæan supremacy, but throughout the Assyrian and the later Babylonian period. It is in the main a city of tombs." *

Neither the remains of this temple nor any other remains of the early period indicate much taste in architecture. The edifices were more solid than beautiful. There being no stone in the whole plain, the only building material was brick, formed of the clay which abounded in the alluvium ; and the bricks were either kiln-burned or sun-dried, the burnt material being much more solid and durable than the other. The better class of dwelling-houses were built of this material. But the mass of the people had to content themselves with humbler dwellings. The reeds, which in the marshes grow to a height of even twelve or fourteen feet, might be easily formed into walls or bent into arches, and covered with mats of flags or sedge. Such houses might be made to last for half a lifetime. If palms were substituted for reeds, and wattles plastered with mud for rush mats, the house would be stronger and snugger. In such a house very probably Abraham was born and bred ; and if such was the home of his youth, it might prepare him for his after life, when he had nothing better for a dwelling than a movable tent.

The temple to the moon-goddess was the great building of Ur ; it was conspicuous from all parts of the city, and like the Temple of Diana at Ephesus in an after age, it indicated the enthusiasm with which the goddess was worshipped in whose honour it was reared. It is believed to have been the work of two kings, Rubu-tsiru and his son Dungi. In the reign of the latter it is probable that Abraham was born. It could not have been easy for Abraham to break away from a worship signalized by so magnificent a temple, and supported by the authority and enthusiasm of

* Smith's "Bible Dictionary," article *Ur.*

two successive kings, who were probably as intolerant of dissenters from the national worship as Nebuchadnezzar in the same plains fifteen hundred years after.

The religion of the Chaldæan people was eminently polytheistic. Our greatest experts have found it difficult to give a connected and consistent account of it. We follow the description of Canon Rawlinson.* The chief god was Il or Ra, of whom we

MAN-BULL, EMBLEM OF THE GOD NIN.

hear little; next came three—Ana, Bel or Belus, and Hea or Hoa, corresponding to Pluto, Jupiter, and Neptune. Each of these had a wife—Anat, Mulita, and Davkina. Then followed a further triad—Sin or Hurki, the moon-god; San or Sansi, the sun; and Vul, the god of the atmosphere. Each of these likewise had a wife. Then came five deities representing the five planets—Nip

* "Ancient Monarchies," i. 112, etc.

or Ninip (Saturn), Merodach (Jupiter), Nergal (Mars), Ishtar (Venus), and Nebo (Mercury). These constituted the principal gods; after them came inferior deities, almost without number. Of the appearance under which these gods were conceived the Assyrian monuments furnish us with striking representations. Nin, the fish-god, is represented by a figure whose back consists of a large scaly fish, the mouth of the fish being the crown of the head. The man-bull, so familiar to us in the Nineveh remains, is another emblem of Nin. The man-lion, with his vast wings, is the

MAN-LION, EMBLEM OF THE GOD NERGAL, OR MARS.

emblem of Nergal, the Mars, or god of war, of the Chaldæans. Doubtless Abraham was familiar with these figures; he would constantly see them receiving the homage of his countrymen,— and in his youth, before he was enlightened from above, he may have bowed the knee to them himself, as his fathers had done before him.

It is not easy to distinguish the popular religion of the

Chaldæans from the theory of religion that may have been entertained by the priests or wise men of the nation. It may be that
at first these deities were merely set forth as poetical symbols of
the powers of nature. Nor was the recognition of them incompatible with a theoretical belief in a supreme God. But if they
originally stood for the powers of nature, it is certain that they
soon came to be looked on as personal beings ; and whatever may
have been the sentiments of the more learned or thoughtful of the
people, the Chaldæan religion came practically to be very de·
graded. Charms and spells were used to cure or ward off diseases,
the arts of sorcery for bewitching and exorcising, and omens and
other appliances of divination for discovering the unknown. A
sensual element, too, was blended with the worship, and wherever
this occurred its tendency was not to elevate but to degrade the
worshippers.

But if the popular religion of Chaldæa was thus corrupt and
unsatisfactory, the legends of the past which probably prevailed
in Abraham's time came much nearer to the truth, and carried
the mind much more definitely to one supreme God. It is from
certain fragments of Berosus, a historian of Chaldæa who flourished between two and three hundred years before Christ, that
we get our knowledge of the Chaldæan cosmogony and early
history of the race. Under a fantastic garb, which was probably
regarded as symbolical, it delineated a process of creation not
unlike what we have in the first chapter of Genesis. In the
beginning all was chaos and water, in which living creatures
of monstrous forms disported themselves, ruled over by a woman
named Omorka — in Chaldee Thalatth, in Greek Thalassa, the
sea. Belus appeared and split the woman in two : of one half
he made the heaven, of the other the earth ; the heaven and
earth were then divided, and the animals formerly existing
perished. Belus then commanded one of the gods to cut off
his head and mingle his blood with the earth. From this mixture animals sprang up, and man, a partaker of divine wisdom.
Belus then made the stars, the sun, and the moon, and the five
planets.

The legends of the Flood and of the Tower of Babel are of similar tenor, with a substantial resemblance to the narrative of Genesis, but with circumstantial variations. According to Berosus, some portions of the ark remained in his time in Armenia, in the Gordiæan (Kurdish) mountains; and persons scraped off the bitumen from it to bring away, and used it as a remedy to prevent misfortunes. Of the Tower of Babel he says: "The earth was still of one language when the primitive men, who were proud of their strength and stature, and despised the gods as their inferiors, erected a tower of vast height, in order that they might mount to heaven. And the tower was now near to heaven, when the gods (or God) caused the winds to blow, and overturned the structure upon the men, and made them speak with diverse tongues; wherefore the city was called Babel."

The Chaldæan inscriptions recently deciphered in Assyria give a fuller account of the Creation and of the Flood than that of Berosus. We see clear traces of a prevalent polytheism, to which the narrative has been adapted. Generally, these narratives are marked by a tendency to wordy embellishment; they are a contrast to the severe simplicity of the narrative of the Bible, which furnishes evidence of truth.

One of the most important additions to our knowledge of Chaldæan traditions which the Assyrian monuments have given us relates to the Sabbath. It appears that "the month was divided into two halves of fifteen days each, these being further subdivided into three periods of five days. But a week of seven days was also in use from the earliest ages. The days of the week were named after the sun, moon, and five planets; and our own week-days may be traced back to the active brains of the long-forgotten people of Chaldæa [the Accadians]. The seventh, fourteenth, twenty-first, and twenty-eighth days of the month were termed 'Sabbaths' or days of rest, when the king was forbidden to eat 'cooked fruit' or 'meat,' to change his clothes or wear white robes, to drive his chariot, to sit in judgment, to review his army, or even to take medicine should he feel unwell."*

* See Sayce's "Babylonian Literature," pp. 54, 55.

Two lines of one of the Assyrian tablets are thus rendered by
Mr. Talbot, an eminent Oriental archæologist :—

> " On the seventh day he appointed a holy day,
> And to cease from all business he commanded."

This author adds that " it has been known for some time that the
Babylonians observed the Sabbath with considerable strictness." *
Abraham could have had no cause to reject the Sabbath as an
idolatrous invention ; it came down from the Creation as a divine institution, and we may well believe that the whole course of his life
was marked by a careful and devout observance of the day of rest.

The wide alluvial plain of Chaldæa was deficient in elements
of interest and variety. But it was of singular fertility : according to Herodotus, it was the most fruitful in grain of any part of
the world, two hundredfold being the common yield, and sometimes three hundredfold. The graceful foliage of the date-palm
was the chief object that relieved the monotony of the plain.
While the alluvial soil was so admirably adapted for grain crops,
there were tracts also more fitted for pasture at a greater distance
from the river. In one of these it is probable that the family of
Abraham was settled. The name Ur may have comprehended
some such region adjacent to the city, where Abraham may very
probably have spent the early part of his life.

There is still a considerable amount of uncertainty about some
parts of the history as derived from the monuments ; but there
seems no reason to doubt that the scene of Abraham's birth and
early life was far more advanced in civilization than we have been
accustomed to suppose. We have, indeed, no cause to think
that Abraham, like Moses in Egypt, was learned in all the wisdom
of the Chaldæans ; but neither are we to think of him as ignorant
and uneducated. We should not be doing him justice if we
thought of him merely as an Arab sheik, rejoicing in the exercise
of his despotic power, and with an ever greedy eye to the increase
of his cattle. The heavenly bodies from the first attracted the
special interest of the Chaldæans, and, we may well believe, that

* " Transactions of the Biblical and Archæological Society," v. 427.

of Abraham among the rest. There is a tradition preserved by Josephus that when Abraham went to Egypt he taught the Egyptians arithmetic and astronomy. It is probably an idle tale ; but it is more than likely that he was in full possession of any knowledge that was then possessed of astronomical science, and that when God afterwards brought him forth abroad, and said, " Look now toward heaven, and tell the stars if thou be able to number them," Abraham gazed on objects with which he was quite familiar, and the number of which he had often tried in vain to count.

But by far the most interesting and significant fact in Abraham's early life was, that in the midst of universal polytheism and idolatry he came to believe firmly in one God, and to worship him alone. It was not that his family had kept the primitive faith pure from the days of Noah ; for Joshua says expressly, " Your fathers dwelt on the other side of the flood in old time, even Terah, the father of Abraham, and the father of Nahor: *and they served other gods"* (xxiv. 2). In his very father's house, Abraham had been brought up in an atmosphere of polytheism and idolatry. Under the shadow of this fact there must lie a history of struggle and final victory which might peradventure rival in thrilling interest all that we know of the struggles of Augustine, of Luther, or of Bunyan. The Bible does not enter on it, and the fragments of tradition bearing on it, preserved by Jewish, Arabian, and Christian writers, are neither very trustworthy nor interesting.* In some way, and it could not but have been a most interesting way, Abraham must have made his escape from the meshes of his traditional faith and traditional worship, and come out, probably alone and unbefriended, to the knowledge and worship of the one true God.

That the revelation of the truth came to him supernaturally from God himself, goes without saying ; but whether by flashes of external revelation, or by a gradual process of inward illumination and struggle, we are not told. We are prone to think that it was by sheer supernatural power that God lifted up men

---

* The principal sources of tradition respecting Abraham are noted in Smith's "Bible Dictionary," and in Dean Stanley's "Eastern Church."

like Abraham to the lofty faith which they came to hold. But it is more in accordance with God's ordinary method to bring his children gradually into the light, and thus prepare them for the great decisive struggle through which they must pass. That the current notions of the existence of many gods were false, that there was but one God, supreme, infinite, and all-sufficient, may at first have come into Abraham's mind as a vague hint, a kind of dream flitting before him like a shadow. But once admitted to his mind, the thought could not be got rid of. The more he thought on the subject, the more he felt his own needs, the more scope he gave to his aspirations, the more he observed the unity of nature, the more he tried to grasp certain traditions of the past that had not yet quite melted away,—so much the firmer hold would his new view take of him. At first it may have frightened him; for if it should prove true, and he should have to avow it publicly, he would become the object of universal condemnation— every mouth would be opened against him. Was he alone right and all the world wrong? Was the opinion of a young farmer to be set above the convictions of a learned and renowned priesthood that had presided for ages over the worship of the gods? Was the great Temple of the Moon, which had been constructed in Ur at such cost, to be discredited and dishonoured because Abraham, the son of Terah, had come to believe that there was no such deity as the moon-goddess? It is easy to conceive his mind agitated by a tremendous conflict, and pressed by very grievous temptations. But whatever the preparatory process, it ended in the firm, God-given conviction that there was but one God, and that he only was to be worshipped. "Here I stand," we can conceive Abraham exclaiming like Luther afterwards; "I cannot do otherwise. God help me."

In this decision the fortune of the whole world was involved. The clouds of polytheism and idolatry were closing over it on every side, and Abraham remained the only clear, firm, outstanding witness to the unity and spirituality of God. There were indeed men like Melchizedek holding the same faith. But they could not have grasped it with the firmness of Abraham, for then it would not have passed away.   Abraham came to grasp it as the very treasure of his soul.   His name stands high in that list of great men who have stood alone against all around them as dis-coverers of truth and benefactors of the world.   On that choice of his, instrumentally, depended the preservation of the knowledge of the true God for long centuries, with all the moral and spiritual blessing, all the comfort and joy and hope, all the purifying and elevating influence on human life and character which are involved in the belief.   By thus preserving the great fundamental truth of God's unity, he kept in its integrity the only foundation on which, two thousand years after, the revelation of the gospel could be reared.   " If," as Max Müller has remarked, " from our earliest childhood we have looked upon Abraham, the friend of God, with love and veneration......his venerable figure will assume still more majestic proportions when we see in him the life-spring of that faith which was to unite all the nations of the earth, and the author of that blessing which was to come on all nations through Jesus Christ.   And if we are asked how this one Abraham passed through the denial of all other gods to the knowledge of the one God, we are content to answer that it was by a special divine revelation......granted to that one man, and handed down by him to Jews, Christians, and Mohammedans......to all who believe in the God of Abraham......We want to know more of that man than we do ; but even with the little we know of him he stands before us as a figure second only to One in the whole history of the world."

The impression we derive of the strength and greatness of Abra-ham's character, from the position he thus assumed as the first great Reformer of the religion of the world, is very powerful.   For, as Canon Mozley has remarked, " a divine revelation does not dis-pense with a certain character and certain qualities of mind in the man who is the instrument of it.   A man who throws off the chains of authority and association must be a man of extraor-dinary independence and strength of mind, *although* he does so in obedience to a divine revelation : because no miracle, no sign or wonder which accompanies a revelation, can, by its simple stroke, force human nature from the innate hold of custom, and the adhesion to, and fear of, public opinion; can enable it to confront the frowns of men and take up truth opposed to general prejudice,— except there is in the man himself, who is the recipient of the revelation, a certain strength of mind and independence which concurs with the divine intention."

It was impossible for Abraham, when he came to the clear perception of the truth, to keep it to himself. He must at the very least cease from taking part in idolatrous worship, and when asked his reason, acknowledge that he has ceased to believe in the gods. For in Chaldæa the practice prevailed of recognizing a Supreme Being without renouncing the worship of the other deities. To this Abraham could not assent. A prayer to the God of Ur recently deciphered from the monuments may exemplify that theoretical recognition of the Supreme Being which admitted nevertheless of subordinate gods :—

" Lord and prince of gods, who in heaven and earth alone is supreme,
　Father Nannar, Lord of the firmament, Prince of the gods......
　Merciful one, begetter of the universe, who founds his illustrious seat
　　among living creatures ;
　Father, long-suffering and full of forgiveness, whose hand upholds the life
　　of all mankind ;
　Lord, thy divinity, like the far-off heaven, fills the wide sea with fear......
　Father, begetter of gods and men, who causes the shrine to be founded,
　　who establishes the offering......
　First-born, omnipotent, whose heart is immensity, and there is none who
　　may discover it......
　Lord, the ordainer of the laws of heaven and earth, whose command may
　　not be (broken),
　Thou holdest the rain and the lightning, defender of all living things ; there
　　is no god who at any time hath discovered thy fulness.
　In heaven, who is supreme ? Thou alone, thou art supreme.
　On earth, who is supreme ? Thou alone, thou art supreme.
　As for thee, thy will is made known in heaven, and the angels bow their
　　faces.
　As for thee, thy will is made known upon earth, and the spirits below kiss
　　the ground......
　As for thee, thy will hath created law and justice, so that mankind has
　　established law......
　King of kings......whose divinity no god resembleth, look with favour on
　　thy temple ; look with favour on Ur thy city." *

　　　　　* Sayce's " Hibbert Lectures," pp. 160–162.

To the supremacy of the one true and living God, and to the duty of rendering all worship to him, and in no way recognizing any other, it was the great distinction of Abraham's life that he was called to be a witness. But it was not as a preacher or propagandist that he was to bear this witness. He was to maintain it within his own family — destined to become a nation — and to protect it from all mixture with neighbouring idolatries. By preserving the truth pure at home he was to make it efficacious abroad. As Dean Stanley has well said : " It is rather as if he were possessed of the truth himself, than as if he had any call to proclaim it to others. His life is his creed ; his migration is his mission. But we can hardly doubt that here the legendary tales fill up, though in their own fantastic way, what the Biblical account dimly implies. It may be an empty fable that Terah was a maker of idols, and that Abraham was cast by Nimrod into a burning fiery furnace for refusing to worship him. ......We may be forgiven if we supply the void by a well-known legend which has left its traces in almost every traditional account of the life of Abraham. The scene is sometimes laid in Ur, sometimes in the celebrated hill above Damascus. The story is best told in the words of the Koran : ' When night overshadowed him, he saw a star, and said, This is my Lord. But when it set, he said, I like not those that set. And when he saw the moon rising, he said, This is my Lord. But when the moon set, he answered, Verily, if my Lord direct me not in the right way, I shall be as one of those who err. And when he saw the sun rising, he said, This is my Lord. This is greater than the star or moon. But when the sun went down, he said, O my people, I am clear of these things ; I turn my face to Him who hath made the heaven and the earth.' " *

* Stanley's "Jewish Church," i. 14, 15. The legend reminds us of that magnificent passage in Augustine : "Interrogavi terram et dixit, Non sum ; et quæcunque in eâdem sunt, idem confessa sunt. Interrogavi mare, et abyssos et reptilia animarum vivarum, et responserunt, Non sumus Deus tuus, quære super nos. Interrogavi aures flabiles, et inquit universus aer cum incolis suis : Fallitur Anaximenes, non sumus Deus. Interrogavi cœlum, solem, lunam, stellas : Neque nos sumus Deus quem quæritis, inquiunt. Et dixi omnibus iis quæ circumstant foras carnis meæ : Dixistis mihi de Deo meo quod vos non estis ; dicite mihi de illo aliquid. Et exclamaverunt voce magna, Ipse fecit nos !" (I asked the earth, and it said, "I am not he ;" and all things in it confessed the same. I asked the sea, and its

If Abraham's mission was not to be that of an active propagandist (for which the world was not ripe), but rather that of a personal witness to the sublime truth to which he had attained respecting God, it was not advisable that he should remain in a community so wedded to idolatry and polytheism as Ur. He must enjoy some protection from influences that would have been perpetually assailing him in his native place, and which, though they could not have prevailed against him personally, might have disturbed and corrupted his household, and impaired the testimony of their united practice. He must be transplanted to some place where he would be practically independent, and not subject to the authority of a great kingly and priestly power like that of Chaldæan Ur. What his next move should be would doubtless have been very embarrassing if he had had no one but himself to guide him.

But the God whom he had come to know was now more than an abstraction to him. Already that fellowship had begun which procured for him the title applied by St. James (ii. 23), and universally bestowed on him at the present day in Mohammedan countries—El-Kalil, or Khalil-Allah, "the friend of God." Here is the index to another great but unknown chapter in the spiritual history of Abraham. To grasp intellectually the truth that there was a God, one living and true God, was one thing; to know him as a friend, and to be on terms of loving fellowship with him, was another. It would seem that in Abraham's case the revelation of God's nature, and the revelation of God as his friend and father, were not far separated. In making himself known to him as the one God, God made himself known also as interested in his welfare, ready to forgive his sins, and to bless him with all spiritual as well as temporal blessings.

And the faith of the patriarch enabled him to take in both

depths, and its shoals of living creatures, and they answered, "We are not thy God ; seek for him above us." I asked the floating breezes, and the whole atmosphere with its tenants said, "Anaximenes is wrong; we are not thy God." I asked the heaven, the sun, the moon, the stars. "Neither are we the God you are seeking for," was their reply. And I said to all the creatures that stood outside my flesh : "You have told me of my God that you are not he ; do tell me something about him." And with a loud voice they exclaimed, "It was he that made us !")

these revelations.  He had a receptive nature, disposed to accept what came to him on divine authority ; and he reaped his reward. Even at this early period of his life " he believed God, and it was counted to him for righteousness."  He found in God a companion and a friend that raised him far above the level of common life, and made him consciously a citizen of a higher country.  Of the play and movements of his inner life we have hardly a note in Scripture; but if we knew all, we should probably find that his experience had many resemblances to that of his son David, one of the few Hebrews whose soul is thrown open to us, and whose varied moods of hope and fear, of trouble and of trust, are so often reflected and repeated in every age.  Strangely swayed by the combined feeling of high dignity and deep humility, Abraham would go about among his neighbours manifesting a spirit which they could not explain.  They could not know the difference between the cold, hard feeling of the worshipper of idols, and the serene and joyous trust of one who was in deed and in truth the friend of God.  This being his frame, he received a communication from him that left no doubt as to his future course : Ur of the Chaldees was to be his home no more.

# CHAPTER II.

## ABRAM'S CALL AND MIGRATION TO CANAAN.

(GEN. xi. 27-32, xii. 1-5.)

THE start of the Hebrew nation on its very peculiar career was unlike that of any other great nation recorded in history. Like other nations, the Hebrew had its distinguished fathers, who were to it as the heroes were to them ; but the Hebrew fathers had this peculiarity—they were related to each other as father, son, and grandson. No other triad resembles that of Abram, Isaac, and Jacob. The heroes of the "Iliad"—Agamemnon, Achilles, and Ulysses—have no such relation. Sometimes brothers were associated in the honours of heroship, as in Indian legends, Rama and Lakshmana, Krishna and Bala ; and again, Judhishthira, Bhima, and Arjuna *—a circumstance that may remind us of the "three brothers" that figure so largely in the traditions of modern Americans on the origin of their families. But there is no other instance of a great nation sprung from three men who were the single representatives of three successive generations. The family, it is said, is the root of the state, and the best states are those which have most of the family character. The Jewish nation was designed to have much of the family character, and this peculiar feature of its ancestry contributed to this result.

Necessarily the history of the first period of the Hebrew race is the history of a family. And while every feature of family life is introduced, each member is marked by so strong an individuality as to seem designed to be a type of his species. In nearly every

* See Ewald's " History of Israel."

feature Abram is a model father and Isaac a model son. Sarai, notwithstanding her impatient temper, is a faithful, affectionate wife, who accepts her husband's *rôle*, and is his attached and beloved companion to the end. Isaac is like his father in many ways, but lacks his greatness and his power. Jacob is a strange mixture of good and bad, but the good predominates at last. He is an interesting and a powerful character, and he has this remarkable fortune, that while in their youth his sons as a whole show all his bad qualities in an aggravated form, they learn, further on, to follow him in much that is good.

Then, besides the relations of husband and wife, father and son, we have in this story nephews, and uncles, and fathers-in-law, and cousins. Abram becomes a father to Lot, his fatherless nephew ; Jacob falls in love with his cousin, but has no satisfaction in his father-in-law. And passing beyond the bonds of blood, we have servants of a very high order introduced as members of the family. Eliezer of Damascus is the faithful steward of Abram, and Deborah the much-loved nurse of Rebekah. But perhaps the most remarkable feature of all is the place which women occupy in this family circle. Sarai, Rebekah, and Rachel are all prominent, holding places of honour, and exercising a much more marked influence on the family life than any female in the household of Moses, or David, or Solomon, or indeed any other Old Testament hero. Was not this a foreshadowing of the Christian household, and an indication that under Judaism the family life generally would have been of a very high type, had not its natural development been checked by contrary influences ?

And this leads to the remark that the tendency to degeneration from the true type was seen actively at work in the patriarchal home. Lot is the counterpart of Abram, lured by worldliness into vice and misery. Hagar is the counterpart of Sarai, a slave-concubine rather than a wife, looking only to the interests of herself and her son. Ishmael is the counterpart of Isaac, as reckless and pugnacious as Isaac is prudent and peaceable. Esau is the counterpart of Jacob, much more like the son of Ishmael than the son of Isaac. Esau's Hittite wives are the counterparts of Leah and Rachel—a grief of mind in many ways to Isaac and Rebekah. The one element wanting in the patriarchal family is sisters. And when at length a sister appears in the family of Jacob, it is not for good to herself or to others. The patriarchal family was not a poetical paradise without a tempter and without sin ; it was a battlefield where good and evil were in perpetual conflict. By sifting away the more active elements of evil, and bestowing a large blessing on the chosen seed, God kept the three fathers comparatively pure, and thus provided for future generations an example enshrined in their earliest traditions which always encouraged whatever was estimable and good.

It is with the founder of this family that we now leave Ur of the Chaldees, as he sets out to go to the land he was afterwards to receive for his inheritance.

We find two statements in Genesis respecting the emigration of Abram—to Haran in the first instance, and thereafter to Canaan. Toward the close of the eleventh chapter it is said, " Terah took Abram his son, and Lot the son of Haran his son's son, and Sarai his daughter-in-law, his son Abram's wife; and they went forth with them from Ur of the Chaldees, to go into the land of Canaan ; and they came unto Haran, and dwelt there." Again, in the beginning of chapter xii. it is said, " Now the Lord said unto Abram, Get thee out of thy country, and from thy kindred, and from thy father's house, unto the land which I will show thee : and I will make of thee a great nation, and I will bless thee, and make thy name great ; and be thou a blessing " (Revised Version).

Some have thought—and the impression at first sight is a natural one—that it was Terah that devised the emigration from Ur to Haran, and that in so doing he was prompted simply by a desire to improve the circumstances of his family ; further, that it was in Haran that the divine call came first to Abram to separate himself from his kindred and his country and his father's house, and that the removal of Abram and his household from Haran was his first act of faith, his first movement in compliance with the divine commandment, when " he went out, not knowing whither he went."

But a more careful examination of the eleventh chapter will modify this conclusion. For it is expressly stated (ver. 31) that Terah's party "went forth from Ur of the Chaldees, *to go into the land of Canaan.*" Haran was not the destination of that emigrant band; it was only a halting-place by the way. Again, in Gen. xv. 7 it is said, "I am the Lord *that brought thee out of Ur of the Chaldees,* to give thee this land to inherit it." This shows that the divine plan which ended in Abram's being brought to Canaan began when he left Ur of the Chaldees, and that the same divine hand that laid hold of him there guided him all the way. It must have been in Ur, therefore, that he first received the divine command. And in the speech of Stephen before the Sanhedrim this is expressly stated : "The God of glory appeared to our father Abraham, when he was in Mesopotamia, *before he dwelt in Haran,* and said unto him, Get thee out of thy land, and from thy kindred, and come into the land which I shall show thee." So convinced were the translators of the Authorized Version that this was the true view, that they threw the statement in Gen. xii. 1 into the pluperfect tense—"Now the Lord *had* said to Abram." This alteration has not been retained in the Revised Version, but that does not mean that the revisers did not hold this view.

It would appear that the first part of the narrative (Gen. xi. 31, 32) is designed to present the transaction in the aspect in which men saw it; the other (Gen. xii. 1–5) goes deeper, and makes known how it originated—the motive by which it was prompted, and the authority to which it was due. As far as appeared to human eye, the migration took place under the direction of Terah, Abram's father, and Abram simply appeared to act the part of a dutiful son, accompanying his father in his emigration. Perhaps, in an Oriental narrative, it would have been counted unseemly to give a secondary place to the father; nominally he must head the expedition. Most readers will agree with the very decided view of Calvin : "That Abram had been called of God before he moved a foot from his native soil, is too plain to be denied."

Two questions naturally arise here, although it is not easy to answer them directly. In the first place, how came Terah, Abram's father, to take part, and apparently a prominent part, in the migration? And in the second place, how came the party to halt at Haran, and remain there (as it seems likely) a considerable time, when Haran was but a station, and an out-of-the-way station too, on the way to Canaan, and no special blessings were promised to Abram there?

To the former of these questions it is natural to reply that probably Terah had been impressed by his son's convictions, and had come to share in his faith. He had renounced his early polytheism, and become a worshipper of the one God (comp. Gen. xxxi. 53). He had been led to associate blessing with his son, and it might be a desire to share that blessing that led him to accompany him. It was not a new thing for a father to look on his son as a channel of coming blessing. Lamech, after a hundred and eighty-two years' experience of the toils and vicissitudes of life, when his son was born, "called his name Noah, saying, This same shall comfort us concerning the work and toil of our hands, because of the ground which the Lord hath cursed." Faith in the divine blessing as promised to some individual or race became not uncommon in after-times. Witness the faith of Rahab of Jericho in the coming exaltation of Israel. Witness the faith of Abigail in the divine promise of David. Or in the New Testament, the faith of the centurion of Capernaum, or that of the Syrophenician mother, in Jesus as the fountain of healing power. Why should not Terah have believed in his son as a divine channel of blessing? It is comparatively easy for fathers to believe in a great future for their sons. Doubtless the demeanour of Abram commended his faith in his father's eyes, and gave reality to his profession. What a happiness it would be to himself if his father entered through his instrumentality into the same blessed relation to God! And how would this react on Abram's own faith, and help to give it its wonderful firmness and tenacity! We may not be warranted to conclude absolutely that it was so; but two facts are sufficiently plain—first, that the divine call to Abram was the true cause of the migration; and second, that Terah accompanied his son.

The other question—Why did the party halt at Haran?—is also difficult to answer. Haran was not in the direct road from Ur to Canaan, but a long way further to the north. The more direct route would have been by Damascus, through which Abram doubtless had to travel afterwards when he left Haran on his way to Canaan. The most probable answer is, that God permitted the halt to be made at Haran by way of gradually training and preparing Abram for the ulterior step. In God's great operations, men are taken at first as they are, and gradually prepared for the crisis of their life. God might easily have enabled the Israelites, when they left Egypt, to advance to Canaan by the nearer route, through the land of the Philistines; but lest the hitherto untrained people should be afraid when they saw war, he led them by the way of the desert. It broke the severity of the trial for Abram to halt at Haran. Perhaps the faith and possibly the infirm condition of Terah were not equal to any further effort at the time. But having experienced God's goodness at the half-way house, Abram would be encouraged in due time to gird himself for the next stage of his pilgrimage, when he went forth to dwell among more complete strangers, "not knowing whither he went."

There were two other companions of Abram's pilgrimage not to be overlooked if we would realize his surroundings. These were Sarai and Lot. His attachment to Sarai was evidently of the warmest. There had been a time in his youthful history when his heart thrilled with a strange sensation for his young and beautiful relative, as his grandson Jacob's did afterwards for Rachel. Then came the happy day of union, and the linking of their lives together, sealing the union of their hearts in a fellowship of which they never tired. And best of all, their hearts were one in their deepest feelings—in their faith and in their worship; they could kneel together at the same altar, and pour out their thanksgivings and confessions, their desires and their hopes, into the ear of Him whom both knew as Father. Sarai is called Abram's sister— "the daughter of his father, but not the daughter of his mother" (Gen. xx. 12). She had been a daughter of Terah by another wife, or possibly, as Josephus says, a grand-daughter of Terah and a sister of Lot; such connections were not then regarded as beyond the circle of marriage. Lot, Abram's nephew, was probably not much younger than himself; evidently they were much attached. Perhaps through sympathy on Lot's part, as well as by personal conviction, Lot accepted his uncle's faith; but there was a shallowness in his character that must have made Abram anxious, and uncertain how he would act in any great crisis of his life.

And now the migration has begun. Michael's vision describes it :—

> " I see him, but thou canst not, with what faith
> He leaves his gods, his friends, and native soil,
> Ur of Chaldæa ; passing now the ford
> To Haran. After him a cumbrous train
> Of herds and flocks, and numerous servitude ;
> Not wandering poor, but trusting all his wealth
> With God, who called him, in a land unknown."

The distance from Ur to Haran is about five hundred miles, and the route is along or near the banks of the Euphrates, over a plain which presented no special difficulty to the transportation either of men or cattle. Attempts have been made to trace the course of the caravan as it moved slowly along the plain, and to indicate the principal places at which it might halt in its northward career. In the space of four thousand years the channels of the rivers may have changed greatly, but the sites of the chief cities and the general features of the country remain the same. About forty miles from Ur they would arrive at Erech or Warka, a famous city (Gen. x. 10), possibly conspicuous even then for its huge temple of Anu. Fifty miles further would bring them to Calneh—Gen. x. 10 ; Amos vi. 2—(Greek, χαλάνη), the modern Niffar, another of the ancient capitals of Chaldæa, its name supposed to be formed from the name of the god Anu or Ana. After another sixty miles they would reach Babylon, passing at a little distance the huge building at Borsippa called Birs Nimrod, "the Stages of the Seven Spheres," which, if it really was "the Tower

of Babel," would impressively remind the company of the early
fruits of disobedience to God's command and defiance of his will,
and strengthen them in that purpose of obedience which had
carried them so far on their way.   Twenty miles beyond Babylon,
Sepharvaim would be reached, the "double city," divided by the
river, afterwards to be one of the scenes of the captivity of the
ten tribes (2 Kings xvii. 24), and to acquire a peculiar character
of infamy from the cruelty of its idolatrous sacrifices (2 Kings
xvii. 31).

Hitherto the pilgrims have travelled along the flat alluvial
plains of Shinar (Gen. xi. 2), but they would now strike into a
more hilly or highland region, through which they would find the
Euphrates rushing at a speed very different from its almost imperceptible movement in lower Chaldæa.   About two hundred
miles north-west of Babylon they would come on the river Chebar,
long supposed to be the river on whose banks Ezekiel had his
visions; but this view has been mostly given up, because this
Chebar was not in Chaldæa, and it is believed that Ezekiel's
Chebar was a stream nearer Babylon, the name of which has not
been preserved.   Crossing the Chebar, the road would lead them
along its banks through a green and beautiful region, bounded by
a range of gentle hills; and following its western branch, they
would proceed toward Haran, which for the present was to be the
termination of their wanderings.

Haran is one of those places which retain their names for
centuries.   It is supposed to be derived from the Accadian language, and to mean "a road," implying that it was situated on
the highroad from east to west, along which the stream of traffic
usually passed.   In Ezek. xxvii. 23 it is enumerated among the
great commercial marts that dealt with Tyre.   It lay in a plain of
great fertility, "strewed at times with patches of the brightest
flowers, at other times with rich and green pastures, covered with
flocks of sheep and of goats feeding together, here and there a few
camels, and the son or daughter of their owner tending them......
The air is so fresh, the horizon so far, and man feels so free, that
it seems made for those whose life is to roam at pleasure, and who

BIRS NIMROD.

*Page 20.*

own allegiance to none but themselves." *       It would appear that
the family of Nahor, the brother of Abram, who had remained at
Ur when his father, brother, and nephew left it, afterwards made
Haran their permanent abode; for when Rebekah directed her son
Jacob where to find her relations, it was to Haran in Mesopotamia that she sent him.   About two thousand years after Abram
occupied it, it acquired notoriety in Roman history as the scene of
the defeat and death of the Roman general Crassus in his encounter with the Parthians.   The present village is a poor place,
inhabited by tribes of Bedouin, consisting of a few conical houses,
like bee-hives in shape, clustered together at the foot of a ruined
castle.

Haran must have been in many ways an inviting place for
settlement; but though Abram remained in it till his father's
death, he resisted the temptation to make it his permanent home.
Probably it was the description of it sent back to Ur that induced
Nahor and his wife Milcah to migrate to it.   It is certain that they
prospered greatly, but they were not so strong in faith as Abram,
and did not wholly renounce the idolatry of the country.   (See
Gen. xxxi. 19, etc.)   At his father's death Abram was seventy-
five years of age.   His wife Sarai was childless, so that there was
no apparent prospect of the fulfilment of the promise that God
would make of him a great nation.   It is likely that the divine
call which he had received at Ur to go forth to a land that God
would show him came to him a second time at Haran, urging him
to go out now on the second and more perilous journey.   It was
now that his faith was most severely tried.   The migration from
Ur to Haran, to use a common phrase, had been "plain sailing,"
for Haran could not but be well known at Ur, and the road to it
was a well-frequented highway; but when he left Haran he literally "went forth, not knowing whither he went."   It could only
be with a shiver of heart of the natural man that he would set out
from the snug home comforts of Haran into the bleak and barren
desert.   There was nothing but his faith in the divine promise to
support him, whether he looked for a place of abode for himself

* Malan, *apud* Deane's "Abraham: his Life and Times," p. 23.

and his dependents, or thought of the promise that God would make of him a great nation, or of the assurance that in him all the nations of the earth would be blessed.

It would be to ascribe to Abram a superhuman steadiness to suppose that he never had any questionings, or anxieties, or fears in connection with God's promises and his own duty under them ; what we know is that at decisive moments, when it was necessary to act, his faith stood firm.    In the haze of distance, and under the influence of the supernatural halo that surrounds him, we are liable to forget that he was a man of like passions with ourselves ; but we should try to place ourselves in his position.    We need to think of men like General Charles George Gordon, or David Livingstone, or, to go further back, of devotees like St. Francis of Assisi, or Joan of Arc, to understand what numberless cravings of the natural heart for ease and security and earthly enjoyment the sense of a divine call had first to encounter and overcome, and how it was only after these temptations had all been swept clean off the field that faith became so miraculously strong.    " Here am I," said Gordon, " a lump of clay.    Thou art the Potter.    Mould me as thou in thy wisdom wilt ; *never mind my cries.*"    No doubt Abram came to feel that he too was absolutely in God's hands, and was enabled to repose in perfect calmness on the divine direction. He too must have learned to say to God, " Never mind my cries ; " but it must have cost him preliminary struggles of unknown intensity to attain to this perfect trust.

The preparations had all been made.    " Abram took Sarai his wife, and Lot his brother's son, and all their substance that they had gathered, and the souls that they had gotten in Haran ; and they went forth to go into the land of Canaan ; and into the land of Canaan they came."    He had evidently prospered in Haran, and gathered a considerable establishment, which made it all the greater trial to leave the place.    His neighbours would call him a fool and a madman.    It has been computed by Kitto that the possessions of Abram and Lot were at least equal to those of Job (i. 3).    But he left nothing behind ; he had not the slightest intention of ever returning.    " If he had been mindful of the country from which he set out, he might have had opportunity to return;" but his hopes were far higher—"he looked for the city which hath the foundations, whose builder and maker is God" (Revised Version).

Manners and customs change little in these Eastern countries, and a graphic writer, founding on what may be seen to-day, gives a lively picture of the commencement of Abram's journey :—" All their substance that they had gathered is heaped high on the backs of their kneeling camels. The slaves that they had bought in Haran run along by their sides. Round about them are their flocks of sheep and goats, and the asses moving underneath the towering forms of the camels. The chief is there; amidst the stir of movement, or resting at noon within his black tent, marked out from the rest by his cloak of brilliant scarlet, by the fillet of rope which binds the loose handkerchief round his head, by the spear which he holds in his hand to guide the march and to fix the encampment. The chief's wife, the princess of the tribe, is there in her own tent (Gen. xxiv. 67), to make the cakes and prepare the usual meal of milk and butter (Gen. xviii. 2–8) ; the slave or the child is ready to bring in the red lentil soup (Gen. xxv. 34) for the weary hunter, or to kill the calf for the unexpected guest......

" In every aspect except that which most concerns us, the likeness is complete between the Bedouin chief of the present day and the Bedouin chief who came from Chaldæa nearly four thousand years ago......The more we see the outward conformity of Abraham and his immediate descendants to the godless, grasping, foulmouthed Arabs of the modern desert......the more we shall recognize the force of the religious faith which has raised them from that low estate to be the heroes and saints of their people, the spiritual fathers of European religion and civilization. The hands are the hands of the Bedouin Esau, but the voice is the voice of Abraham, Isaac, and Jacob—the voice which still makes itself heard across deserts and continents and seas; heard wherever there is a conscience to listen, or an imagination to be pleased, or a sense of reverence left among mankind." *

* Stanley's " Jewish Church," i. 9, 10.

At what time it was revealed to Abram that the land of Canaan was to be his destination we are not informed. The knowledge of this was certainly concealed from him at first, for it was one of the trials and triumphs of his faith that he went out "not knowing whither he went." But when he left Haran the direction in which he was to proceed, at the very least, must have been made known to him. He moved in a south-westerly direction into the bare and lonely desert. It was probably impossible for him to take a straight line through the heart of the desert to Damascus, for no Tadmor (Palmyra) had yet been built as a half-way house, and it is likely that he would pass along the northern frontier. There is much significance in the fact that on leaving Haran his first march was into the desert.

For the desert has often played a prominent part in the pilgrimages of God's people. The first march of Abram's descendants when they left Egypt was through another desert, where, instead of a few weeks, unbelief kept them for forty years. It was in the wilderness that David was taught the art of ruling, and enabled to establish a great kingdom in after years. When the divine Son of Abram had been invested with his sublime commission by the Holy Ghost, he was led up immediately of the same Spirit into the wilderness. Elijah had to be reanimated for new service in the desert of Sinai, and Paul prepared for his apostleship in some lonely part—perhaps the same part—of Arabia. And in a time yet coming, when the long faithless bride—she whose name has sunk from "Israel" to "Jezreel"—is to be brought back in deep penitence to her long-suffering Husband, the way of her return is to be through the desert : "I will allure her into the wilderness and there will I speak comfortably to her" (Hosea ii. 14).

The wilderness, as all devout travellers tell us, while it produces a vivid sense of loneliness and dependence, draws the true heart upward to God. Abram was now preparing to lay the foundations of an empire compared with which that of Alexander or of Cæsar would be but trifling and ephemeral. He was about to found a nation and a religion having as its corner-stone the unity and all-sufficiency of God—the only foundation on which either a religion or a nation can rest securely. He was intrusted with the administration of the one great force that, by bringing man into fellowship with God, would elevate and purify his nature, and instead of a wild savage or a selfish tyrant, make him a saint and a hero. For such a purpose an inflexible faith in God was needed—a faith that no temptation could shake; and the experience of the lonely wilderness, where, alone with God, he and all his company were in manifest dependence upon him, was a fitting discipline for the supreme attainment.

After skirting a long and weary desert, Abram would at last reach Damascus, which even then, with its flowing streams and fruitful orchards, was a place of importance, and from which he seems to have obtained Eliezer, the servant who became the steward of his house (Gen. xv. 2). Josephus, on the authority of a historian, Nicolaus of Damascus, says that "Abraham reigned at Damascus, being a foreigner who came with an army out of the land above Babylon, called the land of the Chaldæans. After a time he rose up and removed to Canaan." Josephus adds that there was a village in the suburbs of Damascus named after him "The Habitation of Abraham." There is no probability in the tradition of his reigning in Damascus. Certainly he brought no army, and the purpose of his pilgrimage would never have allowed him to play the king. As Josephus makes no mention of the stay in Haran, it is likely that the residence in Damascus was substituted for it, while the idea of his reigning may be just an exaggeration of the place of pre-eminence which he held in the former community.

Leaving Damascus, Abram would proceed by one of the ordinary caravan routes that passed, as they still pass, through Palestine to Egypt. It is likely that he would reach the land of Canaan on its northern frontier, and get his first view from some of the northern heights in the Lebanon, either on the east or the west side of the Jordan. At whatever point he crossed the stream, he would feel that a new chapter of his life had begun. This was the land that God had promised to his seed. This was to be the scene of those blessings that God had promised to him.

It was from this centre that the precious influence would go forth which would verify these marvellous words, " In thee shall all families of the earth be blessed." How would Abram's heart thrill when he set foot on the further bank of the Jordan, and actually stood in the land of promise ! With what keen and sparkling eyes would he and Sarai gaze on every side, filling their eyes with the goodly prospect, and exclaiming—" The land of our pilgrimage, and the home of our children to be ! "

## CHAPTER III.

ENTRANCE INTO CANAAN—SHECHEM AND BETHEL.

(Gen. xii. 6-9.)

THE land in which Abram now became a sojourner differed widely from the Ur where he had spent his youth, and from the Haran of his later years. Instead of an alluvial plain, it was a land of limestone mountains that broke up the surface into innumerable heights and hollows, and gave it, on the whole, a somewhat bare and ragged appearance. It has been remarked, and with considerable probability, that when Abram first saw the country it had much the same appearance as it has to-day. In its more prosperous and settled days the hills were terraced for vineyards and orchards, fruit trees and other trees were abundant, and each homestead had a trig and comfortable aspect; whereas now, as at first, the hills are bare, and fragments of rock and loose stones, strewed everywhere, give a neglected appearance to the whole. But the practised eye of Abram would readily perceive that, notwithstanding the unfavourable contrast with the level plains of the Euphrates and the Tigris, there were many parts of the country well adapted to the pasturing of flocks, while here and there, in the valleys between the mountains, there lay green plains of great beauty and fertility, adapted both for orchards and arable farms, so that it needed but care and labour to make it a most desirable and productive land.

Approaching Canaan in a south-westerly direction from Damascus, the first object to attract his interest would be the grand chain of Lebanon, with its snow-clad ridges glittering in the light of the setting sun. Lebanon, with its two parallel ranges running north and south, and the valley between, was the northern boundary of the country—a highland rampart thrown up by nature to protect it on the quarter from which the most vigorous enemies commonly came. The days had not arrived when men admired mountains for their picturesqueness—there was no poetry in them then; but they were always esteemed as emblems of stability and as bulwarks of defence.

The next great feature of the country to attract notice would be the valley of the Jordan. This river, while it forms the eastern boundary of Palestine proper, is the great drain of the country, both on the east and the west, carrying to the Dead Sea nearly all its superfluous water. It runs through a very singular valley; but if Abram struck the valley far north, its peculiarity would not be observed at first. If he came upon it near the "Sea of Merom," or what is now the Lake Hûleh (close to which he afterwards defeated the confederate kings who had carried off Lot), he would find a fertile plain, in which the three branches of the Jordan unite, covered, if it was the season, with heavy crops of grain, and bright with a flora unlike that of Chaldæa, in which special notice would be claimed by the fine Hûleh lily ("the lily of the valleys," and the lily of the Sermon on the Mount), raising its triple petals to form a gorgeous canopy, "such as art never approached, and king never sat under even in his utmost glory."

Passing the Waters of Merom, he would next skirt the Lake of Galilee reposing amid its calm surrounding hills, but showing a depression (though Abram would not be aware of this) of above six hundred feet below the level of the Mediterranean. But as he followed the windings of the river southward, he must have had his attention turned to the gradual deepening of the valley in which it flows, now ascertained to be so great that where the Jordan enters the Dead Sea it is thirteen hundred feet below the level of the Mediterranean. He would perceive what a valuable protection that deep valley afforded to the country on the west, the more especially that the mountains on either side rose up to a considerable height, forming an elevated plateau of irregular surface, broken up by lateral ridges and valleys running down into the valley below. When Abram became better acquainted with the country, he would see what an important feature this elevated plateau formed. It constituted a kind of backbone or dorsal ridge, admirably adapted for the sites of cities, and forming the key to the dominion of the country.

Further observation would reveal the low and fertile plain which ran on the west between the base of the plateau and the Mediterranean, which might well be called the "great sea" in comparison with the Persian Gulf, the only piece of salt water that Abram had hitherto known. When he afterwards followed the Jordan to the Vale of Siddim, he would observe the splendid capabilities of that part of the valley, where the leafy palm, thick-spread and luxurious, revealed a climate equal to that of more southerly lands. And when he surveyed the country at leisure, he would see that its hilly terraces were equally adapted for the culture of the vine, its valleys for wheat and other grain crops, and its breezy, hilly ranges for the pasture of flocks and herds. Small though it was, insignificant though the Jordan was compared with the Euphrates, and contracted though the valleys were compared with the vast plain of the Chaldæan rivers, it was a compact, an interesting, a promising country, capable of rearing a remarkable population, with more active habits and a more enterprising character than the monotonous fertility of Chaldæa was likely to produce.

We may believe that one of Abram's first employments after setting foot in the land was to turn over in his mind the promise that had been given to him in Ur, and to think what it meant: "I will make of thee a great nation, and I will bless thee, and make thy name great; and thou shalt be a blessing: and I will bless them that bless thee, and curse him that curseth thee: and in thee shall all families of the earth be blessed."

To make of him a great nation was not necessarily a desirable thing, for a great nation, fired by mad ambition, would be a source of much mischief and misery; but when the promise was attended with such explicit assurance of the divine blessing, it gave truly a magnificent prospect. And not only was God to be favourable to him and his seed, but he was to count Abram's friends as his friends, and Abram's enemies as his enemies—the greatest proof of friendship which kings in their treaties ever give to one another. Nor was Abram to be a mere recipient of good things. He was to exemplify the divine saying, "It is more blessed to give than to receive." "Thou shalt be a blessing." He was to be a channel of benediction to others. "When the eye saw him it would bless him, and when the ear heard him it would bear witness to him; the blessing of him that was ready to perish would come upon him, and he would cause the widow's heart to leap for joy."

And not only was he to be a channel of blessing, but, in his seed, a source of it. "In thee shall all families of the earth be blessed." We know how to interpret these words from the commentary of St. Paul in the New Testament (Gal. iii. 8, 16). But how did they appear to Abram? Our Lord helps us to answer. "Your father Abraham rejoiced to see my day; and he saw it, and was glad" (John viii. 56). There can be no reasonable doubt that Abram attached a Messianic meaning to the words. The Messianic tradition of paradise and later revelations had not yet died out, and this promise was evidently an expansion of it. To one like Abram it was most suggestive and full of glory, though it may have been a vague glory, more like the glory of an autumn sunset than the clear and clean-cut landscape of a winter morning. It affords the key at once to his readiness to leave the land of his fathers and come to this distant Canaan, and to the immovable steadfastness with which he and his sons clung to the country, save only when inexorable hunger compelled them to go elsewhere for a time for bread.

The inalienable attachment of the patriarchs to the land of Canaan is a fact of history that defies any reasonable explanation, except that it was founded on the Messianic hope. We shall see that when famine drives Abram to Egypt, the king loads him with wealth and honour; but forthwith he returns to Canaan. A burial-place has to be provided for Sarah, but he does not think of laying her remains in the sepulchre of her fathers ; he purchases a field and a cave from the sons of Heth. A wife has to be found for Isaac, and his confidential servant is sent to Padan-aram, the residence of his brother Nahor. His servant foresees that even if he find a suitable maiden, her family will be very unwilling to send her to Canaan, and may propose that Isaac should go to her, not she to Isaac. Abram deprecates the thought ; it is not to be entertained for a moment. If the damsel will not come to Canaan, the matter must end. Jacob quarrels with Esau, and flies to Laban. He marries his daughters, and prospers in his employment, and everything, save Laban's temper, seems to point to his settling in some part of that country ; the anger of Esau is a real and very terrible source of alarm ; but, in spite of all, Jacob dares every risk and ventures back to Canaan, because it is the land of promise and of blessing. When Jacob hears of Joseph being ruler in Egypt, he cannot comfortably consent to leave Canaan and go down to him till he has got the divine permission. On the death of Jacob, his body is carried by his sons to be buried at Machpelah, in the sepulchre of his fathers; and when Joseph is dying, he takes an oath of his brethren that when God visits them, they will carry up his bones to Canaan. Centuries of bondage pass in Egypt, but the one consideration that rouses the people to attempt to escape from captivity is, that a blessed future has been promised them in that land ; and hurried though their departure is, they do not forget to carry the bones of Joseph with them. No explanation of such transactions can stand for a moment that does not proceed on the ground that it was a divine communication that first drew Abram to Canaan, and that held the hearts of his descendants for centuries by its wondrous spell, and that the pre-eminent glory of that message was, that in his divine Descendant all families of the earth were to be blessed.*

When Abram came to Canaan, he did not find it an Australia or a Manitoba, comparatively empty of inhabitants, and only waiting to be occupied. It was already in possession of others.

---

* See this argument stated more at length in my " Witness of Palestine to the Bible "— *Present Day Tracts*, No. 10.

But it does not seem to have been densely peopled ; there was but a sprinkling of inhabitants ; and these did not hold so tenaciously to their rights as to prevent a stranger, where there was room for him, from at least pasturing his flocks among them. This, however, was the full extent of a stranger's privilege. There was a strict land tenure as regarded possession ; so that when Abraham, after a long residence, desired to procure a buryingplace for his dead, he could not acquire a right to it without going through an elaborate form of conveyancing, and publicly paying the stipulated price to its acknowledged owners.

The inhabitants of Canaan in Abram's time are variously designated in Scripture. In Gen. xii. 6, xxiv. 37, etc., they are simply "the Canaanites." In Gen. xv. 16 they are "the Amorites." In Gen. xv. 19, 21, ten nations are enumerated—" the Kenites, and the Kenizzites, and the Kadmonites, and the Hittites, and the Perizzites, and the Rephaims, and the Amorites, and the Canaanites, and the Girgashites, and the Jebusites." More frequently six nations are enumerated—the Canaanites, the Hittites, the Amorites, the Perizzites, the Hivites, and the Jebusites (Ex. iii. 8, 17, xxiii. 23, xxxiii. 2, xxxiv. 2 ; Josh. xii. 8). Once the Perizzites are omitted, making the number five (Ex. xiii. 5), and once the Perizzites and the Hittites, reducing it to four (Num. xiii. 29). On the other hand, in Deut. vii. 1 the Girgashites are added to the six, and the whole are described as "seven nations, greater and mightier than thou." Other varia- tions in the enumeration are also found.

The natural explanation is, that those whose names occur most frequently were the most conspicuous and powerful, while the others held a subordinate position. On this principle, we conclude that the most powerful were the Canaanites, the Amorites, the Hittites, and the Jebusites. Let us endeavour to state what ancient records and modern research have to tell us concerning these.

Of the Canaanites proper we are told that they dwelt "by the sea and by the coast of Jordan" (Num. xiii. 29). The term Canaan is derived from a root which signifies to be low, and is thus appropriate to the two regions specified in this passage—

the Shefēla or maritime plain of the Philistian and Phœnician coast, and the Arabah or plain of the Jordan.    But there is another and perhaps more natural derivation of the term—from Canaan, the son of Ham ; for " Canaan begat Sidon his first-born, and Heth, and the Jebusite, and the Amorite, and the Girgasite, and the Hivite" (Gen. x. 15–17).    We may thus see how the inhabitants as a whole were called Canaanites ; but when more specific designations were employed, the term was restricted to the inhabitants of the low tracts.    And this restriction appears in the New Testament, the woman from the coasts of Tyre and Sidon, whose daughter our Lord healed, being called "a woman of Canaan" (Matt. xv. 21, 22).

The Amorites "dwelt in the mountains" (Num. xiii. 29), the Hebrew name denoting an elevated place, the opposite of "Canaan." They were a particularly powerful and warlike people.    They took a conspicuous part in wars with earlier inhabitants, especially in Bashan and Gilead ; for in the time of Moses two very powerful Amorite kingdoms, those of Sihon and Og, had been established there by the power of the sword, and the name of the people had become proverbial (Num. xxi. 27–30).

The Hittites and the Jebusites were also highlanders, at least in their earliest settlements (Num. xiii. 29), the Jebusites being a powerful people in the south, whose great fortress, Jebus, afterwards Jerusalem, defied all the efforts of the Israelites to take it, until at last it yielded to the prowess and skill of David.

From the earlier references to the Hittites one would hardly suppose that they differed much from the other tribes.    It is only when we come to Joshua that we learn that "the land of the Hittites" embraced the whole tract "from the wilderness and Lebanon unto the great river, the river Euphrates, and unto the great sea toward the going down of the sun" (ch. i. 4).    It used to be alleged that Bible history had here introduced a great empire of which ancient history knew nothing.    But of late years it has been made plain from Egyptian, Assyrian, and Hittite monuments likewise, that the references of Scripture are literally correct.

Before proceeding to state what we have recently learned respecting the Hittites, it is necessary to point out that in the Bible the names of the various tribes are not applied in a precise manner. They are indeed often used interchangeably. Thus the city of Hebron is at one time connected with Amorites (comp. Gen. xiii. 18, xiv. 13; Josh. x. 5), at another with Hittites (Gen. xxiii.), and at another with Canaanites (Judg. i. 10). Jerusalem is Amorite in Josh. x. 5, 6, but Jebusite in Judg. i. 21; 2 Sam. v. 6, etc. The Canaanites of Num. xiv. 45 are Amorites in Deut. i. 44.* It is evident that the line of demarcation between the tribes was anything but precise. Evidently they did not preserve carefully their distinctions of race, but mixed freely with one another.

Few results of recent archæological research are more interesting than the light thrown on the empire of the Hittites as it existed in early times. It is as if another Pompeii had been disinterred. The discovery is even more striking than the revelations we have had of Assyria and Egypt, because from of old it was known that these were great empires, but it was hardly surmised that the Hittites were more than a Canaanite tribe. The fullest account of this people, and of the steps by which they have become known, is to be found in the work of Dr. Wright.† His conclusions as to the Hittite inscriptions were at first disputed, but are now more generally accepted. In Brugsch's work on Egypt,‡ and other books on the monuments, much information on the history of this people will be found.

Our information regarding the Hittites is derived from certain inscriptions in Hittite character which have been found in Hamah, Aleppo, Carchemish, etc., as deciphered by Professor Sayce, but more fully from Egyptian and Assyrian monuments.

Very early Egyptian records refer emphatically to certain enemies across the north-east frontier of Egypt under the name

* See Smith's "Bible Dictionary," article *Amorites.*
† "The Empire of the Hittites." By William Wright, D.D., F.R.G.S.; with decipherment of Hittite inscriptions, by Prof. A. H. Sayce, LL.D. 1886.
‡ "A History of Egypt under the Pharaohs, derived entirely from the Monuments." By Henry Brugsch-Bey. 2 vols. 1879.

Amu (herdsmen), and of these two are very prominent, the Akharru or Phœnicians, and the Khita or Kheta (the Khatti of the Assyrian monuments), or Hittites of Scripture. The monuments give us reason to believe that the empire of the Khita or Hittites existed before that of Assyria, and that before Abraham's time it dominated northern Syria, extending over the whole region which, as we have just seen, is assigned to it by Joshua. Its two principal cities were Kadesh, on the Orontes, and Carchemish, on the upper Euphrates. It became so strong a power that it was a formidable rival to Egypt. We find notices of great battles between the two powers in the territories of both. Thothmes III., the Egyptian Alexander, a little later than the time of Abraham, conducted a great campaign against these Khita in the region of Mesopotamia. Rameses II. also signalized himself by his wars with them, and, while victorious, paid a compliment to their greatness and their prowess by marrying a daughter of the Khita king.

Palestine lay out of the way of both the Hittite capitals, Kadesh and Carchemish, and the Hittites residing in it do not seem to have differed much from the other tribes. The resident tribes of Canaan appear to have been under local sheiks or kings, who ruled over their own little territories, but combined together on extraordinary occasions. In Abram's time they do not appear to have been quarrelsome or troublesome to strangers. But Abram was at great pains to avoid all that might excite their opposition or suspicion. His part was a difficult one; he was really an intruder among them, and it is a wonder that they never rose against him or tried to drive him out. He must have borne himself towards them with extraordinary patience and tact. He always impresses us as a man of remarkable self-control, and wise, careful demeanour. But for this, he would have been liable to constant squabbles with the original inhabitants. Towards them he no doubt exercised the same peace-loving spirit as he showed when strife arose between his herdsmen and Lot's, often giving up his rights—though not probably in the too-yielding spirit which was characteristic of Isaac (Gen. xxvi. 17–22).

The religion of the Canaanites was of a corrupt type. In its

leading features it resembled the Chaldæan, from which it originally came. Its leading principle was personification of the powers
of nature, as if every object or phenomenon in nature possessed a
spirit, either benevolent or malevolent. As the sun is by far the
most glorious object in nature, so the worship of Baal, the sun-
god, was the leading feature of the religion. Whatever calamity
befell the people, it was ascribed to the displeasure of Baal. It
became necessary to propitiate him by appropriate rites. The
sun-god demanded a sacrifice by fire. Children were burned alive,
garlanded with flowers, amid music and other signs of joy. With
Baal was associated Ashtoreth, the goddess of the moon. By some
means not easily explained, she was connected, too, with the planet
Venus, and became the Astartë of the Philistines and the Aphrod-
itë of the Greeks. In connection with her
worship the vilest sensuality was sanctified,
and an unbounded pollution of morals ensued. When religion thus became the pa-
tron of all grossness, the very foundations
of society were destroyed. Innumerable
other gods were worshipped by the Canaanites. Abram and his company seem to have
faithfully resisted all compliance with these

ASHTORETH.

practices, but in after times the Canaanitish idolatry proved a
fatal snare to Israel.

It is said that after arriving in Canaan, Abram "passed through
the land unto the place of Sichem, unto the plain of Moreh."
Sichem is the Shechem of later times. Abram would reach it by
passing down on one side of the Jordan, as we have supposed, and
when about midway between the Lake of Galilee and the Dead Sea,
striking westwards or south-westwards till he reached the valley
of Shechem. This vale has usually been the theme of special admiration by travellers in Palestine. "I was ravished," says Van
de Velde, "with the beauty and loveliness that here surrounded
me on all sides. Nothing that I had seen yet in Palestine appeared
to me so charming as that dale......Here there is no wilderness,
here there are no wild thickets; yet there is always verdure,

always shade—not of the oak, the terebinth, the garoub tree, but of the olive grove, so soft in colour, so picturesque in form, that for its sake we can willingly dispense with all other wood. Here there are no impetuous mountain torrents, yet there is water— water, too, in more copious supplies than anywhere else in the land ; and it is just to its many fountains, rills, and water-courses that the valley owes its exquisite beauty......If somewhere in the neighbourhood of Shechem the oak grove of Moreh stood, it is no wonder that Abraham, on seeing the place, thought it good and inviting for pitching his tent......The valley is far from broad, not exceeding in some places a few hundred feet." In approaching Shechem, " for the last quarter of an hour you pass through fruit gardens. Here there are walnut, mulberry, apricot, almond, fig, and pomegranate trees, among the branches of which clusters of grapes hang down in wreaths and festoons. Brooks gurgle through these orchards from all sides. And those hills to the right and left of the valley that raise their highest summits around the town, what are they ? They are Ebal and Gerizim, the mountains from which Israel's curses and blessings were pronounced." *

Stanley's description of the valley is not quite so glowing, but has an interest of its own. " The traveller descends into a wide plain, the wildest and the most beautiful of the plains of the Eph- raimite mountains—one mass of corn, unbroken by boundary or hedge—from the midst of which start up olive trees, themselves un- enclosed in the fields in which they stand. Over the hills which close the northern end of this plain, far away in the distance, is caught the first glimpse of the snowy ridge of Hermon. Its western side is bounded by the abutments of two mountain ranges, running from west to east. These ranges are Gerizim and Ebal ; and up the opening between them, not seen from the plain, lies the modern town of Nablous. This is one of the few instances in which the Roman or rather the Greek name has superseded in popular language the ancient Semitic appellation — Nablous being the corruption of Neapolis, the ' New Town,' founded by Vespasian after the ruin of the older Shechem, which probably lay further

* Van de Velde's " Syria," i. 385, 386.

THE VALE OF SHECHEM.

Page 18.

eastward, and therefore nearer to the opening of the valley. A valley green with grass, gray with olives, gardens sloping down on each side, fresh springs rushing down in all directions ; at the end a white town embosomed in all this verdure, lodged between the two high mountains which extend on each side of the valley—that on the south Gerizim, that on the north Ebal ;—this is the aspect of Nablous, the most beautiful, perhaps it might be said the only very beautiful spot in central Palestine." *

We all know how our permanent feelings about a place are influenced by first impressions, especially favourable impressions. God seems on purpose to have guided Abram to this select spot, in order that his face might be the more radiant and his heart the more thrilled as he listened to the promise, " Unto thy seed will I give this land." We are told that Abram had his place under the oak or terebinth of Moreh (see Revised Version; in Authorized Version, " the plain of Moreh "). Few will agree with Van de Velde that where we have the olive we do not miss the oak. The oak has now disappeared from Shechem, but in Abram's time it was one of those conspicuous trees that marked out a neighbourhood. There seems to have been no " white town embosomed in the verdure " in those days at the end of the vista between the two mountains. The oak or terebinth was the monument of the place ; and standing with its gnarled trunk behind him, and its spreading branches above, Abram might find a symbol of the promise very helpful to his faith. Old and hard though the trunk of the tree was, it could yet send out young sprigs of vegetation, and so might he and Sarai yet have seed. And these vigorous branches that spread out so far in every direction—might not his posterity one day resemble them, and cover the whole land on whose soil he now stood ? Happy posterity, if it should be their lot to dwell peacefully in this peaceful valley ! In the contemplation of that prospect, the toils and troubles of the journey from Haran to Shechem would be forgotten, and the heart of Abram would seek an outlet for the grateful feeling that welled up to his God.

And that outlet he found. " There he builded an altar to the

* " Sinai and Palestine," pp. 233, 234.

Lord that appeared to him." Under that oak many idolatrous rites had probably been performed of old ; it was now to be dedicated to a higher worship. A pillar might have been a suitable record of his gratitude, but something more sacred than a pillar was called for. An altar was a symbol of sacrifice, a place on which to present an offering. The fact of its being a simple altar in the open air was a testimony to the simplicity and spirituality of Abram's religion : no temple was necessary, and no image was lawful—a plain altar was all. In every true heart signal mercy rouses the sense of signal unworthiness. It brings sin to remembrance, and quickens the desire for a sinless condition. Abram's altar served many purposes : it was a testimony for the people of the land to that one living and true God whom Abram served ; it was a memorial of his gratitude for His wonderful mercy ; and it was a token of trust in forgiving and redeeming grace through sacrificial propitiation, and of longing for that purity of heart which would err from God's ways no longer, but obey and love him evermore.

But it seems to have been little more than a glimpse of Shechem that Abram got now. It was too choice a spot to be at his disposal. The Canaanite was then in the land, and he knew the value of land too well to leave Shechem to adventurers. So Abram "removed from thence unto a mountain on the east of Bethel, and pitched his tent, having Bethel on the west, and Hai on the east : and there he builded an altar unto the Lord, and called upon the name of the Lord." The spot is described with great minuteness, and the identification of it has been easily accomplished. "Immediately east of the low gray hills," says Stanley, "on which the Canaanitish Luz and the Jewish Bethel afterwards stood [and where, we may add, the three or four acres of ruinous Beitin are to-day *], rises—as the highest of a succession of eminences now marked by some vestige of ancient edifices—a conspicuous hill, its topmost summit resting, as it were, on the rocky slopes below, and distinguished from them by the olive grove which clusters over its broad surface above." †

---

* Robinson's "Researches," i. 448.　　† "Sinai and Palestine," p. 218.

Here was the first spot in Canaan where it is expressly said that Abram pitched his tent. This seems to confirm our view that it was but a flying visit he paid to Shechem. The high ground, says Robinson, " is one of the finest tracts for pasturage in the whole land."* Here, probably, he might remain unmolested for a time, till his large flocks had consumed all the available nourishment, and it was necessary to hie him to " fresh woods

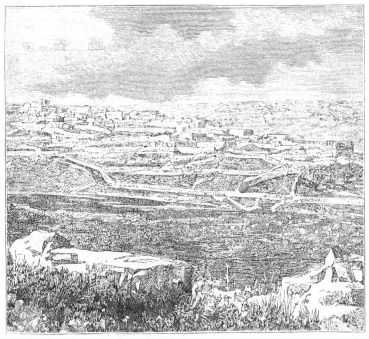

BEITIN (BETHEL).

and pastures new." And here, too, " he builded an altar unto the Lord, and called upon the name of the Lord." For he was neither forgetful of his God nor ashamed of his religion. The words describing his worship are simple but expressive. There is an infinite difference between the religion that is satisfied with the outward form, and that of the heart which is so full of God that the form is but the drapery of the devotion that breathes within.

* " Researches," i. 450.

If he did not make it his business to convert the natives of the country to his faith, neither did he conceal his religion from them; his altar stood before their eyes, and they might readily see the kind of service which he rendered. And if they asked him aught concerning his religion, he would doubtless tell them of his own early idolatries, and of the struggle through which he had renounced Baal and Ashtoreth; and he would let them know how much happier and more satisfied he was now, worshipping Him who made earth and sun and stars alike, who had revealed himself to him as his Friend and Father, and had given him a promise that in his seed all the families of the earth would be blessed.

But even Bethel could not supply permanently what was needful for his flocks, and "Abram journeyed, going on still toward the south." The southern road from Bethel would lead him through many places afterwards to become famous in the history of his race. First Ramah, then Gibeah, then Jerusalem, then Bethlehem, and then Hebron and Beersheba. There is no reason to suppose that any one of these places would attract his special attention, except, perhaps, that he might be struck with the grand situation of Jerusalem, and think how, as the mountains were round about it, so the Lord was round about his people. Possibly he met with Melchizedek as he passed his capital. On the whole, it is best for us all that the future of ourselves and our families is concealed from our view; and it was well for Abram, as he passed Mount Moriah—whether that was Mount Gerizim, near Shechem, or the mount beside the fortress of the Jebusites—that he had no foreboding of what was afterwards to be enacted there.

But now a new and terrible experience befell him. "There was a famine in the land." It is easy to conjure up the horrors that must have resulted to an establishment so large as Abram's, where both men and children and cattle required to be fed, and food was not to be found. "He has to look on his herd melting away, his favourite cattle losing their appearance, his servants murmuring and obliged to scatter. And in his dreams he must have, night after night, seen the old country—the green breadth of the land that Euphrates watered, the heavy-headed corn bending before the warm airs of his native land ; but morning by morning he wakes to the same anxieties, to the sad reality of parched and burned-up pastures, shepherds hanging about with gloomy looks, his own heart distressed and failing." *

It is not difficult to conceive the sore trial to Abram's faith. The situation was somewhat similar to that of the Israelites in the desert of Sinai when they murmured against Moses, and charged him with bringing the host into the wilderness to kill them with hunger.    But whatever fears and misgivings may have occasionally stolen into his heart, Abram appears to have maintained his calmness, and thought deliberately and carefully what was best to be done.    Whether or not he came to his conclusion in the spirit of pure regard to the will of God we are not told, but his resolution was to go down to Egypt.    It was the granary of the world, and bread was to be found there when it could be got nowhere else.    Besides, it had numberless other attractions to a man like Abram.    Now that he was in the south of Canaan, he was near Egypt; he would stay only for a little time, and return at the earliest possible moment.    This seemed the only solution of the difficulty.    His tents are struck, his camels are loaded, his flocks collected, and such stores for the journey as he could obtain are provided ; and by the same route probably as his great-grandchildren in the days of Jacob, he directs his steps to the land of the Nile.

* Dods on *Genesis*, " Expositor's Bible."

# CHAPTER IV.

## ABRAM IN EGYPT.

### (GEN. xii. 10-20.)

IN the succinct notices of Abram's life in Scripture there is much room for reading between the lines. The narrative gives no place to human feeling. The movements of the man are recorded, but not the movements of his heart. The pangs of distress at all the suffering around him during the famine, the sleepless nights, the efforts to comfort timorous hearts, the eager outlook for signs of rain, the hope against hope that relief would come, the wrestlings in prayer, the assaults of unbelief, the return of the soul unto its quiet rest, are all left to the imagination of the reader.

The visit to Egypt is one of the least satisfactory chapters of Abram's life. Neither Godward nor manward does he appear in a favourable light. But if we would be fair we must put ourselves in his place, and think how we should have acted if we had been tossed and driven by the sea of troubles which now bore upon him. Abram was at his wits' end for the very necessaries of life for a great company of servants and cattle, and therefore under great excitement. We are so apt to make angels of the good men of old that we need something startling to remind us that they were men of like passions with ourselves.

The compact with his wife, as they drew near to enter into Egypt, has from the first an ugly look. The divine promise that had brought him to Canaan, though it did not include Sarai by name, included her very really. It was a promise of seed, and

Sarai must be the mother of that seed. How could God mean, when he was about to confer an unspeakable honour and blessing on Abram's house, that this was to be effected through the humiliation and rejection of the beloved partner of his youth, the woman to whom his heart had been united as it never could be to another? In a moment of unbelief afterwards, both Sarai and Abram fancied that the promised seed might come through a slave-concubine; but it was a moment of unbelief. And unbelief was now at the bottom of Abram's proposal to Sarai. Why did they not stick like true spouses to each other? Why did they not commit themselves together for life or death to Him who is a present help in every time of need, and who is ever more ready to honour the simple word of truth than the subtle tale of self-protecting sophistry? And why did not Abram fortify himself and declare his faith by building there an altar to the Lord?

The purpose of the stratagem was very one-sided. Two things impressed Abram—first, that if Sarai, whose person still retained in a remarkable way the charms of youth, went into Egypt as his wife, the Egyptians would kill him in order to get hold of her; and, second, that if she posed as his sister, though she might be taken, his life would be saved.

The first impression was the fruit of sheer unbelief, of forgetfulness of the promise, "I will bless them that bless thee, and curse him that curseth thee." How could the Egyptians kill him if he was the special object of divine protection and promise? Some may ask, how was it possible, after so explicit a promise, for such a fear to find a place in his heart at all? But the answer is easy. There are moods and times when, through collapse of faith, the word of God ceases, even to the best of men, to be a reality, and no voice is heard but that of worldly interest or other carnal consideration. There are times of weakness when God himself seems but a far-off abstraction, and the forces immediately around one play on one's soul with irresistible power. Prayer becomes a form and religious service a mere thing of habit. Most probably it was now such a time with Abram. It was just the same feeling that afterwards overcame David in his conflict with Saul when he said in his heart, "I shall now perish one day by the hand of Saul." How can one perish whom God has pledged himself to protect? Such a man must surely be "immortal till his work is done."

The proposal made to Sarai is very staggering. To propose that she should commit an act of deceit was bad enough, but to propose what would humiliate her, with a view to her husband's safety, was even worse. " Say, I pray thee, thou art my sister : that it may be well with me for thy sake ; and my soul shall live [that is, my life shall be spared] because of thee." It is wholly in Abram's interest that this is proposed to be done. Probably he reasoned that Sarai would be taken in any case, and that if so, it would be better that he should escape than that he should be killed. But what was to become of Sarai ? what outlet from the difficulty and danger was possible for her ?

Our very instincts so rebel against the first aspect of this transaction that it is no wonder that commentators have tried hard to find some explanation that would place it in a better light. But Scripture narratives are so frank and ingenuous that we must take the story as it stands. And, in order to understand it, we must remember the strong sentiment of the time that invested the head of the house with an extraordinary authority and privilege. To him servants, children, and wife were alike in a position of entire subordination. He was a kind of divinity, compared to whom all of them were insignificant ciphers. Lot was ready to give up his daughters to the men of Sodom ; Isaac offered no word of remonstrance when his father was about to lay him on the altar ; Jephthah's daughter would not dream of life when her father had made his vow to God. The head of the house was the one centre of authority, the one element of importance. Abram was the person to whom God had made promises : his life must be protected by whatever means. The submission of Sarai is extolled in Scripture—" She obeyed Abraham, calling him lord ;" asserted no rights for herself beyond what the sentiment of the age permitted ; was willing to sacrifice herself to save her husband : for the position of woman was far indeed then from what, through Christ, it has since become.

This ought not to prevent us from weighing carefully any suggestion that may give another complexion to the proposal of Abram. And the suggestion of some commentators well skilled in the ways of Oriental life is, that in the event of Sarai being sought for as the wife of some Egyptian, Abram might have been able to spin out the customary negotiations till the famine in Canaan should be ended, and he might make his escape with her before she was taken. This, however, is not in keeping with the fact, afterwards recorded (Gen. xx. 13), that the compact between them was not for one occasion merely, but " at every place whither we shall come." It was to be the ordinary arrangement, and Abram could hardly have supposed that it would always be carried out without dishonour to Sarai.

It is not necessary to inquire at this stage, Who was king of Egypt at this time? was he a member of one of the old dynasties, or was he one of the shepherd-kings by whom we know that about this time Lower Egypt was invaded and occupied? The better place for considering such questions will be afterwards, when we come to the period of the entrance of Joseph into Egypt, and of Jacob with his other sons.

The " snare of beauty" was not long of drawing Sarai into its toils. She must have been a very striking figure, for at once she won the admiration of the princes of Pharaoh ; but not one of them sought her for himself. A prize so rare was worthy only of royalty. Passing by themselves, they commended her to Pharaoh, " and the woman was taken into Pharaoh's house," and Pharaoh proceeded to act toward her supposed brother with a rude, barbaric justice that we cannot but esteem. He remunerated him well for giving up his sister. " He entreated Abram well for her sake : and he had sheep, and oxen, and he-asses, and menservants, and maidservants, and she-asses, and camels." We can well believe that never did gifts carry with them a more uncomfortable feeling. " The price of my beloved Sarai !" we may conceive Abram saying to himself, as he flung himself into his tent, after having dismissed the servants of Pharaoh with silken phrases of gratitude and respect. It is difficult to conceive a man nearer to despair—the desire of his eyes taken from him at a stroke, but with such profuse conventional acknowledgments that it would have been impossible for him even to show that he had been most cruelly wronged.

But God does not forsake his servants even when they have been thoughtless and faithless. Who knows but the very depth of his calamity roused his slumbering faith, restored his trust, and sent him back to his God and Father? Be this as it may, God came to the rescue. "The Lord plagued Pharaoh and his house with great plagues because of Sarai Abram's wife." Some may ask, was this just? Pharaoh did not know that she was Abram's wife; he had the best authority for believing her to be only his sister. Why should he be visited with great plagues because of a sin which he was not conscious of committing? The answer is, that even if Sarai had only been Abram's sister, Pharaoh was committing a sin in taking her to his house, to make her no doubt, in due time, a member of his harem. Whatever sanction of usage this custom might have, it was essentially unjust. It was not after this fashion that God designed the relations of the sexes to be conducted. God did not heap wealth on some men that they might bribe and lure a multitude of women to pander to their lusts. God did not raise kings and princes to their elevation that they might spread a net for female virtue, degrading the lives and polluting the souls of their victims. No doubt Pharaoh had drawn a line for himself—at least so he said; he would not thus deal with any man's wife. But there is no line more difficult to keep than a line to regulate sinful indulgence. When one begins one cannot stop. In this case Pharaoh, if he spoke the truth, did not consciously transgress the line he had drawn; nevertheless, though under false pretences, a man's wife had been brought to his house. The whole system was iniquitous, and the "great plagues" which befell him now, while Sarai was the particular occasion of them, were designed to rebuke a custom which was pre-eminently disgraceful in kings, though it was by kings that it was most commonly practised.

Next comes the remonstrance of Pharaoh with Abram. And it must be owned that Pharaoh appears in the whole matter to greater advantage than Abram. In calling his wife his sister Abram was foolish as well as wicked. Pharaoh protests that had he known she was his wife he would not have laid hands on her. This may have been a mere speech got up for the occasion—very probably it was, but it must have made Abram look very foolish and guilty. Reference has sometimes been made to a very old Egyptian record found on a papyrus, containing "The Story of the Two Brothers," now in the British Museum, where the Pharaoh of the time is represented as fetching by means of a military force a beautiful woman to his court, and murdering her husband. If cases of this kind occurred, they account for Abram's fears. In any case he could not have breathed freely till his back was turned on Egypt, and his caravan was again in motion toward the bare hills and parched pastures of Canaan.

Abram, if he was in circumstances to look about him at all in Egypt, must have been interested in a state of things which, socially and religiously, was in many ways unlike what he had left behind him in Chaldæa, and certainly what he had found in Canaan. We know now that many marvellous monuments of Egyptian enterprise and skill were already there. Perhaps the Great Pyramid looked down on him precisely as it does to-day; while some of the great temples reared their massive forms, embellished with the beauties of Egyptian architecture, and preserving the records of the national glory. In regard to worship, it is probable that he found a less glaring departure from his own monotheism than in Chaldæa; although already honour had begun to be paid to that innumerable multitude of gods for which Egypt became remarkable, and the miserable worship of the sacred bull and other animals may already have prevailed. Egypt is admitted to have preserved the knowledge of the one supreme God longer than Chaldæa and other countries, at least as an esoteric doctrine, for it was not commonly taught to the people.

But there was one feature of Egyptian religion which could not but impress Abram—the prominence of the doctrine of a future life. " It was the universal belief in Egypt," says Canon Rawlinson, " from a date long anterior to Abraham, that immediately after death the soul descended into the lower world (Amenti), and was conducted into the Hall of Truth, or of the Two Truths, where it was judged in the presence of Osiris and of his forty-two assessors, the lords of truth and judges of the dead. Anubis (Anepa), the Director of the Weight, son of Osiris and Nephthys, brought forth a pair of scales, and after placing in one of the

FINAL JUDGMENT—WEIGHING A SOUL.
*(From the Egyptian Monuments.)*

scales a figure or emblem of truth, set in the other a vase containing the good deeds of the deceased—Thoth, the Divine Wisdom, standing by the while with a tablet in his hand whereon to record the result." If the good deeds preponderated, the soul was conveyed in the boat of the Sun to the Elysian Fields ; if the evil, it was doomed to a series of transmigrations, which terminated either in its annihilation, if its sinful tendencies proved permanently incurable, or in its return to its former body, to live once more a human life on earth. This was an Egyptian edition of the covenant of works, not grace ; but however erroneous in its ground of acceptance, it was something that it so emphatically recognized a life to come, and a judgment-seat at which men would be judged "according to the deeds done in the body, whether they were good or whether they were evil."

This topic is one of intense importance, and it is well to dwell on it a little. It is true that while Abram was in Egypt, his mind must have been full of that discreditable plot to which he unhappily resorted to screen him from danger, so that he was in no spirit to profit by Egyptian revelations of a future state. But when calmer times came, and his mind was in a better frame for peering into the unseen, the Egyptian doctrine, if he did not need its help, would at least be regarded with lively interest. Surely it is a shallow theology that looks on the patriarchs as practically unacquainted with a future state, and as limiting all God's promises to the life that now is. That certainly is not the view of the author of the Epistle to the Hebrews. It could not be under the influence of such a spirit that Abram "looked for the city which hath the foundations, whose builder and maker is God" (Revised Version). There was but one city in the universe that answered to this description, and that was capable of being the true fulfilment of Abram's hopes. To that city, which we know as "the new Jerusalem that cometh down out of heaven from God," his heart habitually turned, especially in times of weariness and sadness. Doubtless, it would be one of his grounds of self-reproach in better times how little he had been thinking when in Egypt of that city.

On the whole, in leaving Egypt, Abram could have had little satisfaction with himself. He had been in a community where the worship of God was less corrupt than in any other country with which he had had to do; he had seen religion more allied to morality, and in some degree influencing the ordinary conduct of men; and he had found faith in a life to come, connected no doubt with much error and superstition, but vividly and power-fully presented as a great motive in favour of good and against evil. He had been treated with no ordinary generosity in connection with his stratagem concerning Sarai. He had heard the king of the country repudiate as a gross sin the taking of another man's wife; while he had not only believed him capable of that crime, but also of murdering the woman's husband, that he might not be an obstacle to his guilty pleasure. Was it not eminently in such circumstances and in such company that he had been bound to show the higher and purer effect of the religion which he had been divinely taught? Yet not only had he lost his opportunity, but now he left Egypt conscious of having gone down to a lower moral level than that asserted by the Egyptians themselves. How often, through fear and faithlessness, do even good men prove traitors to the cause of truth!

In this episode of Abram's history we see in miniature a chapter of the history of his posterity. First, driven into Egypt by famine; next, treated unjustly by Pharaoh and the Egyptians, who reduced them to slavery and deprived them of their due recompense for their labour; then divinely vindicated by the plagues of heaven falling on the king and his people; and finally driven away as dangerous neighbours, but laden with Egyptian spoil.

## CHAPTER V.

RETURN TO CANAAN—SEPARATION FROM LOT.

(GEN. xiii.)

NOTWITHSTANDING all that he had lost by the effects of the "grievous famine," Abram prospered again, and with his resources greatly increased through the profuse liberality of Pharaoh, who would scorn to take back what he had once given, returned to "the south" "very rich in cattle, in silver, and in gold." But he does not seem to have lingered in "the south" —the neighbourhood of Beersheba and Hebron. "He went on his journeys from the south even to Bethel, unto the place where his tent had been at the beginning, between Bethel and Hai; unto the place of the altar, which he had made there at the first: and there Abram called on the name of the Lord." There is great significance here in the expressions "at the beginning," "at the first." They shadow a state of mind delineated very vividly by the prophet Hosea, when, after unholy endeavours to better her condition, the backsliding wife returns to her first husband, "for then it was better with me than now," or that of the prodigal son resolving, "I will arise, and go to my father." Abram had not gone so far aside as either of these, but he is eager, in more senses than one, to be back where he was. He sees that he has made a mistake—that journey to Egypt should never have been undertaken. He should have remained where he was, trusting his flocks to God. And now he seems eager to retrieve his error, desirous, as far as he can, to erase an unfortunate chapter from his life, to tear out a blotted leaf, and begin again as before. It goes without saying that his spiritual life had suffered by that visit to Egypt. His deceit, his distrust, his selfishness had made a gulf between him and his God. He sighs now for the happiness and peace of former days; and with the hope that the old place would help to bring back the old feeling, that the hallowed associations of former days would facilitate the return of communion with his Father, he goes back to the place of the altar which he had made there at the first, and calls upon the name of the Lord.

And if we may judge from his future conduct, he did not call in vain. Personally, he seems to have regained his old place side by side with God; but the effects of his error on others do not appear to have been so easily rectified. A good man may err, may conform to the world, may engage in a lucrative but pernicious business, without sacrificing his own standing with God; but what of his son, what of his nephew, whom he has brought up to the business, whom he has initiated in his ways? It is here that the Nemesis of Providence often appears. The father or uncle may keep his position; the son or nephew slips and falls. The devil gets a foothold at the very beginning, and he speedily improves it to gain the whole man. We cannot affirm with certainty that the visit to Egypt increased the worldliness of Lot, or that the eclipse of Abram's faith was followed by a profounder eclipse of his nephew's; but the coincidence is remarkable, for there came now a decisive moment in Lot's life, and he did not act like a man of God.

All this time Abram had been accompanied by his nephew. Though constantly together, the two friends kept their establishments apart, having separate flocks and herds, and separate herdsmen to look after them; and now the cattle had grown to such numbers that it was no longer convenient for them to remain together. Strife arose between their servants. The better and more convenient pastures would naturally be sought by both, and the contention evidently rose to an unbecoming warmth. Its effect on the native inhabitants was not edifying. Abram could not bear that the Canaanite and the Perizzite should see them quarrelling.  He had been sufficiently humiliated in Egypt by the king's rebuke of his unworthy artifice, and by the thought that the worshipper of the true God had appeared in a more unworthy light morally than the inhabitants of the country.  Such a thing must not occur again ; at any sacrifice, his strife with Lot must be brought to an end.

Abram is himself again ; and now he acts with a magnanimity which is just as striking as his deceit and selfishness in Egypt were pitiable.  As the elder of the two, the uncle of Lot, the leader of the enterprise, and, above all, the man to whom God had revealed himself and to whom he had promised the land, he might most reasonably have demanded the first choice, if the two establishments were to be separated.  But peace and a good example to the natives were more to him than convenience or gain.  His personal interests do not count in the matter.  Well would it have been had all settlers in new countries been as careful of the moral impression of their actings on the natives !  With Abram we naturally couple men like William Penn, who was so careful in the settlement of Pennsylvania to do nothing unworthy in the eyes of the natives, so eager to give them an impression of Christians as men "that did justly, that loved mercy, and that walked humbly with their God."

So Lot gets the first choice, and finds the whole land before him.  In the neighbourhood of Bethel there rises one of the highest hills in Palestine, commanding an extensive view.  Dean Stanley describes the scene with his usual graphic power :—"From this height Abraham and Lot must be conceived as taking the wide survey of the country, 'on the right hand and on the left,' such as can be enjoyed from no other point in the neighbourhood. To the east there rises in the foreground the jagged range of the hills above Jericho ; in the distance the dark wall of Moab ; between them lies the wide valley of the Jordan, its course marked by the tract of forest in which its rushing stream is enveloped ; and down to this valley a wide and deep ravine, now, as always, the main line of communication by which it is approached from the central hills of Palestine—a ravine rich with vine, olive, and fig, winding its way through ancient reservoirs and sepulchres, remains of a civilization now extinct, but in the times of the patriarchs not yet begun. To the south and the west the view commanded the bleak hills of Judea......and in the far distance the southern range on whose slope is Hebron. Northward are the hills which divide Judea from the rich plains of Samaria." *

The locality in all this amphitheatre that fascinated Lot was "the plain of Jordan." It was so rich and well-watered, probably by artificial irrigation, that it looked like "the garden of the Lord," and reminded him of the land of Egypt. But we must not take the description too literally; for there is no hill near Bethel where a full view may be got of the whole valley of the Jordan.† The cliffs that rise on its western side prevent the valley from being properly seen. But whether Lot could see the Jordan valley from Bethel or not, he must have known its distinguishing features, its great fertility, and its remarkable fitness for all agricultural and horticultural purposes.

In those days it was a more attractive and productive valley than it is now. But this may readily be understood. Contrasting its present condition with what it might yet be, the author of "The Land and the Book" remarks :—"Jericho was called 'the city of palm-trees,' but the one only palm that a quarter of a century ago stood, like a solitary sentinel, near the old tower is gone, and thus has passed away the last vestige of that great forest which gave name to the city. The forest, however, might be restored, and then the best dates would come again from Jericho. The soil and climate are admirably adapted to this tree; and, indeed, *there is nothing required but cultivation and irrigation to make the whole plain of the Lower Jordan fruitful as the garden of the Lord.* Every acre of it might be watered from the strong brook in Wady Kelt, from the great fountain Es Sultan, from those of Wady Dûk, and from the Jordan itself......The valley of the Jordan could sustain half a million of inhabitants. Cotton, rice, sugar-cane, indigo, and nearly every other valuable product for the use of man, would flourish most luxuriantly......Now how desolate and barren ! Just around

* "Sinai and Palestine," p. 218.      † Conder's "Handbook to the Bible," p. 238.

'Ain es Sultan, and between it and Riha, the plain is covered with a forest of thorn-trees; but look elsewhere, and the eye aches from the glare of naked sand-fields glowing beneath a burning sun." *

We shall afterwards have occasion to inquire into the nature of the changes which this region underwent at the time of the destruction of Sodom and Gomorrah. Meanwhile our business is with Lot and Abram. Lot in Scripture is called "a righteous man" (2 Peter ii. 8); but he had the infirmities of his race. The temporal advantages to be enjoyed in a region so favoured by nature blinded him to the moral putridity with which it stank. One would have thought that such a place as Sodom was the last spot in creation where he would have thought of settling with his family of young daughters and all his servants, male and female, over whose morals he was bound to watch with paternal care. But, on the one hand, the sin of the people was so common that it ceased to be thought much of; for in the moral as in the material world men may get used by lapse of time to what is disgusting, so that it ceases to shock them. Moreover, greed seems to have been Lot's besetting sin. The vision of multiplied wealth not only dazzled but overcame him. It carried him captive, as helpless as if he had been in chains. There are lusts of such intensity that when the opportunity of indulging them starts up, conscience is paralyzed, and all power of resistance vanishes. Such a lust was greed in the case of Lot. Nothing could carry him past the mine of gold which now lay at his feet.

So Lot parts from Abram, his life-long friend and companion, his spiritual father likewise in all probability, his guardian angel in many an hour of weakness, the best and noblest friend he could have had. It could not have been a happy parting. Lot could not have been unmoved at the loss he was about to sustain, and though he would not let himself think much of it, at the moral risk he was about to run; and Abram could not have been unmoved to see him descending into a society of unexampled impurity, accompanied by a wife who, whatever the good points of

* "The Land and the Book," pp. 621, 622.

PLAIN OF JERICHO AT THE PRESENT DAY.

*Page 67.*

her character, was more likely to inflame than to check his worldliness, and who was capable of imperilling the moral welfare of her daughters for the sake of rich connections and splendid marriages.

Of the previous history of the people of Sodom and the other cities we have little knowledge. Their genealogy is given in Gen. x. 15–20, but beyond the fact that they were Canaanites, and that their country was the limit of Canaanite territory on the south-east, we know nothing. "The border of the Canaanites was from Sidon, as thou comest to Gerar, unto Gaza; as thou goest, unto Sodom, and Gomorrah, and Admah, and Zeboim, even unto Lasha." Of this place Lasha, which was the farthest limit of Canaanite territory, we have no knowledge whatever, unless it was another name for Zoar. The group of cities were five in number, each with a king or sheik of its own. Sodom was evidently the foremost of them. It was "toward Sodom" that Lot first pitched his tent (Gen. xiii. 12). Afterwards he seems to have had his residence in the town (ch. xix.). Sodom seems to have excelled the other places in wickedness, for its name retains a special taint of infamy, and it was on it that the divine judgment fell first. There can be but one explanation of Lot's selection of it for his headquarters—the worldly advantage of its situation must have been greater than that of any of the other cities.

Leaving Lot to enjoy his choice, if it was possible for him to do so, we return to Abram. It was not long before his generosity in giving Lot the first choice was rewarded, and a new reason presented to him for prizing the comparatively bleak hills about Bethel, where he was to remain. God renewed the promise and the covenant to him in a more specific form. He bade him "lift up his eyes, and look from the place where he was, northward, and southward, and eastward, and westward," and promised to give him all the land which he saw, to him and to his seed after him for ever. Formerly he had promised to make him a great nation, but now he intensifies the language: "I will make thy seed as the dust of the earth: so that if a man can number the dust of the earth, then shall thy seed also be numbered." And as if it were not enough to see the land with his eyes, he bids him "arise, walk through the land in the length of it and in the breadth of it; for I will give it unto thee."

This was a very seasonable announcement to Abram. He had been accustomed hitherto to look on Lot's family as much the same as his own. Possibly, when no offspring was given to himself, the thought sometimes occurred, may not Lot be counted as my son, and may not the blessing come to me through him? If ever such a thought presented itself, it can be entertained no longer. It is not to Lot, who has now left him, but to his own seed that the land is to be given. And this gracious assurance of God further shows to Abram that, notwithstanding Egypt, God is reconciled to him, is still his friend; he is his covenant-God as of old. Abram's generous readiness to let Lot have his choice is thus rewarded. Lot has chosen his corner, but it is not a corner that will be blessed. The whole land remains, and that is to become the property of Abram's seed. And Abram need have no scruple in going to whatever part of the country it suits him to go. If he prefers to go southward, by all means let him go. Encouraged by these gracious assurances, "Abram removed his tent, and came and dwelt in the plain [by the oaks —Revised Version] of Mamre, which is in Hebron, and built there an altar unto the Lord." This was the first consecration of Hebron. The most part of what remained of Abram's life was spent either there or at Beersheba, which was part of the district so well known in the Old Testament as "Negeb," or "the south."

Hebron—sometimes called Mamre, after the chief man of the place (ch. xxiii. 17, 19)—afterwards attained to great and manifold distinction, first as the burial-place of the patriarchs, afterwards as one of the cities of refuge, and finally as the first capital of the kingdom of David. In the time of Moses it was an old city, "seven years older than Zoan in Egypt" (Num. xiii. 22). It had probably been occupied by the founder of Egypt, Mizraim, in his migration southward, till, learning of still richer fields on the banks of the Nile, he had directed his course to Egypt, and laid the foundation of Zoan, its earliest capital. It was half-way between Jerusalem and Beersheba, about twenty miles distant from each. A former name was Kirjath-arba (Judg. i. 10). It was then the city of Arba, the father of Anak, the progenitor of the Anakim, the giant race of whom we hear so often afterwards. Its present name is El Khalil.

Mamre, after whom both the city and the oak, which marked the place of Abram's encampment, were sometimes called, was an Amorite, the proprietor of the land in the neighbourhood. If it be asked, how was Abram permitted to pitch his tent by the oak of Mamre, not only using Mamre's pastures, but the very spot which was pre-eminently associated with his name? it may be said that probably Abram in some way remunerated Mamre for this privilege, as he afterwards paid Ephron the Hittite a substantial sum for the ownership of the cave of Machpelah. But there is another consideration to be taken into account. The very presence of a man like Abram brought advantages with it in those wild times. If the servants of Nabal could represent to him the commercial value of David's presence in the neighbourhood of Carmel, much more probably might Abram's neighbours feel that they were the better for him. When Isaac was in Gerar, the king and his officers went to him and urged him to make a treaty with them, because they saw that the Lord was with him. This may have been merely the result of a superstitious dread toward one who was evidently in partnership with the Almighty, but it counted for much on Isaac's behalf; and no doubt the same feeling prevailed towards Abram, and helped to secure for him that peaceful life at the hands of the native inhabitants which he appears uniformly to have enjoyed.

Situated at the head of a valley, on a high table-land afterwards known as "the hill country of Judah," Hebron was celebrated then, as it is still, for two things—the excellence of its pastures and the luxuriance of its vines. When Dr. Edward Robinson, the distinguished author of "Biblical Researches," visited Hebron in 1838, he paid a visit to a chief who was residing by just such an oak as that under which Abram lived some four thousand years before. "The venerable oak," he says, "to which we now came is a splendid tree; we hardly saw another like it in all Palestine—

certainly not on this side of the plain of Esdraelon. Indeed, large trees are very rare in this quarter of the country. The trunk of this tree measures twenty-two and a half feet around the lower part. It separates almost immediately into three large boughs or trunks, and one of these again, higher up, into two. The branches extend from the trunk in one direction forty-nine feet, their whole diameter in the same direction being eighty-nine feet, and in the other at right angles eighty-three and a half feet. The tree is in a thrifty state, and the trunk sound. It stands alone, in the midst of a field; the ground beneath is covered with grass, and clean; there is a well with water near by; so that a more beautiful spot for recreation could hardly be found.

"I am not sure whether this is the tree which Sir John Mandeville saw near Hebron, of which he relates that it was green in Abraham's day, but dried up at the time of our Saviour's crucifixion, like all the other trees then in the world......This cannot be either the tree of Abraham or its successor; for his terebinth probably stood more towards Jerusalem, and had already disappeared in the days of Jerome."*

Thankful for so much mercy, Abram and Sarai pursued at Hebron the even tenor of their way, but under the silent restlessness of an unfulfilled hope. The flocks and herds would give full and interesting employment to the one, and the other would find an interest in her embroideries and other needle-work, and in kindly attentions to her female servants and their children; but in both an unsatisfied heart-hunger would ever and anon ruffle their tranquillity. Nor could they be free from anxious thoughts about Lot and his family—all the more that they had appeared so little sensible of their spiritual danger, and so thoroughly captivated with the riches of Sodom.

* "Researches," ii. 81, 82.

# CHAPTER VI.

## THE RESCUE OF LOT.

### (GEN. xiv.)

THE choice of Lot, when he separated from Abram, brought troubles on him and his household that he had not taken into his calculation. He had forgot that where the carcass is, thither the eagles are gathered together, and that the richer a country is, the more likely is it to be attacked and plundered. There was another consideration even more important than this that he does not appear to have thought of. The valley of the Jordan forms part of the direct route between the north and the south, between the region of the Euphrates and the region of the Nile, and the command of this valley was essential for those men of the north who desired access to Egypt, whether for purposes of commerce or for purposes of war. Before Lot settled in Sodom a confederacy of northern kings had attacked and overcome the kings or chiefs of Sodom and the neighbouring cities or states, and for twelve years the Canaanite kings remained quietly in subjection, paying no doubt the stipulated tribute. In the thirteenth year they rebelled, and in the fourteenth came Chedorlaomer and his allies, for the purpose of subduing the rebellion and regaining their control of the Jordan valley.

The chapter which contains this story has all the appearance of a separate narrative, written perhaps at the time, and afterwards incorporated into the Book of Genesis. Lot is introduced as " Abram's brother's son," as if we had not been told this before. Abram is called " the Hebrew," and we are told that he was living in the plain of Mamre— facts which would have been assumed in a continuous narrative. In the interval between the two writings, some places had changed their names, and we are told that Bela is the same as Zoar, the vale of Siddim is the Salt Sea, and En-mishpat is Kadesh.

Respecting these confederate kings little is known. Chedorlaomer of Elam was evidently the leader of the second expedition, showing that Elam was then superior to Babylon. Now, the Elamites, as we have seen, were a people of Semitic race, while the Canaanites were Cushite ; so that the expedition was in the line of those Semitic conquests which had already subdued the Cushite Accadians, and it had for its object more and more to assert Semitic supremacy in the East. The Canaanite kings of Sodom and the plain were the natural foes of the Shemites ; the northern confederates could not count on their friendship in any expedition which drew them towards Egypt. They had consequently made war on them, and obtained by the sword the control of their country. But the kings of the plain could not brook subjection, and some time after Lot came among them they rebelled. If they reckoned that Chedorlaomer would not undertake a distant expedition for an object of so pressing importance, they were mistaken ; Chedorlaomer and his allies mustered in force, and by a circuitous route set out to compel the submission of the plain.

Crossing probably from Mesopotamia to Damascus, the allies first attacked the Rephaims in Ashteroth Karnaim—that is, Ashteroth of the two horns or crescent—a city that derived its name from Ashtoreth or Astartë, the Phœnician goddess of the moon. This place comes afterwards into notice as a chief city of Og, King of Bashan (Deut. i. 4 ; Josh. xii. 4), and was included in the territory of the transjordanic half tribe of Manasseh. As the invaders marched southwards, the Zuzims in Ham and the Emims in Shaveh Kiriathaim were next attacked—formidable foes in what was afterwards the tribe of Reuben ; and then the Horites or cave-dwellers in Mount Seir, inhabiting the rocky mountains afterwards occupied by the descendants of Esau, whose chief city, Petra, still exhibits remarkable samples of houses excavated from the rock.   It was the policy of the invaders to subdue these tribes on the east of the Jordan, in order to prepare the way for their getting undisturbed possession of the Jordan valley itself.   They then attacked the Amalekites and Amorites on the south border of Canaan ; after subduing whom they turned northward as far as Hazezon-tamar, afterwards Engedi, on the west of the Dead Sea. All was now ready for the encounter with the kings of the plain. In their march from Engedi to Sodom the invaders must have passed within a few miles of Abram, for Hebron is less than twenty miles west of Engedi.

The battle was fought "in the vale of Siddim, which is the salt sea."   "The vale of Siddim" is one of those expressions which have always puzzled commentators.   Neither the word itself nor any notice elsewhere throws light on its precise situa- tion.   If we take the words as they stand, they would seem to imply that it was a plain now covered by the Dead Sea, as Josephus asserts ; but whether at the northern or southern end is uncertain.   The northern kings, flushed with their successive victories over the Rephaims, the Zuzims, the Emims, the Horites, the Amalekites, and the Amorites, at last encountered the King of Sodom and his allies.   The vale of Siddim was full of slime- pits, or pits of bitumen, and may have been chosen by the Sodomite kings, as Bannockburn with its concealed pits was chosen by the Scots, as likely to embarrass an enemy ignorant of the ground.   But the invaders made their attack with such deter- mined vigour that the pits designed to entangle them proved the destruction of the defenders.   The result of the battle was the total rout of the Sodomite allies and the abandonment of their homes and all that they contained to the enemy.   Everything capable of removal was carried off by the victors.   Lot, who does not appear to have been engaged in the battle, was carried off, probably mounted on one of his own camels, or driven on foot with his hands tied behind his back.   Demoralized by sensuality, the people of the plain seem to have made a wretched resistance, such of them as were not killed flying to the mountains without any attempt to rally, and leaving their families and possessions to the tender mercies of the enemy, which were, no doubt, cruel enough. Neither bravery nor chivalry could be looked for among a people so utterly degraded as these were by sensual vice.

For the invaders everything seemed to succeed to a wish. But just as their triumph was complete, danger came to them from a totally unexpected quarter. "One that had escaped came and told Abram." He was living some twenty miles from the scene of the disaster; but to render any assistance to his nephew was a serious matter. Abram had never been accustomed to war; his people were shepherds, no doubt trained when necessary to encounter wild beasts, and skilled in weapons used against them, but not accustomed to fight with men. And the flocks could not be left long to take care of themselves; they needed day by day the care of the shepherds. And how could Abram expect success in battle against these confederate kings? Had they not swept foe after foe before them, and triumphed on every successive field? Was it not just to throw away his own life and the lives of his people, to attack an enemy of such valour and vigour? Was not the calamity of Lot the retribution of Providence on his foolish choice, and ought he not to be left to reap as he had sown?

It was just a case in which an ordinary man would have folded his hands and said, "I told you so." But the nobility of Abram's soul rose to the occasion. That Lot had treated him shabbily was nothing. That he was now reaping the fruit of his own folly was nothing. That Abram's servants were needed for other work was nothing. That the enterprise was dangerous and difficult and even impossible was still nothing, if God should be with them. The one thing clear to Abram was, that an attempt should be made to rescue Lot. Blood was thicker than water; his brother's son must not end his life as a slave; his old associate and friend must not be abandoned without one blow struck in his behalf.

Very chivalrous and highly sentimental considerations, some would say, but utterly impracticable, and therefore most unreasonable! Not unreasonable to Abram, however, for he had the faith that removes mountains. If God called him to this undertaking, he would strengthen him and carry him through. Abram was the father of the faithful; and the faith which now triumphed under the oak of Mamre was of the very same calibre with that which a thousand years later fortified the young shepherd on the adjacent mountains of Bethlehem to attack the lion and the bear, and a little further to the west, in the valley of Elah, to advance fearlessly with his sling and stones against the giant of Gath.

Abram has the happy knack, like other unselfish men, of making friends wherever he goes. He is happily on excellent terms with his Amorite neighbours, Aner, Eshcol, and Mamre. He induces them to take part with him in his rescue expedition; arms his own servants to the number of three hundred and eighteen; and making such arrangements as he can for his flocks and his family, sets out in pursuit of the now retiring invaders. It is a new character for the shepherd-chief, the man of peace, to whom strife is so obnoxious. But even the rule to live peaceably with all men is qualified by the condition, "inasmuch as lieth in you." From Hebron to Dan is a distance of more than a hundred and twenty miles, to traverse which, whatever expedition he might use, would demand several days. But, unencumbered as he was, he could travel much faster than Chedorlaomer's army, and by calculation he might find that they would reach what was afterwards called Dan about the same time as himself. The eastern kings would advance the whole way by the valley of the Jordan and the lakes; Abram would take the more western route, and would be screened by the mountains from observation. Night is always the best season for sudden and unexpected attacks, when the enemy, wearied and disposed to rest, cannot know the extent or resources of the attacking party. So also the division of an attacking force into sections is likely to increase the panic. Adopting this plan, and attacking the enemy in the dark at various points, Abram seems to have gained a complete and easy victory. Many of the confederates were slain, including, it would seem, Chedorlaomer and the other chiefs (see ver. 17); the rest of the forces fled in confusion, and were pursued by Abram to Hobah, on the left hand of Damascus. It was altogether a most brilliant affair: everything that the enemy had carried off was

PLAIN OF MEROM, THE SCENE OF ABRAHAM'S VICTORY.

*Page 78.*

recovered; Lot was rescued from captivity; all was done that could be done to retrieve the disaster.

We cannot tell what Lot's feelings were—the narrative is silent on the subject; but the fact that he returned to Sodom, settled there as before, and probably resumed his former occupation, does not tell in his favour. After receiving such a warning from Providence, we should have thought that he would be eager to get out of Sodom; and we cannot doubt that had he expressed this desire to Abram, the generosity that had rescued him at such expense and risk would have permitted him to settle in his neighbourhood as before. But no desire seems to have been expressed by Lot either to get out of Sodom or to return to Abram. If this man is to be saved in the end, he will have to be pulled out of the fire with still greater violence.

We meet with a new and great surprise as we return with Abram towards Hebron. That he should be met by the King of Sodom, who had not been carried captive, was only natural; but another royal personage presents himself to the conqueror — Melchizedek, King of Salem, priest of the most high God. No great man was ever introduced in the page of history with such a want of explanation or connection. Who was he? How came he to possess the symbolical name Melchizedek, "king of righteousness"? and where was Salem, the city of "peace," where he reigned? How did he come to be a priest as well as a king, and not a priest of Baal or Ashtoreth, but a priest of Abram's own deity—a priest of the most high God? Who were his forefathers? and who came after him? Some of these questions, and especially the last, are extremely puzzling. There is no known family, or place, or office where we may naturally place Melchizedek. We can only think of him as one who had preserved the primitive religion of Noah in its simplicity and integrity, and had rejected all the polytheistic and idolatrous practices that had grown up, north, south, east, and west. Though called a king, he had little influence on the people of the country, dwelling apart, it would seem, from all his neighbours. That he was the patriarch Shem, as some have conjectured, seems out of the question, not only on chronological grounds, but also because there was no reason why this should not have been stated if it was true, and because it was impossible that Shem should have been settled amid a population almost exclusively Canaanite.

Many other explanations, equally unwarranted, have been suggested regarding him. At the present day it is generally thought that he was a local prince, of the family of Shem, who had come with his people into the territories of the Canaanites in much the same way as Abram himself, but without Abram's call or mission. His being called a king does not imply much, for the head even of the little city Zoar was called by the royal title. The only greatness of Melchizedek was a moral greatness, the greatness of his priesthood; and it was for this that even Abram, in all the flush of victory, and at the head of a troop that had routed and slaughtered the mighty kings of the east, acknowledged his superiority and paid him tithes. But for anything that we know of Melchizedek before or after, he might have fallen from the clouds. It is this mystery of origin, this absence of all genealogical connection and historical explanation, this sudden breaking in of a visitor who vanishes into the darkness with equal abruptness, that makes Melchizedek such a historical puzzle.

But our ignorance of so many things about him ought not to blind us to the significance of what we do know. His personal name and the name of his kingdom are both significant. Unlike the mass of Oriental rulers, he honoured "righteousness" as the foundation of his government, and "peace" founded on righteousness as its end. To most Eastern kings the end of royal power was to gratify their own inclinations, to humour their pride, and to surround themselves with luxuries and pleasures; or if they thought of benefiting their people, it was mainly by war and rapine, by carrying fire and sword into the territories of their neighbours, and enriching their own nation through the plundering and murdering of their foes. Of this style of government Chedorlaomer and his allies had just been furnishing a characteristic specimen. To these Melchizedek was a great contrast. In his view justice lay at the foundation and peace was the crown of all good government. He foreshadowed that Divine Ruler of whom it was afterwards sung, "The mountains shall bring peace to the people, and the little hills, by righteousness."

That Salem was the place afterwards called Jerusalem seems probable, not only from the resemblance of the name, but also because it lay in the line of Abram's homeward march. But as we have said, Melchizedek's great distinction was that he was priest as well as king. He worshipped the same God as Abram, and doubtless mainly after the same manner. If Salem was Jerusalem, it was barely twenty miles from Hebron, and Abram and Melchizedek could hardly be unknown to each other. Abram may have been under obligations to Melchizedek for spiritual instruction and for wholesome spiritual influence. If we knew all the circumstances, the narrative that now seems so mysterious might be all natural and plain. According to Josephus, Melchizedek fed the army of Abram; to himself, as we learn from Genesis, he gave bread and wine. It has sometimes been attempted to give a mystical and sacramental meaning to this bread and wine, but surely the obvious meaning is the true one—they were refreshments provided for Abram, and possibly for his people, very necessary, and doubtless very grateful, after the strain and toil of the last few days. Bread and wine represented all the products of the soil which God had given for the welfare of man. They were, therefore, fit material symbols of the blessing which Melchizedek was about to pronounce on Abram; and they were well adapted to that sacramental use to which they were first applied two thousand years afterwards, when they were made to symbolize all that has been brought to man by Him whose "flesh is meat indeed, and whose blood is drink indeed." It was not merely as a friendly neighbour in sympathy with Abram that Melchizedek now presented himself—not merely in the relation in which Barzillai met David in his flight from Jerusalem. His real object was to bless him. He met him as a priest. "He blessed him, and said, Blessed be Abram of the most high God, possessor of heaven and earth: and blessed be the most high God, which

hath delivered thine enemies into thy hand." No such benediction had fallen on Abram on his return from Egypt. "Them
that honour me I will honour," is the rule of divine blessing.
Abram had sacrificed his own interests and had risked everything
on a mission of mercy, and now he learns how pleasing such service and sacrifice are in the sight of God.

Next, Abram gave Melchizedek tithes of all. This was a very
substantial and practical recognition of his priesthood. Whether
it was a single act, or whether it had been or now became a practice of Abram's thus to recognize Melchizedek and honour his
God, we cannot tell. In the present case, it was a tithe of the
spoil recovered from the enemy that Abram presented. But the
narrative is so expressed as to imply that this was no novelty—
that the payment of tithes as due to God was an acknowledged
obligation; an obligation which, on this occasion, Abram would
be all the more forward to discharge because he had been so conspicuously helped by God, and had won his victory so easily and
so completely.

The practice of paying tithes, to which this is the first reference in Scripture, was a very general one, not only among the
Hebrews, but in other nations both of the East and the West.
The Egyptian monuments record some remarkable cases of kings
returning from war offering to their gods immense gifts out of
the spoil swept from the enemy's lands. We know how Jacob
afterwards promised at Bethel to give to God a tenth of all that
God should give to him, and the whole Mosaic legislation shows
what an important place the tithe held in the Hebrew economy.
" Numerous instances are to be found of the practice in heathen
nations—Greeks, Romans, Carthaginians, Arabians—of applying
tenths, derived from property in general, from spoil, from confis-
cated goods, or from commercial profits, to sacred and quasi-
sacred, and also to fiscal purposes, namely, as consecrated to a
deity, presented as a reward to a successful general, set apart as a
tribute to a sovereign, or as a permanent source of revenue." *
" The Phœnicians and Carthaginians sent to the Tyrian Hercules,

* Smith's "Bible Dictionary."

yearly, a tithe (Diod. Sic. xx. 14) ; the Lydians offered a tithe of their booty (Herod. i. 89), as also the Greeks (especially to Apollo) and the Romans (to Hercules) applied a tenth to the gods." * The word tithe has acquired by use an unsavoury meaning. Viewing it as an offering to God, it has a very different aspect according to the spirit of the offerer. To one, it is like life-blood wrung from him by the force of law, a slice of the most valuable property he possesses taken for a purpose in which he does not believe or in which he has no interest. To another, it is the loving acknowledgment of innumerable blessings, and of a personal interest infinitely more precious than gold and silver—an offering which it is a relief and a delight to present, because the blessings of which it is the acknowledgment are so overwhelming, and leave the offerer after all such an infinite debtor. It needs not to be said in which of these lights Abram regarded the tenth which, through Melchizedek, he offered to God.

Next comes Abram's transaction with the King of Sodom. Salem, if it was Jerusalem, was the place where they would naturally separate, the king to return to the plain on the south-east, Abram to Hebron on the south-west. The proposal of the king was that Abram should take all the spoil, restoring only the persons who had been carried off. To this Abram, with a self-denial which some would almost grudge, and a warmth of feeling which they could not understand, would not listen. And this was not a mere matter of feeling, a mere whim of generosity, but a solemn religious determination. " I have lift up mine hand unto the Lord, the most high God, the possessor of heaven and earth, that I will not take from a thread even to a shoe-latchet, and that I will not take any thing that is thine, lest thou shouldest say, I have made Abram rich." What was the religious principle that moved Abram to this very solemn resolution ? It was his loyalty to his God, the possessor of heaven and earth, from whom cometh down every good and every perfect gift. First of all, Abram is too generous a man to enrich himself through the misfortunes of others. But besides that, he sets too high a value on the covenant

* Herzog and Schaff's " Encyclopaedia."

between him and God to accept of gifts or boons from men. If Abram is to be enriched, it is from the hand of his God that his wealth must come ; not a thread will he take from the King of Sodom. This he has vowed. He has been thinking of the matter before, and lest he should be persuaded to do otherwise, he has fortified his resolution with a vow. God had promised to bless him, and God alone should fulfil his promise. He would not be indebted to man for what he knew he was to get from God. He was destined to prosper, that he knew ; and he would not put it in the power of the King of Sodom to say that his prosperity had in any degree come from him. Nothing should be allowed to obscure the fact that the prosperity of Abram had come from the God he served. His testimony to the one God, the possessor of heaven and earth, must be clear, convincing, indubitable.

Only two things were excepted from the application of this rule. The first was the tithe, already paid to Melchizedek, but paid on the principle that it belonged to God already. Morally, the King of Sodom had no control over that; it was God's, and to God's priest it behoved to be paid. The second exception relates to "that which the young men have eaten, and the portion of the men which went with me, Aner, Eshcol, and Mamre ; let them take their portion." Actual outlay for food he will take back, for the repayment of that will not make him richer ; and the portion of the spoil due to his Amorite allies may be paid, for he has no right to place them under his own self-denying ordinance : but not one farthing more. He will return to Hebron as he came. Men will call him a fool for not availing himself of such a splendid chance of riches ; he will tell them that clean hands and a pure conscience are better than the biggest hoard of gold and silver.

Did Abram always act in this magnanimous way ? Did he act on these high principles in Egypt when he accepted Pharaoh's gifts in return for Sarai, and came home " very rich in cattle, and in silver, and in gold " ? Certainly not. His meanness in accepting Pharaoh's gifts was as great as his magnanimity in refusing the King of Sodom's. But in the one case Abram was not himself—or rather, he was himself, but himself apart from all the higher motives and impulses which fellowship with God imparts. In the other case, his fellowship with God had been regained; hence his self-denial, his faith, his nobility. Perhaps the very shame with which he looked back on his Egyptian baseness was what impelled him now to lift up his hand to God. Happy the man everywhere, and especially the Christian, who, from the very weaknesses and surrenders of the past, can derive strength and courage for the future, and thus "on the stepping-stone of his dead self rise to higher things."

The references to Melchizedek both in the Psalms and in the Epistle to the Hebrews do not throw any light on the mystery that surrounds him. Rather, perhaps, the mystery is increased, because a fresh testimony is borne to the exalted nature of his priesthood, and to the greatness of the man "to whom even the patriarch Abram gave the tenth of the spoils." His priesthood is dwelt on as of a higher order than that of Aaron, and thus a fit emblem of the priesthood of the Lord Jesus Christ. A full thousand years after his meeting with Abram, a son of the patriarch's reigned in Melchizedek's capital. It was natural for David's thoughts to travel back to that early scene in the history, and think with wonder of the man whose remarkable priesthood made him greater than the great founder of the nation himself. And then, under that remarkable influence by which the natural was often merged in the supernatural, this superiority of Melchizedek was made the basis to David of a revelation respecting the royal Son who was to be raised up of his seed, and the divine voice was heard proclaiming, "Thou art a priest for ever after the order of Melchizedek." What made Melchizedek so much greater than Abram, who was himself the priest of his family, remains and must remain a mystery. The announcement to David respecting Messiah's priesthood was peculiarly solemn, for it was made with an oath. And thus the double lesson was conveyed—that the priesthood of Messiah was to be a priesthood of a most exalted order; and that this was a fact of the utmost importance to mankind, inasmuch as the Lord, in constituting him priest, did so not by a simple affirmation, but with the formality and solemnity of an oath.

Probably Abram was the bearer of his own news to his household. Sarai must have had an anxious time, for to a peace-loving shepherd and his company Chedorlaomer and his allies were a most formidable foe. It must have been a happy hour when he told her of his wonderful victory ; then of the release of Lot, and the meeting with the King of Sodom ; and last, not least, of the meeting with Melchizedek, the mysterious representative of a greater Priest, whose blessing symbolized mercies that only Heaven could bestow.

# CHAPTER VII.

## THE DIVINE COVENANT.

### (Gen. xv.)

"THE morning cometh, and also the night." We are reminded of this description of the sudden contrasts of life when we find Abram, after the brilliant events of the last chapter, seemingly in a dull and despondent mood. After the strain of excitement the reaction of languor naturally comes; but in Abram's case there is not only physical exhaustion but mental depression. He seems to have felt as though he had but gone through another act of that perpetually recurring drama, "Vanity of vanities." No doubt he has defeated the eastern kings; he has rescued Lot; he has got the thanks of the King of Sodom; he has got the blessing of Melchizedek; and last, not least, he has kept his hands clear of the stain of greed and his heart loyal to his God. But he has not advanced the purpose of his life; he has not realized the great desire of his heart; as far as the end for which he left his native country is concerned, all appears to have been done in vain. Nay, this very victory may become his destruction: that eastern confederacy is not likely to take its defeat quietly; another year, and a great horde of warriors may cross the Jordan, ravage the whole country, and in one fell massacre consign him and all that belongs to him to destruction.

In this hour of depression he receives a new communication from God. "The word of the Lord came to him in a vision." This is a more explicit statement of the mode of communication than has hitherto occurred; for the first time we find the formula

so often repeated afterwards. For the first time, too, we catch
that divine lullaby, "Fear not," which drops at intervals from the
divine lips with such soothing power over the whole Bible from
Genesis to Revelation. For at best we are but children, haunted
by fears, sometimes real, oftener imaginary; and it is good to hear
One who knows all, and who can do all, saying to us, "Fear not."
If Abram was at all troubled with apprehensions of an attack
from the eastern kings, these words were well adapted to dispel
that fear. If he was vexed for the apparent failure of his family
hopes, they suggested a coming fulfilment. They did not indeed
bring to him at once what he desired, but they brought him the
assurance of a divine friendship capable of performing all that had
been promised.

The object of the assurance, "Fear not, Abram, I am thy shield,
and thy exceeding great reward," was to turn his mind from the visible
to the invisible, from the promise to the Promiser, from appearances
to realities. If Abram was depressed, it was because appearances
were so much against him. For this, God might have provided a
remedy in two ways—either by causing appearances to turn in his
favour, or by opening his mental eye to those divine realities which
were the only solid ground of peace and joy. In our weakness,
when appearances are against us, we do naturally crave that they
may be turned round in our favour; but it is a higher experience
to which we are called when God bids us trust in him as our shield
and exceeding great reward. Abram did not question this—ultimately he received the assurance gladly, and rested on it most
trustfully; but at first he could not but direct God's attention to
the actual state of things, and to their depressing aspect. "And
Abram said, Lord God, what wilt thou give me, seeing I go childless, and the steward of my house is this Eliezer of Damascus?
And Abram said, Behold, to me thou hast given no seed: and, lo,
one born in my house is mine heir." The hunger of his heart
*would* express itself. And God graciously replies to this. He
assures him that his heir shall be of his own flesh and blood; and
he brings him forth abroad, bids him look toward heaven and
number the stars, and declares that his seed shall be like them for

number. A very gracious emblem, surely. Formerly the dust of the earth had been the symbol, now it is the stars of heaven ; and if the dust suggested insignificance, the stars signify glory. Not only are the stars numberless, but they are near God—they are preachers of his glory, they are witnesses to his wisdom and his power. The simile implied that besides being more numerous than could be counted, the posterity of Abram would play a prominent and very brilliant part in the future history of the world.

And now Abram got above the mood of mind dominated by the visible. Faith triumphed over sight. "He believed in the Lord, and he counted it to him for righteousness." His faith placed him in the same relation to God as if he had been personally righteous. What he believed was that, of his free and infinite grace, God was about to bestow on him a great gift—a gift of overwhelming magnitude, to which he had not the slightest claim. In the Epistle to the Romans, the apostle shows that this faith is of the same kind as that by which a sinner apprehends God's gracious provision for his needs in the gospel of Jesus Christ. This, too, is faith in God's free and infinite grace, coming near to us with his glorious gift, and urging us to accept it, not as a gift to which we have the slightest claim, but simply because he is infinitely gracious and loving. Whoever exercises this faith in God's unspeakable gift comes into the same relation to God as if he were personally righteous. Trust in his revealed grace is the spirit which God ever desires to engender in us, and it is the spirit that, when it rules our heart, receives his everlasting blessing.

Abram seems quite disposed to receive the assurance as to the multitude of his seed ; but with regard to the promise of the land, he ventures to crave some token that this, too, will be implemented. Not that he distrusts God, for that would be to renounce the spirit that God has so approved ; but as God has given him the stars as the emblem of one part of his promise, so perhaps he would give him a similar token for the other. In this connection God gave what he asked, but far more than he asked. Abram probably expected a sign, a material token. But God entered into a solemn covenant with him. He transacted with Abram as he

seems never to have done with any human being since the days of
Noah, when the human race started on its new history, and Noah
stood alone, the father of all that survived the Flood. And further,
he gave him some details respecting the future history of his seed
that showed that everything was planned, and that though centuries of trial were first to run, his posterity in due time would
possess the country in all its length and breadth, from the river of
Egypt to the great river, the river Euphrates.

The transaction into which God entered with Abram is called
a covenant (ver. 18), like that of Noah (Gen. ix. 11), although it
had not all the ordinary features of a covenant, being exclusively
a promise on the part of God, without any express stipulation to
be fulfilled by Abram. This form, however, was adopted in order
to make the greater impression on Abram—to convince him
more thoroughly of the certainty of what God undertook. The
covenant, as became any transaction between sinful man and the
holy God, was by sacrifice. And here we have the first elaborate
detail of the method of sacrifice as prescribed by God, and in
substance observed by the patriarchs till the Levitical economy
was introduced. The animals are a heifer of three years, a she-
goat and a ram of the same age, a turtle-dove, and a young
pigeon. Mystical reasons have been advanced by some for the
age of three years, as if there were some allusion to the Trinity ;
but surely it is better to regard the age as denoting the period of
life when the animal was at its best. The animals being slain
were divided into two and set over against each other. This
seems to have been the method suitable for a covenant, where
each of the contracting parties was represented by the half of the
sacrifice, and it was signified that both were equally bound to
their engagements. If the pigeon and the turtle-dove were not
divided, it was because the pair were counted one offering, and
further division was unnecessary. Abram had his place amid
these offerings, not for a passing minute, but for a continuous
stretch of time ; for the vultures, attracted by the smell, began
to hover about, and Abram had to drive them away. It was a
strange position for him to stand for hours between the divided

carcasses of the three beasts.  During all these hours he might
be impressed by the thought that it was only by sacrifice that
man could draw near to God ; and if the worth of the sacrifices
seemed very inadequate to the weight of man's sin, he might
perhaps receive a glimpse of the truth that a worthier sacrifice
would yet be provided, though how, or where, or when, Abram
hardly knew.

At length darkness enveloped the scene, and Abram fell into
a deep sleep.  And in that deep sleep " an horror, a great darkness " (Revised Version) fell upon him.  His condition seems to
have been a supernatural one, combining two experiences which
are not otherwise reconcilable—deep sleep, yet with a certain
consciousness, a consciousness of great darkness, and that darkness
a symbol of distress.  The experience must have been like that
of a dismal and oppressive nightmare, like that of one seeming
to be lying under a frightful weight from which he cannot escape.
But above the horror the divine voice is heard again, sad yet
comforting.  There were hard and trying experiences in store for
Abram's children before they should be settled happily in the
land.  For a period of four hundred years they would be strangers
in another land, slaves to a foreign master, victims of grievous
tyranny.  How must Abram's kind heart have shivered to hear
thus of the long bondage of his children !  But God would not
leave their persecutors unpunished ; his judgments would rebuke
their inhuman conduct, and Abram's children would ultimately
leave the country laden with its spoil.  For himself, he would go
to his fathers in peace ; he would be buried in a good old age.
Four periods of time or " generations " would pass before this
deliverance should be achieved.  The reason was that the land
promised to Abram's seed was not yet ready for their possession ;
the iniquity of the Amorites had not yet reached its climax—it
had not yet become so odious and incurable as to call for the
destruction of the race.

The vision now takes a turn from darkness to light : " Behold
a smoking furnace, and a burning lamp that passed between
those pieces. "  This is a token that the gracious presence of God

will in due time chase away the sorrows of the night—a brighter day will dawn on Abram's seed. Then the divine voice is heard again, and the promise of the covenant sounds out in a form more comprehensive than heretofore, assigning to Abram not only the little strip of land between the Jordan and the Mediterranean, but the vast country between Egypt and the Euphrates, and displacing for him the desert tribes on the south as well as the nations then in possession of what was to be emphatically " the land of Israel."

Four hundred years was a long vista, and it must have been most painful to Abram to think that a period of that length had to elapse before his children would enjoy a comfortable life in a land of their own. Fathers instinctively desire to see their children comfortably settled in the world; and even the experience which most good men have of the necessity of trial does not quench the hope that their children may be spared the bitter discipline of sorrow which they themselves may have had to undergo. But God's rule, though it may have exceptions, is uniform on the whole. " It is good for a man that he bear the yoke in his youth." And what is good for a man is good for a nation. The seed of Abram was to have an unusually long experience of the yoke in its youth. But this, so far from being a token of God's indifference, was designed to mature and strengthen the highest qualities to which a nation could attain. Our vision is too limited to embrace periods of such length. It is God only, to whom one day is as a thousand years and a thousand years as one day, that can manipulate periods of such magnitude, and weave them beneficially into his schemes. If it seemed strange to Abram that God should ordain four long centuries for a nation's preparatory discipline, it is not less strange to us that he should have ordained another period of nearly five times that length for the same nation's subsequent chastisement and rebuke. But divine wisdom was vindicated in the first arrangement, and it will be vindicated in the other too. Ages of benediction, according to the years wherein they have seen sorrow, may yet be destined for a restored Israel, and the blessings of the future may exceed the blessings of the past "unto the utmost bound of the everlasting hills."

It is interesting in this early vision to find the divine presence and favour set forth by that emblem—a bright light—an emblem which is so conspicuous over the whole range of revelation. Evidently the gloom was at its deepest—"it was dark"—when, "behold, a smoking furnace and a burning lamp" brightened the scene. It was the same element as in the symbol of the burning bush; of the pillar of fire and the pillar of cloud; of the Shechinah within the tabernacle; of the great cloud and the fire unfolding itself, and the brightness like the colour of amber, of Ezekiel's vision; of the glory that shone about the shepherds of Bethlehem; of the light from heaven that shone about Paul on the way to Damascus; and of the light, like unto a stone most precious, even like a jasper stone, clear as crystal, symbol of the glory of God, that shone round "that great city, the heavenly Jerusalem," as it descended out of heaven from God. Was it not just a perverted view of this symbol that induced the Chaldæans to offer divine worship to the sun? Of all material things is not light the most expressive symbol of divinity—light and heat together, warming as well as enlightening, purifying as well as guiding, representing the forces that make the earth fruitful and human life joyous and satisfying? Yet never was the symbol presented by God to human eyes in such form as to invite worship, for it was but the visible emblem of an invisible presence that overawed and humbled the beholder. "The smoking furnace and the burning lamp" drew no act of worship to themselves from Abram; he had learned to look through the material emblem, and reserve his homage for "the most high God, the possessor of heaven and earth."

Two questions—one chronological, the other geographical—demand our attention ere we pass from this remarkable chapter of Abram's biography.

The chronological question bears on the length of the period which was to elapse before the land should be occupied by Abram's seed.

" Know of a surety that thy seed shall be a stranger in a land that is not their's, and shall serve them; and they shall afflict them four hundred years." With this we have to compare the statement in Ex. xii. 40, where it is said, " The sojourning of the children of Israel who dwelt in Egypt was four hundred and thirty years." On the other hand, St. Paul in his Epistle to the Galatians says that the giving of the law in Sinai was four hundred and thirty years after the promise to Abram (Gal. iii. 17). Our first and most natural impression of the words in Genesis is that the bondage in Egypt was to last four hundred years; but how could that be if the entire interval between the promise to Abram and the giving of the law was but four hundred and thirty? The Septuagint inserts a clause at Ex. xii. 40 which alters the complexion of the statement : " The sojourning of the children of Israel which they sojourned in Egypt *and in Canaan* was four hundred and thirty years."

Now, in Galatians Paul seems to have simply accepted the Septuagint statement, perhaps because the precise number of years between the promise to Abram and the giving of the law did not matter for his argument, since all that he desired to prove was that the covenant was long before the law. We fall back therefore on the double statement of Gen. xv. 13 and the Hebrew text of Ex. xii. 40, as showing that the residence in Egypt extended to four hundred years. But if this be the correct view, what are we to make of the statement (ver. 16), " In the fourth generation they shall come hither again "? If this means, as we might suppose, the fourth generation from their going down to Egypt, it is plain that the length of a generation must have been reckoned on a different principle from that commonly accepted by us. Instead of the mere interval between the birth of father and son, the average length of life of each man would seem to have been the basis of the reckoning. Four of our generations would have been an altogether inadequate time for filling up the four hundred years, or for producing the vast multitude which formed the nation at the time of the exodus ; but four periods of the average length of life then prevalent would probably be sufficient for this great increase.

The geographical question respects the limits of the country as promised to Abram. Its boundaries are said to stretch "from the river of Egypt, unto the great river, the river Euphrates." A question has been raised, What is meant by the river of Egypt? It is natural to reply, the Nile—a name supposed to have been derived from the Hebrew word for river, *nachal.* But some have maintained that what is meant is not the Nile, but the Wady el Arisch, called by the Greeks *Rhinocorura,* and so translated in one passage by the Septuagint. This is the bed of a torrent, absolutely dry in summer, in the desert between Palestine and Egypt. But this was an obscure stream, probably unknown to Abram; nor does there seem to be any good reason for supposing that the river meant was not the Nile, the Pelusiac branch of which, according to Strabo, was the eastern boundary of Egypt. The Septuagint is somewhat fantastic in its translation of the Nachal or Nahar of Egypt. It makes it at different times the φάραγξ Αἰγύπτου, or gulf of Egypt; ποταμος, or river; χειμαῤῥος, or torrent. To Abram's mind we can hardly conceive the expression as denoting anything but the Nile; and this is confirmed by the very fitness of things, for we can scarcely suppose that a dominion bounded by a great stream like the Euphrates on the one side should have had only an all but imperceptible streamlet for its boundary on the other.*

But did Abram's seed ever occupy all this territory? On the contrary, when they were settled in the country, were not the limits of each tribe carefully determined by Moses and Joshua, and, except in the case of the tribe of Dan, whom the Philistines hemmed in, did they not, in after years, stick for the most part to the allotments that had been assigned to them at the beginning? This is true; but the extent of an empire is not measured by the extent of land occupied by the original people. The people of the United Kingdom might be described generally as inhabiting Great Britain and Ireland, while territories of far greater magnitude, like India, have long been governed by the British crown. Thus it is quite a current usage of language to describe the

---

* See the subject discussed in Keith's "Land of Israel," ch. ii. and Appendix I.

dominions of a country, not by the land occupied by the original race, but by the whole territory held in subjection. The hundred and twenty-seven provinces forming the Persian Empire in the days of Ahasuerus (Esther i. 1) embraced a whole multitude of subject countries. So also in the reigns of David and Solomon, when the promise to Abram was fulfilled in all its integrity. "Solomon reigned over all kingdoms from the river unto the land of the Philistines, and unto the border of Egypt : they brought presents, and served Solomon all the days of his life" (1 Kings iv. 21). The territories assigned to Abram were thus far greater than the mere confines of Canaan.

No fewer than ten Canaanite tribes were enumerated by God as those whose lands the seed of Abram were to possess. Three of these, the Kenites, the Kenizzites, and the Kadmonites, seem to have been Bedouin tribes inhabiting the wilderness to the south of Canaan. It is not possible to trace their origin with precision. In later times the Kenites come in for a peculiar interest, for Moses' father-in-law was one of them (Judg. i. 16), as was also Heber, the husband of Jael (Judg. iv. 11). One of the Kenizzites, in like manner, stands out from the mass, for Caleb was the son of Jephunneh, a Kenizzite (Num. xxxii. 12). To the Kadmonites we have no clue whatever. It is quite possible that by the time of the exodus some of these tribes were reinforced by descendants of Abram through other sons than Isaac, and may thus have preserved a purer religion and purer morals, so as to escape the doom of the other Canaanites. Cases like those of Hobab and Jephunneh show that, even outside the circle of the covenant, there were men in those times that sought after God, and did not seek him in vain. It is pleasing to think that there was always a door of entrance even for members of the doomed races, if they chose to connect themselves with Israel and worship Israel's God. No community, as such, seems to have availed itself of this opportunity ; but not a few individuals and families accepted the offer, and coming by faith into fellowship with Israel's God, were incorporated with the nation, and enjoyed the protection and other privileges of the people of God.

# CHAPTER VIII.

## HAGAR AND ISHMAEL.

### (Gen. xvi., xxi. 9-21.)

WAITING is sometimes more wearisome than working. And waiting is especially trying when the longer you wait the further you seem to be from that you are waiting for. For ten long years did Sarai wait, till she felt that she could wait no longer. She was sixty-six when Abram left Haran (comp. xii. 4, xvii. 17); now she was seventy-six. It was time for her to be a grandmother or a great-grandmother rather than a mere mother. Perhaps she had set ten years to herself as the limit of her waiting, just as, when you are looking for the arrival of a guest, you fix a time beyond which you will cease to expect him. The ten years had passed, and there was no prospect of a son. Something must be done. If the promise is not to be fulfilled through her, may it not be fulfilled through another?

The Bible narrative is so quiet that it is only when a crisis arises that we see how much has been gone through of which we have no record. How Sarai fretted herself on account of her condition—how intensely she longed, and how constantly her longings were thrust back on her disappointed heart—how her life was darkened, and all her natural enjoyment turned to bitterness, through this unbearable disappointment, we gather very plainly from what follows, though it is not expressly said. For the proposal which she made to her husband to assume Hagar as a secondary wife was one that no woman could easily bring herself to advance. To sacrifice her position as the only wife, to conquer her womanly shame and abdicate her conjugal rights, was an act of extraordinary self-denial which no woman would even think of except under the pressure of irresistible feelings. It is true it was an act very different then from what it would be now. For though Abram was no polygamist, though he had honoured the primitive law that made the man and the woman one, and personally had not even a wish to depart from it, yet according to the usage of the time and even the judgment of conscience, he might take a secondary wife with honour and propriety, as he was now urged to do. Nay, this course was proposed to him (as it afterwards was by Rachel to Jacob) by the very person who might have been supposed to shrink from it with the most sensitive horror. If Abram should get offspring by a slave, that offspring would be counted, like all the slave had, as the property of her owner. Hagar was an Egyptian bondwoman—a present, very likely, from Pharaoh when Abram dissembled to him in Egypt. This, then, was Sarai's proposal: The slave-girl, from the very fact of her being a slave, could never be a rival to her in social position or in the esteem of her husband; through her Abram might get a son; that son should be counted Sarai's, and thus the promise would be fulfilled.

Little did Sarai realize what she was bringing on herself, and on the world too, by the step which she urged Abram to take. Little did she think of the rivalry in her own home that would trouble and imbitter her life in after years, or of the element of strife that was to come into the world through Hagar's child. Little did she think of the two religions that were to spring from the two branches of Abram's seed, of the implacable enmity of the Mohammedan to the Christian, or of the oceans of blood that would be shed in future ages when the fiercest passions of the one should be roused to deadly conflict with the other. This is what came of trying to expedite the movements of Providence. With our narrow notions of time, we are for ever liable to think that the wheels of the chariot move too slowly, like children who dig up the seeds in their gardens because they have not sprung up the day after they were sown. How many anxieties, how many blunders, how many crimes have been committed under this feeling! Sarai's position was undoubtedly trying, but she had yet to wait for other fifteen years before the promise came true.

Presented, as Hagar probably was, to Abram in Egypt, among other valuable gifts that were designed to reconcile him to the loss of Sarai, it is more than a guess that she was a young woman of attractive appearance, and it is certain that the relation in which she was now to stand to Abram would be counted no dishonour to her or to any of those concerned.

The permission of slavery among the Jews, although under conditions that made it very different from pagan slavery, has often been a stumbling-block to belief in the Old Testament scriptures. In reality this is one of those arrangements that evince the progressiveness of the revelation of morality, the gradual evolution of the moral law in its higher bearings, its gradual advance towards the full recognition of the duty of man. Evidently the practice had its origin in war, slavery being the natural fate of the women and children that fell under the hand of the conqueror. In after times, when the Jewish commonwealth was settled, even Hebrews might be reduced to slavery, either from poverty or from crime, but only for a limited period. Their position in other respects was carefully regulated by law. Foreign slaves, too, had a measure of protection and of civil right secured by law at the same period, and their masters were urged to treat them kindly by the consideration that their fathers had been bondmen in Egypt. Hagar, however, had as yet no legal rights of this kind, and no claim to kindly treatment, save what natural compassion on the part of her owners might give her. According to the prevalent view, her owners had complete control both over her and her offspring.

But Hagar was evidently a person of too high spirit to enter into the whole of Sarai's plan, and to renounce all property in her child. She was not prepared to sink her individuality, and let her mistress enjoy all the benefit. Finding herself about to have what had been denied to Sarai, she did not conceal her contempt for the childless wife—her mistress was despised in her eyes.

Evidently Sarai was greatly excited, for the plan she had proposed for making everything smooth was already reacting on herself with unbearable acuteness.

Nor did Sarai retrieve her character by her next proceeding. With equal want of reason and fairness, she threw on Abram the blame of the transaction of which she herself was the author, now that she found it was not to work smoothly. She had been wronged by this woman, she said; her place had been usurped by her when Abram took her for his concubine; let Abram bear the blame and suffer the consequences! She solemnly invoked the name of God—called on him to witness her injustice and to vindicate the right. It is painful to think what liberties men sometimes take with the divine name when excited over some disappointment or trial, and how they will ascribe to some unfortunate relative or servant the mischief of the course which they themselves devised. There are few foes more hostile to truth and righteousness than temper and passion; and whoever allows them to sway him, be the provocation what it may, is sure to rue the day.

Nor was Abram much superior on this occasion in generosity. Instead of remonstrating with Sarai on the one hand, or dealing with Hagar on the other, he renounced both his own rights over Hagar, and Hagar's claims on him, now that she was his concubine, and placed her wholly in Sarai's power. He placed her entirely at the mercy of an excited and jealous woman. And Sarai was not disposed to make a moderate use of this power. She "dealt hardly" with Hagar. How many forms of humiliation and suffering may lie under this phrase we cannot tell; we know the result only—Hagar's life became intolerable to her, and she fled from the face of her mistress.

A desperate remedy, truly, because the wilderness lay between her and Egypt, towards which she would naturally turn her face; and rushing thither without tent to screen her from the sun, or provisions to satisfy the claims of nature, there seemed but one possible termination to her venture, unless she should chance to meet with some friendly tribe from whom she might receive the necessary food and shelter. It is possible that in early days, before she was reduced to slavery, Hagar was accustomed to life in the desert. Following probably the caravan route, she would reach a well-known fountain in the wilderness on the way to Shur. Shur was a place near the frontier of Egypt (Gen. xxv. 18; 1 Sam. xv. 7, 22, 23, xxvii. 8), probably in the kingdom of Gerar, near which Abram subsequently dwelt (Gen. xxi. 1). It was probably the last town reached by caravans before entering Egypt.

But Hagar was only on the way to Shur; she had met with no friendly company; and now, resting at the fountain, she was met by the angel of the Lord and instructed to return to her mistress. It is probable that by this time the madness of her flight had become apparent to herself. But it was a hard name she got—Hagar, Sarai's maid; and a hard thing she was called to do —to return to the very life that she had found intolerable, and to the very mistress who had been the author of all her sufferings. But necessity has no law. Before the angel of the Lord met her she had probably the conviction that the right thing for her to do was just to return to her mistress; and now, when the messenger of heaven calls on her to do so, no remonstrance is offered—she at once obeys.

This is the first time that we meet in Scripture with that heavenly being who is called "the angel of the Lord." In after times his appearances are very frequent. It is evident that he was deemed by Hagar more than an ordinary messenger of heaven, for she speaks of him as God, although, with her Egyptian ideas of gods, this does not necessarily imply that he was *the* God. The language of the historian certainly implies that he was God himself. On this subject, it is pretty well known, commentators are not agreed. By many the view is held that he was a created messenger of God, specially commissioned to deal with men on God's behalf, and that this is the reason why he often speaks in God's name, as though he were God himself. But others hold that his appearance was a real "theophany," and that in point of fact he was the second Person of the Trinity, who, as if to foreshadow the incarnation, assumed for a time that human form which was afterwards to be so emphatically his. Thus, and only thus, might he speak of himself as sent of God, and yet as God in very deed. If our attention were limited to certain passages in which divine attributes are very expressly ascribed to him, we should be at little loss in maintaining this view. But there are other passages in reference to which this can hardly be maintained. On behalf of the view that he was not himself God, stress has been laid on the many occasions in the New Testament when one bearing a pre cisely analogous designation, ἄγγελος Κυρίου, the angel of the Lord, who yet cannot be regarded as the second Person, appears to Mary, to Peter, to Paul, and others. But then, in the New Testament, when the Word himself " was made flesh, and dwelt among us," it was reasonable that the occasional messages of God should be carried by others. Whatever reasons there may be for hesitation as to " the angel of the Lord " in the Old Testament, the preponderance of argument seems to be in favour of the view that on certain occasions, at least, it was the second Person who did thus appear.

The seemingly hard command to Hagar to return to her mistress and submit herself under her hands was accompanied by a prediction that could not but sweeten the order. First, she was to bear a son, whose name she was to call Ishmael ("God heareth"), because the Lord had heard her affliction. She had thought herself friendless, but there was One who had weighed her sufferings and heard her cry. The great joy was given her—a joy that can be rightly prized only by the lonely outcast—of knowing that there was One in heaven who habitually felt and cared for her. And the son she was to bear was to have a name significant of this fact—a name that would be a perpetual reminder to her of God's interest in her, because it would bring back to her this memorable occasion when her extremity proved to be God's opportunity. Thus the lonely fugitive was assured that she would be lonely no more, for up in heaven she had a Friend who ever hears the cry of the afflicted ; while down on earth her child would be a bright companion, gladdening her with the winning ways of infancy and childhood, and in after years making for himself a name that would preserve hers in perpetual remembrance.

Was it a shadow that was cast on this picture when it was added, " He will be a wild man," or as it is in the Revised Version, " He shall be as a wild ass among men, his hand shall be against every man, and every man's hand against him, and he shall dwell in the presence of all his brethren"? The wild ass was neither a discreditable nor an unacceptable emblem. In some respects the wild ass had properties that excelled the domesticated animal. In his famous " Retreat of the Ten Thousand," Xenophon says : " The wild ass being swifter of foot than our horses, would, in gaining ground upon them, stand still and look around ; and when their pursuers got nearly up to them, they would start off and repeat the same trick, so that there remained to the hunters no other method of taking them but by dividing themselves into dispersed parties which succeeded each other in the chase." Another Greek writer describes him as κραιπνὸν, ἀελλοπόδην, κρατερώνυχον, ὀξύτατον θεῖν (swift, rapid, with strong hoofs, most fleet in his running).* The idea in the comparison of Ishmael to the wild ass was that he would be free, daring, and rapid in his movements, full of courage and enterprise, scorning the dull ways of homely, plodding men.

Nor did Hagar probably object to what followed : " His hand will be against every man, and every man's hand against him." Certainly it was a character very different from Abram's—that lover of peace, that had such a dislike to strife in his household that for a quiet life he had let Sarai have her will even with the woman whom he had taken for his concubine. It was not this kind of character that Hagar was disposed to exalt, victim as she had been of her master's softness and of her mistress's rigour. Perhaps the blood of the desert ran in her veins. For though she is called an Egyptian, it is not likely that, being a slave, she was Egyptian by race. More likely she was of some African tribe accustomed to roam the desert,—that, hanging on the skirts of Egypt, made many a foray on its rich settlements, till in an evil hour overwhelmed by an Egyptian force that massacred the males and made slaves of the women and the children.

* Barnes on *Job* (xi. 12).

But however understood by Hagar, the prophecy was a description of the spirit not merely of her son, but of the whole nation that was to spring from him. How true and exact the prediction was and is, has been the marvel of the world to the present hour. "The character which it describes," says Kitto, "was too common in an unsettled age to excite special attention. What is remarkable in the prediction is, that this, in the case of Ishmael, was to remain, as it ever has done in the persons of his Arabian descendants, the character of a race. Other nations have changed their habits of life, and not one retains its original character. The sole exception is in the descendants of this man, in accordance with a prediction published at a time when no human knowledge could foresee nor any human power insure the certainty of its fulfilment. The wilderness, which is incident only to a certain stage of man's social history, has become permanent with them; and although they have been compacted and embodied as a nation for more than three thousand years, they have resisted those changes of habits which it is the effect of civil union so long continued to induce."

There was another clause in the prophecy : "He shall dwell in the presence of all his brethren." Colonies will not go off to a separate locality to cultivate their own fields, conduct their own commerce, and build up a community of homesteads and household gods apart from the old home. So it has proved. "The wild desert," as one writer puts it, "which has the Euphrates valley to the east of it and the Jordan valley to the west of it, has been always tenanted by wandering, hunting tribes of Ishmaelites......who have always scorned the city crowds......Again and again have they been hunted down by invading armies; but neither the Macedonian, nor the Roman, nor the Turk has been able to establish a settled rule over their inaccessible and inhospitable wastes...... Most unchangeable of races, they dwell where they have always dwelt, 'in the presence of their brethren,' stable in their instability, while empire has succeeded empire, and civilization has grown upon the ruins of succeeding civilizations." *

* "Abraham, the Friend of God," by J. O. Dykes, D.D.

The name which was given to the well, if not by Hagar herself, at least in connection with what happened to her there, is such as to suggest that she received a deep impression from the conscious presence of God — Beer-lahai-roi, "the well of the living One who seeth me" (Revised Version). What struck her was that God was a living being, cognizant of her every movement, who knew her sitting down and her rising up, and who had proved a present help to her in the time of trouble. Up to this time her heart may have clung to the religion of her youth, all the more firmly because she was a slave and had been torn from her country. She was now convinced that the God of Abram was the one living and true God, but there is no evidence that her faith was of the kind that transforms the life. She seems, as her after conduct indicates, to have remained much as she was before, —believing in God, perhaps, but not knowing him as her shield and exceeding great reward.

Both history and biography repeat themselves. The only other notice of Hagar in Genesis is in many respects a repetition of this one. It may be convenient to glance at it here, though out of chronological order, because all that is said of Hagar will thus be brought together, and we shall have the more complete view of her history and her character.

When Ishmael was about fourteen the promise was fulfilled to Sarah, and Isaac was born. This event must have been a great trial to Hagar, as it threw Ishmael into the shade, and lessened the hope which she had doubtless long cherished, that he would be the heir of Abraham's possessions. Abraham was evidently fond of the lad, and this would encourage Hagar's expectations. The birth of Isaac changed everything, and placed both Hagar and Ishmael in an unfavourable relation to Isaac. How often in after times has this experience been repeated ! How often has the canker of envy and jealousy come in to ruin the peace of families, because it was likely that the possessions would go one way, while some were passionately desirous they should go another !

It is not likely that Hagar and Ishmael concealed their disappointment. In the Epistle to the Galatians we are told that

Ishmael persecuted Isaac—" He that was born after the flesh persecuted him that was born after the Spirit ; " and Hagar would
naturally take his side. At the weaning of Isaac, when a great
feast was made in his honour, the spite of Ishmael rose to a climax.
Sarah seems to have dreaded that he would do her son a deadly
injury. It was impossible that the two should be brought up together. She made up her mind that Hagar and her son must be
driven from the home. Then she laid the case before Abraham,
who had usually let Sarah have her way. But this thing was very
grievous to him. His heart vehemently resisted. It was only an
indication of the divine will in the matter that overcame his
scruples. There was ground for Sarah's apprehensions, and Ishmael must go. Abraham must agree to sacrifice him. He was
not the child of promise. Isaac was heir to the blessing.

It is not surprising that Abraham should have seen the necessity of sending away Hagar and Ishmael ; but was not a piece of
bread and a bottle of water a sorry provision for them in the circumstances ? Out of his great wealth "in cattle, in silver, and in
gold," might he not have made for them a more adequate allowance ? This is so reasonable that we must suppose that Hagar was
not sent away with an empty purse, or at least without the promise
of such help as would be requisite when she should settle on a place
or a mode of living. This indeed may be held as affirmed in
Gen. xxv. 6, where it is said that Abraham made provision for
the sons of his concubines, among whom was Ishmael, by gifts in
his lifetime. The same thing is implied in the fact that Ishmael
joined with Isaac in burying his father in the cave of Machpelah
(Gen. xxv. 9)—an act of filial piety in which he would not have
been likely to take part had his father virtually cast him off
penniless.

Again, then, after an interval of sixteen or seventeen years,
Hagar turns her face to the desert, following the caravan route,
and expecting at the well-known stations to fall in with wells
where she may replenish her water-bottle. But either the wells
are empty or she has lost her way. No friendly tent is near, and
the water is spent in the bottle. Worse than that, Ishmael has

given in, and is unable to advance a step.   The agonies of thirst
in the desert are terrible in any case; in the case of a youth they
are heartrending.    Ishmael is so utterly spent that his end is
evidently near; but to look on his dying struggles is too much
for his poor mother, and she lays him under a shrub to die.   It
is a pitiful sight : the dying child under the shrub one picture of
distress; the weeping mother, about a bow-shot over against him,
another.    Did she at this moment remember what the name
Ishmael meant?   Did she remember who met her in that wilderness on a former occasion, when her heart was breaking from
another cause?    Perhaps the impression of that meeting had
proved like the morning cloud and the early dew.   It may have
been obliterated from her memory by a long course of worldly
living and of scheming for worldly good.    But the moment of
supreme agony is often a wonderful quickener of memory, and
it may be that she remembered not only the appearance of the
angel of the Lord, but his prediction respecting the child.   In any
case, whether she remembered God or not, God remembered her.
He proved the truth of the child's name, for he "heard the voice
of the lad;" his groan of agony touched the heart of the great
Father.    How blessed the words that now fall on the ear of the
poor mother—"What aileth thee, Hagar?   Fear not, for God
hath heard the voice of the lad, where he is."   Simple words, but
all-sufficient.    If God has only heard, if he has taken up the case,
everything is right.    And how near God may be to us, after all,
when we have been thinking of him as inconceivably distant!
By natural and simple means he extricates Hagar and Ishmael
from their deadly danger, showing her a well of water which
revives her son.

Once more Hagar learns that there is a God in heaven, from
whom, and whom alone, both she and her son have their life.
Did not this conviction work itself likewise into the soul of Ishmael, notwithstanding his wild and warlike life?   And did it not
serve to keep alive that faith in the oneness of God which has
been so uniformly and so fiercely maintained by his Mohammedan
descendants in these later centuries?   It has been observed of

circumcised races generally that, however carnal in spirit, they have been more disposed than others to believe not only in God's unity, but in his separateness from nature and superiority over it; not in the God of the pantheist, but in the personal God who created and who rules heaven and earth.

Yet we must note the vast difference between Ishmael's faith and the faith that worketh by love. There lay here the difference between faith in God as a mere ruler and faith in God as a gracious Father. The one faith may be found where there are selfishness, ferocity, and brutality; the other sweetens and sanctifies the whole being. The one is like the faith of the devils who believe and tremble; the other is the true faith that worketh by love. Both kinds still survive, not only in opposite religions, but in opposite sections of the same religion. God grant that the faith which sweetens and purifies may gain ground over that which delights mainly to controvert, to cast down, and to destroy!

# CHAPTER IX.

## RENEWAL OF THE COVENANT AND CHANGE OF NAMES.

(GEN. xvii.)

WE go back to Abram and Sarai. Sarai had to wait other fourteen years, in addition to the ten that had elapsed between her leaving Haran and her giving of Hagar to Abram. If it was hard to bear the delay of the ten, what must it have been to bear the delay of the fourteen? She seems to have given up entirely the expectation of offspring, and concentrated all her hopes on Ishmael; and Abram probably was in the same mood.

But at last the silence of long years is broken. God appears to Abram when he is ninety-nine years old, and introduces a new communication with the preface, "I am the almighty God; walk before me, and be thou perfect." We note the inseparable connection between God's service and personal sanctity on the part of his worshipper. Religion has so often been divorced from morality that we cannot lay too great emphasis on the inseparable connection between them manifest in all the transactions between Abram and God. It is not in a few things, or in a great many things merely, that he is to obey God: he is to walk before him, to live constantly as in his presence; and he is to be perfect or complete, aiming at a complete righteousness, "walking in all the commandments and ordinances of the Lord blameless."

A new assurance, adapted to new circumstances, is given him as to his seed. Formerly he had been tempted to doubt God's willingness to bless him; now that both he and Sarai are so old, his temptation is to doubt his power. Is God really able to give Sarai this child? Can he really set aside the laws of nature? Is it reasonable for me to be squaring my life by this almost extravagant hope? Must I be always straining to lead the life of faith? or may I not adopt some easier rule, and live more pleasantly, like my neighbours around me?

If any such temptation was hovering in Abram's path, the assurance now given was fitted to raise him above it: "I am the almighty God; walk before me, and be thou perfect." I am possessed of all power to fulfil my promise, all power in heaven and on earth; "walk before me," think of me as at your side, and aim at the perfect life which that thought inspires. Do not fashion your life by maxims of expediency, or measure your hopes by earthly appearances; aim at that highest style of life, in which the divine penetrates and transforms the human, and man lives "as seeing him who is invisible."

The covenant was now renewed with Abram, and on the part of God the three promises were expanded into greater fulness than before. First, the promise of seed was amplified into the promise that he should be the father of many nations; and in token of this his name was changed from Abram, "exalted father," to Abraham, "father of a multitude," as also the name of his wife was changed to be no more Sarai but Sarah, "princess." Next, the promise of blessing was made more explicit: God engaged to be a God unto him (with the untold riches of benediction which that implied) and to his seed after him. And third, the land was again pledged to him and his posterity—"all the land of Canaan for an everlasting possession."

In Hebrew experience the change of name was a significant fact in a man's life. No nation ever associated the names, whether of places or of persons, with religion so much as the Jews. Names like Bethel, Peniel, and Ebenezer were significant of memorable interpositions of God in the history of the people. Of names of individuals no fewer than a hundred have been found to have a religious significance. At birth, names were sometimes given prophetically, like Noah, or Judah, or Jesus, indicative of some important characteristic of the future career of the bearer. But the changing of names, as in the case now before us, was even more significant—significant of a new relation to God that altered the whole aspect of one's life.   When Jacob became Israel, when Oshea became Joshua, when Simon became Cephas, when Saul became Paul, they entered on a new chapter of their lives, in virtue of their new relation to God.   It is thought by some that the introduction of the letter ה (H) into Abraham's name, and into Sarah's too, as one of the radical letters of Jehovah or Yaveh, was designed to bring out this special relation to God.   In any case, the change of name in Abraham's case was peculiarly significant; it impressed him with a new character, a new consecration, and it became to him a new assurance that in God's good time— however far that might be from all human reckoning—the promised seed would come.

But now a new provision is introduced.   "Every man-child among you shall be circumcised......He that is eight days old shall be circumcised among you, every man-child in your generations."

How significant this rite of circumcision was to be in the future history of Abraham and his descendants does not need to be said.   It was the rite to which, of all others, the descendants of Abraham clung most tenaciously ; not indeed through the force of spiritual convictions, but in a large degree because it was the distinction of the race, the outstanding proof of the divine interest in their nation.

It is now surmised from the monuments of Egypt that circumcision did not originate on this occasion, the practice having prevailed in Egypt before Abraham's time.   "An old inscription uses 'uncircumcised' and 'impure' as synonymous terms; and a representation of circumcision occurs on the walls of the temple of Khonsu at Karnak, which was built by Rameses II. some little time before the Exodus.   Herodotus (ii. 104) asserts that the Assyrians and the Palestinians derived the custom from the Egyptians; but this statement was made to him by the native priests in glorification of their claim to primeval antiquity, and cannot be relied on.   Certainly many nations did receive the practice from Egypt—as the Colchians, the Troglodytes of Africa, the

Ethiopians of Meroë; and it is used to this day in the Coptic Church and among Abyssinian Christians......It is difficult to say how far it prevailed among the Syro-Arabian races. The Philistines and some of the Canaanites were not circumcised, as we see from various circumstances mentioned in Scripture; and from the story of Zipporah (Ex. iv. 25) we gather that there was no fixed rule about the matter among the Midianites. Josephus ('Antiq.' i. 2) states that the Ishmaelite Arabs were circumcised in their thirteenth year—a practice connected with the tradition respecting their forefather Abraham. Mohammed found the custom already existing, and was himself circumcised, when he put forth the Koran; and though he himself seems not to have regarded it as a religious rite, and makes no mention of it in his laws, his followers have rigidly observed it as if it were a positive ordinance, and it is now found wherever the Mohammedan faith has established itself." *

In laying hold of the pre-existing rite of circumcision (if it really did pre-exist), and consecrating it as the sign of the covenant between him and Abraham, God acted on the principle on which he made the rainbow the sign of the covenant with Noah, and on which our Lord made baptism the initiatory sacrament of the Church. It seemed right in God's sight to rescue circumcision from the corrupt uses to which it had been put in pagan service, and give it a new and holy character in connection with his own people. "In its heathen significance it was saturated with that worship of the forces of the physical world in which probably polytheism took its rise, and with polytheism nearly all the religions and mythologies of antiquity. It bore very directly on the deification of the generative or reproductive virtue in nature —the foul source of much that was cruel and nearly all that was obscene in the mysteries of paganism. Transformed to holy soil, and attached to a covenant of grace, it implied an acknowledgment that God, who is above nature, and not any physical force whatever, is the true author of physical life and its increase, the

* Deane's "Abraham," pp. 98, 99. Cf. Euseb. "Prep. Evang." ii. 104, iv. 27; "Joseph. cont. Ap." i. 22; "Philo de Circum." i. (ii. 210); Strabo, xii. 824; Diod. iii. 31; Herod. ii. 36, 37, 104.

sovereign giver of fertility, the only quickener of a holy and consecrated life.   It taught that what is born of the flesh can only be
flesh.   It suggested that it is by the painful renunciation of
earthly desire and natural self-confidence man must be surrendered to God's service, as his fit instrument for gracious ends.
Finally, it seemed to point forward to one pure and superhuman
birth, through which alone the fatal chain that links in one the
sinful generations of mankind could be severed, and a new fountain of salvation and blessing opened for the fallen race." *

We ought to observe that Abraham was now called for the
first time by this rite to signify his acceptance of God's covenant.
In the transaction of the divided sacrifices (Gen. xv.) Abraham
had been a passive spectator, not an active agent.   The burning
light, which was the symbol of God's presence, passing between the
divided pieces, was God's pledge that he would do all that he had
promised.   In not calling on Abraham to do anything in the way
of assent or promise at that time, God meant to teach that the
first attitude of the sinner entering into gracious relations with
him is simply that of a recipient, and the state of mind proper to
that act consciousness of inability to do anything toward securing
God's favour, and willingness to be indebted to grace alone.   This
was the state of mind which was so commended in Abraham—this
looking up to God as the sole source of blessing.   "He believed God,
and it was counted unto him for righteousness."   In the Epistle to
the Romans, St. Paul is at pains to show that this was Abraham's
state before the rite of circumcision was given ; he was accepted
in virtue of that faith which looked to God alone as the source of
blessing.   But while it is man's heart that must accept God's
grace and respond to his offer, it is fitting that there should be
some external sign by which this is expressed.   Circumcision was
such a sign, and it had thus a double aspect—on the part of God,
and on the part of Abraham.   On the part of God it was a divine
seal of the covenant ; it was a pledge that God would make good
all that had been offered to faith.   On the part of Abraham it
was an act of acceptance of the grace promised ; it was an

* Dykes's " Abraham."

acquiescing in God's covenant, and an engagement to be faithful to all its responsibilities. It signified his acceptance of the promise, " I will be a God to thee, and to thy seed after thee ;" and it denoted his submission to the rule given for his life, " Walk before me, and be thou perfect."

The rite was not confined to Abraham alone. All his male servants were to undergo it, and at the age of eight days every male child born in his house. In those times the head of the house was held to represent the household, and could command their submission even to religious rites to a degree that would certainly be considered now inconsistent with individual manhood and individual responsibility. But even apart from its religious significance, the right to circumcision could not but be counted a signal benefit : for it connected the participant with the great house of Abraham ; and even if it did not place him in the direct line of the covenant, it indicated that he was nearer to the blessing than those who had never been circumcised.

With the institution of circumcision an explicit promise is given that Sarah is to be the mother of the promised seed, and it is in this connection that her name is changed. The blessing that had formerly been pronounced on Abraham could not but in some sense have embraced her likewise ; but now it is intimated that she, too, shall be directly blessed with " blessings of the breasts and of the womb,"—that she shall become a mother of nations, and kings of people shall be of her. "Then Abraham fell upon his face, and laughed, and said in his heart, Shall a child be born to him that is an hundred years old ? and shall Sarah, that is ninety years old, bear ?" The laugh might be either the laugh of joy, the laugh of humour, or the laugh of incredulity. From what Abraham said to himself, we should judge that it was first the laugh of humour, expressing the sense of the ridiculous, the incongruous. Along with that, or springing out of it, there might be the smile of incredulity. It appeared too absurd to be true. And was it needful ? Had not Ishmael been sent to them—a bright, spirited boy ; and were not their hopes centred in him ? Why pass him over ? Guileless Abraham must utter what he feels : " We are

content with what we have ; O that Ishmael might live before
thee ! "

But no : Ishmael may be a right stirring and noble youth,
and a delightful companion for an old man, but he is the child
of the bond - woman ; his birth was merely natural, and the
promise is not to him. "Sarah thy wife shall bear thee a son
indeed ; and thou shalt call his name Isaac : and I will establish
my covenant with him for an everlasting covenant, and with his
seed after him." At this announcement Abraham's smile of
incredulity passed, doubtless, into the smile of joy ; and it was this
mature, and deliberate, and believing smile, expressing the profoundest sense of the power of "the Almighty God," that gave
rise to the name Isaac (laughter), which the child of promise was
to bear. And now Abraham firmly believes that the promised
seed is to be born of Sarah. "He staggers not at the promise of
God through unbelief, neither does he consider his own body now
dead, nor the barrenness of Sarah's womb ; he is strong in faith,
giving glory to God, and believing that what he has promised he is
able also to perform " (Rom. iv. 20, 21). And possibly he sees that
as his son is to be born out of the course of nature, and as he will
thereby be seen more emphatically to be the gift of God, so his
birth will harmonize more thoroughly with the whole character of
God's covenant, which is wholly of grace,—a covenant to which
man brings nothing, but in which God gives all. To us, with our
added light, that supernatural birth of Isaac seems a fit foreshadowing of another, when, in a way still more marvellous, the
Virgin of Nazareth gave birth to the true Seed, in whom, in very
deed, all the families of the earth are blessed.

And as for Ishmael, he is not forgotten : "Behold, I have
blessed him, and will make him fruitful, and will multiply him
exceedingly ; twelve princes shall he beget, and I will make him a
great nation." His lot would be so distinguished that there would
be but one thing to qualify it—the still greater distinction of
Isaac. The father-to-be of twelve princes need not deem himself
neglected, nor need his father grumble because Ishmael is not to
get more. This satisfaction he might have, looking at things from

an earthly standpoint. But Abraham must have known that there was nothing that would necessarily exclude Ishmael from sharing the spiritual blessing. He might have his share of it, certainly he would, if he had his father's faith; although it was not from his line but from his brother's that the great Hope of Israel was to spring.

One word more and the interview comes to an end. The time is fixed. At this set time next year the son will be born to Sarah. Faith is not to be exposed to further trial or to further waiting; the certainty of the promise is now assured in a visible way. After twenty-four long years, faith at last has its reward.

At once Abraham sets about the circumcision of himself, of his son Ishmael, and of all his household. The tumult of emotions that passed through his heart after this interview baffles all attempt at description. The retrospect of the last twenty-four years must have been checkered. Faith at the bottom of his heart all that time, no doubt; but how many misgivings and fears hovering about! How often it seemed to disappear! When he schooled himself, and fought his doubts, and reasoned on the certainty of the Divine promise, all was well; but when his heart, left to itself, was much absorbed with flocks and herds, with the visible and the temporal, how little account it took of the promise of God! But for one thing he had cause to be thankful—that in the depths of his heart he had been able to believe God's word. He had never deliberately surrendered his faith. And now he finds how blessed a thing it is to trust in God.

It is after a much shorter interval that the next divine visit is received by Abraham. It is very unlike previous visits—not marked by the solemnity of a summons to God's presence, but rather by the ease of a social visit. The reason probably was that this visit mainly concerned Sarah, and had it been more formal, the custom of the time might not have allowed her to appear.

Abraham is sitting in the door of his tent, shadowed by the oak of Mamre, in the heat of the day. At that time the heat rendered the interior of the tent too sultry to be comfortable, and the external shade of the tent, falling over the door-way, was more cool and pleasant. His eye catches a group of three strangers approaching his tent, walking on foot, but evidently of superior station. He shows his appreciation of their rank, first by running to meet them—he would not have run in an ordinary case—and then by bowing himself toward the ground before them. Addressing the leader of the party as "my lord," he asks the privilege of entertaining him, hopes that he and his companions will rest under the tree, and offers the two great requisites for refreshment after an Eastern journey—water for the feet and food for the body. Sarah is summoned to bestir herself, for in those hot climates no store of bread ready for use is kept; she has to take flour and knead it quickly on the hearth, as is done at this very day in the like circumstances. The cakes are long and thin, to be the more easily fired, and the great lady of the establishment, instead of a degradation, counts it an honour to prepare them with her own hands. Then Abraham runs to the herd and fetches a calf, tender and good, which he gives to a young man to dress. It was not the custom of those times to make use of meat on ordinary occasions, and when it was needed for such an occasion as the present, the animal had to be killed as well as dressed. To serve up the whole calf would have required too much time; but portions of it broiled over the fire might be got ready at once. Butter, from the milk of ewes and goats, is an indispensable and very plentiful article in Eastern entertainments, often consumed in great lumps, or made into a sauce and poured over the meat. Milk is a usual article of drink.*  Abraham's entertainment was just such as a Bedouin would provide to-day—the best he had, and the most readily prepared. It was a further token of his respect for his guests that he did not sit down to the table with them, but "stood by them under the tree" while they took their meal. The heartiness of Abraham in the matter is very conspicuous; what a contrast he is to such a man as Nabal in the days of David! Generosity to strangers, from whom you expect nothing in return, may well be called a

---

* See Kitto's "Pictorial Commentary," etc.

ABRAHAM'S OAK.

*Page 117.*

Christian virtue—an unselfish desire to contribute to the comfort of others. It is for this reason that this example has received the high consecration of an inspired writer: "Be not forgetful to entertain strangers; for thereby some have entertained angels unawares."

Sarah had not even presented herself to her guests, partly from modesty, partly from the custom of the time requiring the seclusion of women, and partly because she had been busy preparing the food. The strangers now ask after her, for indeed their visit concerns her chiefly. Her curiosity is excited: she listens at the door of the tent, which is near enough to allow her to hear the conversation. While she is listening, the angel of the Lord repeats to Abraham the assurance formerly given that she shall have a son. Somewhat like her husband in the like circumstances, Sarah laughs within herself at the ludicrous suggestion. It is evident that there was more incredulity in her laugh than there had been in her husband's. The Lord rates her for it— "Why did Sarah laugh?" That laugh implied deliberate distrust, —distrust in the almighty power of God. Sarah was in the tent, the guests were outside—they had not seen her; and with the ready resource of a timid nature she denied that she had laughed. The angel is now face to face with her; he repels her lying apology, and, as we may believe, brings her under that sense of awe which the divine presence inspires, and which makes the sin both of disbelieving and disobeying God appear very terrible. Sarah must have been petrified; but in the fever of her emotion and contrition her incredulity vanished. It was requisite that both parents of the coming son should believe before the gift was sent. And Sarah believes now, as we find it expressed in the Hebrews: "By faith also Sarah herself received strength to conceive seed, and was delivered of a child when she was past age, because she judged him faithful who had promised." Probably this was the first experience of settled faith in the coming birth of her son that Sarah had had for many years. We may fancy the changed feeling in her heart, and the changed look in her face, as she sat in her tent that evening. And if she had the gift of song, we may fancy her breaking out into a magnificat of her own—"My soul doth magnify the Lord, and my spirit doth rejoice in God my Saviour."

Some may wonder why such elaborate dealings took place with Abraham and Sarah about that son of theirs—why he was not allowed to come quietly into the world without all this preliminary advertising, like Augustine, or Martin Luther, or any other man who has been a great boon to mankind. The scriptural explanation may seem to some peculiar, for it rests on the great moral and spiritual value of the grace of faith in the sight of God. There was a fitness that those who in their posterity were to be pre-eminently the benefactors of the world, should be conspicuous as honouring supremely the great Being from whom all blessing comes. Now true faith or trust is the very essence of such honour. And this faith is but rare. "To look at the crowds of persons professing religion," says an eloquent writer, "one would suppose nothing was commoner than faith. There is nothing rarer. Devoutness is common, righteousness of life is common, a contempt of every kind of fraud and underhand practice is common, a high-minded disregard for the world's gains and glories is common, an abhorrence of sensuality and an earnest thirst for perfection are common; but faith? Will the Son of man when he comes find it on earth?......Why, the great majority of Christian people have never been near enough to spiritual things to know whether they are or are not; they have never narrowly weighed spiritual issues, and trembled as they watched the uncertain balance; they say they believe God and a future of happiness, because they do not really know what they are talking about—they have not measured the magnitude of these things." *

God desires that his chosen vessels, those through whom he is to bless the world, shall be men and women of faith. They are so opposite in this respect to those that live by sight that each appears insane to the other: the man of the world seems mad to the man of faith, because he pursues shadows as if they were realities; the man of faith appears mad to the man of the world, because the best things of earth are shadows to him, and all that he cares for is above.

* Dr. Dods on *Genesis*, " Expositor's Bible "

# CHAPTER X.

## ABRAHAM AND SODOM.

### (GEN. xviii.)

THE hospitable spirit that induced Abraham to offer refreshments to the three strangers led him also, when they rose to depart, to accompany them on their way. The road from Hebron toward the Dead Sea passes along the eastern slope of the elevated plateau on which Hebron stands, and there is a spot in the road, formerly called Caphar-berucha, now Beni Naim, at which tradition says that God's purpose to destroy Sodom was made known to the patriarch. A ravine gives a glimpse of the hills round Sodom, and the position is analogous to that of our Lord, when, crossing the Mount of Olives, " he beheld the city," and poured his lamentation over it in connection with its coming destruction. In a very human-like soliloquy, the divine visitor is represented as considering with himself whether or not he will make known his purpose to Abraham. And the reason why he resolves to tell him is very honourable to the patriarch. Abraham's seed is to become a great nation, and he himself is one of those rare men that stamp their image on their family, and train and guide them in their own ways and feelings. It will greatly help Abraham to do this if God now enters into confidential communications with him in reference to Sodom. For it· is not on Abraham alone that a very solemn impression will be made, but through him on his family too, and through his family on the great nation of which he is to be the progenitor. There were other believers in the true God in the world besides Abraham—

Melchizedek, for example ; but, as Canon Mozley says, they may have been content to serve God themselves, leaving the rest of the world undisturbed in their idolatry. " But Abraham was cast in a different mould. He has the future of the world before his mind ; he looks upon all the nations of the earth in connection with the true faith." When he becomes the father of a family, he will bend his whole energies to induce them to become partakers of his faith, and to make them in all religious beliefs and practices like-minded with himself.

But God did not at once tell Abraham the worst of what was to happen. Adapting himself to human ways, he represented himself at this stage as only on an errand of inquiry. A very evil report of Sodom and Gomorrah had come up to him ; he was now on his way to ascertain if it was correct. So much, speaking after the manner of men, he told to Abraham. But an unerring instinct revealed to Abraham what this really meant. He felt instinctively that if his visitor should go to the spot and investigate the rumours of wickedness, no report that had ever gone forth could be so horrible as the state of things he would actually find. It became apparent to him that under the veil of an intended inquiry lay hid the certainty of an awful judgment : Sodom was doomed ; unless, indeed, he could succeed in procuring a respite for the city, in consideration of the righteous men that were still among its inhabitants.

The party now breaks up ; two of the visitors pass on toward Sodom, and Abraham remains before the Lord. Tradition has long marked out the spot where Abraham offered his memorable intercession. It is called Ramah, or Ramel-el-Khalil, and is marked by the ruins of a great building. Here, in former ages, large gatherings of people were held, who brought valuable gifts and offered sacrifices, many casting their gifts into the sacred well, whose waters at that sacred season no one ventured to drink. In room of the superstitious or cabalistic rites which had grown up under the oak of Abraham, the Emperor Constantine built a church, some remains of which may perhaps be seen at the present day.*

* Deane's "Abraham."

Every reader is struck by the combination of deep insight, childlike intimacy, and holy reverence in the intercession which Abraham now made to the Lord on behalf of Sodom. He at once recognizes God's right to punish sin, and to punish it by the destruction of the sinner. He recognizes his right to deal with a city as a whole, and to punish it as a whole. But in this method of dealing is there not a risk of injustice? Will the great Ruler punish the righteous alike with the wicked? Surely if the calamity which he is to bring upon the city is to be a judicial punishment for its guilt, the supreme Judge will take care that those who have not partaken of its sins shall not suffer like those who have. Noah and his family were spared in the flood; could God ordain destruction to the righteous men that might be in Sodom? Abraham appeals straight to God's justice: "Shall not the Judge of all the earth do justly?" What a memorable question! First, he takes for granted that God, his God, is the Judge of all the earth. It is not this deity ruling the sea, and that the dry land; this god judging Abraham, and that the Amorites: the one only God is the one only Judge, and Abraham realizes the vision of his far-distant descendant—"I beheld the dead, small and great, stand before God." Then he recognizes the infinite righteousness of this God: no partiality, no caprice, no shadow of turning in him. He *must* do right; he must be true to himself. "Shall not the Judge of all the earth do justly?" It is the grandest conception of his God that Abraham has ever yet expressed.

And he seems to have felt what a firm footing he had here, on this impregnable rock; for he makes bold to urge his plea again and again, reducing each time the supposed number of good men, but knowing that such reduction cannot affect the principle of eternal justice. And it is not merely for the righteous men in the city that he pleads, but for the city in which they dwell. He takes for granted that a few righteous men are sufficient to redeem a community from the charge of utter rottenness. Their very existence in its bosom is a proof that the place is not so utterly gone in wickedness as to deserve to be swept away by a summary judgment. If there were fifty such men in Sodom, would not their presence show that the place was not ripe for judgment? and would not God spare the city for their sakes?

God answers that he would not destroy it for the fifty's sake.

But Abraham cannot leave the matter there. He is profoundly interested in many of the inhabitants of those cities whom he had rescued from Chedorlaomer, and he had a special interest in Lot, and in his family and dependents. Fifty was an ideal number; most certainly it would be impossible to find fifty righteous men in Sodom. He must try to bring down the ideal to the actual, to get God's consent to spare the city for a much lower number than that. It may seem an offensive thing for a man to be driving a bargain with God, trying to get him to lower his terms, like a greedy Jew of to-day higgling over the price of merchandise. But in Abraham's case there is such profound reverence, there is such a depreciation of himself, who is but dust and ashes, there is such a holy fear lest he should be going too far, lest the Lord should be angry, that we acquit him at once of all presumption. We know, too, that he is not pleading for himself. Personally he can no more derive benefit from the sparing of Sodom, and has no more desire to derive benefit, than after the defeat of Chedorlaomer, when he refused to take so much as a shoe-latchet from the rescued prisoners or their kings. It is the profound compassion of the man that is dealing with God. God has implanted that compassion in him, and he will not complain even of its most extreme exercise. And thus the Lord bears with him, and allows him to bring down his terms to forty, thirty, twenty, ay, even to ten. Below that even Abraham dare not go. A city reeking with wickedness, that has not ten righteous men in it, is certainly ripe for destruction. But though he has not prevailed with the Lord to spare the city, he has so emphatically reminded the Lord, at least by implication, of the case of Lot, that special provision is made for him. Sodom is doomed, the other cities are doomed; nevertheless the divine justice is vindicated: the righteous does not perish with the wicked; the Judge of all the earth does rightly.

Abraham had already saved Lot by his exertions; now he

saves him by his prayers.   Each was appropriate in the circumstances, and the success of each, when employed at the fitting
time, shows that neither the one nor the other is to be regarded
as an unfailing specific; both enter, sometimes apart, more frequently united, into the plans of God.

The parting of the Lord from Abraham must have been within
a reasonable distance of the oak of Mamre, for the patriarch returns to his home the same night.   How checkered his emotions
as he reaches his encampment!   Sarah in such exuberant spirits,
in the sure prospect of motherhood, till she hears of the coming
tragedy; Abraham wholly at one in her exuberant joy, yet unable
to utter one joyful word, because this awful judgment absorbs his
whole soul.

We rejoin the two angels that went on to Sodom.   At evening
they reach the gate of the city, where Lot is sitting enjoying the
cool of the evening.   What has brought him to live within the city?
Has he exchanged an agricultural for a mercantile life?   Has he
disposed of his flocks and herds, his servants and his beasts of
burden, and taken to the business of a trader, which in that situation, on the highway between the north and the south, he might
carry on with great advantage?   It would seem that he must
have done so, for neither now nor afterwards have we any notice
of his cattle.   If his wealth had still consisted in these, and they
were roaming on the neighbouring mountains, Lot and his family
would have had no difficulty in leaving Sodom.   But if the live
wealth of the farmer had been exchanged for the solid treasure
of the merchant; if Lot's place of abode in Sodom combined the
office, the bank, and the warehouse; if besides his accumulated
stores he was carrying on a golden traffic that poured new wealth
every day into his coffers, we may understand how his heart and
his wife's heart would be glued to the place.

Still his hospitality remains, his respect for God's servants
remains, his courtesy remains; and perceiving that the strangers
have a distinguished appearance, apprehending possibly that they
are not mere denizens of earth, he invites them to spend the night
in his house.   To test his sincerity, they at first decline, and pro-

pose to remain in the street; but of this Lot will not hear. They enter his house and prepare to rest.

The historian gives no description of the wickedness of Sodom, but leaves it to unfold itself by a simple but horrible tale.

The strangers who had entered Lot's house were doubtless of young and beautiful appearance; their arrival was soon known over the town, and also the fact that they had gone to stay with Lot. The sensuality of the place had effaced every trace of good manners in its inhabitants. So far from any desire to show attention to strangers, or to respect the laws of hospitality, the men of the place, "both old and young, all the people from every quarter," came rudely to the house of Lot, and demanded of him to give up his guests for the vilest purposes. No more lurid light could be cast on the abominable character of the place. From the king on the throne to the beggar on the dunghill, there seems to have been not one to lift up his voice against wickedness so detestable, against an outrage so horrible. Poor Lot had evidently lost the calmness and the sense of moral propriety needful for the occasion. Like timid and unbelieving men generally, he rushed to the readiest expedient for calming the excited populace, for quieting their filthy hunger. Going outside his door, perhaps that his offer might not be heard within, he offered to sacrifice his daughters in order to save his guests. The offer was as vain as it was horrible. Insult is only added to injury. "This one fellow came in to sojourn, and he must needs be a judge." You forget your place, sir, interfering with us, the real masters of this city, and daring to stand between us and our wishes as to these two men. We will make away with you in a twinkling if you dare to obstruct our purpose. Lynch law would evidently have been applied. What cared they that his uncle, Abraham, had done them such an unspeakable service? What do any men care for past services when their blood is up, their temper raging, and there is a danger of their being cheated out of some coarse indulgence on which they are madly set?

It was now that Lot's visitors resorted to a method of protection which might have been applied sooner if Lot had not taken the matter into his own hands and disgraced himself by his humiliating proposal respecting his daughters. The men pulled Lot into the door, and smote the men at the door with blindness. If Lot had trusted a little more and waited a little longer, he would have seen how present a help God is in times of trouble.

And now Lot is made to understand the awful purpose for which these messengers of heaven have visited Sodom. The cry of it has waxen great before the face of the Lord, and they are sent to destroy it. A thrill of horror passes through Lot's soul as he hears what is about to happen ; but he does not set himself, like his uncle, to arrest the judgment. The angels hurry him away before dawn to the houses of his sons-in-law, to give them a chance ; but his words have no moral weight—he seems to be merely raving. Morning dawns, and they urge him to take his wife and daughters and escape from the coming catastrophe ; but he only dawdles, as if chained by his possessions to the place. It becomes necessary to seize them all by their hands and hurry them out, as the police would hurry offenders to prison, for the moment of the bursting of the storm is just at hand. At length they pass out through the gate where Lot had received his visitors so shortly before ; but still, as if paralyzed, he hangs about the place. Urgent words must still be fired at him. " Look alive ! fly to the mountain—there is not a moment to lose ; not a spot in the plain is safe. Escape for your life ; the fire is just coming ! "

But even such words fall without effect on his ear. The bleak, bare mountain, thinks Lot, how can we ever live there? how can we make our living, how can we carry on any business there? Even in that supreme moment his mind is a blank as to any feeling of God ; he can think only of some scheme of earthly good. At last he does utter something like a prayer ; and what he asks is that he may not be banished to the mountain, but allowed to dwell in the little city of Zoar. Little does he remember that his mountain life had been far the best, when he was feeding his flocks with Abraham, and that if he could only return to that life, the old blessedness might come to him again. But no; his thoughts are still of a town life, where he might resume business, where he might retrieve in some degree the tremendous losses he is now about to suffer, and be a rich man again. What a contrast this to Abraham's prayer! Abraham, without a thought for himself, interceding so earnestly for the whole people of the plain, or at least of Sodom, the dominating city; Lot not offering one petition for the people, nor for his sons-in-law, nor for his married daughters, but pleading only for himself. Yet God is gracious, and grants this petition. Zoar, wherever it is, is to be spared for his sake; and till he reaches the place the judgment on the other cities will be delayed. The sun was risen on the earth, was already well above the horizon, when Lot entered Zoar.

But Zoar was not enough for his wife. "She looked back from behind him," for her heart and her treasure were still in Sodom, and she was caught in the deluge of fire. Some portion of the saline and bituminous matter which seems to have burst in the convulsion into flame caught and overwhelmed her, incrusting her remains like a stone or pillar of salt. Lot and his two daughters reach Zoar, and look round on the catastrophe—with what feelings we can hardly conceive. Such a fiery flood never fell on earth since it was the abode of man. His house, his riches, his acquaintances, his sons-in-law, his married children, are all engulfed in that terrible conflagration; and what is most fearful of all, it is God's judgment on sin and sinners—a proof that "it is a fearful thing to fall into the hands of the living God!"

Anxious and restless, Abraham rose up early in the morning and returned to the place whence, with the angel of God, he had got his view on the preceding evening of the mountains round the plain. When he set out all was quiet, for Lot had not yet escaped to Zoar. But there was a strange restlessness and heaviness about the clouds, and when the sun rose it was not to touch up hill and vale with sparkling silver, but to diffuse a lurid glow over the tumbling clouds, as if one of those terrible thunderstorms was impending with which Abraham must have been familiar. When he got to the place where he stood before the Lord, the catastrophe had begun. When he looked toward Sodom and Gomorrah, and toward all the land of the plain, he saw smoke rising up like the smoke of a furnace. Oh poor Lot, how did his heart go out for him at that moment in prayer! But God had remembered Abraham's anxiety for Lot, and happily he was beyond the sphere of the conflagration. How would Abraham have welcomed him if, instead of beseeching God for a retreat in that wretched Zoar, he had directed his steps to Hebron! We may even fancy him looking out keenly along the road, if by any possibility he might see his nephew coming.

But Lot had gone to Zoar. He had some reason to look for a welcome there, for it was his prayer that had saved the place, and if the people had had a spark of grace or gratitude, they would have received him with open arms. In point of fact, they received him with such bitterness of hatred that he could not dwell among them. Lot had had all along a painful experience at the hands of the people of the plain. He had been their friend, and had tried to do them good; but in vain. His soul had been vexed from day to day with their filthy life and unlawful deeds, and he had no doubt remonstrated with them and tried to bring them to repentance. Emphatically we may believe he tried to do so after the rescue by his uncle, when such a boon had been conferred on them by one so conspicuous for his pure religion and his righteous life that already, perhaps, he was called "the friend of God." It was all to no purpose; for Lot had deprived himself of moral influence by the inconsistency of his life with his creed. The people knew that after all his professions he had brought his family into that wicked circle for the sake of worldly advantage. Why had he left Abraham? Why was he there at all? Simply for the sake of gain. This fact deprived his example and his instructions of all moral pith and power. Men that desire to do good to others must see to it that they are themselves serving God with a pure conscience. And now that Lot has come to Zoar, the people judge him as unjustly as Ahab judged Elijah when he denounced him as the troubler of Israel. Instead of welcoming him as their saviour, they look on him, or on his God, as the cause of all this disaster. They make the place too hot for him; and after all his importunity to be allowed to dwell in Zoar, he is fain to escape to the mountain, and dwell with his two daughters in a cave.

That drunkenness must have been one of the sins of Sodom goes almost without saying; for drunkenness is never far removed from other forms of sensuality. The narrative of Lot and his two daughters would lead us to believe that he had already fallen in some degree under the influence of that sin. His daughters could hardly have prevailed on him to drink to excess on two following nights if the way had not previously been prepared. Like many another, Lot felt the burden of his anguish insupportable, and if he could not find a solace for his grief, he might at least find some means of deadening it for a time. As yet, at least, his troubles had not brought him back to God; there was no comfort for him in that direction. But strong drink had for the moment a soothing power, and his daughters knew his weakness. It must have been very vehement feelings that led them to resort to the horrible plot in which they desired their father to play an unconscious part. Was it jealousy of Abraham? Were they maddened to think of his large and prosperous establishment in contrast to their own loneliness and poverty, and especially to think of that promise of blessing, and of the nations that were to spring from his loins, while their side of the house was reduced to one old man and two single women? But what could they do? Now that the four cities were destroyed, and they were persecuted out of the fifth, there was literally not a man in any friendly community to become the husband of either. If their race was not to become extinct, some novel device must be resorted to for obtaining posterity. Residence in Sodom had familiarized them with every form of sensual vice, and had removed the horror with which unnatural connections would at one time have been regarded. We can hardly suppose that when they plied their father with the bottle they passed it untasted themselves. What is there like drink for inflaming the passions, for destroying self-

control, for subduing conscience, for crushing modesty, for turning
the woman into a beast or a devil? Well would it have been
for them had their family ended with themselves; had they never
had descendants to inherit the infamy of their origin and share
with them an unblest career!

With regard to the means by which the destruction of Sodom
and Gomorrah was brought about, a word may now be said. The
statement in Genesis is, "The Lord rained upon Sodom and upon
Gomorrah brimstone and fire from the Lord out of heaven; and
he overthrew those cities, and all the plain, and all the inhabitants
of the cities, and that which grew upon the ground." Brimstone,
bitumen, and other inflammable substances abound in the neighbourhood; and if these were ignited by lightning, and scattered
abroad by an earthquake or other convulsion, or if some burning
mountain opened its mouth on high and poured down its streams
of fiery lava on the cities below, the description of Genesis would
be realized. What could have been more awful than the recent
catastrophe in New Zealand, where earthquake and volcano combined their fiery forces, swept towns and villages in one night
out of existence, and reduced beautiful and fertile valleys to utter
barrenness and desolation? It is not necessary for God, when he
desires to punish wickedness, to resort to supernatural agencies.
The ordinary forces of nature may be turned on to do the work;
and while it would be unwarrantable to infer in the case of every
such calamity, any more than in the case of the tower of Siloam,
that it was a special judgment on the sufferers, yet when God
announces that he is to punish the sin of some community, and
such a judgment follows, though by purely natural causes, the
effect is the same as that of a supernatural agent. God's hand
is seen clearly in the disaster.

Where, precisely, in the Jordanic hollow, were these cities of
the plain? The question has given rise to much geographical
discussion. It was at one time a common belief that the Dead
Sea now occupies the plain in which the destroyed cities stood.
This belief receives apparent sanction from the statement (Gen.

xiv. 3) that the confederate kings of Sodom were joined together at the time of Chedorlaomer's invasion "in the vale of Siddim, which is the salt sea." The Arabic name of the Dead Sea, Bahr Lût, also lends some colour to the supposition. In connection with this, it used to be believed that previously the river Jordan passed through the Wady el Araba to the Red Sea; that by volcanic action a mountain barrier was thrown up at the base of the present lake, so that the outflow of the Jordan to the sea was arrested, and a great lake formed instead. But later and more careful observations have shown that this theory is untenable. It is quite plain from geological appearances that the Dead Sea is not a recent but a very ancient lake, and that in former times, instead of less, there was actually more water than there is now in the valley of the Jordan. It is to be observed, too, that the narrative in Genesis gives us no reason to suppose that the cities were destroyed by water; the rain from heaven that destroyed them was a rain of fire.

Some have supposed that the cities were near the southern extremity of the lake. But this is unlikely, for many reasons. With the lake intervening, the cities would be too remote for Lot to embrace them in his view when he and Abraham surveyed the land from the height near Bethel; nor would the position have been such that Chedorlaomer and his confederates would have been so eager to command it. Moreover, the description of Chedorlaomer's route going to Sodom from the south, *via* Engedi, refutes the supposition. The author of "The Land and the Book," who at first favoured the southern site, has come round to the northern. All considerations point to the northern end of the lake as the probable site of the cities. If the banks of the Jordan were then artificially irrigated, their fertility must have been extraordinary. If Lot did not actually see these green plains from Bethel, he was near enough to perceive the nature of the locality, and information regarding it had no doubt come to his ears. From the richness of the neighbourhood, and from the nature of the position, Chedorlaomer and his allies could not look with indifference upon it. Not far from where Jericho stood afterwards was probably the site of the doomed cities. The plain is now quite barren. "At the north end of the lake," says one, "you may ride for a couple of hours before you reach the ruins of Jericho; and all the way your horse's hoofs will sink through a salt crust into a friable mould some inches deep, in which nothing will grow." Our Lord must often have passed near or over the plain, and had doubtless a very vivid image of the cities in his mind when he declared that it would be more tolerable for Sodom and Gomorrah in the day of judgment than for the cities of the northern lake that had trampled on all his messages of grace and resisted all his appeals of love.

The Dead Sea that adjoins the plain of the Jordan is one of the most extraordinary sheets of water on the face of the earth. Its waters are so largely impregnated with salt that neither fish nor animal of any kind can live in them; but an old belief, that birds were unable to fly over the lake, but fell down in the middle of their flight as if suffocated, is now found to be a mistake. At what time it acquired this saline character cannot be known. There would seem a moral fitness in the supposition that it was at the time when the cities were destroyed. This can hardly be made out; but it seems to be implied in the narrative (Gen. xix. 25) that it was at this time that the plain was made desolate. In Utah and other portions of North America we find salt lakes, caused by the presence of strong alkaline matter in the soil, and washed down by the streams into the lakes. The salt properties of the Dead Sea must be due to the prevalence of alkaline or sulphurous matter in the neighbourhood; but it may have been the convulsions connected with the destruction of the cities that impregnated the waters of the lake and turned it into an emblem of death.

It is not wonderful that the occurrence of so terrible a catastrophe should have found a record in the traditions of many ancient nations. An old Accadian poem describes a rain of fire similar in character and effect to that which destroyed the cities of the plain. Professor Sayce gives the following translation, remarking that the expedition of Chedorlaomer against Sodom

THE DEAD SEA.

Page 154.

makes it not surprising that the destruction of the place should have interested the Accadians :—

" An overthrow from the midst of the deep there came,
The fated punishment from the midst of heaven descended.
A storm like a plummet the earth (overwhelmed),
To the four winds the destroying flood like fire did burn.
The inhabitants of cities it had caused to be tormented ; their bodies it
  consumed ;
In city and in country it spread death, and the flames as they rose over-
  threw ;
Freeman and slave were equal, and the high places it filled.
In heaven and earth like a thunderstorm it had rained ; a prey it made ;
A place of refuge the gods hastened to, and in a throng collected.
Its mighty (onset) they fled from, and like a garment it concealed (mankind).
They (feared), and death (overtook them) ;
(Their) feet and hands (it embraced),
Their body it consumed.
...... the city, its foundations it defiled,
...... in breath his mouth he filled.
As for man, a loud voice was raised ; the mighty lightning flash descended ;
During the day it flashed, grievously it fell." *

Josephus gives the following account of the tragedy : "Adjoining the lake is the country of Sodom, once a blessed region on account of its productiveness and the many cities that adorned it, but now entirely burnt up. They say that for the impiety of its inhabitants it was destroyed by lightning. Even to this day some remains of the divine fire and shadows [or traces] of the five cities may be seen, and ashes growing in the fruits appear; for while they have the colour and appearance of real fruits, when pulled by the hand they resolve into dust and ashes." † The "Wisdom of Solomon" speaks of the fire which fell down upon the five cities, of whose wickedness, even to this day, the waste land that smoketh is a testimony, and plants bearing fruit that never come to ripeness. Tacitus dwells on the contrast between plains once so fertile and abounding in great cities but now completely barren, and ascribes it to lightning. Strabo speaks of the traces of volcanic action still to be seen in the neighbourhood, and of the

---

* "Records of the Past," xi. 117. Professor Sayce has given a somewhat altered translation in *Monthly Interpreter*, vol. iii., p. 465.
† "Wars of the Jews," IV. viii. 4.

tradition of the natives that a dire catastrophe overwhelmed Sodom and twelve other cities, most of which were swallowed up by the waters of the lake.*

As to the present condition of the shores of the lake, let it suffice to quote the testimony of Canon Tristram : "Sulphur springs stud the shore; sulphur is thrown, whether in layers or in fragments, over the desolate plains, and bitumen is ejected in great floating masses from the bottom of the sea, oozes through the fissures of the rocks, is deposited with gravel on the beach, or appears with the sulphur to have been precipitated during some convulsion."

From this period Lot vanishes from the page of history. That he regained a worldly position seems to be implied in the fact that his two sons became heads of nations. This could hardly have happened if they had not been chiefs of great establishments, including a multitude of servants. Lot's story, with that of his wife, remains a perpetual testimony to the sin and certain retribu- tion of a worldly spirit.

* See Deane's "Abraham," p. 111.

# CHAPTER XI.

## GERAR AND BEERSHEBA——BIRTH OF ISAAC.

(Gen. xx.)

" IT is the unexpected that happens." This remark of a keen observer of men and manners was never more strikingly exemplified than in the incident we now come to in the life of Abraham. It has seemed to some so incredible that he should have repeated the unworthy artifice which he practised before in Egypt, and should again have surrendered Sarah to save himself, that for this and other reasons they have supposed that we have here a different version by a different writer of the incident formerly recorded. To bear this out, stress is laid on the fact that in the former narrative (ch. xii.) the name of the Most High is Jehovah; in the present it is (except in ver. 18) Elohim (God). The theory that in the composition of Genesis there were two writers, a Jehovist and an Elohist, seems to receive some countenance from this fact. But apart from the merits or demerits of that theory, the narrative now before us is so circumstantial, the place, the time, the nation, and the name of the king in connection with whom the incident occurred are so different, and the locality to which Abraham removed afterwards is also so specifically noted, that in all fairness we are compelled to conclude that Abraham was guilty of repeating his former offence. He stands out in many ways such a spiritual giant that we forget the usual conditions even of remarkable piety—how often it is associated with great infirmity.

It was probably more than twenty years since the visit to

Egypt, which may therefore have ceased to be vividly remembered. Stratagems of the kind practised by Abraham may have been very common among the people around, and, being common, not much thought of. But, indeed, is it not the common experience of the best of men that they are sadly liable to forget the resolutions they made while under God's hand, and drift again into the course most natural to their own hearts? And are they not also very liable to argue with themselves when an old temptation returns that there is something different in this case from the last? Some such sophistry probably blinded Abraham on this occasion, the precise nature of which we cannot know. But we find him again in the mire, and again he is humbled before pagans, who show far more generosity and uprightness than himself.

He had left the neighbourhood of Hebron—for what reason we know not—and migrated toward "the south." Gerar, where he halted, was the headquarters of king Abimelech, the official name of a Philistine chief who, like himself, was the head of a pastoral people. It is commonly thought that the Philistines were a people of Egyptian origin, who had lately begun to occupy the Shefela, the level strip between the mountains of Judah and the sea. As yet they were evidently in a primitive condition. Some centuries afterwards, when the Israelites returned from Egypt, they were a formidable people, having five principal cities joined by a league, and considerably advanced in military, commercial, and industrial pursuits. As in other barbarous courts, the harem was one of the appendages of royalty, into which unmarried females of distinction were gathered, sometimes for display as much as for sensuality.

Again, to protect his own life, Abraham pretends that Sarah is only his sister, and again he allows her to be taken to the royal harem. Probably he thought that in her present circumstances divine protection would, beyond all doubt, be extended to her, and that she would come out safe and well. In so far he was right. But the divine protection comes in a way humbling to Abraham. The fact that Sarah is his wife is communicated by God himself to Abimelech, and a threatening of death is conveyed for the outrageous crime of taking a married woman to his harem. The form of Abimelech's first remonstrance is interesting, as showing that the judgment of Sodom had lately taken place, and that Abimelech recognized the source of it—" Lord, wilt thou also slay a righteous nation?" The Philistines were not like the men of Sodom; family ties were not desecrated by them; they might be called in comparison a righteous nation. And as to Abimelech himself, he verily believed that Sarah was but Abraham's sister, for both of them had told him so. And God accepts Abimelech's excuse in so far as it can go, but without exonerating him for indulging in a practice which was liable, though against his intention, of leading to most shocking consequences. He orders him to restore Abraham's wife, especially on the ground that he is a prophet, using that word in its wide sense—a man in supernatural communication with God.

Abimelech loses no time in complying with God's command; and that a due impression may be made on others, he calls his household together to explain what has happened. With Abraham he deals with dignified sharpness. He ought not to have treated a friend as he has done; he ought not to have led him to the edge of a precipice, and exposed him and his kingdom to an awful danger. He calls on him to say what motive he had for so unfriendly and ungracious an act. And Abraham, driven to the wall, can only refer to the understanding he came to with his wife some five-and-twenty years before, " when God caused him to wander from his father's house." He would almost insinuate that it was a necessary step under the circumstances, and that God was responsible for it, not he.

How strange is human inconsistency! How strong was Abraham's faith in great things, how weak in little things! He can believe that God will work a great miracle to give him a son, and yet he cannot believe that God will dispose the heart of one of his creatures to respect the relation between him and his wife. Great trials, great duties, great sacrifices, rally the whole forces of the soul; little trials are looked at with careless eyes, and often lead to humiliating falls. Abraham could trust God to raise his son from the dead; he could not trust him to preserve his own life in a moment of possible danger.

Evidently Abimelech got a great fright when he found that this man, to whom he might unwittingly have done a grievous injury, was the special friend of God. This explains the great generosity of his treatment. In returning Sarah, he gave him "sheep, and oxen, and men-servants, and women-servants," and "a thousand pieces of silver." He gave him the run of his country—Abraham might go wherever he pleased. To Sarah, at the same time, he administered a gentle reproof. "See," he said, "I have given to thy brother a thousand pieces of silver: behold, he is to thee a covering of the eyes, unto all that are with thee, and with all other: thus she was reproved." Abimelech's words have been a standing difficulty to commentators, and many is the explanation to which they have been subjected. It is easy to see his meaning in calling Abraham Sarah's veil; as her husband he would be a protection to her in Abimelech's kingdom, and not a source of danger, and therefore the relation between them ought never to be concealed. The gift of a thousand pieces of silver was fitted to give emphasis to this fact; it might impress on her Abimelech's view of the sacredness of the marriage tie, and deliver her in all time coming from the mean pretexts to which both she and her husband had had recourse.

In some degree Abraham was able to make a return to Abimelech for his kindness. The Lord, by way of signifying his displeasure, had closed the wombs of Abimelech's household; Abraham interceded for them, and the curse of barrenness was removed.

The place of Abraham's sojourn was now Beersheba. It lies on the southern border of Palestine, and in Abraham's time was included in Abimelech's kingdom. When we read of "the wilderness of Beersheba," we are liable to think of a sandy desert; but the term "wilderness" was often used to denote an uninhabited tract, well enough adapted for pasturing cattle. Such was Beersheba. Abraham, we are told, "planted a grove" there—not indeed of oak or terebinth, but of the feathery tamarisk, which the traveller notes as "the first and the last tree which he sees in his passage through the desert." The gentle slopes of Beersheba, covered with green pastures, and its celebrated wells, gave it the attractions which shepherds prized. Dr. Horatius Bonar could find nothing to mark it in any special way. It was a fruitful land, no doubt, but a plain and unambitious territory, very like the men who occupied it. Dr. Edward Robinson notes it as "open, undulating country." When he reached it, "the shrubs of the desert ceased; green grass was seen along the water-courses, and almost greensward; and had it been an ordinary season, the gentle hills would have been covered with grass and rich pastures."

And here, in all probability, Isaac was born. The promise at length became a reality: the son of Sarah was now the heir of the blessing.

And his name was called Isaac (laughter). Not that he was to exemplify that bright, joyous temperament that in the very exuberance of gladness is for ever rippling with smiles or bursting forth into peals of laughter. A much quieter and more sombre temperament was his. But his heart knew the deep, calm joy of which mere laughter is often not the token but the mockery. And as the heir of promise and the forefather of that other Son by whom the blessing would be realized in its fulness, he symbolized the joyous effects of the covenant of grace, and pointed to Him whom the Spirit of the Lord would anoint to proclaim liberty to the captive, and to comfort all that mourn. Thus at this early period, in the very name of Abraham's son, was an implied rebuke given to the spirit that has so often associated the idea of misery with the active service of God; and thus was the great fact shadowed forth which men have been so slow to learn, but so blessed when they have learned it, that the one great antidote to the sorrows of the world, the heavenly balm that can heal every wound, the charm that can make us tranquil and happy under all manner of disappointments, pains, persecutions, and agonies, is the joy that comes from fellowship with the great Son of Abraham— "a joy unspeakable, and full of glory."

Next came the weaning of Isaac, the great feast made by

BEERSHEBA.

Page 191.

Abraham on the occasion, and the expulsion of Hagar and Ishmael for their insulting conduct. We have already considered this incident in its relation to Ishmael. And we have seen how grievous it was to Abraham, whose old heart had been captivated by the winning ways and stirring spirit of Ishmael. It was an experience of life to the patriarch in which, under very different circumstances and in another way, many a one has had to participate since. Just when the highest point of domestic happiness seems to be reached, an unexpected blow falls, carrying bitterness and desolation. When the picture is at its fairest, an ugly blot comes on the canvas. Human joy is never allowed to reach perfection. The full cup is rudely shaken before it is carried to the lips. The day of feasting was to Abraham a day of desolation. Probably he looked his last on Ishmael, and could never again think of the engaging boy without a grievous pang at his heart.

It is but seldom that all the members of families are permitted to grow up together, settle beside each other, and spend their lives amid the scenes of their childhood ; and when such cases do occur, we see that they are but the exceptions that prove the rule. The scattering of families is proverbial—one of the commonplaces of human experience ; even he who earned the title " the friend of God " has to submit to the needful discipline. By the departure of Hagar and Ishmael peace is restored to Abraham's household, but not without a sacrifice deeply felt. Something of Ishmael's stirring nature was just what Isaac wanted ; if only the two could have lived in peace, and the younger brother had imbibed the enterprise without the vehemence of the older, he would have been more of a man afterwards, and more adapted for his position in life.

The intercourse of Abraham and Abimelech did not end when the former was sent away from Gerar. The character and life of Abraham evidently made an impression on the king. Abraham was not a preacher, but his life witnessed for God, and testified that God was with him. Both Abimelech and Phichol, his commander-in-chief, were impressed with this conviction.

Even the man of war was struck by the temporal prosperity of Abraham, and drew the inference that the God whom he served must be a powerful God, whose favour it would be well to secure. Here was one of the best of all triumphs—Abraham's light so shining before men that they saw his good works and glorified his Father in heaven. What extent of spiritual impression was implied in the acknowledgments of these two potentates we cannot say, but the anxiety of Abimelech to be on friendly terms was so strong that it did not extend to himself only; he desired his son and his son's son to enjoy the same privilege. He asked Abraham to seal his friendship by an oath, in which he should engage not to deal falsely with him or with his heirs, but to act toward them in the same friendly spirit in which Abimelech had acted to him. To this Abraham agreed. "As much as lieth in you, live peaceably with all men," is in spirit a precept older than St. Paul; to Abraham, cherishing this spirit, the proposed engagement was one into which he could enter without a moment's hesitation, for he had no plans of conquest in his head either against the king of Gerar or any one else. No doubt it was difficult to show what made him content to be a pilgrim and a sojourner in the land. It was natural for the princes of the country to suppose that he must have some aggressive project, to be carried into effect sooner or later. The readiness of Abraham to enter into the proposed engagement, and thus dispel their fears, was another proof of his remarkably disinterested character—a proof how unlike he was to his worldly-minded nephew, whose eagerness to increase his riches had caused his terrible ruin.

But if the relations of Abraham and Abimelech were thus most satisfactory, it was otherwise in the case of some of their servants. The servants of Abimelech had taken a well by violence, driving forcibly away from it those who had right to it, thus following the wild maxim of the Bedouin, "Might is right." It is one of the many proofs of the value of water in those parts that a single well should be the subject of such contention in the first instance and diplomacy in the second. With some warmth and indignation, Abraham complains to Abimelech. The excuse of the king, if true, was so far valid—that he knew nothing of the matter, and had never heard of it before. Abraham accepts the apology, and in token of his obligations to Abimelech, and of his superior right to the country in which Abraham had been allowed to reside, and where his flocks had been pastured, he presents him with sheep and oxen. This is Abraham's rent, not formally bargained for, perhaps, but a fitting acknowledgment of Abimelech's kindness. Further, the two chiefs make a covenant, in which Abraham's right to the wells would be carefully recognized. Beyond this, the covenant did not consist of definite articles, but was a general expression of good-will and friendship. To confirm the arrangement as to the well, Abraham presented seven ewe lambs to Abimelech. Whether these were for sacrifice or not we are not told, but they were a witness unto Abraham that he had digged the well. Beersheba may mean either "the well of the oath" or "the well of the seven." There can be little doubt that the former was the true meaning, but it was an interesting coincidence that it was capable of the other too.

Some light is thrown on these transactions by the experience of the traveller Bruce when bargaining with Arabs. At a place called Sheikh Ammar, he got a pledge from the Arab sheik that he would not be molested in his journey across the desert to Cosseir. A number of people afterwards assembled at the house. "The great people among them came, and after joining hands repeated a kind of prayer, by which they declared themselves and their children accursed if ever they lifted up their hands against me in the *tell* (field), in the desert, or on the river; or in case that I or mine should fly to them for refuge, if they did not protect us at the risk of their lives, their families, and their fortunes, or, as they emphatically expressed it, *to the death of the last male child among them.*" Thereafter, Bruce says, the people sent down to his boat two bushels of wheat, and seven sheep, intended as a ratification of the covenant.*

The covenant between Abraham and Abimelech is the first treaty of peace of which we have any account. It is interesting

* "Pictorial Commentary," *in loco.*

to come on it, because war was the normal condition of most of these nations, as it certainly was in after times of the Philistines. But wherever Abraham went he seems to have diffused a spirit of peace.  It was his marked and manifest fellowship with God that made Abimelech as well as other neighbours so desirous to be on good terms with him.  The author of the Book of Proverbs could hardly have failed to think of him when he wrote : " When a man's ways please the Lord, he maketh even his enemies to be at peace with him."

In this neighbourhood most of the remainder of Abraham's life seems to have been spent, and all of Isaac's.  Isaac had a particularly quiet upbringing.  It has been remarked that the only child of aged parents is usually of a quiet if not sombre disposition, having no playmates of his own age in the family, while his parents are too old to become his playmates themselves. So it probably was with Isaac.  Of one home-treasure he would enjoy an unlimited supply—parental love ; but of the fellowship that quickens a boy's mind, draws out his humour, spurs him to enterprise, and hardens him for the battle of life, he was probably quite destitute.  On the other hand, there was probably no one about Isaac likely to diminish the effect on him of the holy lives and holy lessons of his parents.

We have no means of determining what effect Abraham's neighbourhood to the Philistines had upon that people.  The Philistines then were not like the Philistines afterwards.  If the peace-loving spirit of Abraham had any good effect, it seems to have been utterly lost long before his posterity returned from Egypt.  Some of the sons of Ephraim were killed in a foray by men of Gath, on a cattle-stealing expedition (1 Chron. vii. 21). And the reason why God would not lead Israel from Egypt to their country by the way of the Philistines was, that they were sure of a warlike reception, which would have a depressing effect on their spirits.  The seeds of kindness sown between Abraham and Abimelech had by this time quite perished from the soil. Nations, like individuals, are apt to have short memories for blessings received.

# CHAPTER XII.

## THE SACRIFICE OF ISAAC.

### (GEN. xxii.)

BEERSHEBA had become to Abraham more of a home than any other place of sojourn had ever been in the land of Canaan. "Abraham sojourned in the land of the Philistines many days." It had become associated with a new interest in his life, and enlivened by fellowship with Isaac, who would readily take Ishmael's place in his heart; as they walked about hand in hand, each object seen through the little child's eyes would acquire a new freshness in Abraham's, and he himself would feel young again. Years upon years of quiet life thus passed away. The trials of former days gradually drifted into the background of memory—his leaving Ur, his breaking away from Haran, his long disappointment under the delay of the promise, his agony at the fate of Lot, his distress at parting with Ishmael; and now it seemed that the evening of life was to be serene and unclouded, and that his sun would go down in peace. Suddenly there shot out from the calm sky a bolt more terrific than any that had yet appeared, and in his old age Abraham was exposed to a trial in comparison of which all that he had hitherto experienced seemed light indeed.

The tremendous difficulties which the command to offer up Isaac raises at the first blush in the mind of every reader have given rise to suppositions with which the narrative as it stands cannot be fairly reconciled. Some have maintained that it was not God but Satan that prompted Abraham; some that

Abraham mistook the nature of God's command, since God could never have intended him to sacrifice his son; some have even resolved the narrative into a vision or a parable; and some have thought that the idea of offering up Isaac sprang out of his own devout but mistaken feelings, and on that account appeared to him like a divine command.

All such glosses on the plain narrative of Scripture are unworthy of our acceptance. It was part of the divine plan of Abraham's life that his faith should be exposed to severe tests at various stages, and it was only in accordance with that plan that the last test should be the severest of all.

If we would understand the narrative rightly, it is essential that we place ourselves in Abraham's position. We must not judge of the command to him as we should judge of a similar command to ourselves. Were any of us at this time of day to receive what seemed a divine command to slay one of our children, we should repudiate the idea with indignation. Both our consciences and the law of God impose on us the duty of preserving and protecting to the uttermost the lives of our children; how, then, could God call upon us to kill them? Moreover, the laws of our country, so far from permitting parents to take the lives of their children, would count such a deed, on whatever pretext it might be done, an unnatural murder, and would punish it with the greatest severity.

But in Abraham's time, and among the people with whom he sojourned, a father had unquestioned control over the life of his child. Centuries after, in the days of Jephthah, the right of a father to dispose of a child's life was not called in question. Among the Romans, too, it was an acknowledged fact. The idea of conflicting duty, therefore, could not arise in Abraham's mind, and hence no remonstrance or hint escapes him on the unlawfulness of the deed.

Further, we must remember that in those days the head of the house was virtually the house itself. If he sinned and suffered, the rest of the household suffered not only with him but for him. If Achan stole the wedge of gold and the Babylonish garment, his

wife and children were stoned to death along with him.   Women
and children were hardly recognized as individuals with separate
rights.   The father was supreme ; the rest of the family were only
appendages.

Another consideration that might dispose Abraham to take a
different view of the divine command than we should do was—the
prevalence of infant sacrifices among the heathen around.   The
investigations of learned writers seem to leave no doubt that this
was practised by the early Hamitic races—the people of Tyre and
Sidon for example.   Professor Sayce thinks that he can trace it
among the Accadian people who occupied Chaldæa before the days
of Abraham.   It belonged to the earlier periods of heathenism,
when the spirit of sacrifice was strongest.   It is a practice that has
left its traces in various forms in the classical legends of Greece, and
in the traditions of other nations.*   It sprang at first out of the
conviction that it is the most precious of all our possessions that
we ought to offer to God.   The sentiment was in some degree
kindred to that expressed by our Lord : " If any man come to
me, and hate not his father, and mother, and wife, and children,
and brethren, and sisters, yea, and his own life also, he cannot be
my disciple."   When the command to offer Isaac came to Abraham,
he would naturally think how readily heathen parents gave up
their children, however dear to them, when their gods were held
to require the sacrifice.   If the heathen were willing, why should
he rebel ?   God had promised to be his portion ; if he kept back
his son, would not that show that he valued him more than he
valued God ?   Loving obedience and trust toward God was his
primary duty ; the claims of affection, compassion for the child,
sympathy for his mother, were all subordinate.   Whatever the
wrench might be, however desolate it might leave his heart, however cheerless his life, the command of God *must* be obeyed.

But in making up his mind to obey, Abraham felt that he did
not give up all hope.   A conflict, indeed, seems to have been going
on in his mind between two sources of hope.   First, that God
might provide a substitute for Isaac : " My son, God will provide

* Creudner, "Symbolik und Mythologie der alten Völker."

himself a lamb for a burnt offering." But even failing that, might not God restore Isaac's life as soon as it was destroyed? He knew that Isaac's life was already the fruit of one miracle, and it was possible that now it might be the fruit of a second.* Isaac was the child of promise, and God must in some way fulfil his promise regarding him. Thus, in consenting to sacrifice Isaac, Abraham does not surrender one tittle of the hopes that hung by him. His is as far as possible from the sullen, angry mood that would have said,—" There, now, let him go, and let every hope go with him! God has only mocked me with promises never to be realized." His faith was more serene and beautiful now than ever. Isaac goes ; but God's word is immutable—in some way or other all shall be well.

It is not difficult in some degree to realize the touching scene, when Abraham rose up early in the morning, and with an ass and a couple of servants, and the wood prepared for a burnt offering, set out with his son in the direction of Moriah. Opinion is divided as to the locality of Moriah, the traditions of the Jews and the Samaritans placing it in different places. The Samaritans naturally claim their own Mount Gerizim as the mount of sacrifice ; but the Jewish tradition has long assigned it to the mountain on which the temple of Solomon was afterwards built, and which is expressly called by the name Moriah (2 Chron. iii. 1). Against this tradition there is really no argument of any weight. That Christ should have suffered in the same place with Isaac was not a consideration that would have influenced the Jews to believe that Moriah was at Jerusalem ; but to Christians there seems a remarkable fitness in the two transactions having occurred, if not on the same spot, at least in the same neighbourhood, the earlier having in many respects so remarkably shadowed forth the later.

From this Moriah Beersheba was distant three days' journey, but to reach Mount Gerizim on foot would have required at least

---

* St. Augustine puts the matter in a forcible antithesis :—" Credidit nasciturum, et non plangit moriturum. Ejus dextrâ eligitur ad sacrificium ut moreretur, cujus cor electum est ad fidem ut nasceretur. Non trepidavit Abraham credere quando promittebatur ; non trepidavit offerre quando exigebatur ; nec fuit religio credentis contraria devotioni obedientis."—*Aug. Homil.*

one day more. On the third day, Abraham, seeing the appointed place in the far distance, left his servants and the ass, and proceeded to the spot with Isaac, who carried the wood for the sacrifice. They seem to have walked on in silence, Abraham occupied with conflicting thoughts too deep to be uttered. Who can fail to be touched with the unsuspecting simplicity of Isaac's question: "My father, behold the fire and the wood; but where is the lamb for a burnt offering?" At last the spot is reached, the rude altar of turf or stones is built; but as yet no lamb appears. Abraham can no longer withhold the awful truth from his son. But instead of remonstrating or resisting, or rushing in consternation down the mountain-side, Isaac submits with silent resignation. He must surely have shared his father's faith, and had the same immovable confidence that God would not suffer him absolutely to perish, but in some unknown way of his own bring about the fulfilment of the promises.

Never was it more clearly seen that "man's extremity is God's opportunity." The knife in Abraham's hand was already uplifted to slay his son, when the angel of the Lord called to him out of heaven. The voice that had required the sacrifice now forbids it. God's purpose was simply to test Abraham's willingness, not to exact the penalty. Now that his willingness is shown beyond all doubt, the divine purpose is fully served. Looking round, Abraham finds a ram caught by the horns in the thicket. He seizes the ram and offers him for a burnt offering. He gives the place an ever-memorable name, Jehovah-jireh (The Lord will see, or The Lord will provide). And then the old promise is renewed to him with remarkable fulness and cordiality. Formerly God had made his promise in the form of a simple affirmation; but now, to make it the more emphatic, at least to our human idea, he gives it the sanction of an oath. "By myself have I sworn, saith the Lord; for because thou hast done this thing, and hast not withheld thy son, thine only son; that in blessing I will bless thee, and in multiplying I will multiply thy seed as the stars of the heaven, and as the sand which is upon the sea shore; and thy seed shall possess the gate of his enemies; and in thy seed shall all the nations of the earth be blessed; because thou hast obeyed my voice."

One cannot but be struck, in reading this narrative, with the calm, serene atmosphere in which it lies. It has sometimes been classed with the hideous scenes when children were burned in the fire to Moloch, amid the wild excitement of their parents, their shrieks being drowned by instruments of music. But the story of the offering of Isaac is marked by a gentle, heavenly tenderness, faith triumphing over sight; and when all is over, love alone is left in command of the field—a fresh gush comes from God to Abraham, drawing forth a corresponding return, while both Abraham and Isaac must have felt toward each other such a love as they never felt before.

It had been in Abraham's thoughts that God might provide a lamb for a sacrifice, or that he might restore the dead Isaac to life. In reality he did both. We read in Hebrews that Abraham "received him back from the dead in a parable" (Revised Version). Why is it said "in a parable"? A parable was a mode of revealing truth to some while others remained in ignorance. What was the truth thus impressed on Abraham? It was the doctrine of substitution—deliverance for the doomed through the death of another. "God intended more by this trial than to test faith. The test was meant to prepare Abraham for receiving a revelation. On Moriah, and ever after, Isaac was more than Isaac to Abraham. He offered him to God as Isaac, the son of the promise. He received him back from God's hand as the type of Him in whom the promise would be fulfilled. Abraham had gladly received the promise. He now saw the day of Christ, and rejoiced."*

Who can tell the marvellous relief with which Abraham must have descended the mountain, and the joy of heart with which, when he reached Beersheba, he would salute Sarah, and present Isaac to her, in the full confidence that all their life their home would never cease to be enlivened by the bright looks and loving companionship of their beloved son? And there was even a deeper joy than this—the joy of imparting to Sarah the knowledge of the

---

* "Expositor's Bible," Edwards on *Hebrews.*

typical character with which Isaac had been invested, and perhaps the glorious truth that salvation was to come to them through the sacrifice of that promised Seed in whom all the families of the earth were to be blessed.   Is it not possible that some foreshadow may have been vouchsafed of the truth so gloriously unfolded by one of their descendants in after ages : " He that spared not his own Son, but delivered him up for us all, how shall he not with him also freely give us all things ? "

As to the influence which the whole transaction must have had on Abraham and his house, it would not be possible to find language too strong to express it.   Even in ordinary life the expected death and unexpected restoration, as if from the very hand of God, of a beloved child, thrills a parent's heart to its very centre.   It brings the unseen world and the invisible God so near that they appear to be the only realities.   How much more profound must have been Abraham's experience !   Before this occurrence his life was holy, and his temper serene and heavenly ; but this must have lifted him up to the very gates of heaven, and made the remainder of his life an almost visible fellowship with his covenant-God.

# CHAPTER XIII.

## DEATH AND BURIAL OF SARAH.

### (GEN. xxiii.)

A FTER many years' sojourn at Beersheba, Abraham, for some reason unknown to us, returned to his former quarters at Hebron. Sarah had reached the age of a hundred and twenty-seven, when the bodily frame that had been so miraculously restored to youthful vigour nearly forty years before succumbed at last—Sarah died. There was an old story that it was Abraham's mission to Moriah that killed her—that she never got over the shock. This is extremely unlikely, partly because a mission that ended so joyously cannot be supposed to have left a deep and permanent shadow, but also because the story would bring up Isaac's age at the time of the sacrifice to thirty-six or thirty-seven—an age when he would have been practically beyond his father's authority, and when it would have been quite unsuitable to call him "the lad."

Sixty-two years have now elapsed since Abraham left Haran, and during that long period no bereavement has befallen him that has come so near to him as this. Long have he and Sarah been companions in life's journey, and pilgrims and strangers as they have been in a foreign country, many is the anxiety and trouble they have shared together. When "he came to mourn for Sarah, and to weep for her," it would be no formal or simulated lamentation. Like most other great men, he had a deep emotional nature, and notwithstanding all his self-control, it must have been with a bruised and bleeding heart that he buried Sarah.

Sarah had been very far from a perfect character. She was evidently impulsive, hasty, impatient, sometimes even cruel and unjust. She was no great help to Abraham in the great discipline of his life, no great help in the art of waiting, for she was more restless than he. She lived more in the present and less in the future, less by faith and more by sight. As Abraham obviously suffered much from her temper in the matter of Hagar and Ishmael, so probably he did in other things of which no record has been left. But he bore her temper with characteristic magnanimity, recognizing her many fine qualities, and loving her with that deep affection which may be ruffled for the moment, but cannot be seriously affected by little provocations. For at bottom Sarah was a true and faithful wife. Her obedience to her husband won for her the admiration of St. Peter, and made her a pattern to wives, who might well deem it an honour to be called her daughters (1 Peter iii. 6). As years passed on, her veneration for her husband must have grown apace, and probably her affection too. In all his wanderings she was his congenial companion. Having him always beside her, she seems never to have complained of the inconveniences of tent-life, nor pined for a settled home of her own. To the last she was a pilgrim and a stranger in the land. Her piety was beyond suspicion. And it is a testimony to the esteem which she has won from succeeding generations, that when Scripture names were common, no female name was more frequently given by devout parents to their daughters. The tombstones in Bunhill, and the records of New England Puritanism, combine to show from this circumstance that Sarah was held in Puritan days in extraordinary honour.

Where was she to be buried? Not certainly at Haran or at Ur, in the sepulchres of her fathers, for from that country she and Abraham had severed themselves for ever. Beersheba would have been a natural place. But besides that Beersheba was at that time in the hands of the Philistines, who were not among the seven nations, it was too near the border, too near what might be often the scene of noisy warfare, to be a suitable resting-place for Abraham's family. We like a quiet spot for our graves.

Hebron, or Kirjath-arba, was not subject to the disadvantages of Beersheba. Abraham knew it well, and doubtless had often inspected its Machpelah, and seen how well adapted the cave or grotto was for the purposes of a tomb. We must remember that in the East the dead were not buried in vertical pits dug in the ground, but in natural hollows, or in shelves scooped out from the sides of rocks or caves. The limestone rocks of Palestine, abounding as they do in cavernous openings, were remarkably adapted for such a purpose. The term Machpelah, derived from the word for "double," has often been rendered "the double cave," which may mean either that it had two entrances, or two chambers suitable for burying. If the term apply to the field rather than the cave, it is explained by the fact that the field is (or was) in the form of a double valley.

This cave, then, was the place which Abraham fixed on as the sepulchre of his family. But it would not do to place his dead there at the risk of the tomb being desecrated, and perhaps the body ejected, if it seemed good to its proprietor or to the people of the land. Nor would he allow the ashes of Sarah to be placed in a grave where the dust of idolaters might mingle with it. He had been content to live in tents, because that was God's command; and if one spot became disagreeable, he could easily move to another. But for a resting-place for Sarah, and by-and-by for himself and his family, he must have a more secure title. To acquire that title to Machpelah he now takes the usual formal steps. These steps are very characteristic, and they show that in this matter at least the usages of the country were highly civilized.

First, Abraham presents himself before the lords of the country, the Hittites or sons of Heth, acknowledges himself to be but a stranger and sojourner among them, and asks them to give him not merely the use but "the possession of a burying-place with you." The first answer, with all its politeness and its acknowledgment of Abraham as "a mighty prince among them," is not satisfactory; any of them, they say, will be glad to let him have the use of his sepulchre, the very choice of their sepulchres, for the burial of his dead. With ready tact Abraham accepts the expression of kindness, but reiterates his request, which is, that he may be not a tenant but a proprietor of a grave; and he begs them to use their influence with Ephron, the son of Zohar, to sell to him, at the market rate, the cave of Machpelah and the field in which it was situated.    Ephron being thus named comes forward, and with great apparent politeness and generosity begs Abraham to accept of the field and the cave as a gift.    Abraham understood Oriental manners too well to suppose that it was really intended to give him the property on these terms; or if that was the intention, he saw that it would place him under an obligation which would make him dependent and uncomfortable.  So he bows down before them, and addressing himself to Ephron, politely declines the gift, but again expresses his desire to purchase.   The price is then fixed on, —four hundred shekels of silver (about fifty pounds, it is supposed, of our money) ; and no coins of specific value being yet in current use, the money is publicly weighed out, in presence of the sons of Heth, and paid to Ephron.    And with all the minuteness and seeming redundancy of modern writs of conveyancing, it is stipu- lated that " the field of Ephron, which was in Machpelah, which was before Mamre, the field, and the cave which was therein, and all the trees which were in the field, that were in all the borders round about, were made sure unto Abraham for a possession in the presence of the children of Heth, before all that went in at the gate of his city."

It was indeed " made sure " unto Abraham for a burying-place. The changes of nearly forty centuries, the tempests, the wars, the dispossessions that have again and again changed so much in that land, have left Machpelah untouched; nor has it ever ceased to be known and honoured as the resting-place of Abraham and his family.   Jew, Christian, and Mohammedan have alike con- curred in doing honour to Machpelah.   Nor is it likely that till the world comes to an end it will ever be diverted from its orig- inal destination.

From time immemorial pilgrims have been attracted to it. Among the earliest records of such visits is that of a Spanish Jew, Benjamin of Tudela, who flourished in the twelfth century ; a great traveller, who had visited (besides Europe) Egypt, Palestine, Assyria, Persia, and penetrated to the frontiers of China. He published his travels in Hebrew, under the title of "Mazaloth" (Peregrinations). The book contains many manifest errors, and its statements are not much to be relied on. The account of Hebron and Machpelah is certainly not correct in all points. " I came to Hebron," says Benjamin, " seated in a plaine; for Hebron, the ancient metropolitan citie, stood upon an hill, but it is now desolate. But in the valley there is a field, wherein there is a duplicitie, that is as it were two little valleys, and there the city is placed; and there is a huge temple there called Saint Abraham, and that place was the synagogue of the Jews, at what time the country was possessed by the Ishmaelites [Israelites?]. But the Gentiles, who afterwards obtained and held the same, built six sepulchres in the temple by the names of Abraham, Sara, Isaac, Rebecca, Iacob, and Lia. And the inhabitants now tell the pil-grimes that they are the monuments of the patriarkes; and great summes of money are offered there. But surely, to any Jew coming thither, and offering the porters a reward, the cave is shewed, with the iron gate opened, which from antiquitie remayn-eth yet there. And a man goeth down with a lamplight into the first cave, where nothing is found, nor also in the second, untill he enter the third, in which there are the sixe monuments, the one right over against the other; and each of them are engraven with characters and distinguished by the names of every one of them after this manner — *Sepulchrum Abraham patris nostri, super quem pax sit;* and so the rest, after the same example. And a lampe perpetually burneth in the cave, day and night; the officers of the temple continually ministering oile for the maintenance thereof. Also, in the self-same cave, there are tuns full of the bones of the ancient Israelites, brought thither by the families of Israel, which even unto this day remain in the same place." *

It is a long leap from the twelfth century to the nineteenth. But Machpelah is not less an object of interest and attraction at this day than it was then. Perhaps it is even more so, because

* " Pictorial Commentary;" quoted from " Purchas, his Pilgrimes," 1625.

while it has been under Mohammedan rule, no stranger has been allowed to enter within the enclosure except under very peculiar circumstances. On the crest of the hill which forms the eastern side of the valley over whose slopes and bottom the town of Hebron is strewn, is seen a quadrangular building of about two hundred feet in length by about one hundred and fifteen feet in width, whose massive walls rise to the height of fifty or sixty feet. Some of the stones are in size and massiveness like the stones of the temple, one having been ascertained by Dr. Wilson of Bombay to be thirty-eight feet long, making it plain that so elaborate a structure could have been built only in very flourishing times. As these walls were standing in the time of Josephus, and are not ascribed by him to Herod, it is not unlikely that they are to be traced back to the days of David or Solomon. Part of the space inside this enclosure is occupied by a Turkish mosque, and the whole is guarded from unbelieving eyes with most sacred care.

In 1862, however, the Prince of Wales, accompanied by Dean Stanley and a few others, succeeded in persuading the authorities to show the tomb. The enterprise was not without danger, because no one could say what an incensed populace might not do to the perpetrator of so gross an outrage on the sanctity of a Mohammedan mosque. On a glance at the mosque it was evident that it was a transformed Christian church. "What are called the tombs of the patriarchs," says Dean Stanley, "do not profess to be the actual places of burial, but are merely monuments or cenotaphs in honour of the dead who lie beneath. Each is enclosed within a separate chapel or shrine, closed with gates or railings similar to those which surround or enclose the special chapels or royal tombs in Westminster Abbey......In the recess on the right is the shrine of Abraham, in the recess on the left that of Sarah, each guarded by silver gates. The shrine of Sarah we were requested not to enter, as being that of a woman.......The shrine of Abraham, after a momentary hesitation, was thrown open. The guardians groaned aloud......The chamber is cased in marble. The so-called tomb consists of a coffin-like structure, about six feet high, built up of plastered stone or marble, and hung with three

MACHPELAH.

Page 160.

carpets, green embroidered with gold......Within the area of the church were shown the tombs of Isaac and Rebekah......On re-questing to see the tomb of Isaac, we were requested not to enter; and on asking with some surprise why an objection which had been conceded for Abraham should be raised in the case of his far less eminent son, we were answered that the difference lay in the characters of the two patriarchs. 'Abraham was full of loving-kindness; he had withstood even the resolution of God against Sodom and Gomorrah; he was goodness itself, and would overlook any affront. But Isaac was proverbially jealous, and it was exceedingly dangerous to exasperate him. When Ibrahim Pasha (as conqueror of Palestine) had endeavoured to enter, he had been driven out by Isaac, and fallen back as if thunder-struck.'" *

It is to be noted that the six bodies said to be interred in the tomb are just those of which the Bible narrative makes mention. Rachel, as we are expressly told, was buried near Bethlehem, while no claim was ever made for Ishmael, whom the Moham-medans would have delighted to honour. There is a tradition, indeed, that the bones of Joseph, first interred at Shechem (Joshua xxiv. 32), were subsequently deposited in the tomb at Machpelah, but this tradition is of no great weight. Why Machpelah was dis-used as a place of burial we are not informed, but very probably it was thought that it ought to be held for ever sacred to the memory of the three great patriarchs and their wives—Abraham, Isaac, and Jacob—and that their pre-eminence in the history of the nation should be for ever marked by this, that no one else was permitted to share their tomb.

The permission so very graciously extended to the Prince of Wales and his attendants was, after all, more nominal than real. Previous travellers had been allowed to stand on the top of the stairs leading to the mosque, and through its open door gaze on the shrines of the patriarchs. All the difference was that the prince and his suite were allowed to enter these shrines. But the real tombs are elsewhere, very probably beneath the shrines. Doubt-

* "Lectures on Jewish Church," vol I., Appendix ii.

less it was on some excavated shelf on the side of the rock that Abraham laid the remains of Sarah. In a similar place Ishmael and Isaac afterwards placed his own. If aught yet remains of them, it is in some such cavity that it lies. There is yet, therefore, the bare possibility of a discovery of profoundest interest ; but after nearly four thousand years, the strong probability is that all that ever remained of them has completely mouldered away.

However great the sadness of Abraham as he buried out of his sight the body of Sarah, and closed a long and happy history of wedded life, he had more than one new thought to give him light and hope. Sarah's career was not closed—death did not end all. She but exchanged her pilgrimage for her home. And Abraham had now an actual stake in the land of promise. By that field and tomb, in name of his descendants, he took possession of the country. He could think with new interest of the development of his race which would take place in Canaan when that long period of bondage in another land which God had announced should have come to an end. He could realize more vividly the blessing that would flow to the world through his seed, and especially through Him whose day, though it was yet far off, his faith enabled him to see. Possibly, too, he could look forward to a day when those that slept in the dust of the earth should awake, some to everlasting life, and some to shame and everlasting contempt.

# CHAPTER XIV.

## THE MARRIAGE OF ISAAC.

### (Gen. xxiv.)

SARAH had been dead three years, and Isaac was now forty. Through him the promised seed was to come, and it was therefore time for him to enter upon married life. It was impressed on Abraham that this was too serious a matter to be left to the chance influence of ordinary events. It was above all things necessary that the family of Isaac should remain loyal to that supreme and only God from whom the promise had come, and should maintain his worship, pure and undefiled, amid the growing darkness and idolatry of the nations. The choice for Isaac was really very limited. Among the surrounding people the drift was towards evil—they were all moving in the direction which had involved Sodom in destruction. No daughter of these doomed nations could be a suitable wife for Isaac. Lot's family, alas! was out of the question. Whoever Melchizedek was, there was no one among his people suitable—possibly because they had migrated to some other place. The only quarter in which he could have any hope of finding a suitable wife for Isaac was among his own relations in Haran. It was to that quarter, therefore, that he directed his view. It is quite in accordance with Eastern manners that Abraham, not Isaac, took the initiative in the negotiations.

Communication with the old country had been rare. The caravans from Haran passing southwards to Egypt would probably not often take the road by Beersheba. It seems to have been a long time before Abraham had any news from Haran after he left it. (See

Gen. xxii. 20–24.) When he did hear, the accounts were interesting and so far pleasing. During the long years when Sarah had been childless, a whole troop of children had been pouring into the home of their brother and sister, Nahor and Milcah. Eight sons had been born, and even the third generation had appeared at Haran before Abraham and Sarah had seen the second. Bethuel, apparently the youngest of the sons, had a daughter, Rebekah. No doubt Nahor and his household had often been the subject of Abraham's prayers. Though they were not living in Sodom, they had great need of divine grace to preserve them from the idolatries and immoralities around them; this Abraham felt, and next to Lot's, there was probably no family on earth for which he had prayed more. To that house, accordingly, he directed his eyes, hoping that some damsel, as yet unspotted by the world, would be found among its daughters.

The journey was too far and too severe for himself to undertake it; he must send a younger man. For a long time prosperity had been his lot; the Lord had blessed him in all things; his establishment was large enough to have a chief servant who might be called to the most delicate negotiations. It was this chief steward of his house that was intrusted with the mission; possibly it was that Eliezer who had been the steward and heir-presumptive at the time of the first promise respecting a son (Gen. xv. 2). If so, it says much for Eliezer that he continued as stanch and loyal a friend of Abraham and his family after the birth of Isaac as he had been before, when the succession was likely to fall to himself. What a pure and beautiful virtue disinterestedness is!

But Abraham could not send him off without binding him by an oath—an oath so administered as to carry additional solemnity to one who had received the sign of circumcision, and who knew something of the momentous covenant relation in which his master stood to God. The oath bound him to take no wife for Isaac from among the daughters of the Canaanites. There might be not a few of them that would have liked well to marry Isaac—young women of Canaan, attractive alike for their charming manners and their personal beauty. But there was that fatal objection—an objection often so little regarded now—difference of religion : there was not one of these Canaanite girls but would have had a most pernicious influence on Isaac, drawing him away from his God, to whom every consideration of gratitude and piety and patriotism bound him by the most sacred ties. Any marriage, however otherwise desirable, that would weaken Isaac's attachment to the service of the holy God, Abraham deemed (as all should deem it) sinful in itself, and most pernicious in its consequences.

It is the very scene often realized at this day at the setting out of a travelling party that we see at the departure of Abraham's servant. The animals employed are camels, partly for their endurance, but partly also for their swiftness. Ten camels, we might suppose, would more than suffice to transport a messenger with his necessary baggage and supplies ; but then, as now, the road was dangerous, and it was necessary, especially for the return journey, to have a considerable party, and likewise to convey an imposing impression of the wealth and style of Abraham. It was a long road from Hebron to Haran. The most direct route was along the west bank of Jordan and the lakes, then through the valley of Cœle-Syria, then out through the land of Hamath to the Euphrates, and thence to Haran.* At length the servant reaches his destination. Cities and villages in those days were usually built in the neighbourhood of copious wells, but at a little distance from them, because round the well there was commonly not a little noise and dust and bustle. In large towns, water was drawn and carried by men, but in smaller places by the women. And then, as now, evening was the time when the women went out for water. Abraham's servant and his animals, with the dust and heat of their long journey upon them, were doubtless eagerly desiring to enjoy the contents of the well. But the servant has more than one reason for delay : it would have been counted rude, if not dishonest, to help himself before getting leave from the people of the place ; and, besides, the crisis of his mission was at hand, and he must seek direction from above as to what he was to do.

* " Land and Book."

The servant is like his master—he believes in God, and he believes in prayer. His way of dealing with God is perhaps more devout than enlightened. In most cases, it would be simply presumption for one to lay out a definite plan, as this man did, and bind God to the course which should be in accordance with that plan. But there was such perfect simplicity and childlike trust in the man's way of doing this, that we acquit him of all presumption ; nor need we wonder that God graciously accepted his plan. Besides, there was more reasonableness in the token by which he sought to find out the proper damsel than we should at first suppose. It was not a quite accidental or arbitrary token. The damsel proposed to be regarded as Isaac's divinely-appointed wife was the one that should make a certain response when he asked leave merely to sip a little water from her water-pot for his own use. Not only would she allow him to do this, but she would volunteer to draw for his camels. Now this was no trifling service. Wells were usually in the valley or wady, and were approached by steps or a sloping path. To go down to the well, draw water for each of the ten camels, place the vessel on her shoulder, carry it up the stair, and empty it into the trough, involved no little labour. It might very fairly be surmised that the girl who should volunteer to do this was at once of a very obliging disposition and active habits—two very important requisites in a wife and the mistress of a house.

There were other qualities still more important, but the situation did not permit the servant to test these. He had not finished his prayer when Rebekah appeared, with her pitcher on her shoulder. She carried in her face a letter of recommendation which the old servant could not but appreciate, for she was very fair to look upon. Possibly the Abrahamic features might be discerned in her. Was it not another point in her favour that she and Abraham's servant had no difficulty in understanding one another—they spoke a Semitic tongue ? And was it not a further recommendation that there was such civility in her words and such friendliness in her acts ? Could courtesy or kindness have gone further than hers when she carried pitcherful after pitcherful of water to fill the trough for these thirsty beasts, that drank as if they would never stop?

The man is carried captive with delight, and he must have rushed intuitively to a conclusion; for though he has yet an all-important question to put, he forgets all caution, and presents Rebekah with a golden ring,* a pair of bracelets, and ten shekels of gold. How foolish he will look if he gets no satisfactory answer to his next question! " Tell me, I pray thee, whose daughter art thou? is there room in thy father's house for us to lodge in?" He seems hardly to have ventured to go further than ask for accommodation. "And she said unto him, I am the daughter of Bethuel the son of Milcah, which she bare unto Nahor. She said moreover unto him, We have both straw and provender enough, and room to lodge in." The straw was not for litter, never being so used in the East, but when chopped and mixed with other "provender"— beans, barley, etc.—formed the usual food for cattle in the house.

When the servant heard that she was of Abraham's kindred, he was simply overpowered. All the conditions and requisites of a wife for Isaac were combined in her person. The Lord had very wonderfully and promptly answered his prayer. And with that devout and godly feeling which ruled his heart, he bowed his head in adoration and praise, and thanked God for his wonderful mercy. " Blessed be the Lord God of my master Abraham, who hath not left destitute my master of his mercy and his truth: I being in the way, the Lord led me to the house of my master's brethren."

His words are overheard by Rebekah, who at once divines whence the man has come; and with her ring, her bracelets, and her golden shekels, hurries home to give the news to her mother. Her brother Laban is at hand, and is much impressed by the earring and the bracelets. Whether pure hospitality, apart from these tokens of wealth, would have made Laban equally pressing, we cannot tell; but he gives to Abraham's servant a cordial

---

* There has been much perplexity among translators and commentators about this ring. Our translators of the Authorized Version have made it an ear-ring; but why should there have been but one? And how should it be put on her face? (ver. 47.) The Revised Version makes it at first simply a ring, but the part of the body to which it attaches it is not the ear but the nose. The nose-ring, that seems to us so strange, was a familiar ornament to Rebekah.

welcome—" Come in, thou blessed of the Lord." This may have
been a suitable acknowledgment of the devout character of the
man, or it may have been the florid language of Eastern courtesy,
or a testimony to that material blessing of which it was evident that
the servant had very much at his command. Strange to say, the
camels were also brought into the house. But this is nothing
unusual in the East. " I have often," says Dr. Thomson ("Land
and Book "), " slept in the same room with these peaceful animals,
in company with their owner and all his family."

The camels being disposed of, and the strangers having had
their foot-bath, it is time that the message of the servant be heard.
Indeed he would not eat until he had told his errand. The tale
is told in the words with which we are already familiar. The
emphatic recognition of the one God, the covenant God of his
master Abraham, is significant. If other gods were acknowledged
in Rebekah's family, it is plain enough that Abraham and his
house will have nothing to do with them. The servant does not
advert to the reason why Abraham had left Haran sixty-five years
before. Neither does he say anything of God's covenant with
him, and the blessings he had promised to his seed. He says
nothing of Abraham's mode of life as a pilgrim and a sojourner
in the country, but states simply that " the Lord had blessed his
master greatly, and that he had given him flocks and herds, and
silver and gold, and men-servants and maid-servants, and camels
and asses." Was there not some indication in this that he saw a
worldly spirit prevalent in the family, and found little or nothing
to appeal to in the form of spiritual earnestness?

The question simply is, Shall Rebekah be sent to Isaac for a
wife? And it is remarkable that the question is settled by the
male heads of the family—Bethuel, the girl's father, and Laban,
her eldest brother—without any consultation with the damsel herself. It is only when the subordinate question of the proper time
is under consideration that appeal is made to the party principally
concerned. As to the destination of Rebekah, it seemed to her
father and brother to be already settled by the fact, on which they
laid stress, " The thing proceedeth from the Lord." Was this a

token that they regarded Abraham's God as the supreme and only Potentate, the disposer of all events, who doeth according to his will in the armies of heaven and among the inhabitants of earth; and further, that his will in the matter having been so clearly declared, all opposition on their part was out of the question? So the narrative would seem to imply, and so we should at once understand it, but for the difficulty in supposing that their views were so enlightened. One would fain hope that the noble stand for monotheism made by Abraham so long ago had impressed Nahor as well as Terah, and that his brother, amid some unworthy concessions to the prevailing idolatry, had held to that faith, at least in such sense as to respond to it when it was boldly presented to him by Abraham's servant. One would hope, too, that they had such confidence in God as to feel assured that what he planned must be right and good. Anyhow they gave over Rebekah to Abraham's servant; and on this a new outflow of generosity took place. Brides were not to be had in those times and countries without a dowry from the bridegroom, nor Rebekah among the rest. For her dowry she got jewels of silver and gold, and precious raiment; and there were copious gifts also for her brother and her mother.

Abraham's servant was in no humour for delay. One night's feasting, and he must be off in the morning. Our sympathies go with the relations when they begged for at least a ten days' delay. But even to that reasonable proposal he would not listen, seeing the Lord had prospered his way. Perplexed by his peremptoriness, they at last resolve to consult the bride. The question which they leave with her to decide is, "Wilt thou go with this man?" The answer does not occupy her a moment—"I will go." It is not mere light-heartedness that makes her so willing—at least there was ample room for other considerations. Why should not she, too, be impressed by the visible finger of God in the transaction? And though the servant had not enlarged on the divine promise concerning Isaac, must not some impressions of that sort have reached the home of his relations, and perhaps some rumour of the strange transaction at Mount Moriah, and the wonderful divine assurances with which it was followed up? Then there was the romance of the thing, the pleasant excitement connected with the new mode of life, so well fitted to affect the imagination of a girl at the time of life when day-dreams are so natural. And who shall say that the symbols of Abraham's wealth, the main part of which was to be inherited by Isaac, made no impression? Rebekah did not turn out to be a woman of very noble character; she did not rise to the level to which we should expect a patriarch's wife to attain. Apart altogether from religion, there was a mixture in her character; probably we shall not be far from the truth if we think of her as a lively, warm-hearted, and attractive maiden, very simple and pleasant, and well fitted to brighten a home, but not proof against the temptations of the world, and not so deeply under the influence of the fear of God as to take a decided stand against every form of evil.

Her people sent her away with a blessing: " Be thou the mother of thousands of millions, and let thy seed possess the gate of those which hate them." It was a kind of echo of the Abrahamic blessing, but with the spiritual part left out. The elements of the blessing invoked were only a numerous seed and success in war. This was all the level of benediction to which Abraham's relations could attain even ideally, looking at the matter as they did apart from the revelation that had been made to Abraham himself. The ideal of happiness in life as worked out by the human mind is very different from the divine. The human horizon is very limited; the divine stretches out and expands till it is lost in infinity.

And so next morning Rebekah and her nurse set out on their long journey toward the south-west on the dromedaries that had been sent to carry them. They have to traverse the whole land of Canaan to its most southern verge. It is after many days that, near the well Lahai-roi, they come in sight of Isaac, walking out in the cool of the evening to meditate. He is alone, absorbed apparently in his thoughts, moving along with downcast eyes. Some noise perhaps arrests his attention, and as he lifts up his eyes he sees the cavalcade—the camels are coming. No vestige of message could have reached him before this from his father's servant, nor could he have had the faintest idea how he had sped. Immediately on learning who he was, Rebekah alighted from her camel. It would have been quite contrary to good manners, as understood in those parts, for Rebekah to remain on the animal while presented to Isaac. "It is a customary mark of respect to great personages that one should alight from the animal on which he has been riding and lead it until the superior has gone by ; and as no conventional superiority is conceded in the East to women, as in Europe, this will show that it would have been highly improper for her to have ridden directly up to Isaac when he was on foot." * So likewise Naaman the Syrian alighted from his chariot to meet the messenger of Elisha, and Abigail dismounted from her ass to prostrate herself before David. In Roman history there is a story, when Fabius was consul, of his father being sent on an embassage to him at Suessula. As his father approached, Fabius directed the lictor to require him to dismount. Springing from the saddle, the father exclaimed, " I was just trying to find out, my son, whether you were sufficiently impressed with your dignity as consul." †

On seeing Isaac, Rebekah made a change on her dress : "she took a veil, and covered herself"—covered not her face only, but her whole person. This would have been a somewhat tantalizing thing in ordinary circumstances, as Isaac, doubtless, was full of curiosity to see her face. We are to remember that this was the costume in which brides were, and in some Eastern countries still are, conducted to their husbands. Rebekah indicated in this way that she was Isaac's bride. She showed her acceptance of the offer which had been made to her,—her readiness now, as when she set out from her home, to be his wife. So far, therefore, from objecting to the veil, Isaac must have regarded it as the token that his father's plan had succeeded, and that a suitable wife had been found for him. All the more would he be pleased when the servant narrated to him the whole transaction. And notwithstanding the unnatural mode of arranging the marriage, as it

* " Pictorial Commentary "                    † Livy, xxiv. 44.

seems to us, and the great risk of disappointment, in this case the marriage was a success. "Isaac brought her into his mother Sarah's tent, and took Rebekah, and she became his wife ; and he loved her : and Isaac was comforted after his mother's death."

"All's well that ends well ;" and Isaac's courtship by proxy had a better ending than we should have expected. His heart flowed out to his bride ; it was a true marriage—a union of hearts as well as hands. The divine bond that most of all sanctifies marriage sanctified Isaac's. For the three years since his mother's death his heart had always had a void ; he had sighed for the love that was gone, and found no earthly thing to supply its place. Now the void is filled ; another sun has come into his firmament ; the winter is past, the rain is over and gone, the time of the singing of birds has come. Life has a new joy, and the buds of hope seem ready to expand into a glorious future. Midsummer night's dream has seldom had a brighter sky.

# CHAPTER XV.

## ABRAHAM'S DEATH.

### (GEN. xxv.)

IT is again the unexpected that happens. Abraham himself is the bridegroom now. From the note of time in the Authorized Version, "then again," it is natural to suppose that his marriage to Keturah took place after the marriage of Isaac. But in the Revised Version the rendering has no note of time : "And Abraham took another wife, and her name was Keturah." This leaves us free to determine the time at which this wife was taken. We certainly escape some physical difficulties by supposing that it was in Sarah's lifetime. For even at the age of a hundred Abraham deemed himself too old to have offspring, and unless his bodily powers were permanently renewed, he must have been more feeble at a hundred and forty. Further, the thirty-five remaining years of his life do not seem to allow sufficient time for Keturah's sons growing up to maturity and being settled in the east by their father.

These considerations have led some critics of note to suppose that Abraham's marriage occurred at a considerably earlier date. It is evident that Keturah did not stand to him in the same relation as Sarah. She is reckoned among "the concubines which Abraham had." The same term is applied to her in a much later book—1 Chron. i. 32. And the fact that her sons did not share their father's inheritance with Isaac is a further proof that they stood legally in an inferior position to him.

Very probably Keturah, like Hagar, was a slave, for there is no hint of her parentage or race. If she became Abraham's secondary wife in Sarah's lifetime, there was nothing more to be blamed in his forming this connection than in the case of Hagar. What surprises us on that supposition is that Abraham should have repeated an experiment which had proved so disastrous before. We wonder, too, how Sarah, who would not tolerate Ishmael, could have endured the whole multitude of Keturah's sons. No doubt we can see how Ishmael, as the child of Sarah's maid, should have been much more a member of the household than any other. But the whole case is surrounded with difficulties, let us take the question of time as we may. It is the extreme brevity of the narrative that causes the difficulty ; and though some may prefer the common view and some the other, it does not appear that absolute certainty is attainable.

Six sons by Keturah are ascribed to Abraham, equal to half the number of the sons of Jacob and tribes of Israel. These were sent away "eastward, unto the east country," and are hence called "children of the east" (Judg. vi. 3). Their homes were in those desert regions stretching eastward from the land of the Philistines, away into Sinai on the south, and into Arabia on the east. They reappear from time to time in Bible history as Ishmaelites or Midianites, although these terms are sometimes used in a wider sense. The name of Sheba is perpetuated as the realm of the queen who came from the ends of the earth to hear the wisdom of Solomon. Dedan is named in Ezek. xxvii. as famous for its merchandise, and in the same connection is associated with Sheba (Ezek. xxxviii. 13). Shuah was the country of Bildad, one of the three friends of Job (Job ii. 11). It is hardly to be supposed that these men could have gone forth from Abraham's household without carrying some of his beliefs with them. They had not been trained in idolatry. They had been taught to revere the one true God, maker of heaven and of earth. Their locality was not an influential one ; they had little opportunity of influencing other peoples. But among themselves they seem to have clung to some parts of the truth with much more firmness than the neighbouring tribes. They did not practise the abominations of the seven nations. And if such men as Job and his friends, Jethro the priest of Midian, and others, were among them, this shows that even beyond the precincts of the promised seed, Abraham was the means, to a quite appreciable degree, of shedding the light of truth, and arresting both the darkness and the wickedness of the world.

The last thirty-five years of Abraham's life seem to have been spent quietly with Isaac and Rebekah, with but one more trial to his faith. For twenty years no offspring of their marriage appeared. To one who had to wait longer for his own son, and at a much more advanced period of life, this trial would not have the sharpness of his own. At last his faith was rewarded by the birth of Esau and Jacob. The line of the succession was once more assured. And once more Abraham's soul would magnify the Lord.

Death came at last. But to one who had ever enjoyed such intimacy with God it could not be death. As his fellowship had been growing closer, his joy brighter, and his faith more vivid; as the sense of the darkness and incompleteness of his life had been begetting higher hopes of a coming solution, was it possible that all should end when the mere bodily frame wore out? Just as his orbit was about to come into contact with God's, was it conceivable that his highest aspirations were to be quenched for ever? We have not one trace of his dying experience, but we may infer it from his life. Surely he who saw Christ's day afar off, and seeing it was glad, had at least as clear a vision as Job: "I know that my Redeemer liveth, and that he shall stand up at the last upon the earth; and after my skin hath been thus destroyed, yet from my flesh shall I see God: whom I shall see for myself, and mine eyes shall behold, and not another. My reins are consumed within me" (Job xix. 25–27, Revised Version).

"His sons Isaac and Ishmael buried him in the cave of Machpelah." Earth to earth, ashes to ashes, dust to dust—the common lot. But what a noble life was represented by these ashes! What faith, hope, and charity! What trust in God, and patient waiting for him, and humble reliance on his word; what generosity of heart and disinterested concern for the welfare of others ; what steadfastness and consistency and serenity amid all life's trials and troubles ! It is pleasant to hear of Ishmael and Isaac joining in this solemn act of burial. It is especially pleasing to find Ishmael returning to pay honour to his father. He might have had his reasons for standing aloof and leaving this duty to Isaac, whom Abraham had distinguished so much above himself. But his magnanimity and filial piety overcame all such reasons. Sometimes among those whose place is outside the covenant we find traces of gratitude and natural goodness that we should hardly have looked for. And we may believe that the feeling that brought Ishmael to honour his father led him to deal kindly by his brother. Little congenial though they were, and little of agreeable intercourse though they could have, they could meet very cordially to bury their father. The grave is a great healer as well as a grievous destroyer. When family feuds have unhappily arisen, there is no such place for burying them as a parent's open grave.

Among the great men of the world, few have obtained such universal honour as Abraham. "Wherever his foot trod or his fame spread, the homage of numberless generations has elevated the Hebrew exile of Ur almost into a divinity." We need not say what boundless honour has ever been paid to him by his descendants in the line of Isaac and Jacob. To be the children of Abraham was the distinction which, in the time of our Lord, was held by his countrymen sufficient to repel all reflections on their spiritual condition (John viii. 39). Nay, the fact of their being Abraham's seed was held to give them a title to God's favour, so that it required all the Baptist's eloquence to warn them against this error (Matt. iii. 9). It was Abraham's bosom that was the haven of the afflicted when they came to their rest in the unseen world (Luke xvi. 22). One of the favourite and almost universal names of the Supreme Being was, "the God of Abraham, and Isaac, and Jacob." When the Jews would rebuke what seemed the unreasonable pretensions of Jesus to be beyond the power of death, they asked, "Art thou greater than our father Abraham, which is dead?" (John viii. 53.) The first thing recorded of Jesus by the first evangelist is that he was the son of David, the son of Abraham. When Paul was disposed to glory in his lineage, it was that he also was an Israelite, of the seed of Abraham (Rom. xi. 1) ; and from points of view so different as those of the apostles Paul and James, the faith of Abraham came in for special commendation (Rom. iv. ; James ii. 21–23), as it did likewise from the writer of the Epistle to the Hebrews (ch. xi. 17–19).

And a similar pre-eminence and honour, though not precisely on the same grounds, has been accorded to him by his other descendants. "To devout Mussulmans, all over the lands of Islam, the name of Abraham ranks in the long calendar of accepted prophets as second only to the name of Mohammed himself" (*Dykes*). The Koran is full of his praise, and can find nothing so powerful for pressing its claims as the pretence that Abraham prayed God to send his descendants an apostle who would teach them the book of the Koran ; on which it triumphantly asks, "Who will be averse to the religion of Abraham but he whose mind is infatuated?"

Among all Christian nations he stands pre-eminent in the ranks of faithful men. The raillery of the sceptic has found in him no ground for his scoff; for the unworthy subterfuge by which, in a day of temptation, he sought to protect himself from the schemes of powerful kings was but the proof that he was a man of like passions with ourselves, and that his great excellence was reached in connection with a nature like our own.

What, then, has given to Abraham this unrivalled pre-eminence? Not renown in arms, though he did one brilliant military exploit ; not the gifts of the musician, the poet, or the sage ; not headship of a mighty empire, for one little field enclosing a cave or grave was all that he owned of the surface of the earth ; not the fame of a great religious reformer, for though he did renounce the errors of his fathers, his church in his lifetime consisted only of his own household, and the rest of the world was but little influenced by his views. The main foundation of Abraham's greatness lay in his relation to God. He believed in God. He realized

all that is comprehended in this profound expression. He so believed God as to be moved to the very depths of his being by all
that God said or did. He believed God's word to be true, though
every probability in heaven and earth might seem to be against
it. He believed God's favour to be a real treasure, the pearl of
great price, worth all being lost for it, if it could be retained.
The fears of his own heart, the impressions of his own senses, the
opinion of the world, the loss, the pain, the agony there might be
in doing God's will, were nothing ; God's will was right and good,
and in the end this would appear.

And this faith brought him a happy experience of communion
with God. He walked with him, consulted him, got light and
comfort from him, joy and peace. Hence his glorious title, by
which to this day he is known through the East, "the friend
of God ;" hence also that other name, hardly less honourable,
"father of the faithful." So conspicuous was his faith, so greatly
did it outshine all that had gone before, that he might be called the
father of all them that believe. His literal offspring was even out-
stripped by his spiritual ; for though literally he might be the
father of "thousands of millions," yet spiritually he was the father
of that countless multitude who are to be gathered "from the
east, and from the west, and from the north, and from the south,
and to sit down with him in the kingdom of God."

Along with this faith in God there was evidently in Abraham
a great power of impressing and influencing others. The very
depth of his convictions almost implied this. But the calmness,
the steadiness, the consistency of his character, his constant kindness and sympathy, and the manifest reality of his fellowship with
God, all contributed to the same result. There are families where
an intuitive and irresistible respect for their father keeps the children, at least for a long time, from questioning any of his opinions
or even dreaming of disobedience to his wishes. His wisdom and
his goodness seem so high above their own that it would be un-
pardonable folly and wickedness to go contrary to him in anything. A large experience may one day modify this conviction,
but it will also probably show that in the main it was right.

Thus it was among Abraham's children while he lived, and even after he died. This profound regard for their great father reached down even to the days of the Pharisees; had it only been accompanied by an enlightened apprehension of what their father really was, it would have been of inestimable value.

But by this time they had substituted an idolatrous worship of his name and his memory for a real succession to his faith. They garnished his sepulchre, but repudiated his hope. They venerated him looking forward wistfully through the ages to Messiah's day, while they rejected and insulted the very Messiah to whose day he had so eagerly looked forward. Substituting the letter for the spirit, they reversed all that he held in honour, and exalted their little rites and their little tithes over the everlasting realities— truth, righteousness, and the love of God. Jesus never found occasion for a sharper rebuke than in connection with this very matter—" If ye were Abraham's children, ye would do the works of Abraham. But now ye seek to kill me, a man that hath told you the truth, which I have heard of God : this did not Abraham " (John viii. 39, 40).

# CHAPTER XVI.

## EARLY LIFE OF ISAAC.

### (Gen. xxv. 11-24, xxvi.)

IF the name Isaac (laughter) was meant to shadow forth a feature of his life, it was more applicable to the effect he produced on others than to any especial experience of his own. Isaac does not give us the impression of a laughing temperament or of a particularly sunny nature. Rather we should suppose his demeanour to have been grave and quiet, befitting the deep reverence for God that distinguished him. But Isaac was well fitted to impart to others the quiet joy that springs from a kindly, inoffensive heart, eager to give pleasure, shrinking from all that causes pain. His gentle, loving ways must have made his parents very happy. The tenderness of his affection for Rebekah would be a perpetual joy in her life. His servants must have been happy under one who was so meek and good, whose commands had nothing irritating, whose very rebukes carried no sting. A soothing, comforting influence dropped from him wherever he went; men felt themselves better of his presence.

It has been said of Isaac that his character was dwarfed and impeded in its development by his having had so great a father. "In him we see the result of growing up under too strong and dominating an external influence. The free and healthy play of his own capacities and will was curbed......Life was made too easy for him." * Perhaps it is in this way that we are to account for the fact that men of great creative energy are usually fol-

* Dods on *Genesis.*

lowed by somewhat feeble sons as successors. What a different
set of men, how vastly inferior, the "apostolic fathers" were to
the apostles! Where, in the age that followed the Reformation,
were there men to class with Calvin and Luther, Zwingle and
Melancthon, Farel and Viret, Knox and Melville? What a contrast there was between Oliver Cromwell and Richard! Nature
seems sometimes to pour her gifts extravagantly upon the father,
and to deal somewhat grudgingly with the son. For it was not
wholly his having a father who shaped everything for him in life
that made Isaac comparatively little; his native gifts appear likewise to have been of very moderate calibre.

It was the passive more than the active virtues that he was
called to exhibit. He had none of that spirit of initiative, none
of that power to assume an independent position and undertake
great enterprises, which characterized his father. One of his
earliest experiences of life was the mockery and persecution of
Ishmael, but we are not expressly told how he bore it. Then
came that most memorable event when his father was commanded
to offer him up as a sacrifice. How meekly and submissively
he bore that unexampled trial every reader instinctively feels.
Next he was tried by the long barrenness of Rebekah; he made
no complaint, but carried the trial to the Lord. Afterwards
came the annoyances and thefts of the Philistines connected
with his wells. Here, too, the man of peace shone out. And
finally, he had the trial of the deceit of Jacob and Rebekah—a
double trial that must have been specially afflicting to one suffering under sickness, defective eyesight, and expectation of death.
These passive virtues are very beautiful; but in the case of a man
we long for attributes, too, of more positive and active quality.
In no one were the passive virtues more beautifully exemplified
than in our Lord; but in his case the manly attributes, too—
activity, courage, enterprise, assault on all that was vile and
pernicious—were equally memorable. This makes the character
far more complete. And the balance of qualities attracts our special
admiration, for in our blessed Lord the one set of qualities did
in no way jostle or interfere with the other. It is the one-sided-

ness of Isaac's character that gives it a somewhat limp and meagre look. We desiderate something of the dash and daring of David and Jonathan, of Elijah and Nehemiah, of Peter and Paul. Quietism and Quakerism are useful and admirable, but they do not realize the complete ideal of humanity; there is a harder and higher element in the complete human soul.

Let us glance briefly at the chief incidents we find in the life of Isaac after his marriage to Rebekah.

Happy though his wedded life appears to have been, and prosperous though he was outwardly under the divine blessing, there was one crook in his lot—his wife was childless. He had doubtless pondered the case of his own parents in similar circumstances, and had learned the lesson taught to Abraham that the heir of the promises was to be the special gift of God. It was the example of his father rather than his mother that he now followed. He gives utterance to no language of impatience, and does not propose any step, as Sarah had done, to hasten artificially the arrangements of Providence. He carries the case to the Lord; and while reminding him, doubtless, of the promise to his father and to himself, he is much moved by regard for the feelings of Rebekah. We might almost suppose that her disappointment was the main cause of his prayer—"he entreated the Lord for his wife." It does not appear that Rebekah was as familiar as Isaac, or as Hannah was afterwards, with this method of obtaining the fulfilment of her desires.

But when she found that she was to bear twins, she deemed the circumstance prophetic, and went to inquire of the Lord. As there was no fixed place of worship then, as afterwards, where God's presence was manifested, the question arises, Whither did she go, and how did she inquire? Was there any priest of the most high God, like Melchizedek, who could deal with God on her behalf? Of this we have not a trace. Either she went to God directly in prayer, having learned from her husband's experience the efficacy of that mode of communication; or she may have submitted her case to Isaac, and got him to inquire; or, perhaps more probably, she may have laid it before Abraham, who was yet alive, knowing how often God had held direct communion with him. The answer showed that there was a real prophetic significance in the circumstance. The children about to be born were to be the ancestors of two nations of opposite characters, one of which would be stronger than the other, but the descendants of the elder would be in subjection to those of the younger.

The appearance of the children when born agreed to some extent with the prophecy. The elder was covered all over with an unusual quantity of red hair—"a sign of excessive vigour and wildness," according to one commentator; "a foreboding of the animal violence of his nature," according to another; "the indication of a passionate and precocious nature," according to a third. The name Esau ("hairy") was accordingly given him. The other, with no such hairy skin, was more remarkable for his attitude than his appearance. His hand seemed to grasp his brother's heel; his name was called Jacob, "heel-catcher," "supplanter." There was no want of dash and enthusiasm in the one; the other was more quiet and domestic. Esau was a great hunter, a man of the field; Jacob was a plain man, dwelling in tents. The attachments of the parents seem to have been determined by the existence of qualities opposite to their own. Isaac, with all his quietness, preferred the enterprising huntsman; Rebekah, who had shown no little spirit and courage in leaving her home, preferred the quiet Jacob. Out of these unwise preferences no small trouble was one day to come.

The next incident in Isaac's life is connected with a famine, similar to that which at an earlier period had driven Abraham to Egypt. Isaac had thought of the same step, but a vision from God deterred him. He was instructed to remain among the Philistines in Gerar; and for his encouragement, God made the same threefold promise to him that he had made to Abraham— that he would give to him and his seed all the countries about him; that his posterity should be numberless as the stars; and that in his seed all the nations of the earth should be blessed. When we read of this very gracious communication, we are surprised to find that in his intercourse with king Abimelech he resorted to the self-same stratagem which Abraham had practised twice before, and on account of which he had been humbled before God and man. It is natural enough for rationalist critics, with the liberties they take so freely with the narrative, to affirm that it is the same incident, but ascribed to a different person by the writer from whom this part of Genesis has come. But we cannot suppose that the writer of Genesis fell into any such mistake. We must remember that well-nigh a century had elapsed since Abraham's visit to Egypt, and a somewhat shorter but still very long period since his visit to Abimelech. To us the two events appear very close to each other, reading, as we do, from the brief Scripture narrative, where we find them in almost contiguous pages. But if a long life actually passed between them, it is little wonder that the first was forgotten. Perhaps Isaac had but a faint report of what Abraham did, or he may only have heard vaguely that his stratagem succeeded. The event seems to have occurred before the birth of the children, for their presence with the parents would have made the fraud transparent.

After all, we are not much surprised at Isaac falling into a snare which Abraham had not escaped. If there was a character-istic weakness in Isaac, it lay in the want of courage. We do not condemn him out and out because in a great emergency his faith proved unequal to the strain. The language of cavillers, who have ascribed to Isaac every odious and selfish quality on account of his behaviour on this occasion, is lamentably unfair. The very incident that discovered the fraud to Abimelech—the fond playfulness in which Isaac indulged to his wife—showed that their ordinary relations were most affectionate.

But the fact that this is the third time within a short space that God's displeasure against the fraud is recorded is significant. It has often been discussed as a question of casuistry whether falsehood is not justifiable when an enemy, sword in hand, is ready to take away life. Moralists like Paley have been disposed to allow considerable freedom with truth in the circumstances. It is not many who, when hunted by enemies thirsting for their blood, have dealt with the question as the Scotch Covenanter, Richard

Cameron, did.    Preaching once on the prevalence of lying, he said there was a form of it too prevalent even among professors of religion.    When soldiers came to the house and asked if such a man was there, what answer was to be given them?    Were they to be told the truth, or were they to be told a lie?    "The truth," said Cameron, "and never a lie!    You may play with them a little to gain time, but on no account are you to lie.    Rather tell them that he *is* there, though you and your house should be ruined by it, though it should tend to the prejudice of the best ministers of the land.    But why so?    Because God, the God of truth, will never thank you for saving any man's life by a lie.    Let us be strict and ingenuous both with God and man."

Next, we find some notices of Isaac's great prosperity.    It is likely that when Abraham divided his property among all his sons, Isaac's share, though described as "all that he had," would be considerably less than what had once been his father's.    But a conspicuous blessing from God fell on him.    One year the increase of his grain crop was an hundredfold.    This would have been nothing unusual in the plains of Chaldæa, but for the wilderness region in which he was dwelling it was marvellous.    And this was not a solitary experience, for steady prosperity came to him, so that he became very great, and excited the envy of his neighbours.    We cannot but connect the habits of his life with his prosperity, as indeed this connection is seldom absent.    Perseverance, patience, piety, steady application to business undisturbed by excess in eating or in drinking, or by fits of laziness or self-indulgence, may have had much to do with the prosperity that followed him, but that did not attend his less steady neighbours.

But instead of imitating, his neighbours envied him.    To annoy and injure him, they resorted to the unworthy method of filling up the wells which Abraham had dug in their country, in spite of the solemn covenant made with the Abimelech of those days.    Then came an offensive message from the king himself, requiring Isaac to strike his tents and betake himself elsewhere.    The good man quietly retired to another part of Gerar.    Abraham had been there before, and had dug wells, but the Philistines had stopped them. Apparently the Philistines were much better at stopping wells than at digging them, just as there are many persons who can do much to mar the work of others, but contribute very little of their own. If the Philistines had shown as much plodding perseverance as Isaac did in digging and clearing wells, or as they did in stopping his, they would have fared much better. To establish his right to the wells the more firmly, he called them by the old names; but in vain. The Philistines made ridicule of the names, calling one of the wells Esek or Contention, and another Sitnah or Hatred, and appropriating both. At last " the invincible might of meekness " triumphs. Isaac digs a well which they do not appropriate, calling it Rehoboth or Room. Strange to say, the name survives to this day, Mr. Rowlands having found in those parts a well called Bir Rohebeh, and the ruins of a town of the same name, which are extensive and in good preservation.* We must remember that Isaac occupied the country on sufferance only, and that the people had a prior right to the water. But even at Rehoboth Isaac does not remain long; he goes up to his old station at Beersheba.

It was not a pleasant life nor a pleasant prospect to be constantly driven from place to place, treated as a football, as it were, by the older residents of the country. God, who adapts himself very graciously to the circumstances of his servants, came to him now with a very reassuring message. " I am the God of Abraham thy father," he said : " fear not, for I am with thee, and will bless thee, and multiply thy seed, for my servant Abraham's sake." This was evidently regarded as a great event in Isaac's life. It was not allowed merely to pass into some remote chamber of his memory. His spirits had probably sunk very low before he got it ; but now, in token of his gratitude, he reared an altar to the Lord, and publicly called on his name. He made no secret of God's visit to him, but proclaimed openly what God had said, and let it appear that he firmly relied on it, and felt sure that he would reap the good of it, whatever men might do. Again his servants digged a well at Beersheba. At the present day there

* " The Land and the Book," p. 558.

are two deep wells, at a little distance from each other, in the Wady es Seba, called Bir es Seba, both built up neatly with solid masonry, and surrounded with drinking-troughs in stone for camels and flocks *—possibly the very wells dug by Abraham and Isaac.

A change, of which we can only guess the particular cause, now came over the spirit of Abimelech in his relations to Isaac. With Ahuzzath, one of his friends, perhaps his privy counsellor, and Phichol, his commander-in-chief, he came from Gerar to Beer-sheba to confer with him. With some reason, Isaac expressed astonishment at this visit, for their recent treatment had shown an unfriendly spirit, and had compelled him to go out and sever himself from them. The reply of Abimelech was, that they had seen that he was certainly protected by God, and that impressed by this fact they desired to make a covenant with him. Could it have been that on the death of Abraham it had seemed to the authorities of Gerar that Isaac was too weak a man to be treated like his father, or to make it worth their pains to enter into covenant with him; but that the appearance of God to him, the divine confirmation of all that had been promised to his father, and the public profession of his faith and trust by Isaac after this appearance, impressed them with the conviction that God would be to Isaac precisely what he had been to Abraham? Was this conviction confirmed by observing the prosperity of Isaac, not-withstanding all they did to injure him, and the remarkable per-severance with which his servants dug wells, and secured the supply of water on which their wealth depended? There seemed to be no way of getting the advantage of him. An unseen pre-sence guarded him, the presence of a God of whom Abimelech stood in no little awe, whether he worshipped him or not.

Badly though Isaac had been treated, he was willing to renew the covenant which a former Abimelech had made with his father. In prescribing the form of oath, Abimelech uses words for which we are not prepared. He claims not to have done Isaac any hurt. Was it no hurt to stop his wells, and deprive him and his flocks again

* Robinson, i. 204.

and again of what was indispensable for their existence? or did he mean that his servants had done all this without his permission? Either he must have been ignorant of what his servants had done, or he must have looked on the stopping of the wells as nothing in comparison of the mischief that might have been inflicted had they proceeded to extremities against Isaac. There were so many worse things they might have done that their actual doings were in comparison harmless, and Isaac had cause only to be thankful that he had suffered no bodily harm. In any case, they saw that he was now the blessed of the Lord, just as his father had been, and they desired to come under the dew of the promise—"I will bless them that bless thee."

Peaceful and amiable, Isaac not only agrees to their covenant, but makes them a feast. They spend the night together in his tent, and next day they swear to their agreement and depart in peace. That very day his servants come to him with good news : water has been struck in the well which they have been digging. The old name Beersheba, "the well of the oath," is again bestowed on it, and Isaac is probably allowed hereafter not only to make use of its waters in peace, but to enjoy the shade of the grove which his father had planted. Thus was fulfilled a promise coeval with God's government of the world, though reserved to be formulated in after times as one of a galaxy of evangelical benedictions—"Blessed are the meek : for they shall inherit the earth."

# CHAPTER XVII.

## ISAAC'S DISPOSAL OF THE BLESSING.

### (GEN. xxvii.).

YEARS pass slowly on without much change in the fortunes of Isaac. When the smooth course of his life is next interrupted, it is in connection with the history of his sons.

Diversities of temperament and character are common enough in families, but it is seldom that in twins the contrast is so marked as in Esau and Jacob. Lordly, selfish, and stirring, yet not without warmth of heart, Esau could not brook the irksome labour of the farm. Let Jacob look after that ; the excitement and pleasures of the chase were what he delighted in, and the richer and more luxurious food that a cunning hunter could procure seemed more appropriate to his fastidious palate. Jacob was the very opposite. He was in his element among the flocks and herds, could give his heart to the work of the place, had no recoil from irksome labour, and was pleased with the quiet life of the tent and with plain dishes of herbs. If his mother loved him better, it was because he had a more domestic disposition. In every way it seemed that Esau must be the head of the house, and that the prediction that the elder would serve the younger could not come true.

But what nature seemed to have denied to Jacob, vigilance and cunning enabled him to attain. Sportsmen had no horses to carry them in those days, and their work as hunters had to be done chiefly on foot, and often at great cost of labour and fatigue. Returning homewards one day from the field in an exhausted state, Esau found his brother with one of his ordinary dishes of food—soup or pottage of red lentils. It is said that in the cooking this dish diffuses far and wide an odour very grateful to a hungry man ; it must have been especially attractive to a hunter so utterly spent as to feel as if he were dying. In the case of two brothers, between whom there is any ordinary share of humanity, not to say brotherly love, it would be impossible for the one to see the exhausted condition of the other without cordially offering him a share of his dish. It gives us a poor impression of the relations between Esau and Jacob that the one had to ask, and the other would only sell, a portion of his food. We have a still worse impression of Jacob from the circumstance that to drive his bargain he took advantage of the apparently desperate condition of his brother. And still less can we think of him for the bargain which he did make. We call it sharp practice when a trader, knowing the high value of an article, buys it for a trifle from one who is utterly ignorant or careless about it. What Jacob bought was the birthright. It is quite likely that Esau was an unbelieving man, and did not attach an atom of value to the promise respecting the seed in whom all the families of the earth were to be blessed. This was the real glory of the birthright. No doubt it included likewise the usual inheritance of the eldest son, the double portion that fell to him, but even this seemed of no consequence at the moment to Esau ; in the spirit of sheer epicurean levity, grasping at immediate gratification at any cost, and spurning all care about the future, he was determined to have the dish, let the cost be what it might. So Esau agrees to sell the birthright. But this is not enough for Jacob, who is a merchant to the backbone, and he must have security. Stamped and signed agreements there are none ; an oath is the security. Esau swears. His want alike of worldly and spiritual wisdom seems very strange. For his spiritual recklessness he is called in the Epistle to the Hebrews (xii. 16) "a profane person, who for one morsel of meat sold his birthright."

How cleverly, yet how offensively, Jacob knows to turn things to his own account, like so many more who trade on the misfortunes of their fellows ! How unlike to Abraham, refusing even a shoe-latchet from the unfortunate! It was, however, but one step he had now gained toward his ultimate object. The transaction with Esau was of little avail unless it could be homologated by his father. How this decisive step was to be achieved was the subject of no little consultation between him and his mother.

Yet we must not condemn Jacob too unqualifiedly. In all cases the rights of primogeniture are trying to the younger brother; and if the brothers are twins, and the one has preceded the other but an hour in his entrance into the world, it is peculiarly trying that on so slight a difference results of very great magnitude should often hang. And no doubt Jacob had suffered again and again from the imperious temper of his brother, and felt it hard that while he remained at home working with all his might to improve the family property, his brother should lead a life of pleasure, and come down on them when he pleased to enjoy the fruits of Jacob's diligence. Where men feel that the law is not a just law, their consciences will sometimes bear a great strain, and wink at very rough methods of compensation. Besides all this, Jacob and his mother knew the divine oracle that had assigned the blessing to Jacob at his birth, and no doubt held themselves not only at liberty but bound to do what they could to carry it into effect. In claiming precedence, Esau was doing what seemed unjustifiable alike before God and man. Ere long a step was taken by Esau in his domestic life which must have appeared alike to Jacob and to Rebekah to show that he was unworthy of the blessing and unfit to be its recipient. This was his double marriage—to Judith the daughter of Beeri the Hittite, and to Bashemath the daughter of Elon the Hittite. Not only did he despise the old rule of marriage which God had sanctioned when he created one woman to be the wife of Adam—which rule, in the main, both Abraham and Isaac had observed—but he utterly set at nought both the spirit and the letter of Abraham's solemn charge when he sent his servant to Padan-aram to find a wife for Isaac. If anything had been made plain by that transaction, it was that the purpose for which God had called and blessed the family of Abraham could not be carried out if they mingled by marriage with the idolatrous, and, in many cases, the polluted daughters of the land. Scornfully disregarding the example, the traditions, the principles of the family, and all the solemn and holy dealings which God had held with them, Esau forms this double connection with the Hittites, to the great grief of Isaac and Rebekah. It would seem that ancient as well as modern times could produce sons as unlike as possible to their fathers, some of them ostentatiously repudiating their church, their religion, and their faith, and flying off to a mode of life diametrically opposed to all to which they had been brought up. Whether the personal character of their new daughters-in-law was offensive to Isaac and Rebekah we are not told; it was enough that they were of the doomed race of the Canaanites, and that they had no sympathy with the end for which God had called Abraham. The glimpse we thus get of Rebekah is favourable to her as sympathizing with Abraham and Isaac in the purpose of their separation. But doubtless all that she saw of these young women and their influence on their husband determined her the more resolutely to scheme and devise how the blessing might be secured at her husband's hands for Jacob, whose views, with all his faults, were much more in sympathy with the great purpose of God.

At last the opportunity came of getting Isaac to bestow the blessing on Jacob. The patriarch was old, prematurely old for those times, and his eyes were dim, so that he could not see. Isaac's years would hardly account for the defect of sight, unless the eyes were in some way diseased. Cataract would easily account for the dimness under which he laboured, and which practically amounted to inability to distinguish one face or one figure from another. Isaac himself was under a presentiment of approaching death, although in point of fact he lived many years after, and was alive when Jacob returned from Haran. It is a singular fact that he had a strong desire to combine the sensual pleasure of eating a highly-seasoned meal with the solemn act of conferring the blessing on Esau. That he should have been so fond of good eating as to deem it suitable to send out his son for venison before imparting to him a great spiritual as well as temporal privilege, seems strange ; but the mention of it is only in accordance with the candour of the Bible, which does not give us perfect heroes, but men with many human infirmities, nevertheless on the whole fitted for the part which they had to perform in the purpose of God.

We need not linger over the unworthy stratagem by which Rebekah, overhearing Isaac's words to Esau, contrived that, unknown to his father, Jacob should take the place of Esau. The device of putting the skins of the kids on his hands and on his neck, in order that the smooth Jacob might personate the hairy Esau, seems to us a very clumsy one, sure to be detected ; and the fact that Isaac did not detect it, although his suspicions were roused, shows how extremely feeble he had become in mind as well as in body, prostrated probably at the time by an attack of illness which prevented him from giving his attention properly to little things, especially as the whole energies of his soul were doubtless absorbed by the great and solemn business that lay before him.   Jacob seems to have acted his part with coolness and deliberation, his only failure being his inability to imitate the voice of Esau.   We can readily enter into the *naïve* remark of Luther : " I should probably have run away in terror and let the dish fall."   Isaac's suspicions were not so much overcome as set aside ; for feeble men distrust their own judgment, and are easily persuaded by the resolute assurances of more confident and strong-willed natures.

There is no difficulty in the fact that while the dish that Isaac expected was venison—probably the flesh of the young gazelle—that which he did receive was the flesh of a young goat.   " The difference of taste of the two," says Kitto, " is not very great, as we know from personal experience ; and a still greater difference would be lost even to persons with senses more acute than Isaac's were at this time, when disguised by the strong flavours—salt, spices sour and sweet—which the Orientals are fond of giving to their more luxurious dishes......The most esteemed dishes are saturated with butter or fat, highly seasoned with salt, spices, garlic, and onions, sharpened with vegetable acids, or sweetened with honey or vegetable sweets......If Jacob's kids had been roasted whole, after being stuffed with raisins, pistachio nuts, almonds, and husked corn or rice, the result would have been a most savoury dish, now much admired in the East, and which a man with all his senses in perfection might not readily distinguish from a young gazelle similarly treated." *

Believing that it was his son Esau, Isaac bade him draw near, that he might give him the kiss of paternal affection, and in doing so smelled the odour of his garments, probably perfumed with aromatic plants like those of the desert. This gave the tone to Isaac's introductory words : "See, the smell of my son is as the smell of a field which the Lord hath blessed ; " the very scent of his garments indicates a divine benediction. Perhaps this was said soliloquizing, as an assurance to himself that he was dealing with the son to whom God's blessing ought to come. Then came the benediction itself, invoking on him first fertility and plenty of the produce of the earth ; then lordship not only over the Gentile peoples, but over his brethren and his mother's sons ; and finally extending the blessing to those that blessed him, and pronouncing a curse on those that cursed him. After all, it was a sort of clipped or contracted blessing ; for it indicated neither the multitude of his posterity, nor the possession of the land, nor the seed in whom all the nations of the earth were to be blessed. There is more of this contained in the blessing afterwards pronounced on Jacob, when Isaac sent him away (Gen. xxviii. 3, 4), and still more in the blessing pronounced on him at Luz from the mouth of God himself (Gen. xxviii. 13–15).

Nevertheless, the solemn act of Isaac, as he received his son's savoury meat, did really confer on Jacob the privilege of primogeniture and the special blessing first conferred on Abraham. How Isaac could deliberately bestow this blessing on Esau, or on one whom he believed to be Esau, knowing the oracle which gave the preference to Jacob, is very strange. We are liable to lay all the blame on Rebekah, and to think of Isaac as the innocent dupe of her ingenious wiles. But all the parties were grievously to

* "Daily Bible Readings."

blame : Isaac and Esau for planning to reverse the divine decree ; Rebekah and Jacob for using the devil's weapons to accomplish God's plan.   If Rebekah and Jacob had had a grain of Abraham's faith when about to offer up Isaac, they would have felt sure that even at the last moment God would intervene to bring the blessing to the predestined recipient.   It was want of faith in God, coupled with the impatience that could not wait till he was ready, that precipitated matters, and gave birth to the lamentable fraud. We cannot but feel for Esau and Isaac ; but they, too, were in a most serious transgression—planning to defeat a divine purpose and reverse a divine choice.

Hardly had Jacob left the presence of his father when Esau returned from the field, and having prepared, in his own tent probably, the dish which his father desired, brought it to give him.   Indescribable confusion and terror seized on the old man when Esau entered.   It seems to have flashed upon him that he had been trifling with the divine purpose and scheming to defeat it, but that God had come in, and at once rebuked and defeated him.   When he trembled exceedingly, it seems to have been at the discovery of his own sin, and of the hand of God that had been stretched forth to defeat him.   He was hardly able to speak articulately.   He could not tell Esau explicitly what Jacob had done, but as one bewildered, asked, "Who and where is he that hath taken venison and brought it to me, and I have eaten of all before thou camest, and have blessed him ? yea, and he shall be blessed." There was no idea now of carrying out his own scheme.   God's plan is the right one ; never shall it be tampered with again. And now the truth flashed on Esau ; he saw that he had lost the blessing conclusively, and he burst into an exceeding loud and bitter cry of mingled rage and disappointment.   But could not Isaac, he asked, bless him too ?   If Jacob's blessing was irreversible, was *nothing* left for him ?

But how came Esau to be so much in earnest about this now ? Had his feelings changed ? had he come to see that the birthright was not the trifle which he had formerly despised ?   In some aspects, at all events, he certainly valued the blessing as he had not valued it before. And fain would his father have met his wishes, especially when they were urged with tears. But whatever he might do for him, he could on no account dream of reversing the priority of Jacob, or the precedence which had been assigned to him. Still, there were some crumbs of comfort for the elder son.

But here comes a difficulty. What is translated (ver. 39), " Behold, thy dwelling shall be the fatness of the earth, and of the dew of heaven from above," is rendered in the margin of the Revised Version, " Behold, away from the fatness of the earth shall be thy dwelling, and away from the dew of heaven from above "—thus reversing the sense. And this rendering has been upheld by some on the ground that the land of Edom, which became the property of Esau's descendants, was not a fruitful territory, but corresponded to the description of Malachi: "Behold, I laid Esau's mountains and heritage waste for the dragons of the wilderness" (Mal. i. 3). In opposition to this consideration, it has been suggested that originally the territory of Esau may have been a fruitful one, but rendered sterile through some later cause. In proof of its ancient fertility, reference is made to the message from Moses, when a passage was sought through it for the Israelites—"We will not pass through the fields or through the vineyards." Also to Virgil's praise of its palms ("Georg." iii. 12),—

" Primus Idumæas referam tibi, Mantua, palmas ; "

and Lucan's (" Pharsal." iii. 216),—

" Arbustis palmarum dives Idume." *

At the best, the lot of Esau was to be very inferior to that of Jacob, and his usual condition was to be that of subjection to his brother. But not such absolute subjection as to make resistance utterly hopeless. There would be times when, like an animal tied up, he would break loose and shake his brother's yoke from off his neck.

Rebekah's scheme was now successful : Jacob had got the

* See Keith's " Evidence of Prophecy."

blessing.   But both Rebekah and Jacob were doomed to find what a miserable thing it is to gain possession of any good gift of God's by wicked means, when they cannot have the approval, but must have the condemnation of the giver.   Esau's rage was so excited that as soon as his father's death should take place he vowed that he would kill Jacob.   And his very mother is fain to send Jacob off to her father's distant abode, where for many long years she can never see him, and where, in spite of his birthright, he must toil for his living as a common servant, exposed to many a hardship, night and day.   No doubt she hoped that in a short time she would have him back.   But her "few days" proved to be many years; and it is hardly doubtful that she never again saw his face in the flesh.

It is said of some Orientals that they never do a thing by straight means if it be possible to do it in a round-about way. Instead of telling Isaac what Esau was threatening, and what she proposed for Jacob's safety, Rebekah made a bitter complaint against Esau's wives, that they were the torment of her life.   If Jacob should follow his example, her life would not be worth living.   It was not a high ground on which to rest her proposal—not for Jacob's welfare, at least in the first place, but her own.   The idea, however, commended itself to Isaac.   He called Jacob to him, and sent him to Padan-aram, to his mother's family, to find a wife from among them.   He renewed the blessing to him in ampler terms than before.   Rebekah was thus left with a decrepit husband, with the son whom she had humbled, and with the daughters-in-law that made her weary of her life.   The transaction had an important effect upon Esau.   Finding that his marriage to Hittite women had been so disappointing to his parents, and that Jacob had been sent off to find a wife among his kindred, he contracted a new alliance for himself, marrying his cousin Mahalath, the daughter of Ishmael *—as if marriage to an orthodox wife could undo the effects of marriage to his two idolaters.   It seemed to him that all that was necessary to please

---

\* There is considerable discrepancy in the names of Esau's wives in the two accounts (Gen. xxvi. 34, xxviii. 9, and xxxvi. 2, 3), as if they had been taken from different records.

his parents and to please God was an unexceptionable connection, without regard to the great spiritual considerations for which the seed of Abraham was to be kept separate, as the guardians for the whole world of the knowledge and the worship of the one true God.

Of the remainder of Isaac's life we know nothing. Many years after, Jacob finds him still alive at Hebron. There he ends his days, at the advanced life of a hundred and eighty years (ch. xxxv. 27–29). Often, perhaps, during Jacob's absence, he might wonder whether he would ever return. His faith may have been tried by the fear that he would become attached to the rich and favoured land to which he had gone; that terror of Esau would likewise keep him from returning; and that thus the divine promise would be in danger of not being implemented after all. It must have been a great joy to the patriarch when Jacob returned, and returned to settle in Canaan. Isaac might not be able to see him, for the dim eyes are not likely to have regained their vigour; but the voice that was so plainly the voice of Jacob would not deceive him again. The aged patriarch was buried with the family honours; his sons Esau and Jacob laid him in the tomb—doubtless in the venerable cave where his father and mother rested, and where with them he still lies, awaiting the resurrection of the just.

# CHAPTER XVIII.

## ABRAHAM'S OTHER SONS.

### (GEN. xxv. 1–18.)

IT may be convenient here, before we take up again the thread of Jacob's life, to glance at what is said respecting the fortunes of Abraham's other son, Ishmael, and of the descendants of Esau.

Of Ishmael we read (ch. xxv. 12–18) that he had twelve sons, who became twelve princes, lords of towns and castles, and founders of nations, or, as we should say, tribes. Ultimately they peopled the peninsula of Arabia, and constituted the nation whom we still call the Arabs, although they were not the exclusive settlers in that region. Among the early settlers in Arabia some were Cushites, and some were descendants of Joktan (called by the Arabians Kahtan), the son of Heber, whose other son, Peleg, was the ancestor of Abraham. But the Ishmaelites became the most prominent of the inhabitants of the peninsula. According to some Arab traditions, Ishmael became Prince of Hedjas, and first pontiff of Mecca, and Mohammed claimed to be his descendant. Penetrating from the Hedjas toward the east, " the descendants of Ishmael spread themselves over the peninsula, and introduced their peculiar manners and customs among the original inhabitants, with whom they became incorporated by intermarriages. This Arabian account does not contradict Scripture ; and whether true or not, there can be no doubt that the descendants of Ishmael form so great and absorbing a part of the Arabian population as to allow us, in a general sense, to consider him as the progenitor of that great and extraordinary nation, which has preserved its integrity, its independence, and its primitive usages from the most ancient times, and which had its turn, after the Romans, in forming one of those gigantic empires that have in different ages astonished the world."*

Mohammedans believe that not Isaac but Ishmael was the child of promise; that when Hagar and Ishmael were expelled by the wish of Sarah, Abraham conducted them to Mecca; that the well that sprang up at Ishmael's feet was the Zemzem well, within the enclosure of the temple at Mecca; that the famous Kaaba or temple was built by Abraham to commemorate the deliverance of Ishmael on Mount Moriah (for it was he rather than Isaac that was to have been offered there). The Kaaba is considered to be the navel or hub of the world. These traditions are manifestly a perversion of the true history, but they illustrate the enthusiasm with which the Arabs claim Abraham as their father, and the honour which this parentage is held to confer on the nation.

The descendants of Esau are enumerated in Gen. xxxvi. 1–19. The country in which they settled is known in Scripture by two names—Mount Seir and Edom. Mount Seir is the tract of mountainous country extending eastwards from a line drawn from the south of the Dead Sea to the eastern arm of the Red Sea, the Gulf of Akaba. Edom denotes a wider territory, of which the descendants of Esau obtained possession at a later time, when the southern part of Judea was depopulated during the Babylonian captivity, and Edom stretched to the Mediterranean on the west, and embraced the southern part of the tribe of Judah. We find from the thirty-sixth chapter of Genesis that at first the Edomites were governed by chiefs, but that afterwards they were consolidated into a monarchy, and had eight kings before there was any king in Israel (ver. 31–39). The first contact of the Israelites with the Edomites was on the march from Egypt, when Edom refused Israel a passage through his borders. In the time of David the Edomites were subdued with great slaughter, and garrisons were placed in their cities. To this, the yoke of Israel, they submitted with great impatience, and in the days of Jehoshaphat they revolted, and made themselves a king. The Edomites joined

* Kitto, " Pict. Com.," *in loc.*

with the Babylonians in the sack of Jerusalem, raising the bitter shout, "Rase it, rase it, even to the foundations thereof" (Ps. cxxxvii. 7). After the return from the captivity they sustained a great defeat from Judas Maccabæus. Herod the Great, Roman king of Judea, was an Idumæan. About the third or fourth century the Edomites, or Idumæans, as the Romans called them,

ROCK TEMPLE, PETRA.

ceased to be a separate people, and were merged with the Arabian tribes.

The country called Mount Seir is thus described by the early traveller Burckhardt. Regarding it as part of Arabia Petræa, "it might well be called Petræa, not only on account of its rocky mountains, but also of the elevated plain, which is so covered with stones, especially flints, that it may with great propriety be called a stony desert, although susceptible of culture. In many places it is overgrown with herbs, and must once have been thickly inhabited, for the traces of many ruined towns and villages are met with on both the sides of the Hadj route between Maan and Akaba, as well as between Maan and the plains of the Haouran, in which direction there are many springs. At present all this country is desert, and Maan is the only inhabited place in it."

Petra, supposed to be the same as Selah, the capital of Idumæa, was a remarkable place, on account of the temples, tombs, and houses sculptured out of the rocks that rise on each side of a narrow gorge. At one time the country was the channel of an immense traffic that flowed between Syria and Egypt. That traffic has now entirely ceased, and the predictions of the prophets regarding the desolation of Idumæa have been literally fulfilled. (See Keith's "Evidence of Prophecy;" "Voyage de l'Arabie Pétrée," par Messrs. Leon de Laborde et Linant; and the works of many recent travellers.)

# PART II.

## Jacob and Joseph.

———◆◆———

## CHAPTER I.

### JACOB AT HARAN.

(GEN. xxviii., xxix., xxx., xxxi.)

WHEN Jacob, under the directions of his father, prompted by his mother, set out for Padan-aram, ostensibly in search of a wife, he left in a very different manner from Abraham's servant when he undertook the same journey on behalf of Isaac. An imposing cavalcade of camels, a suitable body of servants, with all manner of wedding gifts and other gifts, accompanied the one; the other proceeded on foot, unattended by a single servant, with no weapon but his staff, and with no store of jewellery to win consideration for him on his arrival. Whence the extraordinary difference between Abraham's servant and Isaac's son? It might be enough to answer that everything was thrown into confusion and dilapidation by sin. We may believe that both Rebekah and Jacob were afraid of Esau, and judged it best that Jacob should leave as quickly and as quietly as possible; and that Isaac, being far from pleased with Jacob, was in no humour to give him a suitable outfit. It was a flight rather than a journey; very humiliating, we cannot but think, to the heir of so magnificent promises. But while the haste of the journey and the poor plight of the fugitive would seem to show that little faith was placed in the birthright and the blessing he had so strangely secured, there are other features of the case that indicate the presence of something like faith after all. In some rough sense Jacob believed in the family promise. He does not think of taking refuge with any of the Canaanite tribes, but, empty-handed and defenceless though he is, he makes for the distant settlement of Haran. For defence against the numerous marauders of the desert, and the destructive wild beasts that were never far off, he had nothing to look to but his staff, and the friendly interposition of the God of his fathers.

The route for the first two or three days was the same as that of Abraham and Isaac in their memorable excursion to Mount Moriah. Perhaps Jacob was in no mood to recall that marvellous example of filial submission and obedience, which was such a contrast to his own recent conduct. A few hours' walk beyond Moriah would bring him to Bethel. Traditions of Bethel must have been rife in the family—the place of one of Abraham's earliest encampments, and also of his first sojourn when he returned from Egypt; the place where Lot decided to leave him, and the scene on that occasion of the most gracious promise as yet vouchsafed to Abraham and his seed. Jacob must have had a most unimpressible nature if these things did not pass more or less through his thoughts during his walk from Mount Moriah to Bethel. The very remembrance of his venerable grandfather, now in heaven, of his lofty character and spotless life, must have led him to think very poorly of himself, and perhaps inspired the desire to turn over a new leaf and walk in his steps. We can easily believe that during his lonely journey a change came over the spirit of Jacob. On his arrival at Bethel he finds no inn or friendly tent that can furnish a couch for the night; but honest fatigue can woo sleep without any luxurious bed, and Jacob is content to gather some of the stones, covering them with dry grass or whatever else he could find that would fit them for a pillow. Ere long he is in the land of shadows, and he dreams a dream. The dream was supernatural, yet it may have had a natural basis, and may have been connected with the upward aspirations which it is likely he had begun to cherish.

In his dream he sees something like a ladder, set up on the earth, the top of it reaching to heaven, and the angels of God ascending and descending upon it. The term "ladder" is hardly appropriate, for no such article admits of persons ascending and descending at the same time. Any structure with steps from top to bottom answers to the Hebrew word, and what Jacob saw may have been a vast structure something like the Tower of Babel, but accomplishing really that fellowship with heaven which was only attempted by the other. Men could not reach heaven by their own daring, but here was God making a path from heaven to earth, sending down messengers to earth, and receiving them back to heaven. It was a lesson often repeated in after years, to the effect that salvation is not the product of man, but the gift of God—a lesson taught dimly in many a figure, but set forth with glorious clearness and fulness when God's Son came in the flesh with the announcement, "Hereafter ye shall see the heaven opened, and the angels of God ascending and descending on the Son of man." In Jacob's dream the Lord stood above the structure and proclaimed, "I am the God of Abraham thy father, and the God of Isaac: the land whereon thou liest, to thee will I give it, and to thy seed ; and thy seed shall be as the dust of the earth ; and thou shalt spread abroad to the west, and to the east, and to the north, and to the south: and in thee and in thy seed shall all the families of the earth be blessed. And, behold, I am with thee, and will keep thee in all places whither thou goest, and will bring thee again into this land ; for I will not leave thee, until I have done that which I have spoken to thee of."

It was the first time that Jacob had himself received any such communication from God. While ruminating during his lonely journey on the circumstances under which he had received the blessing from his father, he may not unnaturally have wondered whether it was really or divinely valid. After all, could God countenance the fraud which his mother and he had concocted, though it was in the line of the divine promise ? could God sanction such a transaction in any sense or to any purpose whatever ? He did not know how often God makes use of very imperfect instruments, and of their very sins and blunders, in order to accomplish his gracious purposes. But if he had any misgivings on the reality of the blessing, they were speedily and effectually dispelled. From first to last, even in the case of faithful Abraham and the meek Isaac, God had made it apparent that his covenant was a covenant of grace, and that the blessings it conveyed were not the fruit of man's merit, but wholly of God's good pleasure. His appearance now to Jacob, and the words which he spoke to him, emphasized this great truth. At the moment when Jacob was least deserving it, God assured him that the land on which he was lying would be his and his seed's, that his seed would be as the dust of the earth, and that in him and in his seed all the families of the earth would be blessed. More than that, he assured him that he was with him, and that he would be with him in Haran, and would bring him back to Canaan, and never leave him till all these promises should be fulfilled. It was a singularly God-like proceeding, so rich in grace, so comprehensive in its range, so wonderful in its unlimited goodness. It was one of those memorable moments which sometimes occur in the history of good men, when their souls are wrapt in a kind of Elysian balm, as if all God's goodness had been made to pass before them.

Evidently Jacob felt it thus. His first thought on awaking was, "Surely the Lord is in this place; and I knew it not." Only God could have given him such a dream. There is a hint here of the old idea that certain places were divine haunts where the deity sometimes appeared. He knew it not when he lay down; he little thought of any such company when, sad and lonely, he looked up to the cold stars, and sighed to think how far off they were, and how little response they could give to his empty, aching heart. Yet there was One near him, and most gracious to him all the time. And in addition, there were these troops of angels, ready to carry up his prayers to heaven, and to bring down the riches of heaven to his feet. His feeling was one of profound reverence: "How dreadful is this place!" It stirred very solemn feelings, since God had been so near and had spoken such words. "This is none other but the house of God, and this is the gate of heaven."

The utterance denotes one who was not quite a stranger to spiritual experiences. But the intensity of his present feeling had never been equalled; God and Jacob had never been so near.

The event was signalized on his part by a monument, an offering, a name, and a vow.

The monument was the stone on which he had slept, which he turned into a pillar, that in future times the event might be fresh in his memory, and he might be helped to renew his most blessed experience. His feeling must have been that of his psalmist-son: "Bless the Lord, O my soul, and forget not all his benefits." The offering was a portion of the scanty stores which he carried with him for his journey. A burnt offering would have been more suitable in acknowledgment of the promise of grace; but he had no animal for sacrifice, and oil being the most precious thing he had, was used instead. Oil, too, was a suitable emblem of consecration, and therefore of the purpose to which the stone was turned.

The name given to the place was Bethel (the house of God). The time had not yet come when not very far from that spot it should be proclaimed that God's dwelling-place was not restricted to Jerusalem, or to Luz, or to any other individual spot; but Jacob had found God there, and he desired to signalize the place for that reason,—as a place that might indeed be known for many things, but to him was sacred and glorious for this single reason that he had found it to be the house of God.

And the vow was a vow not only to cleave to Jehovah as his God, but to recognize the place as a sanctuary, and to dedicate the tenth part of his substance to God's service. In his vow he lays great stress on one article of the divine promise—that God would bring him again to his father's house in peace. That was the event which he desired most, and about which he had most anxiety. He was not so much concerned about the journey to Haran, with all its dangers, as about the journey back. Would he ever see his father's face again? Would there be yet another and better chapter of intercourse with his father, unstained as the last was by the deceit and the unfilial spirit of which he was now so ashamed? And would he ever return "in peace," without being exposed to the dread of Esau's vengeance? Jacob is in a devout and sanguine state of mind, disposed to see everything gracious on God's part, and to promise all that is loyal on his own. He little knows the immediate future. He little understands what he has yet to suffer from his uncle Laban—what discipline he has yet to pass through, what counterparts of his own deceit and cunning he has yet to experience. Like other sanguine men, he looks for a speedy fulfilment of the divine promise; but as in the case of Abraham and Isaac, a long interval has to pass, and much patience has to be exercised, before the vision of faith is turned into the reality of experience.

Striking northwards from Bethel, he would pass on to the Jordan; and long afterwards it was a thrilling incident in his recollection that the staff in his hand constituted all his possessions as he crossed the ford. Then comes the dreary journey through the Syrian desert; and at last he arrives at Haran. The road brings him to a well, where he finds some shepherds with their flocks waiting till all should be assembled, and the stone rolled away that protected the well. He had not to wait long to get tidings of Laban, or to see his daughter Rachel, the shepherdess of the family, who came with her father's sheep. Feelings of loneliness and home-sickness long pent up but now relieved get the better of him, as he so quickly finds himself among his uncle's people, and actually sees his cousin. Like one overjoyed, he kisses her, lifts up his voice and weeps. And Laban, as soon as he hears of his arrival, hurries to welcome him, and invites him to his house. Jacob is at once among friends; everything looks bright and cheerful, and it seems as if a new era of prosperity and happiness were about to begin.

Laban's is evidently a busy house. No member of it eats the bread of idleness. We may think that life in those patriarchal houses was somewhat dull and monotonous, compared with that of our wealthier classes now, with their refinement, their diversity of recreations, their very ample means of enjoyment. But the habitual activity of the patriarchal households compensated for the want of modern luxuries, and gave a relish to such recreations as they had, a relish seldom known to those whose lives are full of pleasure. The honour paid to labour among the wealthy of those days carries a lesson which ought not to be overlooked. If there be a vice more discouraged than another by precept and example in the Bible, it is idleness. Whoever among the toiling multitude fancies that the religion of the Bible looks on his toil with indifference, can be but poorly acquainted with the book. Whoever forgets that by its doctrine of the infinite worth of every human soul the New Testament lifts up the humblest labourer to the very door of God's household, overlooks the most valuable charter that the children of labour ever received.

When Jacob entered Laban's house, it was to have an experience of hard labour such as probably he had never known, but along with this an experience of a very different kind—the experience of being in love, to which he seems to have been equally a stranger. As to his age, whether it was above fifty, as some think, or above seventy, as appears to others, he certainly was not young in years. But a law, of which there are still some traces, appears to have prevailed, that the longer the term of life, the slower was the development of body and mind; and notwithstanding his years, he was probably not older in constitution and feeling than a man about thirty would be to-day.

The story of the attachment of Jacob and Rachel is the first love-romance in the Bible. Never was the magic of the tender passion more graphically described than in the words that tell us that the seven years of hard bondage which Jacob served for Rachel seemed unto him but a few days, for the love which he bore to her. And we insensibly get a kindlier feeling to Jacob when we read this of him. He becomes more attractive to us when we find in him such an intense affection. In two directions we see his heart becoming better under the influence of love. The great love of God draws him nearer to his heavenly Father ; the love of Rachel softens his heart to men.

In proportion to the vehemence of his love for Rachel was his unspeakably bitter disappointment at the mean trick of Laban when the wife actually given him was found to be not Rachel but Leah. The very possibility of such a thing shows what a difference there was between Laban's ways and ours. Yet amid all Jacob's irritation and indignation at this miserable fraud, one consideration would tend to calm him—it was just the treatment and the trick he had practised on his father. It is often seen that those who use craft and cunning as their weapons find themselves, like Shakespeare's engineer, " hoist with their own petard," through similar deceptions practised on them by others. Whatever injustice Jacob suffered on this occasion from Laban, it could not but silence him to think that the trick was the very counterpart of the stratagem by which he had supplanted Esau. But in truth Jacob found himself in a very school of deceit, where craft was matched against craft, and cunning was the only weapon with which he could think of contending with his father-in-law. Ill though he had been treated, the arrangement turned out better than he could have expected. In the first place, after the interval of a week, spent like the one before it as a marriage feast, the coveted prize came into his hands,—Rachel became his wife, on condition of his giving to Laban other seven years of labour ; and in the second place, little though Leah was thought of, she was after all the chief builder up of his house. As the mother of six of his sons, she contributed more than any other to give that importance and dignity to his family which arose from his being the father of so great a number.

There could not but have been some jealousy of Leah on the part of Rachel when children came to her sister in such numbers, and she herself had none. Rachel's disappointment must have been very bitter, and Leah could no longer have been to her what she was in earlier days. Providence moved too slowly for her patience, and with that blind propensity to repeat the blunders of predecessors of which we have so many instances in this narrative, Rachel repeated the device of Sarah by giving her maid to Jacob. The impatience of her nature was seen in the way in which this was done : she got angry at Jacob, and, like a petted child, threw all the blame of her disappointment upon him. Leah was not to be outdone by Rachel, and her maid was added to Jacob's wives. Thus Jacob found himself the husband of two wives and two concubines without himself having had any desire for more than Rachel. Ten sons were born to him, while Rachel continued childless. At length God hearkened unto her, and she became the mother of Joseph. A second son was born to her afterwards, but dying in childbed, she found that even when Providence gives us our own way, it is often at a sacrifice so serious as to make us ask whether the loss is not greater than the gain.

It was on the birth of Rachel's first son that Jacob proposed to Laban that he should let him depart to his own place and to his own country. He had found Laban a most uncomfortable master. There was no reliance to be placed on him nor on his promises. Jacob had had hard work, long hours, and much exposure and danger, but without any adequate remuneration. A careful and skilful man among cattle, he had been the means of greatly increasing Laban's stock, making him now a rich man compared to what he was. Laban was neither willing to lose Jacob nor to give him adequate encouragement to remain. He was one of those selfish masters who extract the utmost amount of service for the smallest possible remuneration. And he had that shabby way of doing things, that if a servant was once in his power he would prevent him from getting away, or from doing anything to better his situation. He even tried to turn Jacob's good standing with the Almighty to his own secular advantage. He found by experience that the Lord had prospered him for Jacob's sake; but instead of regarding that as a reason why he should the more cordially give himself to God's service, he sought only to retain Jacob in his own. He had a respect for good men, as Balaam had afterwards, and some have still. He saw that God was with them and blessed them; but instead of imitating them, he sought to use them for his own secular benefit, finding that their godliness tended to his gain. His one aim was to enrich himself and get others to enrich him. Like those landlords who have a high opinion of industrious and skilful tenants, because the improvements they effect on the land increase the value of the estate, but who refuse till compelled by law to remunerate them for their improvements, Laban desired to make the most of Jacob, but declined to give him a fair return for his services.

So often had he broken his word that Jacob despaired of making any terms with him, except such as would seem to give to Laban an immense preponderance of benefit. He therefore made a proposal that seemed a silly one for himself. He proposed that only the speckled and spotted of the cattle, and the brown of the sheep, should form his remuneration—a very small proportion, surely, of the whole. Laban accepted the proposal, but forthwith went to the herds and flocks in Jacob's charge, and removed all the animals of that description three days' journey from them, leaving to Jacob absolutely none of that sort. It was a flagrant violation of the spirit of the bargain ; but grossly unfair as it was, Jacob did not remonstrate or despair. Availing himself of a physiological fact with which a dream made him acquainted, he took steps which he deemed likely to increase the number of animals that would fall to him. The plan succeeded to a marvellous degree ; but the dark looks of Laban and the threatening words of his sons showed that more mischief was brewing. A divine communication now came to Jacob, commanding him to leave Haran and return to the land of promise. Leah and Rachel encouraged him to take this course, their reasons being that their father had behaved unfairly to them as well as to their husband, that no part of his substance would ever be theirs, and that it was a waste of time to remain longer in connection with him.

But how was Jacob to get away ? Laban certainly would not willingly allow him to leave, and the force at Laban's disposal was too powerful for Jacob to resist. Moreover, there was a great multitude of cattle to which Jacob had now acquired an undoubted right, that could move but slowly, and might be overtaken very easily. The difficulty would have overwhelmed a less clever or less venturesome man. If Jacob could not get clear away from Laban, he might at least reach some neutral ground, where, when overtaken, he might treat with him on more equal terms, and from which Laban would find it more difficult to compel him to return.

Availing himself of a time when Laban was occupied with the shearing of his sheep, Jacob gathered all his possessions and stole away. In the East, preparations for a long journey or even migration can be made in a fourth of the time necessary in the like circumstances among us. The tents are quickly struck, and, together with all the movables and possessions, packed on the backs of camels, mules, or asses, and the whole party will very quickly be on its way, leaving not a rag or halter behind. "The order of march in the removal of a pastoral tribe or family seems to be just the same as that which may be traced in the next and ensuing chapter......The sheep and goats usually lead the van, and are followed by the camels, perhaps asses, laden more or less with the property of the community, consisting of the tents, with their cordage, mats, carpets, clothes, skins, water and provision bags, boilers and pots, and sundry other utensils, bundled up in admirable confusion,—unless when all the property belongs to one person, as in the case of Jacob. The laden beasts are usually followed by the elderly men, the women and the children, who are mostly on foot in the ordinary migrations with the flocks, which must be carefully distinguished from a caravan-journey or a predatory excursion across the deserts. The very young children are carried on the backs or in the arms of their mothers, who in general are on foot, but are sometimes mounted with their infants on the spare or lightly-laden beasts......The chief himself brings up the rear, accompanied by the principal persons of the party......It would seem as if most of Jacob's people went on foot; it is only said that he set his wives and children upon camels." *

So cleverly had Jacob made his arrangements that he was well on his way before his departure became known; and although Laban set to work immediately, and, unencumbered with flocks or children, pursued his son-in-law at the very top of his speed, Jacob had reached the outskirts of Gilead before he was overtaken. Gilead, as is well known, was the name of a very fertile region east of the Jordan.

Whatever Laban's intentions may have been—whether to try

* "Pictorial Commentary," *in loc.*

to compel Jacob to return, or to exact of him such a fine as would in some measure compensate for his extraordinary share of cattle—he was prevented from taking either step by a message from God, received in a dream, warning him against saying one evil word to Jacob. When he came up to him, therefore, he had to be silent on the subject that no doubt was uppermost in his mind—the vast number of his flocks and herds, which was certainly far beyond what either of them could have expected. Laban could only reproach him for the suddenness of his flight, and the affront done to himself, as a man of courtesy and an affectionate father, by his not giving him an opportunity to make a feast on the occasion, and to kiss his sons and his daughters. But the cloven foot comes out in the announcement, " It is in the power of mine hand to do you hurt." A coarse-minded man, Laban cannot but shake his fist in Jacob's face, asserting his superiority, and thus inflicting a wound on his feelings that makes his complaint of discourteous treatment by Jacob ridiculous. But he frankly tells him that much though he might desire to chastise him, he is restrained by the vision of the previous night and the solemn charge of God. He reckons on God as a powerful force, that happens to be on the side of Jacob, but he shows no disposition to regard him as the blessed and only Potentate, or to seek for himself the blessing of dwelling under the shadow of his wings.

On the contrary, he makes a complaint of Jacob that shows that neither he nor his family, not even Rachel, had given up all idolatrous practices. He accuses Jacob of stealing his images— " the teraphim that were her father's." The teraphim were small images, used in houses, sometimes placed in niches with lamps burning before them, not primarily or necessarily designed to receive worship, but rather to remind the worshipper of the true object or objects of worship. Various reasons have been supposed why Rachel should have taken them. But the most obvious explanation seems also the best—that neither Laban nor Rachel had abandoned all the superstitious and idolatrous practices of the country, and that Rachel thought that the possession of the images would bring prosperity to her house, and would enable her to continue the worship to which she had been accustomed. That she had no countenance in this from Jacob is evident from the fact that he was ignorant of the transaction. In replying to her father, Rachel, who was really sitting on the images, had recourse to the family weapon, deceit, both in excus-

TERAPHIM.

ing herself from what was deemed most disrespectful—remaining seated before her father—and in denying all knowledge of the missing articles. Laban was baffled in his search, becoming in this, as in other matters, the victim of the habit of deceit which he had so often practised on Jacob, not only at his marriage, but on all the other occasions on which he had defrauded him.

Believing the charge of theft to be baseless and trumped up for the purpose of insulting him, Jacob loses his temper, and under the excitement of anger gives Laban a few lines of his mind. What was the value of these trumpery images, about which he made such a fuss, compared to all that Laban had unjustly deprived him of during the last twenty years? What cause had Laban to take up a complaining tone, when his whole course of proceeding toward him all that long time had been one of injustice and oppression? Jacob, on his part, takes an extreme view of Laban's proceedings, and, as angry men are prone to do, omits everything more favourable and friendly. He forgets how Laban took him in when a stranger and a fugitive, and gave him his daughters in marriage. He sees nothing but injustice in all the transactions of the twenty years. One feeling certainly is emphasized by this means in Jacob's mind —how much he owes to the divine protection; how absolutely penniless he would have been if the God of his fathers had not taken his side.

Laban has lost his pains; he must return without son-in-law or daughters, without even a single ox or sheep from Jacob's store. But it would not do to return without seeming to have accomplished anything. So he proposes that the two should make a covenant—an empty enough transaction, seeing that there could be no securities for enforcing it, and seeing that Jacob's life was about to be spent at such a distance from Laban that practically there could be no intercourse between them. But if it be any satisfaction to Laban to hear Jacob promise that he will treat his daughters well, and if it be any comfort to Jacob to be assured that Laban will leave him alone in the future, the covenant at Galeed, and the pillar and heap of stones which commemorate it, may be viewed with satisfaction on both sides. At any rate the covenant is an amicable transaction between them, and it gives them a tangible opportunity of shaking hands and parting in peace. Their last words will not be words of recrimination, flung out by the one and tossed back by the other. The solemnity of a divine transaction is given to the covenant. Laban appeals to the God of Abraham, Jacob's grandfather, and of Nahor, his own grandfather, and the God of their father Terah, all of whom would thus seem to have been worshippers of the one true God. Jacob swears by "the Fear of his father Isaac"—an expression that denotes the great predominance of reverence in the piety of Isaac. And Jacob, as priest of his family, offers sacrifice on the mount. He recognizes the need of approaching God and invoking his blessing on the footing of sacrifice. Probably he recalls that transaction at Hebron between God and Abraham, when the heifer and she-goat and ram, the turtle-dove and the young pigeon, formed the sacrifice that ratified their agreement. Whatever defects we see in the character of Laban or of Jacob, we must respect the honour paid by both to the divine Majesty, and the solemnity with which they felt that their covenant was invested, from being formed in the face of the Most High.

Twenty years had now elapsed since Jacob left his father's

house, intending to return in a few days, when his brother's anger should have quieted down. "Man proposes, but God disposes." There were many drawbacks to his happiness during this period of his life. Yet, on the whole, he had received much mercy. In the love of Rachel a new brightness had entered his life. If during the first fourteen years he had acquired no property, he had prospered during the last six beyond his utmost expectations. Above all, he had received new assurances of the presence and protection of the God of his fathers. We see his natural character undergoing new developments : we see his dogged perseverance and cunning cleverness in pursuing his ends, especially when he has to contend with superior power ; but we see what is better—a steady family affection, and a heart that never swerved from its early love. The birth of so many children had given him a new tie to life, and had created new obligations to work for their welfare. Probably his trials and disappointments had chastened the impetuosity of his spirit, and given him more self-control. With much that was painful in his Haran life, he must have been able to see even more that was gratifying, the retrospect of which, now that he was bidding the place a final farewell, might well lead him to "thank God and take courage."

## CHAPTER II.

(Gen. xxxii.)

"ONE woe is past; and, behold, another woe cometh quickly." Jacob has settled with Laban; but Esau has to be dealt with yet. Rough though Jacob was in many things, he had continued loyal to God at Haran, and had honoured him in his way. And God does not leave him without encouragement. A vision of angels comes to him at Mahanaim, reminding him of his vision at Bethel twenty years before, as he was leaving Canaan, and of God's gracious dealings with him then. It was a magnificent forecast of the divine protection in the troubles that were yet before him. He gave the place the name of Mahanaim ("two hosts"); and it continued to retain it, having been the capital of Ishbosheth, son of Saul, and the scene of the memorable battle between David and Absalom. But no mention is made of it afterwards; unless, indeed, it be referred to in the passage, Song of Sol. vi. 13, "What will ye see in the Shulamite? As it were the company of two armies" (*margin*, "Mahanaim," Authorized Version). In the Revised Version we have, "Why will ye look on the Shulamite? As upon the dance of Mahanaim" (*margin*, "two companies"). It is supposed that there were sacred dances at Mahanaim, similar to those at Shiloh (Judg. xxi. 21), used here as the emblem of pure and graceful activity. But if there be a reference to the old meaning of the name, Mahanaim would be the symbol of angelic beauty and joyful praise.

And now, having parted finally from Laban, Jacob is able to

direct his whole mind to Esau, and to consider how he is to deal with him. In the plans he makes for this purpose, some of his most characteristic features come out—his firmness of purpose, his cleverness of policy, his power of sacrificing the present for the future. In the first place, in order to find out in what mood he is to find Esau, he determines to send him a friendly message announcing his approach ; and in this message, so far from assuming the superiority which had been divinely conferred on him, he addresses him as "my lord Esau," and styles himself "thy servant Jacob." To show, moreover, that he is not returning as a beggar, and that there is no risk of his laying claim to anything that was Esau's, or that Esau might look for from their father, he informs him that he has ample possessions, oxen and asses, flocks, and men-servants and women-servants, and that the sole object of the message which he now sends is to bespeak a friendly reception. To this humble message Esau deigns no reply, and the mood he is in may be inferred from his setting out to meet Jacob with four hundred men. If anything could mean war, surely it is this.

No wonder that Jacob was "greatly afraid and distressed." Notwithstanding, his self-possession did not forsake him. Deliberately considering the situation, he set about the best means of protection he could devise, dividing his company into two sections, so that if Esau were to come and massacre the foremost of them, the other might have some chance of escape. Then recognizing God in a way, but not (as we shall see) so fully as he ought to have recognized him, he implores the divine protection on himself and his company, reminds God of his command to him to return to Canaan, gratefully acknowledges the goodness and mercy that had followed him since he crossed the Jordan, with his staff as his only property, owns his terror of Esau, and rehearses the promise that his seed would be as the sand of the sea. This shows the reality of Jacob's piety ; but there was a reserve in his mind, as if he did not feel an absolute dependence on God, or cherish an absolute assurance of his protection, but was trusting more to a plan of his own, which he thought would gain over Esau and remove all difficulty.

To fight with him and his four hundred men was out of the question; his policy, therefore, must be a policy of conciliation—as it is needless to dream of force, he must try to attain his end by a great profession of love. Esau must be disarmed as the traveller in the fable was divested of his cloak—not by the wind, but by the sun; not by boisterous threatening, but by the arts of gentle affection. Jacob does not propose to make any reference to the expressed mind of God as to the relation of the two brothers to each other. His plan is to buy up his brother, anger and all, by a stupendous act of bribery. The bribe is to be on such a vast scale as by the very mention of it to take away Esau's breath, and at once overwhelm him. It must have cost Jacob, who liked his property so much, a tremendous effort to decide on so costly a scheme. The present which he sent forward consisted of no less than nine parcels of animals, amounting in all to five hundred and fifty. Camels, goats, oxen, sheep, and asses, all carefully sorted and arranged, and containing, doubtless, many a beautiful animal, were sent on in nine detachments, with an interval between each. The servants in charge were instructed to offer them for Esau's acceptance, no doubt with profound and studied courtesy, with an announcement that Jacob himself was coming after them to pay his respects to his brother. We can understand how dumfounded Esau must have been. No doubt he saw through the pretext of affection and the purpose of the gift; but he could not fail to be impressed with the largeness of his brother's ideas, and with the substantial addition to his own wealth which the gift implied. Selfish though Jacob was, he could do things on a large scale when the occasion demanded; he was not like the miser in the storm, who preferred to sink clutching his bag of gold; he had a gift of calculation, and could sacrifice much where his interest required it. His ability to part with property on so vast a scale, though no proof of true generosity, indicated a strength of character far above the common level.

Such was Jacob's plan. He was now near the confluence of the Jabbok with the Jordan, for in his prayer he speaks of "this Jordan," as if he were close to it (ver. 10); and we are expressly told that at night he sent his wives and children over the Jabbok, remaining himself alone on its other bank. The Jabbok is a considerable stream, flowing through a deep, rocky ravine, and entering the Jordan about forty miles south of the lake of Galilee. Our Lord must often have crossed it, probably at the same spot, in travelling, as he often did, through Perea, on his way to Jeru- salem from Galilee, or in returning northwards. The name Jabbok is thought to mean a wrestler, from the circumstance that the stream has to fight its way through the hard and jagged rocks that obstruct its course. An obstruction like that which the stream encountered from the rocks Jacob was now about to experience from a very different source.*

After all his company had been sent across, as we have seen, he remained alone on the northern bank. He had need of rest and solitude, and he had yet to consider what course he would take if the present for Esau failed of its purpose. No doubt it was a magnificent present; but then Esau had never cared for cattle, and perhaps he would treat his offer with scorn. What would Jacob do next? Suddenly his thoughts were thrown into a very different channel. A man appeared, as if on purpose to obstruct him, and wrestled with him until the breaking of the day. Whence this strange opposition on the part of one whom Jacob afterwards recognized as the divine angel of the Lord himself? Could it be that in his plans for conciliating Esau, and finding unimpeded access to the land of Canaan, Jacob was placing too much reliance on his own arrangements, trusting to the devices of his own cleverness and cunning? No doubt he had prayed for God's protection; but a man's prayers and practice do not always agree. Did he forget that it was as God's servant that he was now about to enter God's land; that the whole trans- action was a very solemn one; and that it became him to advance in full recognition of God as his leader and his master? Did not this angel-stranger withstand him because he was coming in his

* Major Conder ("Heth and Moab") has started the idea that Jacob was on the south bank of the Jabbok, and that he sent his children over to the northern bank, in order to have that stream between them and Esau. We are disposed, however, to hold by the older view.

own name rather than in the name of God? And was it not for this that he seemed intent on turning him back—back towards Laban, from whom it had been such a relief to be separated, and with whom he never could have either happiness or peace?

At first Jacob did not apprehend the reason of the obstruction, and sought only to overcome it. He must advance; back to Laban he would not and could not go. He must advance to the land of his fathers, the land of his affections, the land of his hopes, the land of the divine promise, the land in which, with all the ardour of his nature, and not without a measure of faith, he and his children desired to live and to die. As the struggle went on the sinew of his thigh was strained (Revised Version); but with that contempt of pain which has often been shown in desperate warfare, he wrestled on. At what time it dawned on him that it was the angel of the Lord that was wrestling with him, we cannot say. But he did come to know it, and with the knowledge of it a new light fell on the whole situation. Yes, there was reason why the angel of the Lord should obstruct him. He had been pressing forward in reliance on his own subtle schemes and clever projects, and giving but a secondary place to the guidance and blessing of God. But now he feels that this will never do. He must have the blessing of God. That is what he needs; and till he gets that, wounded though he is, he will hold on—he will not let the angel go. For now the relation between the two combatants is changed. The angel now wishes to go, and Jacob will not let him. "Let me go," cries the angel, "for the day breaks." If only he had said "Let me go" sooner, Jacob would only have been too glad. Then it was the angel that would not let Jacob go; now it is Jacob that will not let the angel go. And Jacob prevails. The angel gives him the blessing. Jacob has now nothing to fear; he will march unopposed into the land, not in virtue of his own cunning and cleverness, but because "the angel of the Lord encampeth round about them that fear him, and delivereth them."

And now Jacob achieves a double victory—he prevails with the angel and he prevails with Esau. It is often represented that

Jacob's prevailing with the angel is a proof of the efficacy of persevering prayer. The last part of the transaction does show this, when Jacob said, " I will not let thee go, unless thou bless me ; " but this was not said till the day was breaking, at the very close of the combat. The intense ardour of Jacob during the night was directed towards removing the obstruction which the angel seemed to be throwing in the way of his entering the land. In a sense, both the angel and Jacob succeeded : the angel got Jacob to feel the need of the divine blessing ; and Jacob overcame the obstruction, and obtained divine blessing from the angel.

But the incident shows the benefit of persevering in action as well as in prayer. Jacob is the symbol of a man addressing himself earnestly to his work, even while the forces of both earth and heaven seem to be opposing him. The case has often been repeated in Hebrew history and in other history : in the case of Moses persevering in his great task till he brought his people to the Jordan ; in the case of Gideon contending with Midian— " faint, yet pursuing ; " in the case of Nehemiah building the walls of Jerusalem, with his implement in one hand and his weapon in the other ; and highest of all, in the case of our blessed Lord, with his face set so steadfastly to go up to Jerusalem. And in more recent years, have we not had similar instances of inflexibility of purpose—in Christopher Columbus, persevering in his strange enterprise amid the mutiny of sailors and the nameless perils of unknown seas ; in Martin Luther, holding on to his views despite all the terrors of Church and State ; or in David Livingstone, re- solved to open Africa or perish in the attempt? Such men may at times have been obstructed, and the obstructer, unknown to them, may have been an angel from heaven ; but the effect of the ob- struction was to make them persevere more resolutely and appeal more earnestly for the blessing of God. The more they were opposed, the more pertinaciously did they move, not backwards, but forwards and upwards, seeking the strength that is made per- fect in weakness. Perseverance in prayer is no doubt one of the lessons of this transaction, but not less perseverance in effort too ; in a right course we must not turn back, be the difficulties what they may. The rule of the kingdom is, "He that endureth to the end, the same shall be saved."

But Jacob in this conflict prevailed with man as well as with God. By this we understand that the opposition of Esau was overcome directly through God influencing his mind, but indirectly through Jacob's unyielding attitude at the beginning of the struggle, and his successful prayer at the end. His conciliatory policy would probably have failed. The five hundred and fifty cattle might have been scorned by a high-minded man like Esau as a contemptible bribe. But among other results of the blessing brought to Jacob by his victory, one was, that by some unseen force the heart of Esau was so moved that he let his brother alone. The promise afterwards to be recorded came true : "When a man's ways please the Lord, he maketh even his enemies to be at peace with him." The sudden change on Esau is one of the most notable incidents of the occasion. It could not have been a herd of cattle, however big, that changed the vindictive purpose that had smouldered in his breast for twenty years, and was burning fiercely only a few days before. Another power must have been at work in subduing Esau. He that rules the waves uttered his "Peace, be still." Esau yields to the invisible power. "He maketh the storm a calm, so that the waves thereof are still. Then are they glad because they be quiet; so he bringeth them unto their desired haven."

The victory of Jacob is commemorated by a change of name : "Thy name shall be called no more Jacob, but Israel [a prince of God] : for as a prince thou hast power with God and with men, and hast prevailed." A change of name by divine direction always indicated an important crisis in a man's history, and his entrance on a new chapter of his life or a new aspect of his character. So it was when Oshea became Joshua, and Simon became Peter. After this transaction Jacob stands on higher ground, and seems to lead a higher life. Not that the old man is entirely swallowed up by the new ; not that Jacob is wholly superseded by Israel ; but tricks of carnal policy cease to be his usual method, and the spirit seems to gain ground that afterwards comes out so strongly in his blessing to his sons, especially in the expression of the attitude which his spirit of perseverance took in the end : " I have waited for thy salvation, O Lord."

As the angel had dealt with his name, so he inquires after the angel's ; but he gets no answer. For whatever significance the people of those days might have attached to names, and whatever interest Jacob might take in connecting this transaction with such divine name as the angel might have given, the mere name, after all, was but a frivolous matter. Jacob showed that he knew quite well who his antagonist was, and therefore that the question needed no answer, by the name which he himself gave to the place : " He called the name of the place Peniel : for I have seen God face to face, and my life is preserved." God had been near to him, not as a mere name, but as a great reality. Never let him lay his plans for the future without reckoning with him ! This meeting with God is the more striking because his life is preserved. Self-confident and foolish though he had been, God had not scornfully swept him out of the way, but had condescended to him and dealt gently by him. Peniel was henceforth a sacred place ; but in its after history we find little to remind us of this. Twice only do we meet with the name again, and on both occasions in no very favourable connection : once in the history of Gideon, who, to punish its disloyalty, broke down the tower and slew the men of the city after his defeat of Midian (Judg. viii. 17) ; and once in the days of Jeroboam, who, among his other undertakings, rebuilt the place (1 Kings xii. 25).

All his life Jacob carried with him a memorial of this night : the strained sinew did not recover its elasticity—" he halted on his thigh." This furnished a perpetual reminder that it was by God's grace he had conquered—" out of weakness he was made strong." He was like St. Paul after his trance-visit to the third heaven, when the thorn in the flesh was sent to afflict him, " lest he should be exalted above measure." Those who have enjoyed near fellowship with God stand in as much need as the Roman general, amid the glory of his triumph, of a slave to stand behind and remind them that they are mortal.

# CHAPTER III.

(GEN. xxxiii.)

THE experience of Jacob at Peniel was more fitted to refresh him than the soundest sleep. In the morning he crosses the Jabbok, and is encamped on the bank of the Jordan, when he sees Esau with his four hundred men advancing to meet him. After arranging his wives and children in proper order, he passes over before them and pays profound obeisance to Esau. The meeting was as friendly as if all their lives they had been the dearest friends. It seemed as if an old fountain of brotherly love had suddenly burst forth from Esau's heart : he ran to meet Jacob, and embraced him, and fell on his neck and kissed him. Nothing could have been more cordial. Then kindly inquiries are made and answered about the wives and children, who come in due order, one batch after another, and repeat the homage of Jacob. And then, on the subject of Jacob's gift, the brothers engage in a friendly contest of politeness and generosity. Esau cannot deprive his brother of all that drove ; he has enough already. But Jacob is not to be outdone ; he urges Esau to keep the present, and with ready tact represents that if there were no other reason for it, this very friendly and brotherly reception deserved the acknowledgment.

It is now Esau's turn to press Jacob, and he invites him to go with him and pay him a visit. Jacob has not courage to say no, as he would fain do ; he excuses himself on the ground that his company cannot travel so fast as Esau's, and gives him to understand that he will follow him to Mount Seir, as fast as the condition of his caravan will allow. It is not very plain whether Jacob carried out this proposal or not. The strain of the narrative would lead us to suppose that he did, but nothing to this effect is directly stated. If Jacob did go to Mount Seir to visit his brother, he could hardly have taken his flocks with him. Perhaps the booths he is said to have built at Succoth were designed to shelter his cattle till his return. It would be very hard to fancy that after all that he had experienced at Peniel he would be guilty of an open breach of his word to Esau, or that he would expose himself anew to his brother's anger by failing to pay his visit, which would have been an act of the grossest discourtesy.

Jacob next proceeds to Shechem, purchases a field, and digs a well. This, too, was a questionable transaction. It did not amount to disobedience or open unbelief, but it showed a carelessness as to his old vow at Bethel; for now that God had brought him back in safety, we should have expected that his first act would be to go there and rear some memorial of his gratitude to him. Apparently his zeal for God is not yet equal to his regard for his own interests. He is in no haste to go to Bethel. He is captivated by the attractions of Shechem, as Lot was captivated by the attractions of Sodom. Perhaps, too, his sons were urgent in begging him to remain where he was, and they had now to be taken into account. He accordingly proceeds to settle on the field which he has purchased. Considering that his sons were but boys when he entered Canaan, but had become strong men before he left Shechem, we must believe that he remained ten or twelve years at that place. That he should have dug a well at such a place may seem strange, because Shechem is a well-watered valley, and natural streams abound. But it was reasonable for him to desire to have a permanent supply of water within the limits of his field.

What is called Jacob's Well remains to this very day. At the foot of Mount Gerizim, half-an-hour from Nablous (the ancient Shechem), all travellers go to see Jacob's Well. And there can be little doubt that the tradition is true. It is called Jacob's

JACOB'S WELL.

TAYLOR

Page 228.

Well in that remarkable narrative which records our Lord's conversation with the woman of Samaria. The position of the well agrees with the circumstances recorded in the Gospel, and the tradition that it was at this spot that Jesus spoke to the woman goes back to the days of Eusebius. The interest of the field and the well in Jacob's time is superseded by its far more notable connection with our Lord; yet fancy can draw a bright picture of the earlier time when Jacob's household were all astir about the place, and little Joseph, in his mother's hand, might have been seen in all the glee of childhood charmed with the scene.

But retribution overtook him at last for trying to settle at Shechem before he visited Bethel. His light-headed daughter Dinah, mixing with the people of Shechem, had fallen into temptation, and thereafter she was sought in marriage by Shechem, son of Hamor, prince of the country, who urged his suit with the most vehement passion. And Jacob's conduct in the matter was not straightforward. One would have thought that, reminded of Lot's experience in Sodom, he would have been all haste to escape from Shechem, and reach some place where the morals of his family would be exposed to no such risk. But the alliance of such men as the Shechemites, Canaanites though they were, would be a great boon to him in a temporal sense. When he consulted his sons, Simeon and Levi, they proposed a compromise,—deceitfully, as was shown afterwards; and their father agreed. Their real plot was nothing short of diabolical, showing an extraordinary combination of carnality, craft, and cruelty: carnality, because they represented that a fleshly rite would wipe out a moral stain; craft, because under this pious guise was hid a murderous intention; and cruelty, because their real design was to put the Shechemites to death when they were unable to resist. "In them first," remarks Dr. Marcus Dods, "we see how the true religion, when held by coarse and ungodly men, becomes the root of all evil. We see the first instance of that fanaticism which so often made the Jews a curse rather than a blessing to other nations. Indeed, it is but an instance of the injustice, cruelty, and violence that at all times result where men suppose that they themselves are raised to quite peculiar privileges, and to a position superior to their fellows, without recognizing also that this position is held by the grace of a holy God and for the good of their fellows."

The cruel, treacherous, and hypocritical scheme of Simeon and Levi for the destruction of the Shechemites was executed to the letter. We cannot but wonder at the truculence and savagery of the deed, and ask how it was possible for these very young men, usually engaged in the peaceful occupation of shepherds, to perpetrate so horrid a crime. The answer is, it was the fruit of their intercourse with the people of the land. Among them they had come in contact with massacres as common occurrences—sometimes of a caravan, sometimes perhaps of a whole tribe—and had seen them carried out in cold blood, rousing no more feeling of compunction than the slaughter of sheep and oxen at the shambles.

Jacob's dreams of an advantageous connection were now scattered to the winds. His field, his well, and all that had been built for his accommodation, were rendered useless; for he could no longer live in a place where, apart from other considerations, the law of blood revenge must claim him and his family as victims. More than that, his reputation as a neighbour was ruined, and the credit of his religion was shattered. How different his position from his father's, when Abimelech came to make a covenant with him because of the holy atmosphere around him— because he perceived that God was with him ! A sadder plight could hardly be for the head of a family whose besetting sin was the desire, at any cost, to prosper in the world. But no doubt his bitterest thought was, that the cunning and treachery of his sons were of a piece with his own conduct in early life, although their truculence was a new thing in the family. It was more like the spirit of Ishmael or of Esau, casting the first dark shadow over the history of a house that for three generations had been unstained by treachery or bloodshed in its intercourse with the outer world. We see in Jacob's children that element of ferocity which seems to lie deep in the Eastern nature, ready to burst forth whenever provocation comes. That divine Spirit which had subdued it in

Abraham, Isaac, and Jacob had not as yet conquered it in the sons. We often find it at work in after times in individual members of the race, like Ehud, Abimelech, Ahab, or Jehu, but not on the awful scale on which it appeared in the Assyrians, the Babylonians, and the Idumeans. But it took a long education to infuse the love of mercy into the Hebrew character : all the more striking was the result when One who, according to the flesh, was of the same blood, not only taught, " Blessed are the merciful," but exemplified in himself the best quality of mercy, and exalted it to the very highest rank as an element of human character. Many a page of missionary history presents the threefold view,— first, ferocity rampant ; then ferocity modified by incipient but growing mercy ; and, finally, mercy triumphant and ferocity all but extinct.

In this rude and terrible way Jacob was driven out of Shechem. For the third time in his history he is a fugitive from his home. But though the expulsion came through his sons, there was a needful lesson from heaven for himself. Jacob's dull ears at last heard the divine voice calling him to Bethel. He awoke to a sense of the carnal, self-seeking spirit in which he had been living ; felt, doubtless, that the first thing he ought to have done was to rear an altar to God there ; and proceeded at once to fulfil his neglected duty. The experience of Shechem showed him that the pure service of God must have a more prominent place in his heart and in his life. Perhaps he had never till now told his family of the vow he had made at Bethel some thirty years before.

But even before they go up to Bethel there is a duty to God to be performed from which they must not flinch. Contrary to all that prevailed among the heathen, the worship claimed by his God was an undivided worship. There must not be the faintest recognition of other gods. All the objects and images of idolatry, therefore, must be surrendered and destroyed. The order to this effect was given, and, strange to say, it was readily obeyed. When his sons had had time to think of their crime, they were stricken with terror for the vengeance of their neighbours, and were thus the more ready to obey their father. All the images and the ear-rings which they had worn openly were surrendered and buried under a well-known oak in Shechem. If the ear-rings had been mere ornaments, their surrender would have been unnecessary; but probably they bore figures of the heathen gods, or some symbols of their power, and it was an evidence of the concern of the family for past unfaithfulness that they were so readily given up. The whole family, male and female, had got a fright at the wicked rashness of Simeon and Levi. But God remembered his covenant, especially in this hour of penitence: "the terror of God was upon the cities that were round about them, and they did not pursue after the sons of Jacob."

The altar was built at Bethel, and the name of the God of their fathers invoked, in tardy fulfilment of Jacob's vow. But another affliction befell them: a beloved servant of the family died—Deborah, Rebekah's nurse. There is no room in Genesis to dwell on her virtues, but the fact that she is mentioned in the history at all is a great testimony to her worth; and the name given to the oak under which she was buried, Allon-bachuth (the Oak of Weeping), shows that she was one of those faithful women who take a deep hold on the hearts of a family, and when they die, cannot be thought of without tears.

But the death of Deborah was but a prelude to a further and deeper sorrow. Bethel seems to have been found by Jacob, as it had been by Abraham, insufficient for the permanent pasture of his flocks and herds; so that, like Abraham, he was induced to move on in the direction of Hebron and Beersheba. The company had passed the heights of Jerusalem, and were come near to Bethlehem, when "Rachel travailed, and had hard labour." In giving life to Benjamin she lost her own. She would have named him Benoni (the Son of my Sorrow); but his father, not desiring him to bear a name so ominous, called him Benjamin (the Son of my Right Hand). Rachel had been Jacob's right hand—affectionate, faithful, and helpful; and the name of her son perpetuated the memory of her life.

With what feelings Jacob buried Rachel we may easily conceive. To him Bethlehem was ever after associated with the

gloom of death : to how many, in after ages, has it been associated
with the joy of life! It was not merely the pillar which he placed
over the tomb of Rachel that served to keep her memory alive.
Though in the after distribution of the country Bethlehem fell to
the share of Judah, Jerusalem was in Benjamin's lot, and there,
in after ages, the memory of Rachel as a warm-hearted mother
continued to be cherished; for when the prophet Jeremiah drew
his frightful picture of the massacre which Nebuchadnezzar was
to inflict, by a fine poetic figure he introduced Rachel weeping for
her children, and refusing to be comforted, while Matthew, in his
Gospel, repeated the figure in connection with the massacre of the
babes of Bethlehem. In a wild and solitary spot there rises at
this day a small square building, surmounted by a dome which
bears the name of Rachel's tomb. It cannot be the pillar reared
by Jacob, but in all likelihood it marks the place of her burial,
the spot where one of the deepest wounds he ever suffered was
inflicted on the heart that had loved her so well, and had deemed
his heaviest labours and troubles light for her sake. Why
Rachel's bones were not laid in the cave of Machpelah, which was
but twelve miles further on, we are not told. Possibly Jacob was
uncertain whether he would get access to it; more likely it was
because Rachel was not his first wife, and therefore not entitled
to be buried in the family tomb. The privilege was conferred on
Leah.

We may hope that this sore trial, added to all that had gone
before, was not unproductive of spiritual benefit, but served to
chasten and purify Jacob's heart. We cannot but feel deeply for
him now, in an experience which has very often been repeated.
When he has got what he has been so eager for—got back to the
scenes of his youth, which for many long years it had been the
height of his desire to visit—and when he might have reasonably
looked for a time of peace and enjoyment, his deepest trials only
begin. What was all that he suffered from Laban compared to
the heart-bitterness that came on him now? And bruised as his
heart was, a further pang was inflicted on him by the profligate
and unnatural vice of his eldest son. The stern moral purity of

TAYLOR

RACHEL'S TOMB.

*Page 234.*

Abraham and Isaac, and we may say of Jacob too, is disappearing; here already is the second flagrant deed of lust among Jacob's children. If no strong testimony is borne to purity, and no standard lifted up against vice, the seed of Abraham will soon become as corrupt as any. It is manifest that the family, as well as Jacob himself, are needing chastening; but God will take his own way to effect his purpose.

Meanwhile Jacob reaches Hebron—how many years after his flight we can hardly say—and finds his father still alive. No hint is given as to what took place at the meeting of father and son after the long separation; nor have we even a glimpse of Jacob's feelings on returning to the place of his birth and the scenes of his youth. Everything was changed, and he was changed himself. Rebekah seems to have been some time dead; and it could not be long after his return that Isaac too passed away, full of years, and leaving behind him a memory fragrant with the odour of gentleness and goodness.

The scene at the death of Abraham is renewed—Jacob and Esau bury their father in the cave of Machpelah. The old sores are not reopened; the brothers are content to follow the lines marked out for them. They return to their vocations with that feeling which the death of the last survivor of a generation makes so vivid—the sense one has of being now in the foremost rank in the march of life, and the next, as things usually go, to pay the debt of nature and be gathered to one's fathers.

## CHAPTER IV.

### JOSEPH'S YOUTH AND CAPTIVITY.

#### (GEN. xxxvii., xxxix.-xli.)

WITH grown-up sons to take the burden of the flocks, Jacob could now lead a quieter life, directing the operations of the family from within, and withdrawing from the toil and exposure which made his Haran life so hard. Nearly seventeen years had now elapsed since he left Laban, so that even Joseph might at least accompany some of his elder brethren, and bear a part in the care of the flocks. It was with the sons of Bilhah and Zilpah that Joseph associated chiefly—possibly because there was more jealousy between the families of Leah and Rachel, or rather, perhaps, because the sons of Leah were known to be wild (see ch. xxxiv. 25, xxxv. 22, and xxxviii. 15). But if Jacob thought that Bilhah's and Zilpah's sons were better, the report of them that Joseph brought showed him to be mistaken. Jacob was very unlike Abraham in one thing—in his inability to impress his sons with his own views and character. It is easy to account for this: Abraham on the whole was consistent, unselfish, and upright; while Jacob, trying often to serve two masters, did not seem thoroughly sincere. Even in those distant times that subtle source of unbelief was in full play which is so active in our own time—inconsistency, selfishness, and worldliness on the part of prominent champions of the truth.

It was not unnatural for Jacob to have a special affection for Joseph, not only because he was the son of his old age, nor even because he was the son of Rachel, but because that interesting mixture of grace and talent which afterwards shone out in him so remarkably, and which was such a contrast to the coarseness of his brothers, had won his heart, and had knit the souls of father and son into a wonderful unity. But surely it was not wise to show his partiality so openly, and especially by such a token as the coat of many colours. For this kind of garment was a sign of great distinction, and was not worn by the ordinary members of a family. The work was done elaborately with the needle, patches or threads of various colours being sewn or embroidered on the plainer robe, as we read how the attendants of Sisera's mother assured her, when impatient for her son's return, that he was coming with "a prey of divers colours, a prey of divers colours of needlework, of divers colours of needlework on both sides, meet for the necks of them that take the spoil." Already, in the eyes of his brethren, Joseph was silently recognized as above themselves, and hated accordingly. Their hatred and jealousy were deepened yet more by the dreams which he not very prudently, but probably with a measure of boyish pride, if not with some presentiment of the truth, made known to his brethren—how their sheaves stood round his sheaf, and the eleven stars made obeisance to him. But the deepest cause of their hatred, although they might not let themselves think it, was the conviction that in character Joseph was better than they. His ingenuous frankness, his chaste spirit and pure life, due in some measure, we may hope, to Rachel's teaching and influence, were a perpetual rebuke to their license, and always roused a dissatisfied and intolerant feeling against him. Some have blamed Joseph for carrying the evil report of his brethren to their father. But if there was a deep sympathy between Joseph and his father, it would have been impossible for him to keep back anything in which he was deeply interested. The anguish of heart caused by their coarse, unscrupulous wickedness may have been overwhelming and peculiarly distressing to the youngest of them all; for, as has been well said, while "an elder brother, if he will, may more effectually guard the innocence of a younger brother than any other relative can, he can also inflict a more exquisite torture." Possibly Joseph thought that the best thing he could do for his erring brethren was to let their father know how they were living; for young persons are apt to believe in something like the omnipotence of parental influence, and to suppose that if only the parents know what is wrong, it will be sure to be put right. It is only experience that teaches us what a task it often is for parents to move the hearts and control the habits of their sons.

The elder sons had gone to Shechem to pasture their flocks. One would have thought it the last place they would have cared to go to; but Shechem was a wide district, and they would not necessarily come into contact with the families of the men they had massacred. On the other hand, we learn from Eastern writers that even after massacres, tribal feuds, like the quarrels of children, are often quickly healed. Believing his brethren to be in that neighbourhood (about three days' march from Hebron), Jacob, thinking it well that Joseph should have an errand of kindness to them, sent him to inquire after their welfare. But they had gone northwards to Dothan, and Joseph followed them thither. In the clear air of the East, his brethren recognized him while yet at a considerable distance—perhaps because he was conspicuous for the coat of many colours. We get an awful glimpse of their wickedness in their cold-blooded conspiracy to put him to death. Neither his youth, nor his being their brother, nor his being the comfort of their father's old age, could stem their passion. Reuben was more merciful, in outward form at least, but hardly in fact; he would have had him starved to death in an empty pit—one of the reservoirs for water, common in the country, that had run dry. Pits of this kind exist to this day, sometimes with a narrow mouth, while the sides bulge out like those of a wide jar or carboy, defying all the efforts of any one who may fall in, or be driven in, to escape. To such a pit Joseph was consigned; whether to that which is called Gib Youssouf (the Pit of Joseph), at this day, or another, we do not know, and need hardly inquire. "In such a place he was left to die—under the ground, sinking in the mire, his flesh creeping at the touch of unseen slimy creatures, in darkness, alone; that is to say, in a species of confinement which tames the most reckless and maddens the best balanced spirits, which shakes the nerve of the calmest, and has sometimes left the blankness of idiocy in masculine understandings. A few wild cries, that ring painfully round his prison, show him he need expect no help from without; a few wild and desperate beatings round the shelving walls of rock show him there is no possibility of escape. He covers his face, or casts himself on the floor of his dungeon to escape within himself; but only to find this also in vain, and to rise and renew efforts he knows to be fruitless. Here, then, is what is come of his fine dreams. With shame he now remembers the beaming confidence with which he had related them; with bitterness he thinks of the bright life above him, from which these few feet cut him so absolutely off, and of the quick termination that has been put to all his hopes." *

But soon a new experience would come. "No doubt he would think of Isaac and Isaac's God, till between himself and the impenetrable dungeon walls the everlasting arms seemed to interpose, and through the darkness of his death-like solitude the face of Jacob's God appeared to beam upon him; and he came to feel, what we must by some extremity all be made to feel, that it was not in this world's life but in God he lived, that nothing could befall him which God did not will, and that what God had for him to do God would enable him to do."

But even the most reckless men cannot do deeds of this kind without some compunction, for "conscience makes cowards of us all." The appeal of anguish which Joseph made to his brothers, and to which they would not listen, haunted them ever after, and flashed with lurid vividness into their memory some twenty years later, when their own lives were trembling in the balance (Gen. xlii. 21). Probably some twitch of this kind induced them to listen to the proposal of Judah to sell him as a slave for twenty pieces of silver to a travelling company of Ishmaelites, or Midianites, that happened to be passing along. Reuben, who had been absent at the time, returning to the pit, and finding that Joseph was not there, was in great trouble, and showed more emotion

* Marcus Dods, D.D., "Expositor's Bible."

than we should have expected : he rent his clothes. The necessity of pacifying his father had come home to him, as the eldest brother, as well perhaps as the magnitude of the crime—or perhaps timidity had restrained him from avowing his feeling before the rest; but now he was in despair. The clumsy device resorted to in order to deceive Jacob—dipping his son's coat in blood, and making him believe that he had been torn in pieces—was just a new application of the deceiving policy which Jacob had practised to Isaac. In this case the effects were overwhelmingly tragical : Jacob's heart was broken, he refused to be comforted, the remainder of his life seemed wrapped in darkness, nothing remained for him but a dismal journey to the tomb.

The trading company to whom Joseph was sold is said in one place to have been Ishmaelites and in another Midianites. They must have been of mixed origin, Ishmaelites and Midianites preponderating; some of them probably cousins of Joseph himself. Dothan was on one of the highways between Syria and Egypt, and even at this day it would be by no means remarkable to see a caravan on the same route, conveying merchandise to Egypt. We recognize the suitableness of the articles for Egyptian purposes—spices and myrrh for embalmment, balm or frankincense for the temples. Joseph's brethren, of course, would not make known his family to the traders ; and for himself, it was needless to do so. Money had been paid for him, and more money, if possible, must be made out of him. Who he was would make no difference in a commercial point of view ; the only consideration was how to get the best price for him.

That there was something superior about him—a gentleness and refinement above the calling of shepherds that fitted him for the higher grades of slave-service—may be inferred from his being purchased as a house-servant by Potiphar, captain of the guard to Pharaoh. Whatever anguish he may have suffered in being dragged from his home and sold into slavery, the natural elasticity of youth, the healthful buoyancy of his nature, and the fellowship with God which he had learned to enjoy, enabled him to adapt himself with wonderful equanimity to his new situation. The

(393) 16

Lord was with him, as his master saw, and made all that he did
to prosper in his hand.   He was the true representative of Abraham and Isaac, a true child of Abraham in the faith as well as
according to the flesh ; and captive though he was, all that he did
was marked by that outward prosperity which in those days was
the usual token of divine approval and blessing.

An episode in the life of Judah, Jacob's fourth son, which
comes in at this point of the sacred narrative, is one which it is
most painful to dwell on ; but it is introduced, in the truthful
and honest spirit of the Bible, for an important purpose.   Judah,
regardless of the spirit of Abraham's solemn charge to his servant,
not to fetch a wife to his son from the daughters of the Canaanites, regardless, too, of the example of Esau, whose Hittite wives
were a grief of mind to Isaac and Rebekah, had married a daughter of Shuah, a Canaanite.   It is to give us a picture of Canaanite profligacy, and the shameful results of such connection, even
on one who was well brought up, that the narrative of Judah's
wickedness is introduced.   An additional touch of horror is thrown
over the picture in the margin of the Revised Version by the
literal rendering of the term which denotes the supposed calling of
the woman seen by Judah sitting at the wayside—*kedesha*, " a
temple harlot "—indicating a class of women devoted to lust in
connection with religion, and thus marking the lowest point to
which it is possible for religion to descend.

Painful though the narrative is, it is full of instruction.   In
the first place, it vindicates the purpose of God to sweep away
those Canaanites from the face of the earth.   When people come
to regard the vilest profligacy as an act of divine service, it is plain
that they have corrupted religion beyond recovery ; the salt has
lost its savour, the moral sense is overwhelmed ; there is nothing
left for the moral Ruler but to sweep such a community away.
Further, we see a good reason why the descendants of Abraham
should be removed for a long period from a country which was
now exerting on them so pernicious an influence.   In Egypt there
was much profligacy, but family life was on the whole purer than
in Canaan.   The first three generations—Abraham, Isaac, and

Jacob—had kept themselves pure; but the fourth was evidently acquiring the prevailing taint of the country. It needed to be broken off from the vile habits it was forming, and started anew on a more wholesome footing. In particular Judah, who was the strongest man of the older brothers, and to whom a splendid *rôle* was to be given in the future history of the country, who was also an heir of promise, needed some strong, uncompromising discipline to turn him from the course on which he had entered so thoughtlessly when he allied himself by marriage to the Canaanites. Judah appears at this time to have broken away from his brothers and set up an establishment of his own in the midst of the heathen. His moral danger was therefore most imminent. He seems to have allowed himself the license of the country; and had he not been plucked by a strong hand out of the fire, he would have probably sunk in the mire, and become as bad as the Canaanites themselves. The great truth that had already been made plain in the national history had to be specially demonstrated in his case—that it was not nature but grace that made him heir to the blessing.

We now follow the fortunes of Joseph to Egypt. Potiphar, his master, was captain of the guard, or captain of the executioners—that is, he was employed to execute the sentences against offenders, on which account he seems to have had control of the prisons. It is specially said of him that he was an Egyptian, which would have been a superfluous piece of information had the population of Egypt been all of one race. We shall afterwards see the significance of the fact that Potiphar was of the old nationality. It is not certainly known in what city of Egypt Potiphar dwelt. Tradition has fixed on On, called by the Greeks Heliopolis (the City of the Sun), as the scene alike of Abraham's visit to Egypt, of Joseph's captivity, and of the education if not the birth of Moses. Others, and with more apparent probability, regard Zoan or Tanis, near the land of Goshen, as the abode of Pharaoh (see after, page 270).

The first picture in Joseph's Egyptian life is a pleasant one, everything in Potiphar's house prospering on his account—a prosperity which we are not to ascribe wholly to supernatural causes, but rather to the superior qualities which he brought to his work. For among other abilities that seem to have been hereditary, we must reckon that remarkable talent for the orderly and successful conduct of business which has now become proverbial in the Jewish race. It is a quality that stands opposed alike to carelessness and to fitfulness in work; it implies a power of fixing attention earnestly on the whole work to be done, planning wisely how to do it, and applying oneself steadily to it, until all is accomplished. It is usually accompanied by a placid temper and a calm demeanour. How much Abraham excelled in it is apparent from the success with which he performed all his undertakings, especially his expedition for the rescue of Lot, sudden and unusual though it was. Of Jacob's turn for business we have ample proof, apart altogether from the craft and cunning which he often brought to bear on it. Evidently Joseph inherited the talent, but in connection with a more unselfish purpose and a more equable temper than his father. There is little inducement to a slave usually to devote himself very energetically to his work. Joseph's spirit was not broken by his grievous trial, and the force of conscience was evidently strong in him, with an unselfish desire to do what he could to further the welfare of his master's household. If to this we add a habit of prayer, a consciousness that God's eye was ever on him, and a resolute desire to please God as the highest reward to which he could aspire, we shall understand the principles on which his work was done, and the blessing with which it was crowned.

But no Eden can remain long unvisited by the serpent. The form in which it came to Joseph and desolated his paradise was peculiarly trying, because his ruin had its origin in his immovable fidelity. We may believe it was no ordinary temptation when day after day the mistress of the house, " expert in amorous arts," came to spread the net, with every allurement which her skill and her passion could devise. We may conceive how even Joseph might be moved by the thought that, slave though he was, he had attracted the admiration of a woman of such rank, and how the vision might flit before him that through her influence he might recover his liberty and in a bright career realize his dreams after all. We can understand how the abounding sensuality of his native land and the lax morality of Egypt might blunt his early horror of sensual sin. How beautiful the spirit that at one stroke sweeps every form of temptation from his path with the thought, "My master hath put all that he hath into my hand; neither hath he kept back anything but thee, because thou art his wife: how then can I do this great wickedness, and sin against God?" How beautifully does he combine gratitude to man with loyalty to God, and challenge the possibility of his dashing through such a two-fold barrier to sin! It is the aspect of the sin as ingratitude to Potiphar that he chiefly dwells on—what would be emphatically *his* sin. As a slave, it would not have been his part to remonstrate with his mistress on account of *her* sin, or to wound her self-respect more than was requisite to vindicate himself. Joseph knows well the maddening effect which his refusal will have on the disappointed woman; her passion may turn in a twinkling to rage, calumny, and revenge.

Coming as Joseph did from a country notorious for licentiousness, there might seem some probability in the charge which she brought elaborately against him; though, on the other hand, it must have been strange to Potiphar that a slave, and one, too, who was so exemplary and dutiful, should have been guilty of such insane presumption. That he did not at once order him to a capital punishment, even though his wrath was kindled, could only be because he had not the power of putting slaves to death. Joseph was probably detained for trial at some future time. At first his punishment seems to have been very severe. The rehearsal in the 105th Psalm says that "his feet they hurt with fetters; he was laid in iron," or as it is in the margin, "his soul came into iron."

Yet in this new affliction, as in the past, his cheerful self-composure does not desert him. He accepts this as he had accepted his former humiliations, as coming from the hand of God, and as designed for a gracious end. And what is very wonderful, he submits in silence to his punishment and his disgrace, though a single word uttered to Potiphar revealing the truth about his wife might have turned the tables on her and set him free. It is because Potiphar has trusted him and been kind to him that he restrains himself from so much as hinting to him the real state of the matter; he will not vex a man to whom he owes kindness. How inimitable this generous self-control!

It was not long before his capacity and trustworthiness became known to the jailer. The rigour of his bondage was relaxed; the jailer obtained his help in the prison, and in this new capacity the old blessing attended him. Ere long the whole charge of the prison was committed to him; its nominal keeper was left free to indulge or amuse himself as he pleased, without thought or trouble about prison affairs. It seemed a strange and most incongruous situation for Joseph, yet doubtless it was most useful for him in view of his future employment. He would gain an amount of knowledge of the laws and ways of the country and the character of the people which would be of the greatest use to him when at last, at a moment's notice, he became the governor of the country.

On an Egyptian papyrus a story has been found somewhat parallel to that of Joseph, entitled the "Story of the Two Brothers." Anepu, a married man, while in the fields, sends his younger brother on an errand to his house. While engaged in attending to the message, he is solicited by the wife of Anepu, as Joseph was by the wife of Potiphar. He replies:—" 'Thou, O woman, hast been like a mother to me, and thy husband like a father; for he is older than I, for he might have been my father. Why this great sin that thou hast spoken to me? Say it not to me another time, then will I not tell it this time, and no word of it shall come out of my heart to any man at all.' In the evening, when Anepu returns, he finds his wife in great apparent trouble, and when the cause is asked, she says that the younger brother has made dishonourable proposals to her." *

Meanwhile, under Joseph's management, two distinguished officers of Pharaoh's household are committed to prison, the chief

* Brugsch's "Egypt under the Pharaohs."

of the butlers or cup-bearers, and the chief of the bakers or confec-
tioners. According to a Jewish tradition, they had been found
guilty of a plot to poison the king; but if this had been true, they
would probably have been dealt with in a more summary way.
Herodotus says that the culture of the vine was not known in
Egypt. But the statement is erroneous, as some things in Herodotus himself show; and besides this, the monuments bear abundant
evidence that the cultivation of the vine and the art of making
wine were well known from a very early time. Both prisoners
seem to have been on intimate terms with Joseph, and from both
of them he might derive much valuable information respecting the
royal household and the character and aspirations of the king and
his court.

On the same night each of these officers had a dream which
they both regarded as prophetic of coming events, but being unable
to find a key to the meaning in the morning, both looked sad and
disconcerted. It was impossible that Joseph should not be reminded of his own dreams. As yet these had proved but vanity
and vexation of spirit; and had Joseph been a man of hasty temper,
he would have laughed at the dreams of Pharaoh's servants as
nonsense, and at the dreamers as fools. But his own unfavourable
experience had not disturbed his faith in dreams, nor in his God as
able to interpret them. "Tell it me, I pray you," he said to each
of them, in the hope that God would enable him to solve the
riddle. In the dream of the butler, there appeared a vine with
three branches, on which, with that disregard of time which is so
common in dreams, the buds at once became blossoms, and the
blossoms clusters of grapes, and the grapes were squeezed by the
butler into a cup and given to Pharaoh. Joseph was able to
interpret that in three days the butler would be restored to his
office; and to this information the very reasonable request was
added that, when restored, the butler would think of Joseph, and
represent to Pharaoh the double wrong which made him an inmate
of the prison. The baker's dream was similar, and no doubt he
looked for a similar interpretation; but it turned out very different.
After three days it was the doom of the baker to be hanged, and in

his case the horror of death would be aggravated by the fate of his body after it,—it was to be torn and devoured by the birds of the air. Thus early was that remarkable saying of our Lord exemplified which has had so many fulfilments throughout the world's history : " One shall be taken, and the other left." Pharaoh's birthday happening three days afterwards, both inter-pretations were verified. But no relief came to Joseph. The chief butler was too full of his own good fortune to have any thoughts to spare for his Hebrew fellow-prisoner. Another saying, recorded afterwards (Eccles. ix. 15), was fulfilled by an-ticipation : " Now there was found in the city a poor wise man, and he by his wisdom delivered the city ; yet no man remem-bered that same poor man." For full two years more Joseph remained wasting his youth, as it seemed, in an Egyptian dungeon.

But " the longest lane has its turning," and the captivity of Joseph came at last to an end. And now it became clear that in keeping him in bondage during these two weary years, God was doing for him the best thing possible, because the upshot was in-finitely more in his favour than anything which the chief butler could have secured if he had remembered him. It was now Pharaoh's turn to have a prophetic dream. On the bank of the Nile, the one river of Egypt, there came up out of the river seven well-conditioned kine, that fed " in the meadow,"—literally, " in the reed grass," which, though it has now disappeared, we know to have been then very abundant on the edge of the river. Seven lean kine followed, which devoured the fat cows, without becom-ing any the fatter. To see the full significance of the symbol, we must bear in mind the sacredness of the cow in the Egyptian religion. A second dream changed the cows into ears of corn ; first, seven full and good ears appeared on one stalk, followed by seven empty and blasted. It was manifest to Pharaoh that the dream was supernatural and prophetic ; but none of his wise men —the order of Egyptians that devoted themselves to magic and astrology—were able to show what it meant.

Now was Joseph's time. The chief butler at last remembered

the Hebrew prisoner who had explained his dream, and Joseph was sent for from the prison. It was a strange place for Pharaoh to find a royal counsellor. Hastily Joseph changed his prison dress and shaved himself; for though, as a Hebrew, he had let his beard grow long, the Egyptian practice was to cut it close. On coming into Pharaoh's presence, before even hearing his narrative, he at once disclaimed all power to interpret of himself; God only could remove Pharaoh's anxiety. Then, on hearing both dreams, he declared them to have the same signification, as indications from God to Pharaoh of what was about to happen. The explanation which he gave of the double symbol—as denoting seven years of plenty to be followed by seven years of famine—was so natural, so simple, so satisfactory, as to bear internal evidence of its truth. And the advice that followed was as manifestly sound as the explanation was true. Let proper arrangements be made for storing the surplus during the years of plenty, so as to meet the deficiency when the years of want should follow. Let some fit man be appointed to superintend the whole process, with others under him to attend to the details.

Joseph's advice was admirable to Pharaoh; he resolved at once to follow it. And not less decided was his conclusion to make Joseph himself the superintending officer. In the glow of his gratitude, and with some shame perhaps that a man like Joseph should have been the inmate of a dungeon during so many years, the king now constitutes him the second ruler in his kingdom, and presents him with all the insignia of office. " He is invested with the golden chain or necklace, as with an order, exactly according to the investiture of the royal officers, as represented in the Theban sculptures. He is clothed in the white robe of sacred state, that appears in such marked contrast on the tawny figures of the ancient priests. He bears the royal ring, such as are still found in the royal sepulchres. He rides in the royal chariot that is seen so often rolling its solemn way in the monumental processions. Before him goes the cry of an Egyptian shout (*Abrech !*), evidently resembling those which now in the streets of Cairo clear the way for any great personage through the crowded masses of man and beast."* Never had there been so sudden a change from a dungeon to a chair of state, from absolute slavery to dominion over an empire. And Joseph might now see quite plainly that all his trials, all his unjust treatment, all his shameful experience of evil, were necessary links, divinely planned, in the chain of his advancement. If he had not been sold into Egypt, if he had not been sentenced to the dungeon, if the chief butler had not forgotten him, if he had not been still a prisoner when Pharaoh dreamt his dream, he would not have been called before him, nor have had the opportunity to reveal what was about to happen. If ever, during the long years of his unjust captivity, he was disposed to blame God for his hard fate, how eagerly would all such complaints be recalled in this moment of triumph ! If he was enabled all the time to cherish that patient faith of his fathers Abraham and Isaac, but hardly Jacob, how would he feel himself rewarded for his patient waiting, and bless God, who, in his own time, ever shows himself the avenger of the oppressed, and never forsakes any that put their trust in him ! It is interesting to mark the complete and sudden *dénouement* of God's plans. We see many instances of this in the schemes of providence, and it is a great encouragement to patient waiting, for the reward may be as sudden as complete.

One cannot pass from this chapter of history without remarking the significance of dreams. Three times in the narrative this is pressed on our attention. The early dreams of Joseph were symbolical of his coming exaltation. The dreams of the butler and the baker prefigured their respective fates. And now the dream of Pharaoh indicates a remarkable series of events in the history of his kingdom, and enables him to make timely preparation for them. That these dreams were really supernatural intimations of the divine will can be doubted by no one who believes in the supernatural power of God, and in the events of Scripture history as forming a supernatural revelation of his will. That God was pleased at certain times so to influence the thoughts of men during sleep as to convey to them supernatural knowledge, all must

* Stanley's "Jewish Church."

acknowledge who accept the Bible as the inspired record of his will. The instances of such dreams are far too numerous to be accounted for in any other way.

It is a more difficult question whether God does not sometimes convey supernatural knowledge in this way still. Admitting that men of superstitious temperament are morbidly prone to multiply instances of supernatural communications, and admitting also a fact, which recent inquiries have emphasized, that very seldom do we possess an authentic record of prophetic dreams made before the date of their fulfilment, nevertheless we cannot deny that there have been dreams too remarkable to be accounted for by natural causes. But in such cases we find certain peculiar features that take the dream out of the category of common events. The great minuteness of the impression, or the repetition of precisely the same dream twice or oftener, or some other circumstance that baffles all ordinary explanation, may stamp on the dream such a character that no one can help regarding it as an abnormal event.

And thus, at last, Joseph's patient continuance in well-doing was rewarded. He had not had the same specific promises made to him as his fathers, for his was not the line of the promised seed; he had only the assurance God gave to them, that he would be a God to them and to their seed after them. As the narrative goes, we have no such notices of Joseph's personal communion with God as we have of Abraham's or of Jacob's. We have no record of a single prayer. But what we have shows very clearly that Joseph had the same belief as they in God's personality, and in his interest in all that concerns his children. It was Joseph's God that gave Pharaoh the key to his dream; it was he that showed Pharaoh what he was about to do. It was he whom Joseph had such a horror of offending when temptation came on him in the house of Potiphar. Personal attachment to the living God is as much the key of Joseph's conduct as it is of theirs. It was no strange thing that he too should have his severe trials, or that his faith and patience should be tested like theirs. Perhaps there was in him, naturally too, as the favourite child of his father, a certain tendency to think of himself more highly than he ought, which needed to be subdued. But the stern discipline of his youth enabled him to bear his honours, when they came so suddenly, with admirable calmness. His withstanding of temptation, his calm endurance of wrong, his silence as to Potiphar's wife, and his faithfulness in every duty, constituted a noble victory —one of the noblest in Scripture.

> " Heaven thus early tried his youth,
> His faith, his patience, and his truth;
> And sent him here through hard assays
> With a crown of deathless praise."

## CHAPTER V.

JOSEPH RULER OF EGYPT——VISITS OF HIS BRETHREN.

(GEN. xli.-xlv.)

THE entrance of Joseph into Egypt as a slave must have greatly impaired the interest which such a country was fitted to awaken in a youthful and intelligent mind. The change from the rude simplicity of Canaan to the refinement and elaborate monuments of Egypt would indeed have been most striking, if he had had the opportunity to observe it as other men. The children of Ham had a wonderful skill in the arts of construction, and in all that tended to make human life civilized and refined. Already, in all likelihood, the Great Pyramid reared its vast form in the plain of Gizeh, and temples, tombs, and other works of elaborate design and workmanship arrested attention on every side. It was a new experience for Joseph—something, as has been said, like that which greeted the northern nations in the Roman capital. But to a slave confined in a prison—and prisons or dungeons in those days were not like the model prisons of modern times—the existence of numberless works of great beauty and interest around him, which he could not see, was fitted only to make his situation more irksome, and with a less patient nature than Joseph's would have caused him to chafe the more, and, like an imprisoned bird, dash himself fiercely against the bars of his cage.

But now Joseph is released, and everything is changed. And Joseph shows a wonderful power of accommodating himself to his new situation. He was not like the French prisoner who had

spent so many years in the Bastile that, when at last he was liber-
ated, everything around him was so strange that he besought the
jailer to take him back to the place which long familiarity had
made to him something like a home.   It is a wonder indeed to
find one whose horizon hitherto had been so contracted—who had
been used to nothing greater than the management of flocks in
Canaan, and of houses and prisons in Egypt—able to take a comprehensive view of the needs of an empire for years to come, and
to form his plans accordingly.   Joseph, we see again, must have
had a marvellous talent for the transaction of business, and a remarkable degree of that power of adaptation to the circumstances
of other nations which has enabled the Jews, in subsequent ages,
to live and flourish in every country of the globe, and even to
accumulate wealth where the native population has been hardly
able to live.

It was with almost absolute power that Joseph was intrusted
by Pharaoh.   There is not a hint that he abused his power.
During the years of plenty he occupied himself in building storehouses in the suburbs of every city in the land.   His marriage to
Asenath, daughter of the priest of On, was followed by the birth
of two sons, Manasseh and Ephraim, whose names were symbolic
of his banishment on the one hand, and his prosperity on the
other.   The grateful reference which he makes to God as the
author of his remarkable lot indicates that, like his great-grand-
father in Chaldæa, he continued faithful in the service and worship of the one true God.

At last the famine came.   Famine in Egypt is so rare, even
when it prevails in neighbouring countries, that its occurrence has
always been marked as a specially memorable event.   The failure
of rain in the upper regions of the river is the only cause from
which it can spring.   In one of the ancient monuments mention
is made of a somewhat similar famine.   In a tomb at El Kab, in
Upper Egypt, the tomb of one Baba, there is an inscription which
Brugsch holds to belong to the seventeenth dynasty.   Baba gives
an excellent account of himself, of his mildness, of his benevolence,
and his prosperity.   Then he adds: "I collected the harvest, a

THE GREAT PYRAMID AND SPHINX.

Page 252.

friend of the harvest-god; I was watchful at the time of sowing; and now, when a famine arose, lasting many years, I issued out corn to each city, lasting many years." The conjecture of Brugsch

is, that at the time when Joseph was acting as steward and administrator in the Delta, Baba was employed in like manner in Upper Egypt, either under Joseph, or under a king of another dynasty, then ruling that part of the land.

In more recent times, famine has been very rare in Egypt. "Twice only, in the eleventh and twelfth centuries of the Christian era, such a calamity

STORING GRAIN IN ANCIENT EGYPT.

is described by Arabian historians in terms which give us a full conception of the calamity from which Joseph delivered the country. The first lasted, like that of the time of Joseph, for seven years; of the other the most fearful details are given by an eye-witness......'The poor ate carrion, corpses, and dogs. They went further, devouring even little children......As for the number of the poor who perished from hunger and exhaustion, God alone knows what it was......A traveller often passed through a large village without seeing a single inhabitant......The road between Syria and Egypt was like a vast field sown with human bodies, or rather like a plain that has just been swept by the scythe of the mower. It had become as a banquet-hall for the birds, wild beasts, and dogs which gorged on their flesh.'"*

Such were the horrors from which Joseph delivered not only the people of Egypt but those of neighbouring lands. "When all the land of Egypt was famished, the people cried to Pharaoh for bread: and Pharaoh said unto the Egyptians, Go unto Joseph; what he saith to you, do. And the famine was over all the face of the earth: and Joseph opened all the storehouses, and sold unto the Egyptians; and the famine waxed sore in the land of Egypt. And all countries came into Egypt to Joseph for to buy corn; because that the famine was so sore in all lands."

* Stanley's "Jewish Church."

Thus it was that the sons of Jacob went down to Egypt to buy corn. Whether, being married men and heads of families, they had by this time gone off, like Judah, to form establishments of their own, or whether they were still living in one patriarchal encampment, we do not know; but the authority of their father was still acknowledged when he told them to go down to Egypt and procure a supply of food. It is strange to think of them travelling along the same caravan route by which the Ishmaelites had taken Joseph, and arriving at the city to which he had come as a slave, and where he was now reigning as a prince. We mark a great difference in respect of language. Abraham could converse with the king of Sodom, and Jacob with his uncle and cousins at Haran; Melchizedek, Chedorlaomer, Eliezer of Damascus, and Rebekah and Rachel, when they came to Canaan, seem to have had no trouble about language; but the speech of Canaan requires an interpreter to be understood in Egypt. And this may probably explain how it happened that Jacob's sons had never had even a hint that the new ruler of Egypt was originally from their country. However he may have accommodated himself in dress, manners, and speech to the Egyptians, traditions of his marvellous history could not fail to be still afloat; and in his worship of the God of his fathers we should fain hope Joseph still made plain the difference between him and the people of the land. Being strangers and foreigners, and unaccompanied by their wives, they could hear little or nothing of the gossip of the place. Intent on one thing only, they limited their intercourse to the one matter of business.

It seems to have been the rule that strangers applying for supplies should appear personally before Joseph, and the ten brethren came and bowed themselves before him with their faces to the earth. Could the ruler of Egypt help a grim smile as he thought of his dream—the sheaves coming round about and doing obeisance to his sheaf?

It certainly was no freak of despotism that made him assume a rough demeanour, and accuse them of being spies, for his heart was as tender as a child's (ver. 24), but a desire to find out their real character, and especially to know how they would now act

(393)     17

when one of their number was in trouble. Do we not find a suggestion of the craft of the family in his scheme for bringing out their character? First, he must give them all a taste of the prison, confining them for three days, and threatening to keep them all there till one of them should go up and return with their youngest brother. Then, as they had somewhat mitigated his doom when instead of killing him they sold him, he relaxes theirs, permitting the nine to return, and keeping but one, Simeon, in bondage. (Was Reuben, the eldest, passed over because it was he that said, "Let us not take his life"?) How it was that in this season of distress they recalled their own treatment of Joseph, and especially the cruelty that refused to listen to his cry of anguish, can only be explained on the supposition that their crime, during all the long interval, had hovered like a restless ghost about their consciences, and ever came up to accuse and terrify them in times of trouble. The condition of Simeon in their absence is to be no mere pretence of imprisonment; he is bound before their eyes with just such fetters as those by which Joseph had been himself confined.

Then the nine take their sorrowful journey homewards. And on opening their sacks and finding their money in the sack's mouth, they know not whether to be pleased or terrified. At length they reach home and tell all to Jacob. And Jacob does not relieve the situation. He protests that he will never allow Benjamin to go to Egypt. Thus the brethren have saved their lives, but they have brought a new burden on their minds. The remembrance of Simeon's fetters cannot be got rid of. Jacob is immovable in his protestation that he will never let Benjamin go down. How shall they ever be extricated from this trouble?

But when famine places men in its fearful grip, few resolutions formed in easier times can stand out against it. Jacob, after long resistance, is forced to yield; Benjamin is sent down to Egypt with the nine, and the party is despatched with a touching moan from the father—"If I am bereaved of my children, I am bereaved." One can see a great change on all the brethren, but most of all on Judah. His heart must have been touched by a higher power than human. He is as much concerned for his father's comfort now as formerly he was indifferent. He takes upon himself the whole responsibility for Benjamin, and comes under every form of engagement that can be thought of for his safe return. And the result showed that these engagements were not mere words to gain over his father; the time came when they demanded an unprecedented sacrifice, and that sacrifice—a sacrifice, as it seemed, of himself for life—Judah was prepared to make.

Once before, Jacob had been in great trouble from the expected wrath of his brother Esau, and on that occasion he had acted on the belief that gifts are a very useful ally in conciliating a possible enemy. Diplomatic and pawky, he reverts to the same policy now. There are still a few products of the country that will be much esteemed in Egypt—honey, spices, myrrh, nuts, and almonds. Of these his sons are to take for the ruler of Egypt; also double money in their hand, for fond of money though Jacob is, he would be the last man to take advantage of an oversight in such serious circumstances as the present.

Again the brothers arrive in Egypt, and again they are presented to the great ruler of the country. The eye of Joseph is quickly caught by Benjamin, and instructions are given to the steward to prepare dinner for the party in Joseph's house. A new terror falls upon them; never were consciences so uneasy: they are called into Joseph's presence on account of the money in their sacks; it is just a plot against them to justify their being seized as bondmen! Before they would go into the ruler's presence they carefully explained the matter to the steward, and showed their sincerity by the offer of double money. The steward appeases their fears, and shows his sympathy with their religion by assuring them that the money in their sacks, though it had come through him, was a present from the God of their father. It appears soon that they are not only to dine in the ruler's house, but in the ruler's presence. Not indeed at the same table, for Egyptians had a dread of dining with foreigners, chiefly because they knew not but they had partaken of the flesh of the cow, their sacred animal.

When Joseph came in, and inquired for their father, and spoke to Benjamin, his feelings overpowered him; "he sought where to weep." At dinner they were handsomely entertained, according to Egyptian usage. They sat at meat, as the Egyptians did, and as the Hebrews did then, though afterwards they reclined. Great was their surprise to find themselves arranged according to their ages—an Egyptian custom probably; but how had their ages been ascertained? When it is said that Benjamin's mess was five times as large as theirs, it is not meant that he was expected to eat more food, but that the tray from which he supplied himself contained five times as many dishes, affording him thereby the greater variety of food and drink. One might suppose that the drink flowed rather freely at the feast: "they drank, and were merry with him," or as it is in the margin, "they drank largely." The words do imply that they drank up to the point of exhilaration, and that comes pretty near to the point of intoxication. We are not called to defend all the ways of Egypt.

But for some reason Joseph was not yet quite satisfied as to the spirit of his brethren. His ultimate intentions towards them were singularly generous, but unless their own spirit was entirely changed from what it had been, such generosity as he proposed would not benefit but only spoil them. He deemed it necessary, therefore, to subject both their filial and their brotherly affection to a further test. Hence the stratagem of the cup. With this cup commentators have been not a little concerned, wondering how Joseph could have given any countenance to those arts of divination for which such cups were constantly employed. We need not concern ourselves with such inquiries, for evidently it was part of the plot to make out that the theft was an aggravated offence, and that the cup had a sacred character, being used for divination by Joseph himself. The standard of truth laid down in the Sermon on the Mount would not admit of such deception, but Joseph had not heard the Sermon on the Mount. Authorities give us some curious details of the manner in which among many nations cups were used for divination. "Small pieces of gold or silver leaf or thin plate were thrown into the cup, intermingled with precious stones, on which certain characters were engraved. Then the inquirer repeated certain forms of adjuration and invoked his gods. The answer was variously given. Sometimes a voice was heard; sometimes certain of the signs engraven on the stones were seen reflected in the water; and sometimes the image of the person respecting whom inquiry was made appeared therein. This mode of divination is said to have been common to the ancient Egyptians, Assyrians, and Chaldæans."*

But it was in a very different manner that Joseph in this case was to use his cup for divination. His object was to find out what impression would be made on the men's hearts by the misfortune of Benjamin. If they were satisfied to leave him to his fate, if they showed themselves unconcerned alike for his welfare and for the feelings of their father, who could not but be reduced to the lowest stage of anguish on hearing that Benjamin was detained as a bondman in Egypt, then plainly they would be unworthy of the treatment which he contemplated, and had best be left to grapple with the five remaining years of famine as best they might.

So conscious were they of the innocence of the whole party that, with the utmost confidence, they proposed that if the cup should be found in any of their sacks, the culprit should be put to death, and they all would become bondmen to the Egyptian ruler. To the consternation of all, it was found in Benjamin's sack. The stratagem was successful, for the true character of the men came out. So far from trying to escape, they all make common cause with Benjamin, rend their clothes in token of their grief, and return to the city. Judah is the spokesman of the party. He is thoroughly overwhelmed and nonplussed. His conscience is troubled, as it has been these many years. He feels that at last that great family crime is to meet its retribution at the hands of God. He can only surrender at discretion. They had undertaken that if the cup were found in the sack of any of them, he should be put to death, and all the rest become bondmen. Judah cannot repeat the first offer—it is too horrible; but he stands to the rest.

* Kitto's "Daily Bible Illustrations."

They will all become slaves. Nay, says the viceroy, not all; only the one who has done the wrong. The rest may go back to their father; Benjamin only will remain a slave in Egypt.

Few more noble or more beautiful scenes have ever been enacted in the world's history than that which followed. It is again Judah that speaks. If his heart showed the touch of divine grace before, it is now manifestly penetrated by it through and through. The thought of their going back to their father without Benjamin is too staggering, too overwhelming to be entertained under any conditions whatever. Very touching are his words detailing the circumstances under which they had come down to Egypt. Every syllable thrills with concern for the old man their father. What a change from the time when they were willing to let him think that Joseph had met with a cruel and horrible death! Every pang of his father's heart tears Judah's tenderest fibres. There is no pain to which he will not submit, if it is to free his father from pain. He does not recoil from his solemn promise that he will be surety for Benjamin, and that if he do not bring him back he will bear the blame for ever. He knows that Benjamin is indispensable to his father's happiness, and that he himself is not. It may be an unreasonable prejudice of the old man, and certainly it is not flattering to Judah; but there it is, and it must be reckoned with. Jacob was now an old man, with a foot in the grave; Judah was in the prime of life, with possibilities of long life and enjoyment before him. It might seem a most unequal bargain for the young man to sacrifice his life or his liberty on behalf of the old. But it was implied in his undertaking to his father; and now that it has become necessary, he does not flinch. "Now therefore, I pray thee, let thy servant abide instead of the lad a bondman to my lord; and let the lad go up with his brethren."

"Judah, thou art he whom thy brethren shall praise!" Joseph is now satisfied, and more than satisfied. No wonder, for nobler words were never spoken in this world, and nobler offer never made, till the Son of God himself came from heaven to die for men, and "give himself for us, the just for the unjust, to bring us unto God."

And now came the *dénouement*. It was too touching a scene for the presence of any but the brothers. The pent-up feelings of Joseph could bear it no longer ; he wept aloud. It was a touching scene when Esau wept over Jacob, but how much more so when Joseph weeps over his brethren. How refreshing, amid the numberless proofs of the weakness and wickedness of humanity, to come upon such redeeming features ! Still more, to find Joseph, in his anxiety to save them pain, dwelling on the one bright aspect of their treatment of him—the only aspect which was at all satisfactory—that it had proved a link in the chain of causes that had saved them from a miserable death by famine. Fancy the bewilderment and consternation of the brethren, confronted with their long-lost brother amid such a flood of graciousness and affection, showing that no trace of bitter feeling, nothing but the purest love, remained toward them in his heart ! Like Saul on the way to Damascus, hearing from the lips of Jesus only words of affection, they found their injured brother heaping coals of fire upon their heads.

And Joseph's kindness was not confined to amiable words. He had a plan for his father and all the family which, if it could be reconciled with the divine intention regarding them, was certainly a most hopeful and comfortable one. Father, children, children's children, flocks, herds, and all they had, were to be transported to Egypt, and provided for in the land of Goshen, a convenient and most productive section of the country. And when the matter was brought under Pharaoh's notice, he was as cordial as his viceroy in his invitation to Jacob and his house. Nay, he went a step further, and ordered waggons to be sent for them from Egypt to facilitate their removal. The brethren were despatched each with a change of raiment ; Benjamin with five, and three hundred pieces of silver besides. The gift, though less munificent, was of the same quality as that which Naaman the Syrian took with him to the land of Israel—ten talents of silver, six thousand pieces of gold, and ten changes of raiment.

We may be sure that not an hour would be lost in that journey to Hebron. It were hard to say which of the brothers would

be in the most exuberant spirits—Simeon, after his long captivity, the unwelcome fetters no longer galling his limbs; Benjamin, released from his hideous nightmare, the charge of an
impudent robbery, so like an ugly dream, but at first a very
dismal reality; Judah, happy in his own freedom, happier still
in Benjamin's, and happiest of all in the thought of the intense
relief and satisfaction that would brighten his father's heart; all
the rest jubilant and happy, dwelling on this feature or on that
of their experience with such wondering gladness, and feeling so
cordially to each other, under the influence of their marvellous
good fortune. It was hardly possible, even for the most scep-
tically inclined among them, not to see the finger of God in the
events that had befallen them. We may hope that their hearts
were pervaded by a new sense of the faithfulness and the goodness of the God of their fathers, and new resolutions to be faithful
and earnest in his service.

For the most remarkable effect of this wonderful episode was
that it recalled to God the straggling band that had been wandering away from him in the land of Canaan, forgetting the example
of their fathers, and going after the ways of the heathen. At the
very least it gave them a new lesson of trust and reverence for
their God. The twelve brothers were not merely Jacob's family;
they were the heads of the nation of Israel. It is delightful
within the sphere of the family to mark how the filthy rags of
lust and selfishness have disappeared, and the fair garments of
filial love and dutifulness have come in their room.

But the change is far more important when viewed in its
effects on the coming nation. It was Joseph pre-eminently that
was the influence for good in the family. What an example and
power must his self-denying purity and steadfastness to God
have been amid the temptations both of Egypt and Canaan!
What a striking testimony his life bore to the excellence of the
rule, "Not slothful in business, fervent in spirit, serving the
Lord!" What an inducement he supplied to perseverance in
well-doing, even amid injustice and oppression—never despairing,
never thinking ill of God, but ever assured that in the end of the

day right would triumph and faith would have its victory! What vitality is revealed in the divine promises, in the relation of God to Israel, in the certainty of his rewarding fidelity to the covenant! Not but that the forces were still very active that dragged the people away from God ; nevertheless, the influence of Joseph, besides being a strong counteraction in his day, must have passed into generations following, overcoming many a temptation, and confirming in many a young heart the purpose to cleave firmly to the ways of God.

## CHAPTER VI.

### JACOB AND HIS SONS IN THE LAND OF GOSHEN.

#### (Gen. xlvi., xlvii.)

IT is no wonder that Jacob was incredulous when he heard the news of Joseph. Strong man though he was, "his heart fainted;" it seemed to stop through the shock he experienced. It was the sight of the waggons that led him to believe the news. No wheeled conveyance of the kind was in use in Palestine; they were known to be Egyptian. They are familiar objects in the monuments—small two-wheeled carts, more adapted to the level plain of Egypt than to the undulating surface of Canaan. One would have thought that the ten asses laden with the good things of Egypt, or the changes of raiment which his sons had brought, would have been more convincing. But there is a touch of nature in the statement that it was the waggons. His sons would be so eager to give him the news that they could not wait till any of their goods had been unloaded; the waggons were the first thing that told of Egypt, and told of a plan by which he and his family were to remove to that country, as his sons had said. There is a beautiful simplicity in the old man's confession of his new faith : " It is enough ; Joseph my son is yet alive ; I will go and see him before I die."

It is somewhat singular that in inviting his father to go to Egypt, Joseph does not appear to have borne in mind the promises connected exclusively with the land of Canaan. For it was not a brief visit that Joseph invited the family to pay—they were to " dwell in the land of Goshen;" and when Pharaoh confirmed

the invitation, he assured them that "the good of the land of
Egypt was theirs." It may be doubted, however, whether these
expressions were meant to denote permanent residence, or only a
residence till the famine, which had yet five years to run, should
have come to an end. But however that may have been, Jacob
could not but have deemed it a serious matter to go even for a
time to the country where Abraham had fared so indifferently,
and to which Isaac had been actually forbidden to go. For
Jacob's faith in the gift of the land was one of his strong points.
His eagerness to leave Laban and return to his own country, and
the firmness with which he carried that purpose into effect, in
spite of what he dreaded from Esau, showed that to him Canaan
was a sacred land, and that residence in it was deemed essential
to one who should inherit the promises.

At first, accordingly, Jacob thought only of a visit to Joseph :
" I will go and see him before I die ; " but at Beersheba, after a
solemn sacrifice had been offered, God gave him full permission to
go down, and an assurance that he would bring him up again, not
indeed personally—" for Joseph shall put his hand upon thine
eyes," ministering to him at his death—but in the person of his
descendants. And we know that ultimately Joseph himself was
profoundly impressed by the promise of the land, taking an oath
of his people before he died that when God should visit them they
would carry up his bones.

We have seen that there was need for Jacob's family being
removed from Canaan, as some of them were becoming much
tainted with the idolatry and pollution prevalent there. No
doubt in Egypt, too, they would be exposed to idolatry ; but,
on the whole, life was purer. Further, if they had remained
among the Canaanites, and multiplied into a nation, they would
have excited such jealousy that they would not have been allowed
to live in peace. The Canaanites might despise their claim to the
land while they were a mere family, but they could not despise it
if they were increasing by leaps and bounds. In Egypt, on the
other hand, they occupied Goshen merely by the permission of
Pharaoh ; and when they did multiply there so as to excite the

fears of the Egyptians, it was not because they were likely to seize their land, but to join their enemies.   Then there was a risk of their amalgamating by marriage with the doomed Canaanites ; but the Egyptians were so different a race that there was no such risk with them.   To be among the Egyptians would also be a benefit to them in other ways, for they would learn much from a people so skilled in all the arts of life and so superior in civilization. Jacob did not know and possibly did not surmise that this removal to Egypt would lead on to that dark chapter in their history of which God had spoken to Abraham : " Know of a surety that thy seed shall be a stranger in a land that is not theirs, and shall serve them ; and they shall afflict them four hundred years."   By a merciful arrangement our entrance on disastrous epochs of our history is generally hid from us : " Sufficient unto the day is the evil thereof."

It is not easy to ascertain the precise number of persons who went down with Jacob to Egypt.   The number is given in Genesis as seventy ; by Stephen, in Acts vii., as seventy-five.   The differ- ence, which must arise from different modes of reckoning, is of no practical consequence.   We see at once the great preponderance of the children of Leah and her maid ; they were more than two- thirds of the whole.   It is remarkable that, without a single exception, the sons were all of the same occupation—shepherds. One sees in this an evidence of the uniformity of taste and habit prevalent in the East.   In what Western household should we find ten or eleven sons all addicted to the same pursuit ?   We are not to suppose that the seventy or seventy-five souls constituted the whole emigration.   We have to add the servants, the number of whom greatly exceeded that of the masters.   If Abraham was able to arm three hundred and eighteen servants of his house for the rescue of Lot, and if the establishments of his descendants bore any proportion to his, the emigration to Egypt must have amounted at the very least to three thousand souls.

The meeting of Jacob and Pharaoh is another dramatic incident.   It is a matter of importance even to Joseph that his family should make a favourable impression on the greatest of

earthly kings. He picks out five of them (the best looking, perhaps), along with his father, and presents them formally to his
master. The questions put by Pharaoh seem to show nothing
higher than the play of curiosity, or the commonplace style of
courtly civility. Even when Jacob, in the exercise of his patriarchal
authority, blessed Pharaoh, no suspicion seems to have entered the
royal mind that this was more than a kindly ceremony, or a
characteristic of the Hebrew nation. The Hebrews were received
by Pharaoh with the condescension of a great man wishing to be
agreeable to humble strangers; not with the deference due to a
family whom God had chosen to discharge a function in the world,
that threw all the achievements of the great kings of Egypt utterly
into the shade.

But what was the condition of the country into which Jacob
and his family now came? Who was this Pharaoh who occupied
the throne? What was the prevalent religion of the country, its
learning, its social life, and the character of its people? And
what kind of influence was exerted on the family of Jacob during
the four centuries of their residence on Egyptian soil?

The valley of the Nile is known to have been one of the earliest settlements of the human race, as it was also, perhaps, the
most distinguished in all the arts of civilized life. As we have
already said, it constitutes naturally a part of the great desert
that stretches over the north of Africa and the central part of
Asia; and it owes its fertility solely to the river Nile, the annual
inundations of which fertilize the land on either side of its banks,
creating a soil of unexampled fertility, which is stimulated to its
utmost capacity by a climate of unrivalled excellence.

The first period of what is called Egyptian history is of that
mythical character which mingles gods and men in the affairs of
the country, and even thereafter a haze of obscurity hangs over
the narrative. According to Manetho, the great Egyptian historian, of whose history we have only some fragments preserved
by Josephus, thirty dynasties of kings ruled Egypt in succession.
On the whole, the monuments confirm this statement, and furnish
considerable additional information respecting several of the kings.

The late Dr. Brugsch, a German writer, who spent a great part
of his life in Egypt, purposed to compile a continuous history of
the country from the monuments alone—from Menes, the first
king, to the present day—part of which intention he fulfilled
in a work entitled, " Egypt under the Pharaohs." The question
that more immediately interests the student of the Bible in the
days of Jacob and Joseph is, Under what dynasty, and under what
king, did Jacob come into Egypt ? Who was the Pharaoh that
dreamt the dream of the kine and the ears of corn ? Is anything
recorded of him on the monuments ? Is further light thrown on
his history and his character ?

Now it must be owned that we are not quite out of the region
of conjecture when we deal with these questions. And one prob-
lem in particular is very difficult. We learn from Manetho and
Josephus that at an early period Egypt was invaded and taken
possession of by conquerors that bore the name of Hyksos, or
shepherd kings. These conquerors are believed to have been of
Semitic origin, perhaps a mixed multitude in which the Hittites
predominated. Their dominion was chiefly in Lower Egypt—that
part which is nearest to the mouths of the Nile. After a considerable time—Manetho says upwards of five hundred years—they
were subdued and expelled by the ancient Egyptian people, and a
dynasty of the old race was placed on the throne.

The question has been keenly debated, Were these Hyksos, or
shepherd kings, in power during the whole or part of the time
when the Israelites were in Egypt ? It would not be suitable to
occupy these pages with the arguments that have been urged on
either side of this question. It is now generally believed that the
shepherd kings were in power during at least part of the residence
of the Israelites, and to us it appears that there is much to be
said in favour of the opinion that the Pharaoh of Joseph's time
was one of them. Nothing can be inferred from the name
Pharaoh, because it was the official name of all the kings of
Egypt. If the king in Joseph's time was one of the Hyksos, we
can understand the favourable reception and kindly welcome
which he gave to Jacob and his sons, shepherds though they were,

even at a time when to Egyptians of the older stock every shepherd was an abomination. The very fact that shepherds were
" an abomination to the Egyptians" proper, would seem to imply
some grievous calamity inflicted by them on the country, because
the fact that the Egyptians were devoted to the agricultural side
of farming life would not in itself account for so keen a hatred
to those that pursued the other branch. When, in after times, a
king arose " that knew not Joseph," we can understand how
this opposition to Joseph's people should have arisen from a
change of dynasty, and very probably from the expulsion of the
Hyksos kings. For if the Israelites, as being shepherds, were
congenial with the Hyksos, they would naturally come in for a
share of the national hatred when the Hyksos were expelled.
This, too, may in some degree explain why few traces of the
residence of the Israelites in Egypt are found on the monuments.
The successors of the Hyksos kings would naturally be disposed to
destroy the records of their domination. At one time it was
thought that a picture on a very ancient tomb, that of the Beni-
Hassan, depicted the procession of Joseph's brethren to Pharaoh.
But this opinion has been practically given up. There is no
figure in the procession corresponding either to Joseph or to
Pharaoh. The long strings of ostriches which they are represented
as bringing formed no part of the wealth of the patriarchs. The
inscription is an interesting illustration of the relation of Egypt to
other countries, but not to the family of Jacob.

On their first arrival, the Hyksos appear to have conducted
themselves with the destructive rudeness which barbarians usually
show when they obtain possession of a civilized country. The
ancient temples and other monuments of art and civilization found
no mercy at their hands, but were ruthlessly demolished. But as
their dominion was confined mostly to Lower Egypt, the temples
of Thebes and other cities in the south escaped their ravages. In
the course of time they became more assimilated to the ancient
Egyptians, adopting their language, their religion, and their
customs generally. Even in their earlier and more destructive
period, some monuments, like the Pyramids, were too massive to

be demolished, and others were spared.    Egyptian civilization sustained a rude shock ; but its progress was not arrested, and after a time it advanced under new conditions more vigorously than before.

Canon Rawlinson has come to a very decided conclusion, not only that the Hyksos invasion occurred before the time of Joseph, but that the king whose dream Joseph interpreted was Apepi, the last king of the Hyksos dynasty.    "Apepi stands out from the Egyptian kings of the period as a monarch of distinct individuality and with a marked character.    He built a great temple to Set or Sutekh at Tanis, his principal capital, composed of blocks of red granite, and adorned it with obelisks and sphinxes......But it was in the religious changes which he introduced that Apepi's individuality appears most strikingly......Apepi became a monotheist. Singling out from the multitudinous gods of Egypt one special personage, Set or Sutekh, he made him the sole object of his worship, refusing to serve any other god in the whole land.*    He even became an apostle of monotheism, imposing the worship of a single god on the tributary monarch of Southern Egypt, who held his capital at Thebes......We may regard it as most probable that Apepi, like the later Egyptian monotheists who are known as the disk-worshippers, identified his sole deity with the bright orb of day, the great source of light and life to the universe." †

If this was the Pharaoh under whom Joseph served, and if these were his religious views, we may the better understand how Joseph might retain in Egypt the worship of his father's God, and might marry the daughter of the priest of On, without coming into violent collision with the worship practised by the king.

The land of Goshen was assigned to Jacob and his family as their residence.    It lay along the Tanitic branch of the Nile, being the part of Egypt nearest to Canaan ; and it was a remarkably fertile district.    It is still the most productive part of Egypt, having most flocks and herds, and also most fishermen ; and its products at this day, as enumerated by Mr. Lane, a distinguished writer on Egypt, are much the same as those for which

---

* "Records of the Past," viii 3.    † Rawlinson's "Isaac and Jacob," pp. 165, 166.

the children of Israel lusted in the wilderness (see Num. xi. 5 ; xx. 5). "They consist of millet or maize, milk, new cheese, eggs, small salted fish, cucumbers and melons, and gourds of a great variety of kinds, onions and leeks, beans, chick-peas, lupins," etc.

But the testimony of a much more ancient authority than Mr. Lane has lately been brought to light. Describing Pi-Ramessu, the city of Rameses (a later designation of Zoan), an Egyptian letter-writer, on an ancient papyrus roll, thus speaks : " Its fields are full of good things, and life passes in constant plenty and abundance. Its canals are rich in fish ; its meadows are green with vegetables ; there is no end of the lentils ; melons with a taste like honey grow in the irrigated fields. Its barns are full of wheat and durra, and reach as high as heaven. Onions and sesame are in the enclosures, and the apple-tree (?) blooms. The vine and the almond-tree and the fig-tree grow in its gardens. Sweet is their wine for the inhabitants of Keim. They mix it with honey. The red fish is in the lotus canal, the Borian fish in the ponds ; many kinds of fish, besides carp and pike, in the land of Pu-harotha ; fat fish and Khiptipennu fish are in the pools of the inundation ; the Hanaz fish, in the full mouth of the Nile, near the city of the conqueror (Tanis)." *

It was indeed in "the best of the land" that the sons of Jacob got their settlement. If it be asked how it happened that so choice a region lay open for them, the answer is, that it was nearest to the quarter from which the Hyksos had come ; and that, more than any other part of the country, it had been dispossessed of its former inhabitants, the more especially that it was in the immediate neighbourhood of Tanis or Zoan, the capital city of the new reigning house. It would be the more suitable for the Hebrews that comparatively few Egyptians were now in it, and consequently their occupation as shepherds would excite the less disgust. If it be said that at the time of the exodus the Israelites were dwelling among the Egyptians, and that their houses were so intermingled that those of the Israelites had to be distinguished

---

* Letter of Panbesa in "Records of Past," vi. 11. See the author's "Manual of Bible History," pp. 101, 102.

by the sprinkled blood, we must remember that the Hyksos had by that time been expelled, that the Israelites had multiplied to a prodigious extent and spread over a much wider district, and that the population consequently had become much more mixed.

Zoan or Tanis, afterwards called Pi-Ramessu or Rameses, was the chief city of the neighbourhood, and one of the royal residences. The Hyksos kings seem to have lived much here; and after their expulsion their successors might find it convenient to be often in the city which had been the centre of influence of their predecessors.    It is to be remarked that Dean Stanley, following Brugsch, favours the tradition which made On or Heliopolis, the "City of the Sun," the place of Joseph's residence and the royal city of the Pharaohs.    Of the importance of this city, its magnificent Temple of the Sun, its colleges, and its fame, which drew to it such visitors or residents as Herodotus, Strabo, and Plato, it were hardly possible to speak too highly.    But besides that Zoan was well known to the Israelites (see Num. xiii. 22), its situation corresponds better to the narrative, and especially to the supposition that the Pharaoh of the period was one of the Hyksos or shepherd kings.    Heliopolis or On was at no great distance, and there was easy communication between the cities.

# CHAPTER VII.

## DEATH OF JACOB AND OF JOSEPH.

### (GEN. xlviii.-l.)

SUCH was the remarkable part of Egypt to which the family of Jacob now removed, and in which he himself spent the last seventeen years of his life. It was his privilege to see his descendants exceedingly prosperous; "they grew and multiplied exceedingly." They were now rising to the dimensions of a nation, and the divine promises were receiving, in this respect, a literal fulfilment. The great sorrow that had imbittered so many years of his old age was completely removed, and the one unfulfilled wish to which we may conceive him giving expression was, "Oh that Rachel had lived to share these blessings!" If, when he returned from Haran, he could contrast with a gush of gratitude the "two bands" with his condition when, with his staff, he crossed the Jordan, much more amazed he would be at the contrast, now that his descendants were swarming all around. Free from all worldly care, he had the opportunity to turn his thoughts more fully to those subjects which are emphatically appropriate to old age, lying on the edge of the life to come. That his spirit was in close communion with God, we may infer from the prophetic gift with which he was intrusted, for that gift was seldom bestowed save on men in close sympathy with the holy God. He had been cast down, but not destroyed; and the trials and sorrows of his life, under the sanctifying power of God, had turned him into a better man. Oftener than once he seems to have thought that his end was approaching, and at such times he set himself to utter words given him by inspiration of God concerning things to come.

On one of these occasions Joseph goes to pay him a visit, taking with him his two sons, Manasseh and Ephraim. He finds his father frail, blind, and mostly bed-rid; but by an effort he rouses himself, and sits upon the bedside, leaning on his staff (Heb. xi. 21). His mind goes back to the scenes of his youth, and especially to the memorable night at Luz, when he saw that staircase between earth and heaven, the steps of which he himself was now so soon to climb. Then he touches on his great sorrow— the death of Rachel, Joseph's mother, an event too remote for Joseph to remember, but one that gave Joseph and Benjamin a place in his heart that none of his other sons could rival. It was not in Jacob's power to confer on Joseph the specific blessing which Isaac had conferred on him. But he gave him a very peculiar distinction when he raised his sons, Manasseh and Ephraim, to the level of his own sons, entitling each of them to rank with them in the inheritance of the land. Too blind to see, he does not seem at first to have apprehended the presence of the lads; but when he came to know that they were there, he kissed them and embraced them, and laying his hands on their heads, gave them a prophetic blessing. Nor was it by accident that he laid his right hand on the head of Ephraim. He was guided by a light from heaven that even Joseph did not share: blind though he was, he saw into the distant future, and he knew that Ephraim would be greater than Manasseh. The conferring of the blessing was a recognition of the divine will, an act of worship suitably performed by a frail old man : "he worshipped, leaning on the top of his staff." In the blessing we mark the beautiful combination of piety and love :—

> "The God, before whom my fathers Abraham and Isaac did walk,
> The God who hath fed me all my life long unto this day,
> The Angel which hath redeemed me from all evil, bless the lads !
> And let my name be named on them, and the name of my fathers Abraham and Isaac ;
> And let them grow into a multitude in the midst of the earth."

His last words to Joseph showed his firm belief that God would in due time visit his descendants, and carry them up into the land of promise. And when that land was got possession of, he indicated that Joseph's descendants would inherit one portion above their brethren. There is some obscurity here which we cannot quite remove. This additional inheritance consisted of a portion which he had taken from the Amorite by his sword and by his bow. This could not be the piece of ground which he acquired of the sons of Hamor at Shechem (Gen. xxxiii. 19), because instead of getting that in war by sword and bow, he obtained it in peace by paying down the stipulated price. Many commentators think that Jacob referred by anticipation to the future conquest of the country, which, in the person of his descendants, he was to obtain by sword and by bow. But the reference is evidently to a past transaction, and we must accept the statement as we find it, though unable quite to understand it, not knowing all the circumstances that occurred in connection with the matter. The fact of importance is that the dying Jacob presented a special gift in that land to Joseph, in acknowledgment of his memorable services to the family. His doing so was a striking combination of affection for his son and faith in his God.

Though Jacob had at one time believed himself to be bereaved of three of his sons—Joseph, Simeon, and Benjamin—it was his rare privilege, not long after this interview with Joseph, to see the whole twelve, in obedience to his call, gathered round his death-bed to receive each his last message, uttered by inspiration of God. It was not wholly a message of benediction. It was a prophetic forecast of the future, determined in most cases by the personal conduct of the sons. Reuben, by his unnatural lust, had forfeited his right to the honours of the first-born, and was too unstable to excel. Simeon and Levi came next, but their perfidy and cruelty to the Shechemites were fatal to their claims. Next came Judah, and it was with a glow of delight that the dying patriarch enlarged upon him. He had begun ill, but had ended nobly ; never could his father forget his magnificent self-sacrifice, when he offered himself for slavery in place of Benjamin. "Judah!

thee shall thy brethren praise!" The lion furnishes the symbol of his strength; the warrior, of the fearless energy of his character; the vineyard, with its abounding clusters, denotes the felicity of his inheritance; and far away in the future, while his sceptre still abides, not merely his own tribe and people, but other nations too, are seen flocking to One who is to spring from his loins—that very One in whom all the families of the earth are to be blessed! It was, indeed, a delight to the aged father to leave behind him such a son as Judah.

We cannot pass over, in the blessing of Judah, the new terms in which the Messianic hope is expressed. The old Jewish interpreters understood Shiloh to mean the Messiah; and amid all the modern efforts to find another sense, no other interpretation has been suggested that fits the context. In his far-off vision, the dying patriarch saw a Son of Judah, glorious in His apparel, travelling in the greatness of His strength, to whom not only the tribe of Judah made obeisance, but the peoples, the Gentiles, the world itself gathered to do Him homage. Well might Jacob think of Him as the divine Deliverer, who was to be sent to redeem lost humanity; and well might he rejoice, in the consciousness of all his own sins and shortcomings, that there was such a Deliverer for him! It had been Jacob's privilege, from that night at Bethel when he slept with the stone for his pillow, to be familiar with human features which somehow were identified with the divine Being. He had seen foreshadows of the incarnation. It had been his still greater privilege to experience in his own person the infinite grace and loving-kindness of that wondrous Being in whom God, angel, and man seemed so wondrously blended. Was not the Shiloh, whose day he now saw afar off, just the same gracious Being, now incorporated in flesh and blood with Judah's family, no longer flitting like a meteor, half in heaven, half in earth, but the Word made flesh, dwelling among men? And as he thought of this advent, and of his son Judah as the father from whose loins He was to spring, might he not say, with an emphasis which no other consideration could inspire, "Judah, thou art he whom thy brethren shall praise!"

Of the other sons, with one exception, little is said that rises above a commonplace level. The exception is that of Joseph. But before coming to him, and in the very heart of his discourse, Jacob utters a remarkable exclamation, which comes in like a burst of personal emotion and testimony in the midst of his solemn prophecy : "I have waited for thy salvation, O my God!" Some have understood this as the war-cry of the tribe of Dan, of whom Jacob had just spoken as "an adder in the path, that biteth the horses' heels "—a tribe that used suddenly to fall upon opponents, with a warlike shout, like Cromwell's famous watchword, "Let God arise, and let his enemies be scattered." But the suggestion is as repulsive as the exegesis is unsatisfactory. To call it "an apprehensive sigh lest his strength should be exhausted before his task was completed," or "a prayer that God might speedily effect his painless dissolution," or a device for dividing his benedictions, and separating the group of Judah from that of Joseph, is to fall very far short of the glorious meaning of the words. We recall the blessing of Judah, and the vision of the Shiloh, with men of all kindreds and tribes and tongues crowding around Him, and receiving that blessing which He came to bestow. The surpassing brightness of that vision seems still to linger in the sky, and the dying patriarch, recalling it for a moment, cannot repress the utterance of his personal trust : "This, O my God, is what I have waited for : now lettest thou thy servant depart in peace, for my spirit hath seen thy salvation!" But account as we may for the exclamation in this place, no spiritual mind, entering into the position of the dying patriarch, can deem the words out of place in one who, prophet though he was, felt himself a great sinner—one who was standing consciously very near to the holy Judge, with no justifying plea or righteousness of his own, and who, in that position, was constrained to relieve his soul, with reference to his own personal state, by an exclamation of his long-continued trust in the salvation of God.

When it came to Joseph's turn to receive the benediction, the heart of the dying patriarch surged and swelled as it had done in the case of Judah. Extraordinary fruitfulness and extraordinary strength are ascribed to Joseph, indicating the nearness and favour of Him who is at once the feeding " Shepherd " and the sustaining Rock or " Stone " of Israel. In harmony with the tenor of the prophecy, the tribe of Judah and that of Ephraim, who was reckoned as the elder son of Joseph, became by far the most important and conspicuous in the future history of the nation, and above all the others contributed to render the seed of Jacob the wonderful people they became.

The whole address is pervaded by the spirit of supreme loyalty to God ; and he must have been a very callous son who could listen to it without being thrilled, and without experiencing a new sense of the obligation of loyalty to the God of their fathers.

One closing request came from the dying patriarch : " Bury me in the cave of Machpelah. There they buried Abraham and Sarah his wife ; there they buried Isaac and Rebekah his wife ; and there I buried Leah." It was the last expression of Jacob's faith that all the promises which God had made regarding the land would yet come true. If he was buried there, he would sleep under the benediction of God ; and who knows but he had a glimpse of a glorious awakening and of a life when the promises which he saw afar off should be fulfilled in surpassing glory ? And now his work was done ; he could sing his *Nunc dimittis ;* it only remained that he should gather up his feet into the bed, yield up the ghost, and be gathered unto his people. And Joseph, his beloved son, closed his eyes.

The funeral obsequies were performed with extraordinary care and elaboration. First, Joseph commanded his servants, the physicians, to embalm the body of his father. The art of embalming was practised in Egypt at a very early period, as Herodotus and other early writers have informed us. No other people could equal the Egyptians in this remarkable process. To complete the process occupied forty days. There was also a public mourning for Jacob, which extended to seventy days. Herodotus mentions seventy days as the time during which a dead body lay in nitre, but Diodorus says the process of embalming occupied forty days. The periods may not have been always the same. In Jacob's case the time was certainly a long one. Diodorus mentions seventy-two days as the period of mourning for a king, so that Jacob was treated with almost kingly honours. In the case of a king, the temples were shut up, and there were no sacrifices, feasts, or solemnities all the time. The people rent their clothes, begrimed their heads and jaws with mud; and in this condition men and women went about in companies of two or three hundred, with their loins girded and their breasts bare, singing plaintive songs, reciting the virtues of him they had lost. During the time of mourning they abstained from wine and generous diet. They ate no animal meat, or food dressed by fire, and abstained from their customary baths and anointings.*

More remarkable still, as a tribute of honour to Jacob, was the procession of mourners from Egypt. Not only his own sons and their households, with the exception of their little ones, but all the servants of Pharaoh, the elders of his house, and all the elders of the land of Egypt, went up with the body. Greater honour could hardly have been shown to mortal man. This is the first time that we read of elders, and even now the institution seems to have been an ancient one. Chosen and named first for their age, elders came soon to be selected for their capacity to rule. The institution was adopted by the Israelites, and was a conspicuous feature of Jewish church and state throughout the whole period of their economy.

It is no wonder that the cavalcade made a great impression on the Canaanites, and that they changed the name of the place where they halted for a seven days' lamentation from Gosen-Atad, or the "threshing-floor of Atad," into Abel-Mizraim, or the "mourning of the Egyptians." Chariots and horses were at this time unknown in Canaan, but they had been long in use in Egypt. As to the route by which the procession advanced, there is some uncertainty. When it is said (Gen. l. 11) that Gosen-Atad was "beyond Jordan," it looks as if the company had advanced east of the Dead Sea, and crossed the Jordan near its mouth. But besides that this would have been a very circuitous route, it was quite

* "Pictorial Commentary."

impracticable for the Egyptian chariots. Most probably "beyond Jordan" is to be regarded as a conventional phrase, denoting merely that the place was on the western side of the river. The cavalcade probably advanced through Shur, the usual route, halting at Gosen-Atad, perhaps because the Egyptian chariots could proceed no further. The cave of Machpelah was found probably as Jacob had left it seventeen years before. The embalmed body of Jacob was laid in one of its chambers. The vault where the body was placed has been kept sacred from the gaze of Europeans; all that even the Prince of Wales was allowed to see was the cenotaph in the chamber above. It is quite possible that the embalmed body of Jacob lies in that vault at the present day.

It is singular to find Joseph's brethren giving way to unworthy suspicions of him after his father's death. Probably they dwelt apart, and there was little social intercourse between them. They thought that it was only regard for their father's feelings that had restrained him from punishing them during his life, and that now that he was gone he would be under no such restraint. How slow men are to believe in generosity, whether human or divine! Approaching him under shelter of words spoken by their father, they implored his forgiveness anew; but only to find that their fears were utterly unfounded, that no trace of unkindness lingered in his heart. Joseph then went his way, his brothers theirs. In due time, one after another, they paid the debt of nature. Joseph lived to the age of a hundred and ten years, of which he had spent ninety-three in Egypt. Dying, he took an oath from the representatives of the family that when God should visit them they would carry up his bones, that they might rest in the sacred land. His children had been brought up not as Egyptians but as Hebrews, and seem to have amalgamated readily with their brethren. Neither his long residence in Egypt nor his extraordinary honours had dimmed his faith in the divine promise or obscured its glory. With his fathers he saw something more glorious than material wealth or earthly dignity. "He looked for a city which hath foundations, whose builder and maker is God."

Few studies of character are more interesting than that of

Jacob. At first he appears a quiet, home-loving boy, a contrast to his enterprising brother—one apparently that will never make any figure in the world, or be connected with stirring events. And he is not only quiet but cunning, with a selfish greed for all that he can get, however unworthy the means. We see by-and-by that there is a deep well of love in his heart, by no means universal, but flowing out intensely towards select congenial objects. And further, we find that he has got great strength of desire, and great persistency of effort toward whatever his heart is set on. It seems now as if the quiet youth may yet in his own way become a considerable figure in the world. In addition to all this, he has a sense of religion, but rather as something claiming attention by itself than an imperial force which is absolutely to rule his whole life. In his early years we see these elements surging about in a tumultuous, discordant way. But as years pass, the Spirit of God seems to move over him, and the chaos of his soul falls more into order. Very bitter experiences of deceit and cunning practised on himself reveal the nature of that sin. The strange struggle at Peniel shows him that no step in his life can be safely taken without God's blessing, and that everything must be brought to the touchstone of God's will. With the death of Rachel all the joy of his life seems to be extinguished, and vanity of vanities is stamped on the objects on which he used to set so high a value. The tragic death, as it seemed, of Joseph throws a fresh gloom over this world, and quickens the feelings that look upward and onward for true felicity. All this strange and painful discipline is effecting the chastening of his rugged character and smoothing it out into order and tranquillity. He is gradually coming nearer to God and becoming more changed into his image. That early night of his wanderings, when " darkness was over him, his rest a stone," but in his dreams God was very nigh, became a picture of his life. At last his back is turned to the world that he used to idolize so grievously, and his deepest desire leaps out from his dying lips, " I have waited for thy salvation, O my God ! "

And who would have thought to find this man, so earthly, prosaic, and crafty in his youth, manifesting in old age the prophet's soaring eye, and the poet's flowing tongue, and the saint's holy rapture? Does not grace make some old men young again? Who would have thought that the cunning shepherd, who took such strange methods to get justice from Laban, would be heard, in the far-off evening of life, telling, in the solemn, stately tone of a prophet, all that should befall his sons in the last days? Who would have expected to hear him disposing of them like the vice-gerent of God, comparing them to warriors grasping the neck of their enemies, or telling of garments washed in wine and clothes in the blood of grapes, of fruitful boughs by a well whose branches ran over the wall, of blessings prevailing over the blessings of pro-genitors to the utmost bound of the everlasting hills? Truly it is a great change. He stands now high on the ladder between earth and heaven; his name is no more Jacob but Israel, for as a prince he has power with God, and has prevailed.

Of all the three patriarchs Abraham, Isaac, and Jacob, Jacob was most irregular in his character and most chequered in his career. If the sceptic has found no loose joint in the armour of Abraham or of Isaac, how different it has been with Jacob! But on the whole it must have been a good and powerful character that so gained in the end on these wayward sons, and brought them so much nearer to the character of their fathers. And the unexampled funeral *cortège* that followed his remains to the land of Canaan was a mark of profound esteem, not only for Joseph's father, but for the patriarch himself. But the crowning testimony to him is the fact that it was not Abraham's, nor Isaac's, but Jacob's name—his new name, Israel—that came to denote the nation that sprang from his loins. The causes that brought about the change were probably these: the abandonment of the policy of craft which had been so prominent in his youth; the manifestation of a far deeper affection for his children than he had seemed to possess, and of a holier trust in that God for whose salvation he was seen to be waiting; and finally, a tenderness of compassion, in view of the chequered course of man's mortal life and of the many sorrows of his own—his flight from his home, his harsh treatment by Laban, the death of Rachel, the loss of Joseph, and other troubles which, in his own touching phrase, had seemed to bring down his gray hairs in sorrow to the grave.

Joseph's is a far steadier character, and though outwardly he has a much more varied experience, his inner life is of much more uniform texture. In Joseph's character there is a gradual development—first the blade, then the ear, then the full corn in the ear. There are no signs of revolution here; it is like the shining light, that shineth more and more unto the perfect day. His natural simplicity and winsomeness contrast broadly with his father's cunning and reserve. His early protestation against sin, "How can I do this great wickedness and sin against God?" seems already to indicate the maturity of a saintly soul. His faith in God's promises shows no symptom of wavering. His power of forgiveness is like that of God himself. His tenderness of heart is too great for the rough scenes of life; he must go to some quiet place to indulge it. Adversity did not make him sour and impatient, prosperity did not lift him up. The world did not dazzle him nor hinder him from seeing, beyond all its gilt and glitter, the surpassing glory of the life divine.

One cannot pass from the history of Joseph without being struck by its manifold resemblance, on the human side, to that of the blessed Saviour: his being hated and cast out by his brethren answering to Christ's rejection by his people; his saving their lives through the sufferings they had brought upon him answering to Christ's redemption of his people by the shedding of his blood; his gracious treatment of his brethren, pardoning and blessing when he might have punished and crushed them, so like the gracious reception of all penitent sinners by Christ. The time is coming when Christ, becoming known to his brethren according to the flesh as he whom they have pierced, a reception shall take place the counterpart of Joseph's becoming known to his brethren, and not the house of Pharaoh only but all the world shall hear the weeping. Finally, in Joseph's personal history, first humbled and imprisoned, afterwards exalted to a throne, we have a forecast at once of the humiliation and the exaltation of the Son of God.

Before we pass from the patriarchal period of history, the question naturally presents itself, What was the impression left by it on the Hebrew people? What influence had it on the religious history of the future?

In the main it served vividly to impress two truths. First, the existence of one supreme God, Lord of heaven and of earth, the only fit object of worship, who holds in his hands the life and destinies of every creature that lives. And, second, the relation of this God to men, as it is and as it may be; evinced particularly in the covenant he made with Abraham, with its specific promises, some bearing on the immediate future, but the most important on a distant age; some carrying temporal blessings, others spiritual and eternal; involving, during the interval, a great trial to the faith and patience of his people—a long period, during which God would withdraw himself from view, but would not lose one atom of interest in their welfare, nor fail to reward true faith with the most ample blessings.

This high faith in the one unseen God, as the moral Ruler of the world and the Friend of his chosen people, was the grand object which the dealings with the patriarchs were designed to promote. And this faith the lives of Abraham, Isaac, and Jacob, as well as those of Judah and Joseph, were well fitted to exemplify. At a time when the whole current of thought ran in a different direction, when men were vivifying the powers of nature and turning them into gods, when the notion of one great Ruler was passing away, and the affairs of the world were being given over to lords many and gods many, it was of supreme importance that a powerful witness should be borne to the ONENESS OF GOD, and to the interest which he takes and the government which he exercises in the affairs of men. And it was of great importance for the Jewish nation itself, continually exposed, as it was destined to be, to the temptation of conformity to the neighbouring nations, to have five such men as the fathers of their race, and in their lives to read a perpetual protest against all idolatry, and find the greatest possible encouragement to all who should prove loyal to the God of their fathers.

There were other lessons taught by patriarchal history. It was shown that in the main, though not without exceptions, temporal prosperity went hand in hand with moral and spiritual fidelity. It was further shown that no elaborate and minute system of worship was indispensable to the true service of God. The religious worship of the patriarchs was very simple. The burnt-offering was their method of sacrifice, ever teaching the solemn lesson that always accompanied the shedding of sacrificial blood. Worship and life were vitally connected; men could not serve God acceptably if their lives were not spent in harmony with his will. And men were encouraged to look forward with hopeful expectation : one day God would draw still nearer to men, and the richest divine blessings would flow out from a member of the seed of Abraham, Isaac, and Jacob, in whom, according to the promise, all the people of the earth were to be blessed.

After all, the lesson was poorly learned. There never was a time when Israel did not appear ready to forget it, and go off into idolatry. Again and again champions of the truth were raised up to rally the scattering forces and bring them back to their allegiance. Light and darkness had a struggle during all the Hebrew history, and the darkness seemed ever ready to prevail over the light. Had the fathers of the nation not been the men they were, and had not a succession of men like-minded been raised up from age to age, the grand truths of God's being and government would have been submerged, and the flood of polytheism and immorality would have spread its polluting stream over all the earth, without a single people being left to testify for the unity of God and the spirituality of his worship. We see very clearly that the Hebrew religion was not a development from within, but a seed from heaven, developed and matured by the grace of God.

# PART III.

## Life of Moses.

———◆◆———

### CHAPTER I.

#### BIRTH AND EARLY LIFE.

(Ex. i., ii.)

IT is not easy to tell how long a period elapsed between the death of Joseph and the birth of Moses. We have already (see page 98) adverted to the difficulty arising from the various statements of Scripture as to the duration of the sojourn in Egypt. If we accept the whole period of the sojourn as four hundred and thirty years (Ex. xii. 40), reckoning from the time when Jacob and his sons went down to Egypt, the interval between Joseph's death and Moses' birth would be about two hundred and eighty years. This may seem irreconcilable with the statement in 1 Chron. vi. 3, which makes Amram, the father of Moses, to be a grandson of Levi. But in the genealogical lists we are not to assume that every generation is specified,—cases are known where some of the names are left out. During the greater part of the long Egyptian sojourn, the condition of the people might be called a state of oppression, because they were really servants of a foreign master; but at particular periods the oppression rose to persecution, and it was in one of these periods that Moses was born.

If the king in Joseph's time was the last of the Hyksos, as Rawlinson and others believe, the oppression of the Israelites might have begun very soon, for the restored dynasty could be no friends of a Semitic people. It has generally been held that the king under whom Moses was born, and the oppression of the Israelites rose into acute persecution, was Rameses II., or perhaps his father, Seti I. What that king was most alarmed for was lest the Israelites should join any invading force and imperil the Egyptian supremacy. Invading forces came from the north, as the Hyksos had done, and perhaps some apprehension was felt of a renewed attack from that quarter. If the Hebrews occupied Goshen, the north-east corner of Egypt, they were in the region which enemies from the north would reach first if they should attempt the subjugation of Egypt; and as the Israelites had no goodwill to the Egyptians, it was very probable that they would be disposed to help the invader. At all costs, then, the king felt that the Hebrew colony must be held down, and measures adopted at once to lessen their number and to crush their spirit.

It may be useful here to glance more particularly at the events that had been going on (if we read the monuments aright) previous to the time of Moses, in order the better to understand the great magnificence and power to which Egypt had now attained. "The Hyksos kings" (as we have said elsewhere) "appear to have spared no pains both to establish their authority at home and to extend their influence abroad. One of these, Thotmes or Thutmes III., who is supposed to have reigned about 1600 B.C., has been called the Alexander the Great of Egypt. His foreign conquests were on the most extensive scale. In the celebrated temple of Karnak we find full and important records of his reign. It appears that during a period of twenty years he carried on no fewer than thirteen great campaigns against foreign nations on all sides of Egypt. Among the most important of these were his campaigns to the north-east, including the country called on the monuments Ruthen, and the district of Naharaim or Mesopotamia. Ruthen or Rutenna was the general name of the region comprehending Palestine, Phœnicia, and western Syria. An inscription at Karnak gives a complete list of the towns in Upper Ruthen that had been opposed to him, or rather of the prisoners belonging to them that had been taken in the town of Megiddo. Just as in later times, the plain of Megiddo had been the scene of a great conflict, and the city of that name (which gives the symbolical name Armageddon to the final conflict of the Apocalypse— xxi. 16) had been the scene of one of the earliest military struggles that ever took place in the East. What gives the highest value to the catalogue, in Dr. Brugsch's estimation, is the undisputed fact that for more than three hundred years before the entrance of the Jews into the land of Canaan, a great league of people of the same race, which the monuments call by the name of the Ruthen, existed in Palestine under little kings, who dwelt in the same towns and fortresses as we find stated on the monuments, and who, for the most part, fell by conquest into the hands of the Jewish immigrants.

"The mere lists of booty brought to Egypt after the foreign campaigns of Thotmes III. are elaborate and very imposing documents. Masses of gold and silver and precious stones; vast herds of cattle; stores of wheat, wine, and garments; curiosities of various kinds; and great numbers of men and women, reduced to slavery, were added year after year to the stores of Egypt. This royal scourge of the vast territories which he pillaged was an eminently religious man in his way. He built splendid temples in honour of the gods of Egypt, the famous 'Hall of Pillars' being one of them; he dedicated to them large portions of booty; he instituted feasts, reared obelisks, erected statues to the memory of his ancestors, vindicating his right to the title of 'his holiness,' although he was little better than a wholesale robber and murderer." *

We have said that according to the general belief Rameses II. (or perhaps his father Seti I.) was king at the birth of Moses. This opinion is confirmed by the fact that one of the treasure cities built by the oppressed Israelites was Raamses, so named after the reigning king. Rameses was a great warrior, and the determined opponent of the Khita, or Hittite power, of whose vast influence we have already spoken. He had many campaigns against that

---

* "Manual of Bible History," pp. 103, 104.

STATUE OF RAMESES II. THE PHARAOH OF THE OPPRESSION.
*(Found at Tanis.)*

*Page 289.*

people between the fifth and the twenty-first years of his reign; but, as we have said already, the king of the Khita at last sued for peace, to which Rameses acceded, and he wound up the long campaign by marrying a Khita princess.  The Khita or Hittites had no favour for the seed of Abraham, and it does not appear that the Hittite wife of Rameses did anything to mitigate the rigour of the persecution of the Israelites.

The lands assigned at first to the Israelites in Goshen must

SITTING FIGURE OF RAMESES II.
AT IPSAMBOUL.

have soon become far too narrow for their necessities. Many of them must have gone elsewhere, and found employment otherwise than by tending flocks.  We read of certain families that wrought fine linen, of others who were potters, and of others who dwelt among plants and hedges, and who dwelt with the king for his work (1 Chron. iv. 21, 23). One of the Hebrews married Bithia, a daughter of Pharaoh, and by her had a considerable family; but he seems to have stood true to his own nation, and not to have gained any rise of rank among them by his royal connection (1 Chron. iv. 18).

No doubt there was some exaggeration in the alarm given by the king of Egypt when he said of the Hebrews that they were " more and mightier " than his own subjects.  " More " they could not be actually at that time; for the Israelites could not have much exceeded a million, while the Egyptians were reckoned at six or seven millions.  But they might have been more in that part of Egypt which they occupied ; and " mightier " they certainly were. As a race the Hebrews were more powerful than the Egyptians. That remarkable turn for active business life which had been so conspicuous in Abraham, Jacob, and Joseph no doubt appeared also in many of their descendants. Pharaoh might see at a glance what an industrious, plodding, and withal thoughtful people the Hebrews were, and would readily infer that if they were not kept down they would soon get the upper hand.

The government of Egypt was an unmitigated despotism—the king might do whatever he pleased. His first device was to reduce the Hebrew people to a condition of practical slavery, and lay on them such burdens as would crush their spirit and enfeeble their bodily powers. "Therefore they did set over them task-masters to afflict them with their burdens. And they built for Pharaoh treasure cities, Pithom and Raamses." The treasure cities were designed for storing provisions, or perhaps the munitions of war. Such cities were built of brick, to prepare which was part of the task of the Israelites. The material had to be dug from beds of stiff clay, under the exhausting sun of Egypt, a toilsome and weary task, which would often exhaust the energies of the workers.

It has been conjectured by some that the labour of the Israelites was employed in the building of the pyramids; but there is no mention of this in Scripture. The pyramids, indeed, were of more ancient date, and the enormous toil required for their erection had been drawn from the sinews and life-blood of earlier captives— possibly the people of Ruthen, before the times of Abraham. There is evidence in the monuments of the horror which the building of the pyramids created, and of the bitter curses it drew out against those who had so inhumanly set their captives to it. But the tasks of the Israelites were just as severe. Besides the toil of brick-making and building, they were set to "all manner of service in the field." The toilsome and monotonous task of raising water from the Nile and conveying it to the fields for irrigation would often fall to them. They were treated as beasts of burden; and so far from their labour being lightened by considerate treatment, it was aggravated by reproaches and blows. No day of rest dawned

sweetly on them to recruit their energies.  If they were allowed to
live with their families, they could only see them sharing their
poverty and their misery.  In short, the slavery was so unmitigated
that all the joy was crushed out of their lives, which had become
one continued course of exhausting toil.

Pharaoh and his wise men were ignorant of a law of population
familiar to us now—that hardship tends rather to the increase

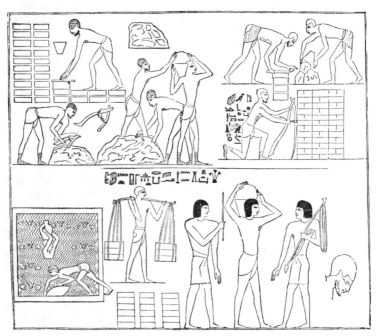

BRICK-MAKING AT THEBES.

than to the diminution of a people.  The poor are usually more
prolific than the rich.  In this country no families are so liable
to die out as those of the aristocracy, and in none do so many
births occur as in those of the poorly-fed Irish and West Highland peasantry.  It was no wonder, therefore, that the more the
Hebrews were afflicted, the more they multiplied and grew.  Some
more violent method must be adopted, if the Hebrew ranks were
to be really thinned.

Instructions were accordingly given to the two principal mid-wives, and through them to the others, that on the birth of Hebrew children the males were to be put to death and the females preserved alive. Infanticide was little thought of in Egypt, and Pharaoh probably reckoned that there would be no great opposition to the execution of this order. But the midwives "feared God;" their vocation, humble though it was, was to save life, not to destroy it. They neglected the king's order, and when challenged for doing so affirmed that, owing to the habits of the Hebrew women, they could not get a right opportunity of killing their children at their birth. The expression "feared God" seems to show that these Egyptian women believed in the divine protection of Israel, and had heard, perhaps, the solemn assurance, "Blessed is he that blesseth thee, and cursed is he that curseth thee." "Therefore God dealt well with the midwives; and because they feared God, he made them houses." The terror of God that was upon the Shechemite cities in the days of Jacob was upon these Egyptian women now. Whether or not they believed in Jehovah as the one Lord of heaven and earth, they certainly believed in his protection of his people, and they were afraid to do anything that would draw down his wrath.

Still a third device had to be resorted to: "Pharaoh charged all his people, saying, Every son that is born ye shall cast into the river, and every daughter ye shall save alive." Pharaoh had become so bold and imperious that it is not likely he would disguise this hideous order, as some have suggested, by the pretext that it was called for as an offering to the river-god. For Pharaoh knew well, and his people also, that if the river-god claimed a sacrifice, it was not the despised children of the Hebrews, but the prized and valued offspring of the Egyptians, that he would look for as his due. It was during the prevalence of this order that Moses was born.

Moses was neither of the family of Judah nor of that of Joseph. His father was Amram, of the family of Kohath, the son of Levi; his mother, Jochebed, of the same tribe, a near blood relation of Amram. It is not apparent how many generations intervened between his parents and Levi.  It is probable that their home was in the city of Memphis, because that was the residence of the Pharaoh of the day, and they were evidently not far from the royal palace.  Already there were two children in Amram's home— Miriam, a half-grown girl, and Aaron, a boy of three.  If Amram had to labour at the grievous tasks of the Hebrews, his house must have been poor and empty, and it could only have imbittered his daily sufferings to return at night and think what must soon be the fate of the beautiful infant that had come among them like a sunbeam from heaven.

The birth and early exposure of Moses are recorded with won- derful simplicity.  One marks on the very surface of Bible history the absence of miraculous embellishments or prodigies at places where mythical writers would have been sure to place them. There is no miracle connected with the birth of Moses.  Josephus has treated the subject very differently.  According to him, a pro- phet terrifies the King of Egypt by the announcement that a boy is about to be born who will inflict a fearful injury on his king- dom ; and the father of Moses sees a vision, and has a communica- tion made to him on the birth and wonderful destiny of his son. What we note in the Bible history at this point is, not miracles, but certain providential coincidences, very striking, but not lying beyond the limits of the natural.  The mother of Moses is more than ordinarily desirous to save him, because he is "a goodly child," "exceeding fair" or "fair to God" (Acts vii. 20), "a proper child" or "a goodly child" (Heb. xi. 23, *Revised Version*).  It was his exceeding beauty that led the mother to brave all risks and determine to try to save him : an inferior motive, and im- probable in such a case, some would say ; a motive very true to human nature would be the more correct judgment of others. The mother needed but to look on that sweet face to make up her mind what she would do.  So beautiful a reflection of God's image could not be given up to destruction.  "The reason," as has been said, "sounds quaint, if not childish.  The parents hid him because he was comely ; yet they hid him by faith.  The beauty of a sleeping babe was to them a revelation—as truly a revelation as if they had heard the voice of the angel that spoke to Manoah or to Zacharias." * After all, why may not God speak to us through the beauty of a child, as well as through the beauty of a flower or the glory of the sun?

As long as his mother could she hid him in the house. This was no easy task, for as Egyptians passed most of their time in the open air, their houses were little more than bed-closets. We cannot wonder that the time came when he could be hid no longer. Jochebed knows where to apply for help. A daring, almost desperate scheme for her child's protection came into her head, which she believed came from God. She knew that the daughter of Pharaoh (whose name by one account was Thermuthis, by another, Merrhis) was in the habit of bathing in a certain part of the river. If only she could see her little son, she thinks his beauty and his helplessness would touch her heart, and that she would resolve to save him. In the very mode which she devises for bringing him under her notice, she shows that she is very far from giving him up as lost. It was an ark in which she placed him, an ark of bulrushes, but still a vessel whose name and shape recalled a simi-

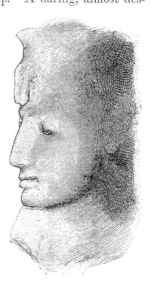

PHARAOH'S DAUGHTER.

lar danger, and seemed somehow to promise that the deliverance which the ark had afforded to Noah would come to Moses too. Miriam is set to watch, and instructed, no doubt, what to say should Pharaoh's daughter discover the child and be interested in him. Everything turns out to a wish. Pharaoh's daughter sees the child, and her heart is touched. A nurse being needed, Miriam, as instructed by the princess, runs for the mother of Moses, and her child is given back to her to be brought up as the princess's son, and paid for accordingly. Thus once more, in the history of

* "Expositor's Bible"—Edwards on *Hebrews*, p. 239.

Israel, faith is conspicuously rewarded. Though it seemed a faith founded on a fancy, founded on the beauty of the child, yet it was a real faith, a faith in God, a faith that inspired venture, and courage, and hope, because God was a real Being, and the child had been committed to him, and he would not suffer him to perish. The name which the princess gave him was significant of his peril when the river seemed about to claim him—" Moses, because I have drawn him out of the water."

An Arab tradition makes a little island in the Nile, called Rhoda, the scene of the exposure of Moses; but the tradition is of no value. It is natural for travellers, as they sail up the Nile, to keep looking out for the bulrushes and flags by the river's brink; and it is no small disappointment to some to discover no trace of either. It would have confirmed the Scripture narrative, they fancy, if these plants had still occurred in abundance; but the truth is that their entire disappearance is a more striking confirmation of Scripture. Other sources of information leave no doubt of their abundance in former times, but Isaiah wrote, when foretelling the downfall of Egypt : " The reeds and the flags shall wither ; the paper reeds by the brooks shall wither, be driven away, and be no more." True to this prediction, all trace of them has disappeared.

The first few years of his life would be spent mostly in his father's house ; the next few at Pharaoh's court, where, though his Hebrew origin was not concealed, he was brought up as the son of the princess. " As a child he probably went about, like other Egyptian boys, without clothes, and with his hair shaved off, except a single lock, which depended on one side of the head. He would be waited on by numerous attendants, would be carefully and delicately fed, kept scrupulously clean, and taught the refined manners of the highest circles." * As Memphis occupied nearly the same site as the modern Cairo, it is easy to place before our minds the scenes amid which the boy would grow up. He would see the three great pyramids standing up against the orange glow of the western sky—vast habitations of the dead, full even

* Rawlinson's " Moses," p. 22.

then of grandeur and mystery. In the streets, shouts and cries would be heard from the noisy charioteers; the busy movements of trade and commerce would enliven the thoroughfares; or religious processions would be seen entering the temples or moving along the highways. On the river, heavily laden vessels would be slowly passing by, or livelier craft darting along with gay sails and bright painted sides. On the temple walls he would be initiated into the meaning of the grotesque hieroglyphical figures, which told many an interesting tale of the past; while in his walks he might occasionally meet the Apis or sacred bull, though he could not be induced to pay homage to the pretended incarnation of God. "The Egyptian religion delighted in openly manifesting itself, in setting itself everywhere and at all times before the eyes of the people, in challenging and compelling their attention. All the grandest edifices were temples; next to the king, the persons most considered were the priests; religious festivals, involving great gatherings and long processions were frequent; men, women, and even children attended them. Moses must have been early familiar with the external aspect, at any rate, of the Egyptian worship, and must have frequently witnessed the revolting rites of the prevalent idolatry." *

There are abundant materials for ascertaining the particulars of Egyptian education for young men destined, like Moses, for civil or military service under the Middle Egyptian Empire. M. Maspero has collected the most important facts in the introduction to his work on a portion of a papyrus of the nineteenth dynasty, entitled, "Hymne au Nil." A summary of his information is thus given in a note in the "Speaker's Commentary:"—"He observes that we know for certain that a literary education was the first condition for admission to the public service; the title of scribe was necessary in order to obtain the lowest appointment in the civil administration or in the army......The education so highly valued began at a very early age......The scholar learned the elements of letters, the rules of orthography and grammar; and, as he advanced, the art of expressing his thoughts in simple and

* Rawlinson's "Moses," p. 24.

perspicuous prose......It was no slight thing to master the quali-
fications of a man of letters. The mere art of writing presented
difficulties so serious, that we find scribes boasting of a thorough
knowledge of the mysteries of sacred letters as a rare and wonderful attainment......The mystic writings, in which ancient truths
were embedded in dark and dreary superstitions, occupied much
of the time not only of the priests but of all men of learning."

The Egyptians had two modes of writing—the hieroglyphic and
the hieratic. The hieroglyphic alphabet represented sounds and
ideas by pictures of objects. Of these picture-objects there were
about a thousand. To know these was in itself no small achieve-
ment. To draw the objects, and to do it quickly, correctly, and
tastefully, was another and by no means easy accomplishment.
The hieratic was a kind of cursive language formed upon the
hieroglyphic, and requiring a knowledge of it. Its forms, too,
were very numerous and difficult to distinguish.

Arithmetic and geometry were important studies in Egypt.
So was music, vocal and instrumental; also harmony or rhythm.
That Moses was skilled in the last appears both from his song
after the passage of the Red Sea, and from the poem in Deuteronomy, ch. xxxii. Astronomy, law, medicine, chemistry, and the
philosophy of symbols, were among the more advanced branches;
but religion, or the sacred books, was the main subject of study.

There were two great universities in the Egypt of those days,
that of Heliopolis and that of Hermopolis; and tradition has it
that at the former of these, about twenty miles north of Memphis,
Moses received his higher education. Heliopolis or On, the City
of the Sun, was memorable for the great temple to that deity.
An avenue of sphinxes led to a colossal gateway, from which
red and blue streamers waved from gigantic flagstaffs. " Before
and behind the gateway stood, two by two, the colossal petrifac-
tions of the sunbeam, the 'obelisks' (spits), of which one alone
now remains to mourn the loss of all its brethren. Thither, it
was believed, came the Phœnix to die. Close by was the sacred
Spring of the Sun, a rare sight in Egypt, and therefore the more
precious, and probably the original cause of the selection of this

remote corner of Egypt for so famous a sanctuary. This, too, still remains, almost choked by the rank luxuriance of the aquatic plants which have gathered over its waters. Round the cloisters of the vast courts into which these gateways opened were spacious mansions, forming the canonical residences, if one may so call them, of the priests and professors of On ; for Heliopolis, we must remember, was the Oxford of ancient Egypt, the seat of its learning in early times, as Alexandria was in later times—the university, or rather perhaps the college, gathered round the Temple of the Sun. Thither Herodotus came to gather information for his travels ; and thither, centuries later, the careful and more accurate Strabo, who was shown the house in which Plato had lived for thirteen years......In the temple there sat in his gilded cage the sacred hawk, or lay crouched on his purple bed the sacred black calf Mnevis or Urmer, each the living representation of the deity of the temple. Thrice a day, before the sacred beast, the incense was offered, and once a month the solemn sacrifice......He was the great rival of the bull Apis at Memphis......The molten calf in the wilderness, the golden calves of Dan and Bethel, were reminiscences, not to be wiped out of the national memory for centuries, of the consecrated calf of Ra, the god Mnevis." *

We may readily understand how the pious mother of Moses, knowing that he was to be brought up in Pharaoh's palace, and amid scenes of idolatry such as those at Heliopolis, would be eager, while she had him, to imbue his mind with the faith which was not only her own, but had been the faith of all the great and good in the nation before her. Probably there never was a great man that owed more to his mother. Most earnestly would she press on him all that was great and glorious in the history of Israel— God's gracious plan to reveal himself to Abraham and his seed, and finally raise up of his race the Deliverer in whom all the families of the earth were to be blessed. And then she would tell him how gladly the fathers had accepted God's covenant, and what noble men they had become under the influence of the faith they cherished ; and she would appeal to him, with all the persuasive

* Stanley's " Jewish Church."

force which love lends to a mother's words, not to forsake their noble example, but bear aloft their banner even in Pharaoh's palace, and cling to the people whom He had chosen, and among whom He had pledged Himself to dwell. And the seed fell into good soil. The deepest devotion of his heart was drawn to God; and for his countrymen, too, there sprang up not only an attachment but a passion that drew him to them irresistibly. They were dear to him because they were his countrymen, but dearer because they were the people of God, "to whom pertained the adoption, and the glory, and the covenants, and the service of God, and the promises."

The early life of Moses at the court of Pharaoh, amid all its attractions and advantages, must have had some drawbacks. Egyptian youths and Egyptian courtiers could not be altogether cordial to the Hebrew boy, who, as the grandson of Pharaoh, enjoyed so exalted a position and received such eminent attention. If he was expected to receive instruction from the priests on religion, there must have been no little opposition on his part to many of their lessons; if, as a Hebrew, he was allowed the benefit of a "conscience clause," and exempted from religious instruction, there would be hardly less of a barrier between him and his instructors. For a boy to hold his own against such influences could not be easy. When he came to receive the more advanced instruction which the priests had to offer—to understand their "philosophy of symbols"—there might be a nearer approach to each other than at the earlier stage. To advanced scholars it was taught that the gods and goddesses of the popular belief were not real existences, but popular modes of representing the various attributes and operations of the one God. It was held necessary to have a popular religion for the populace, but a purer religion for the initiated. On the unity of the one true God, Moses and his instructors might theoretically be nearly at one. But the Egyptians would not sympathize with him in the views which gave such interest to that doctrine in his eyes. They would be slow to believe, would probably refuse altogether to believe, that God had revealed himself specially to his fathers, and entered into covenant with them, making them his people, and constituting them the channel of the richest spiritual blessings which would ever be bestowed on the children of men.

As Moses grew up, it must have been an anxious question for him and his friends in what particular way he was to spend his life. To hang idly about the court as a child of pleasure, amusing himself from day to day with the usual frivolities, would not have satisfied a young man of so high abilities and so active a nature. The priesthood was counted a most honourable service; but of course he could not think of that. Literature, too, was honoured, and Moses had no doubt proclivities in that direction; but it was too quiet an occupation to be the principal business of his life. Then there was the army. King Rameses was a keen, active, ambitious warrior, and would have plenty for Moses to do in that department. That Moses directed his energies to this field is the invariable testimony of tradition. Josephus, indeed, goes further, and specifies an expedition against the Ethiopians as having been intrusted to Moses, when all Egypt was in terror at their aggressions, and as having been completely successful. Stephen, in his speech to the Sanhedrim, says that during this period of his life he was "mighty in word and deed." It would be difficult to conceive how he could afterwards have planned the simultaneous exodus of a whole people from Egypt, and conducted their march through the wilderness, if he had not been accustomed to handle masses of men and provide for their wants. Be this as it may, the language of Stephen shows plainly that he had attained a position of great weight and influence at the court of Pharaoh before he became a fugitive from Egypt.

All the stronger was the temptation to cling to that position. But a time came when he felt he must abandon it. A great struggle arose in his mind. Was he to be an Egyptian, or was he to be a Hebrew? All that the world could offer was on the one side, with a profusion rarely experienced; on the other were poverty, reproach, contempt, and even danger and possible death. Whatever mental struggles Moses may have experienced, he showed no want of decision when he had to make the choice.

What the world would have deemed its greatest prize, he deliberately put aside. Whatever offence he might give, whatever charge of ingratitude he might incur, whatever reproach of idiocy he might draw down on himself, he resolved to throw in his lot with the Hebrews. The principles on which he did so are set forth in the Epistle to the Hebrews : " By faith Moses, when he was come of years, refused to be called the son of Pharaoh's daughter ; choosing rather to suffer affliction with the people of God, than to enjoy the pleasures of sin for a season ; esteeming the reproach of Christ greater riches than the treasures of Egypt : for he had respect unto the recompense of reward."

It is one of the most striking instances that have ever occurred of the triumph of faith over sight. It was the unseen, the distant, the spiritual that moved him, and raised him high above the seen, the present, the carnal.

But his case was not like the ordinary case of a young man called to choose between God and the world. Besides the voice that had called him to serve God personally, to which he had probably responded in his boyhood, another call seemed to come to him to deliver his people from the bondage of Egypt. Dim and distant that voice had been at first, and, as often happens in such cases, it had been dismissed as a mere freak of the imagination. But back it comes, louder and more distinct, though even now what it points to seems so utterly out of the question that Moses cannot fancy it is really addressed to him. Yet the more he ponders the more is he impressed. What was the purpose of that marvellous preservation of his life as an infant, when hardly any other Hebrew boy escaped the jaws of the river? Why had he been brought under the notice of the princess, adopted as her son, and brought up in her house ? Why had he enjoyed so remarkable advantages, become possessed of such influence, and been placed among rulers, making it comparatively easy for him to head a great cause ? The idea that seemed a phantasm at first became at last the ruling idea of his soul : he was called to deliver his people, and that call he must obey !

And the same considerations that had swayed him in his

personal choice were effectual in this also. The passage in the
Hebrews lays emphasis on two. The people were the people of
God, and their reproach was the reproach of Christ. Those toiling
slaves, with their backs furrowed by the bastinado, and their
limbs blackened or bleeding from the kicks and cuffs of their task-
masters, were precious in God's sight; and whoever should be-
friend them in their misery, and rescue them from their bondage,
would be doing service to the people of God. And the reproach
which he would have to suffer was the reproach of Christ. Does
this not mean, as the words seem to imply, that he saw that when
the great Deliverer came he would be exposed to the same reproach
that would now fall on himself? Did he foresee that the Messiah
would have to leave a higher court than Pharaoh's in the execution
of his work, and would be taunted with the miserable condition of
those whom he came to deliver? So far from this reproach being
a drawback in Moses' eyes, he esteemed it greater riches than the
treasures of Egypt; for he had respect to the recompense of the
reward. No sacrifices or losses or reproaches, therefore, would hinder him from accepting the call to be the deliverer of his people.

Moses would come to see afterwards that the work of deliverance was not a thing to be rushed at in a moment of enthusiasm.
Meanwhile, he was full of the thought, and he believed that as
soon as he made it known his countrymen would respond. Under
its influence, "he went out unto his brethren, and looked on
their burdens." If we may judge of the condition of the Israelites from the common treatment at the present day of slaves in
Egypt and other Eastern countries, the sight must have been
very harrowing. Toiling unprotected at the heaviest tasks under
the burning sun and sky of Egypt, they were liable, if they should
attempt to snatch a moment's rest, to be lashed into activity by
the taskmaster's scourge; or if, through sheer exhaustion, they
should fall down, to be cursed and kicked as they lay; and if they
should die, flung out on the sand for the vultures to devour.*

---

* Philo says "that the taskmasters continually became more and more savage; that
many of them were wild beasts in human shape, with hearts as hard as steel or adamant,
utterly pitiless, and unwilling to make allowance for any shortcoming, whatever its cause"
("Vit. Mosis," pp. 86, 87).

Moses was not long among them when he saw a sight that made his blood boil. " He spied an Egyptian smiting an Hebrew, one of his brethren." It may have been a feeble and sickly Hebrew that received the blows ; and the whip or the bastinado, or the blows and kicks from the hands and feet of the Egyptian, may have been laid on so frightfully that Moses could not repress his indignation. A few moments more and the oppressor is stretched lifeless at his feet. A hasty grave is dug, and he is buried in the sand.

Next day, seeing two of his countrymen quarrelling, and cut to the heart that they should be increasing their misery by strife among themselves, he expostulated with them ; but only to be rudely asked by one of them, " Wilt thou slay me as thou didst the Egyptian yesterday ? " Two conclusions rushed from this question into his mind : first, that his life was in danger in consequence of the murder being known ; and second, that no reliance could be placed on his countrymen to respond to his plan for their deliverance, or even aid him by silence. He knew well that should his deed come to the ears of Pharaoh, as in all likelihood it would, there would be no mercy for him. He had not only killed an Egyptian, but he had done so in frustration of the purpose of the king. No doubt he was well watched, probably suspected of rebellious designs. He must consult his safety by flight. And he must get as soon as possible beyond the jurisdiction of Pharaoh. The desert of Sinai, on the eastern shore of the Red Sea, was the only feasible place of refuge. To reach that region Moses now fled, as utterly alone as his father Jacob when he fled to Padan-aram. But Jacob was flying only from the anger of an offended brother, Moses from the vengeance of an offended king. And Moses had no uncle or relative at the end of his journey to receive him. At the best he could but find himself among strangers ; and it was doubtful whether at their hands he would meet with any kindness, or whether he would not rather find himself reduced to the state of slavery in which he had left his miserable countrymen.

It is a very chequered judgment we must form of Moses' conduct on this occasion. While its general course was supremely noble, this specific act was manifestly wrong. It brings before us a strange but undoubted fact in human history—how with the noblest intentions men of the purest character may commit very ruinous blunders. It indicated too clearly that Moses was not yet fully fitted for his work. He was too rash, too impetuous, to be the deliverer of his nation. Like Joseph, the forwardness of his spirit needed to be chastened by a long period of loneliness and trial. It is evident that this act of his was not done in faith. Strange that the wings of that sublime faith on which he had been borne away from Pharaoh's palace were now folded, and the sword of the Lord exchanged for the feeble weapon of man! Faith is a fearless thing; it feels that it is backed by omnipotence, and it does not fear the face of clay. It does not look round, as Moses did, on this side and on that, to see that no man is present before it strikes its blow. It does not fear when it apprehends that its deed is known. It does not rush into concealment when it hears of an exasperated king. It does not abandon its enterprise when it receives its first repulse. When Moses returned to Egypt from the burning bush his faith was of a different temper. The King of Egypt and all his hosts were nothing to him then. Now he has nothing to fall back on. He is like Samson with his locks shorn, and having no heavenly refuge he is weak as other men, and must seek safety in flight.

But, on the other hand, when we look at the general course of his conduct, apart from this mistake, it is noble in the extreme. What could have been grander than to turn his back on Pharaoh's court to take up the cause of a poor, oppressed, enslaved nationality? Let us view Moses' sacrifice in the light of that of the great Master himself. Between Jesus coming to earth to redeem men, and Moses leaving the court of Egypt out of sympathy for his oppressed nation, there was no doubt an infinite difference in one view, but a near resemblance in another. Like Jesus, he could not rest satisfied with an honourable and comfortable position, while his brethren appealed so powerfully to his compassion. Like Jesus, he threw in his lot with his afflicted people, and became for them a man of sorrows and acquainted with grief.   He was of that noble type of men who are ever ready to sacrifice themselves for others, and count no labour and no pain too great on their behalf.   In the divine Son of Mary this type is at its highest.   But in all ages, and notably in our own, we find not a few who have devoted themselves heart and soul to the cause of the oppressed, and found their noblest satisfaction in relieving their burdens and breaking their fetters.   Nothing can ever rob Christianity of this glorious distinction so long as the example of Him retains its power, who, "though he was rich, for our sakes became poor, that we through his poverty might be rich."

## CHAPTER II.

(Ex. ii. 15-iv.)

TO give up a grand mission to which he felt a divine call because the first hasty effort had been a failure, showed that Moses had not yet reached the full stature of his manhood. "He had been taught to rule," says the German Kurtz, "but not to serve ; and the latter was as necessary, if not more so, than the former. He possessed the fiery zeal of youth, but not the circumspection, the patience, or the firmness of age. A consciousness of his vocation had been aroused within him in Egypt; but it was mixed with pride and ambition, with headstrong zeal, but yet with a pusillanimity which was soon daunted. He did not understand the art of being still and enduring, of waiting and listening for God's direction—an art so indispensable for all who labour in God's kingdom." In fact, the faith of Moses was as yet but a brilliant impulse, not a sustained and steady habit. Its movement was like the rush of a rocket, that leaps with a great blaze into the sky ; not like the flight of the eagle, that sustains itself on well-poised wings, even when the tempest is raging around it.

Yet we should not have thought that the long period of forty years would be needed to discipline him for the work of his life. Neither should we have assigned to him, during that long period, the humble task of a shepherd. The whole mental history of Moses while in the wilderness of Midian is a blank to us. Any attempt to fill it up in detail would be merely conjecture. All that we know is that, like his divine Antitype, he learned obedience by the things which he suffered. Somehow, under God's training, the infirmities of his youth were overcome; his faith, his courage, and his judgment were all matured; and when the reluctance caused by long inaction was once overcome, he was enabled with unwavering faith to grapple with the work of delivering his countrymen, and bring it, with God's help, to a glorious consummation.

His route across the desert would be very similar to that by which he afterwards led his people, except that, to avoid the sea, he might now strike eastward by a more northerly path. The district to which he fled was the peninsula of Sinai, a singular and solitary tract, full of barren mountains, lying between the two gulfs into which the Red Sea parts at its northern extremity. He seems in his flight to have gone right across the peninsula to the Gulf of Akaba, where he fell in with a pastoral tribe of Midianites, and accepted the humble situation of shepherd to Reuel, their priest and chief.

The peninsula of Sinai is about one hundred and fifty miles in greatest breadth, and in greatest length two hundred. It is shaped like the letter V. There is some doubt as to the exact part where Moses settled, but probably it was near the eastern border, on one or other shore of the Elanitic Gulf. In the southern part of the peninsula the mountains are crowded together with bewildering confusion, and some of them rise to the height of nine thousand feet. The two great characteristics of the region are majesty and desolation. A modern traveller has described its appearance by comparing it to an ocean of lava, which, while its waves were running mountains high, had suddenly been made to stand still. Another describes the mountains as the Alps of Arabia,—but the Alps unclothed; the Alps planted in a desert, and therefore stripped of all the clothing that goes to make up our notions of Swiss and of English mountains stripped of the variegated drapery of oak and birch, and pine and fir, and grass and fern— wild, bare, rugged, desolate;—truly "a great and terrible wilderness." Still another traveller gives a vivid idea of the desolation by a simple entry in his journal: "Walked six hours; saw two

beetles and a crow." This wilderness is everywhere intersected by ravines or *wâdys* running towards the sea, each of which for a short time in winter forms the channel of a torrent, but during the rest of the year is nearly as dry as the dust of the highway. It is to the absence of water that the desolate character of the district is owing. Notwithstanding, most of these *wâdys* have a thin coating of vegetation, consisting of aromatic and other plants, "the desert's spicy stores" of the poet; and in some spots, under the influence of perennial springs, a richer vegetation flourishes, brightening out here and there into scenes of considerable luxuriance and beauty. It is the business of shepherds to find out all these green spots, and to lead their flocks to them for refreshment and pasture. There is evidence that in the early ages the peninsula was more productive and of greater importance than it is now. Copper and turquoise mines had been worked in it from a very early period, and were probably in full operation in Moses' time.

He seems to have found no one to hold intercourse with till he reached the settlement of Reuel the Midianite. Reuel is said to have been priest of Midian, and seems to have been a worshipper of the true God. Depressed in mind and wearied in body, Moses sat down by a well. The seven daughters of Reuel came to draw water; but unlike Jacob, who in the like case hastened to remove the stone and water the flock, Moses sat still. Nor did he rouse himself till some shepherds came and drove the damsels away. This kindled his spirit, and made him stand up and help the young women to water their flocks. The incident is trifling but instructive. Was it not for a similar act of chivalry that he was now a lonely fugitive? Why should he trouble himself with the affairs of these strangers, when he had burned his fingers so grievously in trying to serve his own people? But there were stronger impulses in Moses than those of prudence and self-interest. He was one of those men that cannot endure the sight of wrong, especially when perpetrated on the weak. One man against a group of shepherds was no doubt a very unequal force. And, after all, the girls were accustomed to their rudeness. But at the sight of injustice Moses sprang to his feet, and the unexpected apparition of a man of such bearing, and probably grand physical form, seems to have struck the shepherds with panic. Reuel's daughters were freed for once, and perhaps for altogether, from the rude selfishness of the shepherds. And Moses' kindness so recommended him to them and to Reuel that he invited him to his house. It is remarkable how often acts of spontaneous courtesy were rewarded in the early history of Israel—Rebekah's, when she offered to draw water for Eliezer's camels; Jacob's, when he rolled away the stone and drew for Laban's flocks; and now the courtesy of Moses. So true is it, according to the saying of Lady Mary Wortley Montague, that "civility costs nothing and buys everything."

Was there a tender chapter in Moses' history now? Was Zipporah to him as Rachel to Jacob? Was the task of shepherd made pleasant by the same magical charm? The future relations of Moses and Zipporah would not altogether warrant the supposition. For Moses seems always to have been a lonely man. The name of his eldest son, Gershom (stranger), shows that the home-sickness had not left him. It is as if he felt that the faces he most loved were not around him, the voices he would fain have heard were silent to him, the thoughts and feelings he would fain utter he must lock up in his bosom for want of kindred listeners. Miriam is introduced afterwards in the story as "the sister of Aaron," as if in her social life she was connected with him more than with the brother whom she had watched on the Nile. And the history of Moses' family ends with himself; they succeeded to none of his honours, nor do they appear to have been imbued with his spirit.

We cannot but be struck with the readiness of Moses to accept the humble calling of a shepherd, and prosecute it for forty long years. He seems to have thought that by his rashness he had destroyed his commission from God as the deliverer of his people, or at least that he never could resume it without a new and special call. Any occupation was good enough for one who had spoiled so noble a chance. He seems quite content to be a servant; shows none of Jacob's pushing spirit; makes no bargain for himself; is still a servant, keeping the flock of Jethro his father-in-law (or brother-in-law ?), apparently for a mere livelihood, when the angel appears to him in the burning bush. The same unworldly spirit shown in renouncing Egypt is still at work; he seeks nothing great for himself or his family. Another resemblance this to the great Antitype, who so patiently accommodated himself to this poor world, and to the lowly society of carpenters and fishermen, full of that charity which "seeketh not her own," coming "not to be ministered unto but to minister, and to give his life a ransom for many."

He had called his eldest son Gershom (stranger), as if to indicate how far he was from congenial human fellowship; but his second son got a more cheerful name, "Eliezer; for God, said he, hath been my help, and hath delivered me from the hand of Pharaoh." This had really been a great danger; and when we think how eager Pharaoh was afterwards to pursue and bring back the people, we may see what a proof it was of divine protection that he did not make a search, or, at all events, that he did not succeed in his search, for Moses when he fled to Sinai. It is pleasing to find that the forty years in the wilderness were not a wilderness of forty years —not a weary night of spiritual desertion, but a time of much divine fellowship, in which Moses learned to say, "Lord, thou hast been our dwelling-place in all generations." As to his feeling regarding the deliverance of his people, that was in God's hands, and until God moved Moses never would. It was awfully harrowing and saddening to think of such scenes being still enacted every day as that which had maddened his soul in Egypt; but God must look to that, and in his own time he would. No step would Moses take of himself, though he should wait till his eye became dim and his right hand forgot its cunning; never again should it be said of him that he had gone a warfare at his own charges, or that he had run, even on a divine and most patriotic errand, before he was sent.

During the forty years Moses silently and slowly ripened for his work. "Come into the desert and rest a while," were words that Jesus used to address to his disciples. The bustle of active life is not favourable to reflection. You cannot well review your life while everything is going on around you with restless activity. You cannot overhaul or repair a machine while it is in motion. His first forty years in Egypt had furnished Moses with much knowledge, but he had not had opportunity to digest it. Now he gets the opportunity of calm meditation, and he seems to have used it admirably. All that he had seen in Egypt of the human heart, all that he had gathered from books, all about religion and government, laws and customs, ordinances and worship, would now be subjected to slow and patient reflection, and turned into maxims of sanctified wisdom. God was leading him, as he leads the blind, by a way which he knew not,—preparing him for his life-work, and likewise for his eternal reward.

In the wilderness, too, he had opportunities and encouragements for fellowship with God that he could not have had in the court of Pharaoh. No contrast could have been greater than that between the objects that surrounded him in Egypt and in the desert. In Egypt all was the work of man ; in the desert, of God. Man had done his utmost in Egypt to rival the works of God. The pyramids in their massive grandeur, the solemn temples with their elaborate ornamentation, the mysterious sphinxes, the tall slender obelisks—what an impression of the power of man they were fitted to convey ! But what were the pyramids to that magnificent Horeb whose summit was lost among the clouds ? What were the statues and the sphinxes to the statuary of nature, those huge granite blocks piled on each other in such fantastic forms, amid which the lightnings played ? What was the grandest temple, with its blue ceiling spangled with gilded stars, to the great azure vault where the Sun ruled by day, and where by night the real Orion came forth in his splendour and Arcturus guided his sons ? A heart like that of Moses could not but be more deeply impressed in such scenes with the supremacy of God ; while at the same time he would attain to closer intimacy with, and peradventure to a clearer knowledge of, God's purpose concerning the seed of Abraham. Thus encouraging him to blend reverence with intimacy and intimacy with reverence, the wilderness of Sinai would prepare him for that unprecedented intercourse which he was hereafter to hold with God on that towering summit which, bathed in the glory of sunset, must often have looked like the very throne of heaven.

During the years that Moses had spent in the wilderness, the children of Israel had also been undergoing a divine discipline. They needed to be prepared for deliverance as much as Moses needed to be trained as deliverer. For a long time they seem to have lived in the hope that a change of ruler in Egypt would benefit their condition. Their hopes were thus turned to man rather than to God. At last the change of sovereign took place, but it brought no relief to the afflicted people. More emphatically than ever, they sighed and cried by reason of their bondage. "And God heard their groaning, and God remembered his covenant with Abraham, with Isaac, and with Jacob. And God looked upon the children of Israel, and God had respect unto them."

Those who deny the operation of a supernatural power in the deliverance of the Israelites are obliged to find an adequate cause of deliverance on the part of the people themselves. It is conjectured that at this time, and under the new sovereign, a movement toward emancipation began among them. The tribe of Levi, Moses' tribe, it is supposed, took the lead in this movement. Remembering what Moses had done long before, their hopes were set on him. His brother Aaron was despatched to Sinai to look for him, consult with him, and bring him back, that he might head the perilous work for which he had offered himself at a time when the people were unprepared to move.

That the longing for freedom had become active among them at this time is evident from the narrative—evident from the fact of their sighing and crying to God. That Aaron was despatched to look for Moses, consult with him on the great subject, and if possible engage him to return and set his people free, is quite possible, and quite consistent with the narrative of Exodus. But that Moses took the matter in hand simply at the urgent entreaty of Aaron, is in the very teeth of the narrative. If ever supernatural influence was needed, it was here.

Still we may find in the circumstances one of those coincidences in Providence which it is always interesting to mark. Just as at a future time, while Cornelius was being prepared to receive a message, Peter was being prepared to carry it, so now, as the children of Israel begin to turn towards the right quarter for deliverance, the preparation is completed of their destined deliverer.

Faithful to the duties of his calling, Moses was keeping his father-in-law's (or brother-in-law's) flock in "the back" or western part of the desert (Gesenius), when the angel of the Lord appeared to him in a flame of fire. At first, what Moses saw was only a strange phenomenon—a bush burning and not consumed. It was as he turned aside to examine it that he became aware of the presence of the angel of God, and heard a voice calling, "Moses, Moses." That it was God who spoke to him was made more clear when he was warned not to come near, and ordered to take the shoes from off his feet, because the place on which he stood was holy ground. And still more when the voice proclaimed, "I am the God of thy father, the God of Abraham, the God of Isaac, and the God of Jacob." Yes, it was God himself who was speaking. "And Moses hid his face ; for he was afraid to look upon God."

What was the precise meaning of this symbol—God appearing as fire, and appearing in a bush which was not consumed? The voice of the Church universal has explained it in one way. The bush, a lowly plant of the desert, was the symbol of Israel enslaved in Egypt ; the fire denoted his trials ; and the bush, yet green and fresh notwithstanding the fire, denoted his preservation from destruction through the power of God. And the symbol has been a favourite emblem of the preservation of the Church of God "in all time of her tribulation"—passing every age through some fresh ordeal, yet surviving all ; showing fresh buds bursting into leaf even when the bush was seemingly dead ; bearing a charmed life which no weapon could destroy; renewing her youth like the eagle, because dwelling under the shadow of the Almighty. And the special lesson of the symbol to Moses would thus be, that the fires of persecution had not destroyed his countrymen, but that the presence of God among them had preserved their vitality unimpaired amid all the efforts of the enemy to destroy them.

That this is substantially the true explanation of the symbol must, we think, be generally admitted; but there is this difficulty about it, that it was the angel of the Lord that appeared in the flame of fire in the midst of the bush—that the fire, therefore, did not properly symbolize the sufferings but the real preserver of the people. Hence some have thought that the fire denoted merely the avenging holiness of God about to be shown in the punishment of the Egyptians. But this leaves the unconsumed bush meaningless. May we not consider the fire and its effects here as an instance of *constructio pregnans*—as denoting, in the first instance, the fiery trials which God *suffered* to fall on the people, because they were an essential factor in his discipline of them? In this sense God was in the fire. On the other hand, the directing power and grace of God so quenched the violence of the fire that it did not consume: as it left the branches green, so persecution had hitherto left the Israelites undestroyed, and it would continue to be harmless to the end. Versed as Moses was in the language of symbols, he could not fail to derive this impression from the marvellous sight. Preservation amid the forces of destruction was the obvious moral of the appearance.

God's first assurance to Moses was that the condition of his people was well known to him. If the form of language should seem to imply that he had but recently become impressed by it, this must be dismissed as out of the question, because "all things are naked and open to the eyes of Him with whom we have to do." We must think of God as having been fully and keenly alive to that long era of persecution, every day of which had witnessed so much wrong and suffering inflicted on his chosen people. The calmness with which God sometimes appears to look upon bitter wrongs and unjust sufferings, and to let them go on unrebuked for years, and generations, and centuries, is one of the features of his providence which it is most difficult for us to understand. But the longer we live the more clearly we see that suffering, sharp suffering, long suffering, is one of the most important of God's agencies for the good of men; and that it is a proof of God's great strength of mind, so to speak, that where great good is to be effected he allows keen suffering to continue so long as it is needed for his great ends.

What, then, does God purpose to do, now that the time to favour his people has at length come? He purposes to send Moses to Egypt to bring forth his people out of the country. It is always human instruments that he uses to effect deliverances, and Moses is to be his instrument now. And what Moses is to do is not merely to make better terms for his people, not merely to secure for them better treatment where they are, but to bring them clean out of Egypt, and settle them in the place of the Canaanites, and the Hittites, and the Amorites, and the Perizzites, and the Hivites, and the Jebusites.

It is no wonder that, being but a man, Moses is astounded at this news. "Who am I, that I should go unto Pharaoh, and that I should bring forth the children of Israel out of Egypt?" Forty years before, Moses had not thought so poorly of himself; he had not been afraid of the work of deliverer then. Now he has learned how utterly unfit he is for such a task; and calling to mind perhaps his miserable failure, he deems himself the last man on earth for such an undertaking.

But it is not as he made the attempt forty years ago that he is to make it now. "Certainly I will be with thee:" thou art only to be my instrument; I myself will undertake the work, and direct it in all its details to a successful issue. And take this proof that I have planned it all out, and that I will see to its being all fulfilled—"When thou hast brought forth the people out of Egypt, ye shall serve God upon this mountain." The assurance conveyed here was of the kind that takes place when, before a crisis, two parties agree as to what they will do after it is safely past; as if a general should overcome the hesitation of a lieutenant appointed to a difficult task, and show his confidence that all would turn out right, by engaging him to dine with him in a certain house after the work should be done.

But Moses was not satisfied. For one who had to persuade a nation in God's name to such an unprecedented course, it was necessary that he should have some special name of God to make known to them, to rouse them and inspire them with the needed trust.  Did Moses call to mind the change of names that had taken place in connection with great events in the history of the fathers—Abram to Abraham, Sarai to Sarah, Jacob to Israel? Did he infer that in such an extraordinary crisis in their history the announcement of some new name *on God's part* would be necessary to secure the due attention of the people?  It is not easy to perceive the precise line of thought that led him to suppose that the people would demand a new name.  But whatever the reason may have been, a new name was given—"I AM THAT I AM."  It was a name that brought out three things—God's self-existence, his personality, and his immutability.  He was not a mere power of nature, or a combination of the powers at work in nature, as the Egyptians fancied, but a distinct personality, a self-existent, unchangeable I—an I that had held special dealings with their fathers, that now sent Moses to them, that was utterly independent of any other being, and that could not by any possibility change so as to be different to-morrow from what he was yesterday.  This I AM THAT I AM was the God of the fathers, of Abraham, and Isaac, and Jacob; and what he was to them he would be to their descendants; what he promised to them stood sure in the history of the future—as sure to stand as the everlasting hills.  This was his name for ever, and this his memorial to all generations.

But Moses was not to go to Egypt in an abrupt and impetuous way, unfurling his standard of a sudden, and trusting to the mob to flock to it in a passion of enthusiasm.  He was not to deal with the mob at all.  He was to gather the elders together, make known his commission to them, and he and they were to go to the King of Egypt in a constitutional way, and make a reasonable and constitutional request of him—to allow the Israelites to go three days' journey into the wilderness, that they might sacrifice to the Lord their God.  Some have represented this as a deceitful and dishonest request.  But there was no ambiguity in reality as to what it implied.  The contest really was whether the Israelites belonged to Pharaoh or to God.  That was a great question; but it might be tried on a small issue, just as the right to a large property is sometimes discussed by trying the right to a small field or a house upon it. On this limited issue, Were the Israelites to obey God by going into the wilderness to sacrifice to him? the whole question as to who was their master was to be decided. For Pharaoh to have yielded this would have been to acknowledge God's sovereignty over them. The contest was quite plainly a religious contest. It was this that made it so clear that "the king of Egypt will not let you go, no, not by a mighty hand." But when the king showed his determination in his way, God would stretch forth his hand and compel submission. And when the people left Egypt, they would not leave it empty. An unfortunate mistranslation in the Authorized Version (rectified in the Revised), substituting the word "borrow" for "ask," has exposed this transaction to a gross misconstruction. The Israelites were not to borrow, but to ask "every woman of her neighbour, and of her that sojourned in her house, jewels of silver, and jewels of gold, and raiment: and ye shall put them upon your sons and your daughters." The Egyptian people had a sense of justice unknown to their king; they had seen how the Israelites had been robbed and insulted, compelled to perform such toilsome tasks with no adequate remuneration, and were willing to give them part of their own jewels, as a rude compensation for the wrongs they had suffered. They would not be led into the wilderness penniless, but with such stores as would for a time amply insure their comfort.

But Moses cannot yet bring himself to consent. Another objection has occurred to him. How shall he persuade the elders that he has received this commission from God? The elders are shrewd and careful men, that must have good grounds for all they are asked to do—how shall he convince them? This objection likewise is met. He is furnished with three symbolic signs. First, the shepherd's rod in his hand is changed into a serpent of such fearful appearance that, accustomed to serpents though he has been, Moses flies from it. The symbol showed how God could make the feeble strong—could turn the harmless rod into a terrible serpent—could make a poor shepherd like Moses so powerful that Pharaoh would cower and tremble before him. Then the sign is reversed : Moses seizes the serpent by the tail, and it becomes a rod. So God could use Moses for converting even a fierce and mighty king like Pharaoh into the most tame and helpless of beings.

The next sign was, that when Moses put his hand in his bosom and drew it out, it became leprous ; when he did it a second time, the hand was restored like the other. The leprous hand might denote the helpless condition to which Moses had been reduced in the wilderness. He had lost his position in Egypt, his influence at court, his acquaintance with the people, and likewise the spirit of enterprise. But that shepherd would yet become a man of might ; that same hand, made strong and stretched out over the waters of Egypt, or over the sea, or over the land, or held up by Aaron and Hur at Rephidim, would work unheard-of wonders.

The third sign was reserved for Egypt, if the other two should prove insufficient. The water of the Nile would be turned into blood. The river that had created Egypt, that had made her the granary of the world, and that was the boast and glory of all the Egyptians, would be turned into a curse. When Moses should appear armed with such a power, how could his people hesitate to follow him, or how could Pharaoh persist in opposing him ?

Moses is hard to satisfy. Yet another difficulty starts up now. He is not a ready speaker. In the desert he has fallen into the slow method that usually marks those who dwell in lonely places. Very likely, in this interview, he has felt that painful embarrassment that prevents one from finding suitable words. " O my Lord, I am not eloquent, neither heretofore, nor since thou hast spoken unto thy servant [as thou mayest see] : but I am slow of speech, and of a slow tongue." Once he had been mighty in word and deed, but his desert life had changed all that. In these objections he is persistently overlooking the fact that it is not Moses but God that is to fight this battle. And as God has made man's mouth, as he has made the dumb, the deaf, the seeing, the blind, surely when he needs a mouth he can adapt it to its pur-

pose—surely he can adapt Moses' mouth for all that he will have
to say.

Moses had now exhausted his objections, but not overcome his
unwillingness. And having no other reasonable plea, he bursts
into a kind of impatient fret, and beseeches God to send any
one rather than him. But this is an abuse of God's forbearance
and condescension. The anger of the Lord is kindled against him,
and his tone changes from meek persuasion to stern rebuke.
Nevertheless, God continues to make arrangements for aiding
him in his duty. "Is not Aaron the Levite thy brother? I
know that he can speak well." They were to form a sort of co-
partnery—Moses directing, Aaron speaking. The two should go
together to Pharaoh, and compel his proud heart to submission.

At length Moses silently assents. But he is not now the Moses
of forty years ago. He has risen on the stepping-stone of his dead
self to higher things.

Called to this work so remarkably of God, it might perhaps be
thought that it was superfluous to ask permission for it of man.
There are men who in such circumstances would have scorned to
go to Jethro and ask his leave to do what God had enjoined.
But the highest order of good men are not so careless of their
fellows. All things must be done in an orderly way, and every
effort made to secure the cordial assent of relatives to arrangements which affect their feelings or their interests. Happily there
was no difficulty with Jethro. He consented at once to his going,
secretly convinced, perhaps, that Moses was fitted for a much
higher post than that of a shepherd, and flattered by the hope
that he would rise again to distinction.

But if all was smooth and easy with Jethro, it was otherwise
on the part of Moses' wife. She agreed, indeed, to go with him
to Egypt; but it turned out that, in consequence of a neglect
of which Moses had been guilty in deference to her, his life was
nearly lost. Some explain her conduct in this way: among the
Midianites it was not the custom to circumcise till the child was
thirteen years old—the age at which Ishmael was circumcised;
and Zipporah, following the family custom, had induced Moses to

defer the circumcision of at least one of her sons, who was under that age. But it is more likely that both sons were above thirteen, and therefore the postponing of the circumcision must have been owing to Zipporah's unwillingness that her sons should cease to be Midianites and should become Hebrews. Moses seems weakly to have yielded to her, instead of circumcising his sons on the eighth day. But now his setting out for Egypt would bring matters to a crisis. He was going to Egypt to claim Israel for God on the divine ground—"Israel is my son, even my first-born. Let my son go that he may serve me ; and if thou refuse to let him go, behold, I will slay thy son, even thy first-born." Pharaoh could not deny that Israel was God's, since each man-child in the nation bore God's mark on his person. On the ground that he was his slave, Pharaoh might indeed refuse to part with Israel ; but God claimed him on a higher ground—because he was his son. But how outrageous it would be for Moses to advance this plea for the nation, if his own sons did not bear the mark of the covenant ! Before he sets out they must be circumcised. How strange the inconsistencies of good men ! Moses is prepared to brave the wrath of the King of Egypt, yet till now he has not had the courage to displease his Midianite wife.

On the way God meets him at some place erected for the accommodation of the caravans that passed that way, and manifests high displeasure. Not a word apparently is spoken ; the conscience of Moses understands the reason, and Zipporah in terror hastens to perform the operation. But as soon as the immediate alarm is past, she gives vent to the mortification of a bitter heart, taunting her husband with having brought her a dowry of cruelty and blood.* Thereupon she vanishes from the story, and it is only afterwards that we find that she did not accompany him to Egypt, but returned to her own people, and did not join Moses until after the contest with Amalek (Ex. xviii. 2).

---

* The whole incident is obscure. It is explained thus in Smith's "Bible Dictionary" : Either Moses or Gershom fell sick on the way. Zipporah connected the sickness with the neglect of circumcision ; took a knife, performed the rite, and flung the instrument at her husband's feet, thinking he had caused the death of her son. On the recovery of her son, she continues to call him a bloody husband, as he had caused the blood of her son to be shed in his circumcision.

Here was another bitter trial to Moses—his heart wounded in the house of his friends, insult and discouragement poured on him for doing the will of God from the very quarter from which one looks for comfort and cheer.

How plain it is from all these things that the undertaking was not of Moses' planning, and that the return to Egypt to contend with Pharaoh was the last thing he would have dreamed of but for the supernatural call of God.

But if one domestic support fails, another takes its place: Aaron meets him in the mount of God. It is a most affectionate meeting, and it brings back a thousand memories of early times. Better still, Aaron accepts God's commission to Moses as true, and hears with interest of the signs which he has given him. For the first time probably in forty years, Moses enjoys the company of a thoroughly congenial heart. As he draws near to Egypt he is able to look without a sinking heart on the old landmarks—the pyramids and temples and obelisks, monuments though they be of Pharaoh's power. And doubtless the two brothers join right heartily in prayers which could not be better expressed than in the words of Moses' psalm—"Let thy work appear unto thy servants, and thy glory unto their children. And let the beauty of the Lord our God be upon us : and establish thou the work of our hands upon us ; yea, the work of our hands establish thou it."

# CHAPTER III.

## THE DUEL WITH PHARAOH.

### (Ex. v.–x.)

IT would be interesting here, if suitable materials existed, to inquire what changes had passed on the children of Israel during the four hundred years they had now spent in Egypt. More particularly, what was now their religious condition? Four hundred years could not but have effected much change on any people. As to their religion, we must bear in mind that during all this period they had no prophets, no priests, no new revelation such as had been made to Abraham and Isaac and Jacob. They had only the tradition of the revelations and promises made to their fathers, and of the simple mode of worship which had been practised by them. The land of Goshen was probably no longer their only place of abode; it is likely that they were much mingled with the Egyptians. And being in such contact with a nation conspicuous for the number of its gods, they could not escape the taint of Egyptian idolatry. There is no reason to think that they had ceased to reverence and to worship the God of their fathers; but it is exceedingly probable that many had learned to worship him through images, and likewise that some of them had begun to conjoin the worship of the Egyptian gods with that of Jehovah. And as the worship of animals, and particularly of the ox, was a prominent feature of Egyptian religion, they had attained a strong proclivity towards that form of idolatry. There are not a few indications in the next chapters of their history that they were deeply penetrated by idolatrous tendencies. But still the tradition of the great God of their fathers must have been a powerful force. Still their hearts would turn wistfully in the direction of Canaan as the home of peace and plenty, and the sphere of spiritual blessing, which had been promised to their fathers. And still they would retain such an expectation of help and deliverance from their national God, that when Moses and Aaron came to them, professing to bring a message from him, they found them by no means unprepared to listen or unwilling to believe.

The first step taken by Moses and Aaron, as God had directed, was to call an assembly of the elders. The people had not been allowed to fall in Egypt into a state of confusion. An orderly national government, a kind of Home Rule in Goshen, within such limits as Pharaoh allowed, had been established, each section of the people having a representative elder. The meeting would probably be held at some central spot in Goshen, and early on the appointed day the elders of each village and country district would be seen trooping to the rendezvous, full of curiosity to see the brother who claimed to have received a divine commission to deliver them. Many of them would feel kindly to him, remembering how nobly he had acted forty years before in leaving the palace out of sympathy for his people ; and a few of the oldest would recall with wonder his deliverance from the Nile, and find it begetting a vague expectation that the symbol would now receive a wider fulfilment, and Israel be drawn out of bondage as he had been drawn out of the water.

"Moses at eighty years of age retained much of the comeliness of his youth. The fire of his eyes was undimmed to a much later age (Deut. xxxiv. 7). He was tall and dignified, with long streaming hair of a reddish hue, tinged with gray, and with a long shaggy beard.* Aaron, at eighty-three, can scarcely have presented a less venerable appearance." Aaron was the speaker, and no doubt in impressive words rehearsed all that God had said to Moses. Then the signs that God had given them were brought

* Rawlinson's "Moses," founded on Artapanus *apud* Euseb. "Præp. Evang.," ix. 27 ; "Diod. Sic.," xxxiv., tr. 1.

forward. The rod became a serpent, and again the serpent a rod. The leprous hand was plucked out of the bosom, and the second time it was whole. Thus the expectations of the elders were so far fulfilled. They saw that the Lord had visited his people; they felt the glow of a new hope; "their mouth was filled with laughter, and their tongue with singing;" "they bowed their heads and worshipped."

The next step was to arrange an interview with Pharaoh. The monarch now reigning was probably Menephthah, son of Rameses II., who had all his father's selfish indifference to the sufferings of others without any of his greatness. Being of feeble character, Menephthah was all the more disposed to plume himself on his official greatness, and to follow the pretensions of his father, who ranked himself among the gods. "There is a legend that he once hurled his spear at the Nile when its floods rose too high, and was punished with ten years of blindness......In another war, he boasts of having slaughtered the people, and set fire to them, and netted the entire country as men net birds." *
The communication of Moses and Aaron was introduced with a formula to which Pharaoh's ears were little accustomed—"Thus saith Jehovah, God of Israel;" and the claim followed, "Let my people go, that they may hold a feast unto me in the wilderness." Pharaoh fired up at once at the mention of the God of Israel. "Jehovah! who is Jehovah, that he should be sending such messages to me? I know nothing of Jehovah; I have nothing to do with Jehovah; most certainly I will not let Israel go." Moses and Aaron had yet an argument. It would be at their peril if they disobeyed the voice of their God; and there was a risk, if they did, that he would bring on them the sword of an enemy, or send among them the curse of pestilence. Army and pestilence were not agreeable words to Pharaoh, for if they came they might spread over a wider territory than Goshen; but in the lips of Moses and Aaron they were mere words—there was no real ground to fear them. Moses and Aaron were told rudely that the only effect of their interposition was mischievous; they were

---

* Chadwick's "Exodus," p. 90.

drawing the people from their work. "Get you unto your burdens," he insultingly exclaimed. That was the only employment for which they were fit, or which would be tolerated by Pharaoh. And so ended the first interview. Moses was prepared for a repulse. God had told him that Pharaoh would not let the people go; but perhaps he expected that some display of divine power would have taken place, that then and there would have compelled Pharaoh to yield.

But Pharaoh has got a fright. Like all tyrants, he does not like the spirit of independence which the words of Moses and Aaron breathe. Something must be done to smother it. The burdens lying on the people are not as yet heavy enough to crush out all thoughts of liberty; their burdens must be made heavier. They must be worn out by greater fatigue. And the way to make their burdens heavier is to withhold the straw hitherto supplied for mixing with the clay—to send them to look for straw, or any substitute they can find, but not to diminish the number of bricks exacted hitherto. In vain the Hebrew officers or foremen remonstrate with Pharaoh on this outrage on all reason and justice; in vain they try to arrest the bastinado, which is applied to them with savage cruelty, even when they are doing their best. All they get is to be taunted with idleness, taunted with desiring to shirk their work on pretence of religion, by going away to do sacrifice to their God. Not a tittle of redress shall be given; the new law shall be enforced with unsparing rigour. Coming away from this dreary interview, the Hebrew officers meet Moses and Aaron. Maddened by the result, they reproach them with being the cause of this new misery. They show none of that noble spirit which would have animated the leaders of a people bent on emancipating themselves. One good result of this experience, however, is that they are turned wholly against Pharaoh; each stroke of the bastinado helps to convert them to the side of Moses.

But their taunts go to Moses' heart. He is greatly distressed, but happily does not allow his distress to work inwards; he carries it to God. "Lord, wherefore hast thou so evil entreated this people? why is it that thou hast sent me?" To a hasty reader the language might seem irreverent; but perhaps it rather indicates a privilege of friendship and intimacy—the privilege of which David often availed himself in the psalms, where, with a thorough conviction that God was really right, he spoke of his proceedings as being, on the surface, very strange, and calling for explanation. God does not give any vindication, for this is but an instance of his method to allow evil to work itself out to its very worst before he fairly grapples with it. This contest with Pharaoh was not to be a mere skirmish, but a pitched battle, in which the earthly king would be allowed to do his very worst against God's people, and to throw every possible obstruction in the way of their leaving Egypt, and would yet in the end be completely and ignominiously beaten.

Before the battle opens, Moses gets a renewed assurance of God's help, coupled with a commentary on the name Jehovah, and some comforting assurances for the future. But when he rehearses these to the people, they are too miserable to take them in. Again God summons him to go to Pharaoh; but when his own people have refused to listen to him, how can he expect Pharaoh to attend? It required a new assurance of the coming deliverance, coupled with an announcement that God would harden Pharaoh's heart, and multiply his signs and wonders in the land, before Moses and Aaron could muster courage to seek another interview with the king.

Ere we go on to the actual conflict, it will be well here to advert to two of God's statements to Moses that have an important bearing on the struggle. The one is connected with God's use of the name JEHOVAH; the other concerns the mysterious influence he was to exert on Pharaoh in hardening his heart.

1. How could it be said to Moses, " I appeared unto Abraham, unto Isaac, and unto Jacob by the name of God Almighty; but by my name JEHOVAH was I not known to them "? Not only does the name Jehovah occur frequently in Genesis, but it occurs as used by the patriarchs themselves, as when Abraham called the name of the place where Isaac was to have been offered Jehovah-jireh (Jehovah will provide). The name Jehovah was even in

use before the days of Abraham—"Then began men to call upon the name of JEHOVAH" (Gen. iv. 26). Some have supposed that it was "the Angel of the LORD," the second Person of the Godhead, that was not known till now as Jehovah—that divine Being who, in these struggles, was so conspicuous as the Guide, Defender, and Saviour of Israel. But it was with that "Angel of the LORD" that Abraham had his dealings at Mount Moriah, and we cannot think that the name Jehovah-jireh was not meant to apply to him. The only explanation that seems admissible is, that the *full significance* of the name Jehovah was not known to the patriarchs. They did not know all the fulness of meaning involved in it; they did not realize to the full extent what it was to have God as their covenant God; they did not experience all that it involved in the form of extrication from deadly evils, from furious oppressors, from an alien land and an alien nation; they did not witness the grandest tokens of Jehovah's supremacy—his superiority to all the powers of nature, to all the might of Pharaoh, to all the fabled puissance of Egypt's gods. But Israel was now to have such manifestations of these things as would throw into the shade all that the fathers had known. For it was not a mere display of the resources of God as the God of nature that would take place, but of God as the covenant King and Protector of Israel; and one of the leading features of it would be this, that the outstretching of his arm would be wholly for the reproof and destruction of Egypt, and for the encouragement and salvation of Israel.

2. The other point requiring explanation is, how the Lord hardened Pharaoh's heart. This seems to ascribe to God an influence for evil inconsistent with his infinite holiness and goodness. The usual explanation is, that the Lord *allowed* Pharaoh's heart to be hardened; and substantially this is the most that can be said. We must remember that though God is never the author of evil, or of evil influences, yet as these do exist in the world, he can take them into his plans, he can turn them to his uses, and bring good out of them. Pride was the besetting sin of Pharaoh. It pleased God now to let him be placed in circumstances that tended to inflame and draw it out, that made him shut his eyes to reason,

and in his blind recklessness persevere in a course utterly disastrous to himself and to his empire. God allowed this state of things to go on. He did not bestow restraining grace to make him truly humble. He left him exposed to the influence of his surroundings. Just as the sun hardens clay, because it is the very nature of clay to harden when not shielded from the sun, so the contest in which Pharaoh was involved hardened his heart, because it is the very nature of a proud heart to be hardened by every assault upon its pride.

The battle is now on the eve of beginning. Moses and Aaron have another interview with Pharaoh, and by God's direction Aaron takes his rod. Pharaoh had heard of it, and wished to see what it could do, and he had called his wise men and sorcerers for a conflict of skill. Thus the first battle was on the arena of magic : could Moses and Aaron on the one hand, or the magicians of Pharaoh on the other, perform the more remarkable wonders? Aaron casts down his rod before Pharaoh, and it becomes a serpent. The magicians, who had heard of this before, and were prepared for it, cast down their rods, and they become serpents too. How they achieved this has been the subject of much conjecture. An old tradition had it that their rods were pieces of rope, having the appearance of rods when laid on the ground, but by some inward contrivance made to twist and wriggle as if they were serpents. Another account is, that the serpents were brought in in a torpid condition, so as to look like rods ; but being roused when thrown on the ground, they exhibited their natural movements. And some think that both rods and serpents were real, and that by legerdemain the serpents were substituted for the rods. The trial might not have been decisive had not Aaron's serpent in the end swallowed up the other serpents, and thus evinced by a sudden and overwhelming proof that Moses was stronger than Pharaoh.

This was, as it were, a mere fancy combat ; but the next was to be of a far more practical and serious nature. Moses was sent forth to Pharaoh in the morning, to meet him as he went to the water—it is not said to bathe ; perhaps it may have been to perform certain religious rites in honour of the river-god. " Possibly it was his duty to recite the mystic hymn, found in a manuscript of the time, where Hapi, 'the hidden,' was acknowledged as the giver of all good things, the source of countless blessings. 'Hail to thee, O Nile,' ran the words of the sacred song, 'that showest thyself in this land, coming in peace, giving life to Egypt. O concealed one, thou leadest the night on to the day, a leading that rejoices the heart! Thou overflowest the gardens created by Ra; thou givest life to all animals; thou waterest the earth without ceasing, from the path of heaven descending. Lover of good, bestower of corn, giving life to every homestead!' The rites were about to be begun, the priests were ready, the courtiers were all attention, when suddenly the monarch found himself confronted by the pertinacious Hebrews." *

Whether this fanciful picture has any foundation or not, certain it is that, undaunted by past failure, the voice of Moses and Aaron was again heard with the same solemn demand on the part of the God of the Hebrews—" Let my people go, that they may serve me in the wilderness." It would have been easy to give the old answer to the old demand, but there was an addition to the former words that must have fallen with startling emphasis on the ears of Pharaoh and his courtiers—" Else I will smite with the rod that is in mine hand upon the waters which are in the river, and they shall be turned to blood." A short pause for a reply, but no reply is given. The rod of Moses is lifted up; before the king's very eyes the water is turned to blood. So also it is in all the streams throughout the whole country, and in the cisterns of wood and stone in which the people were accustomed to gather the water that the mud might subside; they are not able to drink it, for it is putrid and disgusting. And the plague lasts for seven days. The only way of getting pure water was to dig about the river and gather the drops from the soil. What domestic inconvenience and suffering this entailed throughout the country it is not easy to conceive. But every red drop proclaimed the victory of Moses.

* Rawlinson's " Moses."

And domestic suffering was not the only result. The river Nile was not merely held sacred, but actually looked on as a god, just as the Ganges is still regarded by the Hindus. An ancient authority pronounced the god Nilus, or Hapi, as the Egyptian name was, the rival of Heaven, since he watered the earth without rain or clouds. When he overflowed his banks and deposited the mud that fertilized their fields and beautified their gardens, it was looked on as the act of a bountiful father stretching out his arms on every side, and leaving his blessings for his children. But now the time had come for casting contempt even on this much extolled god. Under the rod of Moses the water that had been the medium of life became the source of death. Not only so, but the fish of the river, on which the Egyptians relied as a main article of their food, all died. And some of these were sacred fish. Thus a humiliating blow was struck at "the gods of Egypt." And in this, as in some of the other plagues, a special rebuke was inflicted on that animal worship which was one of the chief forms of Egyptian idolatry.

Great though the manifestation of divine power in this plague was, it made no great impression on Pharaoh. The magicians appeared to be able to produce the same result. And as the water that Pharaoh needed both for drinking and bathing was probably supplied through the method that still remained, he was not much affected personally. The week passed; the river returned to its former condition. Pharaoh's heart was hardened ; he would not let the people go.

We are not to suppose that the plagues followed one another in uninterrupted succession, like the blows of a hammer. There was probably a considerable interval between them ; some notices of time seem to indicate that they were spread over a considerable part of a year. Things had been going on quietly for a time, when one morning, to his great disgust, Pharaoh is again confronted with these two old men, and hears another of their solemn messages from the God of the Hebrews. Another plague is threatened —the plague of frogs. Frogs were at all times abundant in the Nile ; but the plague consisted in so multiplying them that they

SCENE ON THE NILE.

*Page 334.*

were not confined to the river, but spread over the whole country, crowding into the roads and streets and houses in such multitudes that their loathsome forms were continually present. And the frog, too, was a sacred animal, so that the people dared not kill them, under pain of the displeasure of the gods. Heka, an Egyptian goddess, had the head of a frog, an emblem of fecundity and productiveness. We are told by an ancient writer of a plague of frogs in a part of Greece which filled the houses and the streets. As killing them or shutting the doors was of no avail, as even the vessels were full of them, the water untasted, and all food uneatable, as the people could scarcely put their foot upon the ground without treading on heaps of them, and as they were utterly disgusted with the smell of the great numbers which died, they fled from the region altogether. It is not difficult to imagine what an offensive and horrible visitation it was. To feel the cold, clammy skin of the frog wherever one laid one's hands ; to see them leaping on beds and chairs and embroidered coverlets, or nibbling at the choicest dishes on the table ; to feel them crawling over one's face in bed, and hear the everlasting croak of their horrid throats by day and by night, was enough to drive one to distraction. And to think that they came from the sacred Nile, and that they were under the protection of Heka, was indeed a hard thing for the Egyptian idolater. Somehow the Egyptian magicians were able to imitate Moses and Aaron, or to seem to do so, and to bring up frogs on the land ; it did not appear an exclusive power of the God of the Israelites ; but Pharaoh was so much annoyed and disgusted —for the palace was as full of them as other houses—that he promised to let the people go if the plague were removed. The prayer of Moses brought about the removal of the frogs; but all that Pharaoh wanted was to be rid of the annoyance. When they were gone, he broke his promise, and coolly refused to let the people go.

The next plague was accordingly sent without any preliminary warning. The dust of the ground was turned into lice, according to the Authorised and Revised Versions ; into sand-flies, according to the margin of the Revised. Sir Samuel Baker has said that at certain seasons, in some parts of north Africa, lice swarm as if the very dust were turned into them; and that, naturally, the creatures are not larger than a grain of sand, but when filled with blood expand to the size of a hazel-nut. How hateful the plague of lice would be to a people so proverbial as the Egyptians for personal cleanliness may easily be conceived. As the calamity is said to have fallen upon beasts as well as men, the sacred animals of the temple, the Apis of Zoan and the Mnevis of On, may have been affected by it; in which case the perplexity of the people must have been intense, for so far from being able to protect the people from danger, even the sacred animals seemed unable to take care

EGYPTIAN BEETLES.

of themselves. The magicians were baffled in their attempts to imitate this wonder, and confessed that it was the finger of God. But notwithstanding this, it passed away without any effect being produced on Pharaoh.

Moses and Aaron were accordingly sent to announce a fourth plague. Swarms of flies were to be sent—*'arob*, a word which some prefer to render beetles. They are represented as "devouring" the Egyptians—an act hardly applicable to a fly. They were to be sent upon Pharaoh, and upon his servants, and into his houses; but now a difference began to be made between the Egyptians and the Israelites, for the Israelites were to be entirely exempted from them. The Egyptian beetle (*Blatta Ægyptiaca*) " devours every-thing that comes in its way, even clothes, books, and plants, and does not hesitate to inflict severe bites upon man." *  The beetle was sacred, an emblem of the sun-god, who was represented by a beetle, or a man with the head of a beetle. It was therefore unlawful to destroy them. There was no help but to allow them the fullest license. "That it occupied a conspicuous place among their sacred creatures seems to be evinced by the fact that there is scarcely any creature which occurs so frequently in Egyptian sculpture and painting. Visitors to the British Museum may satisfy themselves of this fact; and they will also observe a re-markable colossal figure of a beetle in greenish-coloured granite." †

Again, therefore, the misery of the people arose from one of their gods. This time the heart of Pharaoh yielded for a season : possibly he was impressed by the exemption of the Israelites. He called for Moses and Aaron, and expressed his readiness to let them go and sacrifice to their God—but not in the wilderness, only within the precincts of the land. To this restriction Moses made the most determined opposition. If the Israelites were seen offer-ing as sacrifices creatures like the ox, which the Egyptians counted sacred, they would be held guilty of the grossest sacrilege, and the indignant people might raise a tumult against them. It was a *sine quâ non* that they should go beyond the boundaries of Egypt; and Pharaoh had to yield this also, qualifying his permission by the condition that they were not to go very far away. Perhaps he believed that he could so place his armies as to compel them to return ; but, on further reflection, he seems to have thought that if once they got beyond Egypt they would escape altogether, and when the time came he refused again to let them go.

A fifth plague was therefore announced, in the form of a very grievous murrain "upon the cattle, upon the horses, upon the asses, upon the camels, upon the oxen, and upon the sheep." No species was exempted. And not only was the miserable sight pre-sented of animal sickness, suffering, and death, but a very serious loss was inflicted on the owners of property. The rich man

* " Pictorial Commentary," *in loco.*         † *Ibid.*

counted his losses by scores and hundreds ; the poor man bemoaned the death of his one ass, the useful animal on which he depended for making his living. All the losses and miseries arising from what we know as the cattle disease (it seems to have been the same epidemic) were now witnessed all over Egypt. It is remarkable that " within recent years the murrain has thrice fallen on that country—in 1842, 1863, and 1866 (also sixty years previously)— when nearly the whole of the herds have been destroyed." * Amid this universal suffering in Egypt not one animal of all that belonged to the Israelites was so much as touched. But this visitation, too, passed away, and Pharaoh's heart continued hardened, neither would he let the people go.

A sixth plague had accordingly to be sent. Moses and Aaron were commanded to take handfuls of ashes from the furnace, and Moses to sprinkle them toward heaven, so that they should become small dust, and entering with the air into the bodies of men and beasts, should give rise to boils and blains of a painful nature. The word translated boils occurs as one of the symptoms of leprosy in Lev. xiii. 18, 20, and likewise of the disease of Job. It has been thought by some to denote here the disease of elephantiasis ; but probably all that is meant is a general swelling over the body, breaking into ulcers, without the particular class of disease being denoted. The means taken to bring about this plague were somewhat mysterious—the scattering of dust from the furnace. Perhaps there was only a symbolic connection here between cause and effect. Other plagues had originated in other elements—in water, earth, and air ; this one originated in fire. God was shown to be sovereign over all the elements and forces of nature. But in addition to this, it is not unlikely that the furnaces were connected with the labour of the Israelites—not necessarily the brick-making, but other departments of their toil. Out of their very oppressions punishment now came to their oppressors ; but, like the former visitations, it left the king unsubdued.

A hailstorm was the next calamity. It was introduced with a particularly solemn warning that God was about to send all his

* " Speaker's Commentary."

plagues on Pharaoh ; that, indeed, the object for which Pharaoh had been raised up to his unrivalled pre-eminence as a king, was to show how insignificant his power was as compared with God's ; and that this would be made apparent by the very grievous hailstorm that was now to be sent on him and on his cattle and his people. The previous plagues, though all very terrible, had come quietly—with no such overwhelming rush as usually produces the most vivid impression of human impotence. But this new plague of hail, accompanied with lightning, was of the latter kind. Its effects remained as a powerful tradition in the Hebrew memory, and were referred to again and again when it was desired to recall how God had dealt with the enemies of the nation. "The Lord also thundered in the heavens, and the Highest gave his voice ; hailstones and coals of fire" (Ps. xviii. 13). "He gave them hail for rain, and flaming fire in their land" (Ps. cv. 32). "He destroyed their vines with hail, and their sycomore trees with frost. He gave up their cattle also to the hail, and their flocks to hot thunderbolts" (Ps. lxxviii. 47, 48). There was this peculiarity about this plague, that unlike some of those that preceded it, it was rare in Egypt. Neither hail nor lightning occurs frequently, and when they do occur they are but mild. The idea of destruction was not associated with them in the Egyptian mind. The effect must have been the more overwhelming when these very mild and innocent forces of nature were invested with such terrific violence as to crush everything before them. In Goshen no trace of this appeared.

It is no wonder that for the moment Pharaoh was overwhelmed, and that, amid the furious raging of the tempest, he uttered an expression of penitence such as had never crossed his lips before. "And Pharaoh sent, and called for Moses and Aaron, and said unto them, I have sinned this time : the Lord is righteous, and I and my people are wicked. Intreat the Lord (for it is enough) that there be no more mighty thunderings and hail ; and I will let you go, and ye shall stay no longer." The expression of penitence was met at once by Moses with a promise of help, even though he knew that it was an insincere and superficial confession—the moment he was gone out of the city he would spread out his hands to the Lord, and the tempest would cease. Moses was not living in the city, but somewhere in the neighbourhood, and it would seem that it was only outside of the rebellious capital that he would make his appeal to God. Not that he might not have found God as truly in the very scene of Pharaoh's wickedness, but the fact was made impressive to the Egyptians that the capital was a God-forsaken place, that they had sinned God out of it, as it were, and that it was in the territory of the Hebrews that the God of grace and mercy was to be found. At once the visitation of hail and rain and lightning was arrested; and Pharaoh, once more relieved of the terror and the trouble of a present and pressing evil, hardened his heart, broke his word, and refused to let the people go.

The eighth plague, the plague of locusts, was next announced. What a visitation of locusts was the Egyptians knew very well, for though not very common, they came at times both from the west and the east, from Libya on the one side and Arabia on the other. What was now to fall on them was to be in such aggravated form as to surpass all that had ever been known in previous times—it was to be such as neither their fathers nor their grandfathers had seen since the day when the earth began to be peopled. By this time it was known that Moses never uttered either a false or an exaggerated word. What he now announced, though it seems to have made little impression on Pharaoh, went deep into the hearts of his servants. They had become sensible of the folly of provoking against their country such desolating judgments as those which Moses had from time to time threatened. And they ventured to remonstrate with Pharaoh. "How long shall this man be a snare to us?" They felt that he was luring them on to one form of resistance after another, in order to plunge them into new calamities; and it seemed such madness, that the sooner they got rid of him and his people the better. "Let the men [the males] go, that they may serve their gods; knowest thou not that Egypt is destroyed?" Moses and Aaron are accordingly brought back. A compromise is offered: the males may go, but it is needless to ex-

pose the little ones to the casualties of a long journey; they will
remain behind.   But Moses rejects the compromise with great
decision.   Young and old, sons and daughters, flocks and herds,
all will go, and the feast to the Lord shall be a real family feast
—not one shall be absent.   Pharaoh for the first time loses his
temper, provoked at the unyielding firmness of Moses, when he
thinks he himself has yielded so much : the two Hebrews are
driven violently from his presence.

We may conceive Moses and Aaron exchanging a grim smile as
they leave the city and take the next step.   The rod of Moses is
stretched over the country : an east wind blows from Arabia, and
in the morning the locusts are seen covering the face of the country
and darkening the very sky.   The land has not yet recovered from
the last plague, the plague of hail ; but now the locusts fall upon
every herb of the field and fruit of the trees which the hail had
left, and Egypt bids fair to be left without one green leaf throughout all its borders.

We may form some conception of their ravages from a traveller's account of a similar visitation at Novgorod in 1646 :—
"The ground was all covered, and the air so full of them that
I could not eat in my chamber without a candle ; all the houses
being full of them, even the stables, barns, chambers, garrets, and
cellars.   I caused cannon powder and sulphur to be burnt to
expel them, but all to no purpose ; for when the door was opened
an infinite number came in, and the others went fluttering about.
And it was a troublesome thing when a man went abroad to be
hit in the face by these creatures, on the nose, eyes, or cheeks,
so that there was no opening one's mouth but some would get in.
Yet all this was nothing ; for when we were to eat they gave us
no respite, and when we went to cut a piece of meat we cut a locust
with it, and when a man opened his mouth to put in a morsel he
was sure to chew one of them." *

Once more Pharaoh humbles himself and confesses his sin.   He
brings back the men whom he had driven violently from his presence, and begs them to entreat the Lord only this once that he

* Beauplan *apud* Pusey, " Minor Prophets ; " Rawlinson's " Moses."

may take away this death only. It is the last time he will ever have to make such a request; this is the last evil that God will ever have occasion to send upon him. All is now to be put right; these rebellious proceedings are to cease, and no further obstacle interposed to prevent God obtaining from his people the service that he claims. Once more Moses lifts up his hands: the locusts are carried away as quickly as they came; a powerful west wind sweeps them into the Red Sea—not one remains in the country. And once more Pharaoh proves false to the core; God's demand is resisted as strenuously as ever.

The plague of darkness is now to be tried. In strong poetical language it is "darkness that may be felt" — the "palpable obscure" of Milton. How it was brought about, whether by means of clouds of dust and sand, or by a dense fog overshadowing the country, or by some other means, is of little consequence; probably darkness caused by clouds of dust and sand, such as is still not infrequent in the East, answers best to the description, "darkness that may be felt." For three days and nights it overspread Egypt. It might seem, after all that had happened, that this was a comparatively mild visitation, a mere deprivation of a comfort, but not involving positive suffering, not actively and wildly destructive, like so many of the other plagues. But there is something in darkness, and especially in universal darkness, that has a fearfully depressing effect, creating a nameless horror, not only in children, and not only in the breasts of the superstitious, but in others also who are not easily cowed. It is said that the most hardened and desperate of criminals dread no punishment so much as confinement in a darkened chamber; it takes all the nerve and defiance out of them. Similar to this was the effect which the three days and nights of darkness had on Pharaoh. He sends for Moses and Aaron, and is willing to make another concession. He will let them go with their children now, but not with their cattle. Ought not Moses to accept this compromise, and not have to continue the fight any longer?

But experience has taught Moses the value of Pharaoh's concessions—no sooner made than withdrawn. It would be silly to accept a compromise from a man who only dangles promises at the end of a string, to whip them away as soon as they are made. With great energy Moses insists on the full amount of his original claim. Shylock himself could not have stood more firmly to his first proposition. " Our cattle shall go with us ; there shall not an hoof be left behind ; for thereof must we take to serve the Lord our God ; and we know not with what we must serve the Lord, until we come thither." Was this an honest excuse? Did they not know well enough already what were the animals to be offered to God in sacrifice? But there is a suggestion here of a new ritual about to be prescribed, a foreshadow of the Aaronic dispensation, under which many new sacrifices and ceremonies were to be enacted, the details of which they really did not know, but for which they must be prepared.

But in point of fact, what Moses desired to convey to Pharaoh was that they had no intention of returning. He knew that God was about to fulfil his promise to Abraham that he would give the land of the seven nations to his seed. As we have said, the real conflict was whether Israel was Pharaoh's slave or God's son. Moses would make no vestige of concession that would invalidate God's claim in the slightest particular, or abate by one iota his right to dispose, not only of the people, but of their cattle and all that they had. When Pharaoh made any concession his pride must have undergone a fearful strain. It was infinitely mortifying to find that in spite of this Moses was as inflexible as ever. In a towering rage the king again drove Moses from him, pelting him with insults and with threats : "Get thee from me, take heed to thyself, see my face no more ; for in that day thou seest my face thou shalt die." The reply of Moses is manly and appropriate : " Thou hast spoken well ; I will see thy face again no more," uttered no doubt in a tone that implied that what Pharaoh thus welcomed as a relief he would one day deplore as a calamity. For men that insult and drive away God's faithful servants are not on the winning side.

Thus, then, ended the dealings of Moses with Pharaoh. It is remarkable that till this last moment Pharaoh had never ventured to strike at Moses, or even to threaten him with personal punishment. He dreaded the power behind Moses, and felt that he dared not by an overt crime of that kind rouse it against him. His calm demeanour, on the whole, contrasts favourably with the bluster of such kings as Ahab, Sennacherib, and Nebuchadnezzar when they met with opposition from God's servants. But calmness of temper was, as we know, a habitual feature of Egyptian character, and in harmony with what finds expression on the monuments. Of the great colossal sphinx that lies half buried in the sand beside the pyramids, travellers remark that it has none of that fierce, wild expression which most nations would have given to such a monster, but a look of calm composure the very farthest removed from passionate excitement. It was well for Moses that all through the early stages of his conflict he was kept from the threat of personal violence. At first his faith might have been too feeble for this, but by the end of the day its fibre had become so firm that even the threat of death could no more move him than the clenched fist of a little child. So it was that God led Luther during the early stages of the Reformation struggle: while his faith was but feeble, his person was unmolested; nor was the storm of violence let loose against him till, safe within the refuge, he had learned to smile at its fury.

Moses had found the conflict with Pharaoh infinitely easier than he had expected. So it is with all whom God sends out on his work, when they really trust him. To Zerubbabel the mountain was made a plain. The apostles could not only confront the Sanhedrim but even defy them. Paul could say, "I can do all things through Christ strengthening me." Luther could not only assert his theses but deal with the Pope as antichrist. Doubtless Moses felt deeply ashamed of his attitude at the burning bush, and often mourned that he had been so distrustful, when it was God's enterprise he was called to conduct and God's honour he was called to uphold.

# CHAPTER IV.

## THE EXODUS.

### (Ex. xi.–xv. 22.)

THE last and the decisive wonder against Pharaoh had much that was peculiar to itself. Ample notice was given of it; but unlike the other plagues, no notice of it was given to Pharaoh. It was to the Israelites that it was foretold. And in connection with it, it was announced to them that so far from Pharaoh wishing to keep them longer in the country, he would thrust them out altogether, without any desire for them to return. In the prospect of their departure they were to obtain jewels of silver and gold from their neighbours, not as a loan, but for permanent possession.* The property which they would leave behind them in Egypt would be of far greater value than these jewels. The houses which these neighbours would come to own, the heavy furniture which could not be removed, such of the flocks and herds as were either too young or too old to travel, the vegetables left in the gardens, the fruit in the orchards, and the crops in the fields, were of much more value than their neighbours' rings or bracelets. There was no time for a regular sale or even a valuation or exchange; the transference of the jewels was a rough and ready settlement; it was neither a swindle nor a robbery, but as fair a transaction as was possible in the circumstances.

The final visitation was to be the slaughter of the first-born, both of man and beast, in every Egyptian dwelling. But in connection with it, and before it should take place, a new and very

* See Revised Version.

solemn rite was prescribed to the Israelites. To mark its pre-eminent character, the month then current was to be reckoned the first of the ecclesiastical year. It was called Abib (ch. xiii. 4), afterwards Nisan; it corresponds nearly to our April. Formerly the year had begun with the month Tisri. Among the Egyptians it began in June, with the rise of the Nile. The rite which Moses was directed to institute was the first in that long series of ceremonial institutions which were afterwards prescribed through him. The deliverance now to take place from the long bondage of Egypt was so remarkable that, to commemorate it in all time coming, the ordinance of the Passover was set up. On the tenth of the month, every family, or group of families, was to take a lamb, a male of the first year, without blemish. The animal was to be kept for four days, probably that during that time the minds of the members of the family might be duly impressed with what was about to take place. On the evening of the fourteenth day of the month it was to be killed, and its blood sprinkled on the lintel and door-posts of the house. The body of the lamb was then to be roasted whole, and eaten by the family together. It was to be eaten by them in haste, with unleavened bread and bitter herbs, with their loins girded, with their shoes on their feet and their staves in their hands. On that memorable night, the fourteenth of Abib, the angel of the Lord was to pass through the land and kill the first-born of the Egyptians; and the blood on the lintel and the door-posts of the dwellings of the Israelites was to be the token by which he should know to pass over those dwellings, as being the homes of the Lord's people.

It was hardly the kind of memorial that we should have expected. We should have thought of something more jubilant, more exulting, some service of mirth and festivity, as the appropriate celebration of the deliverance from Egypt, something akin to the triumphant service on the farther shore of the sea, when the song of Moses was sung to the timbrel of Miriam, and the air was rent with the hosannas of a redeemed and triumphant people. But why this solemn Passover rite? Why the painful bleating of the imprisoned lamb, kept for four days, till the chil-

dren came to make a pet and plaything of him? Why the sad
sound of its death-cry, not away in the shambles, but within the
house? Why the sight of its gashed throat and streaming blood
before all the family, male and female, young and old? Why the
unleavened bread, and the bitter herbs, and all the marks of haste
—the shoes on the feet and the staff in the hand? Why, above
all, the stains of blood—those stains which we are generally so
eager to obliterate—on every lintel and door-post, to indicate to
every passer-by that a work of death had just been done within
every dwelling-place of Israel?

Evidently this was the beginning of that long course of education through which the Israelites were taught to connect the
enjoyment of God's favour with the shedding of blood. That they
and not the Egyptians should be in covenant with God was not
due to any difference of nature between the two—Israel was a
sinner as well as the Egyptian; but of his free grace, God had
taken Israel into covenant with himself, and had made him the
heir of blessing. But of this covenant, blood was, and was ever
to be, the token, to indicate that even on Israel, in the sight of
God, there lay the pollution of guilt, to be removed only by the
shedding of blood; and when the light of the New Testament
explained the shadows of the Old, it became apparent that the
only valid propitiation was, not the blood of bulls or of goats, but
the precious blood of the Lamb of God—Christ our Passover sacrificed for us—the Lamb of God that taketh away the sin of the
world.

Moreover, there was something appropriate in the last act
performed by the Israelites in Egypt being an act of sacrifice.
The whole nation, family by family, offered a lamb in solemn
sacrifice on the last night of their residence in Egypt. It was a
great united acknowledgment of the sins and shortcomings of that
period of their history, and an appeal to God to cancel all their unworthiness through his own appointed method of taking sin away.

The sun has but set on that night much to be remembered, the
14th of Abib, when the death-cry of the lamb is heard in every
Israelite house, and before the last streaks of daylight have passed

away, the red drops are crimsoning every lintel and door-post. A bright fire sparkles on every hearth—rare sight for the land of Goshen—and the body of the lamb, pierced by the spit, crackles to the blazing fuel. The whole family have sat down, though in strange garb. The meal is over, and yet they wait. There is no talk of bed that night. The hour of midnight is drawing near, and still they are waiting. How have their Egyptian neighbours been spending that night? Doubtless, ill at ease. They have heard what Moses has foretold, and they know that not one of his predictions against Egypt has fallen to the ground. Keen is the gaze which the fond Egyptian mother fixes on her first-born that night, and warm the kiss with which she bids him good-night. They are an affectionate people, these Egyptians, and much attached to their children. Restless is the mother's head that tries in vain to woo sleep on the pillow. Horrible spectres are flitting through the house, grinning on the trembling parents. Suddenly at midnight a cry is heard from the eldest boy, as of one pierced by a dart. The mother flies to his side, but despair is at her heart; the father flies for help, but at each door where he knocks, at each window he passes, he sees a calamity the same as his own. The whole land resounds with the cry of the dying and the wail of the living. And no one can tell where the calamity is to end. For when sudden death falls on a house, the very cords of life seem all to be loosened, and we know not what is next to happen. It seems as if the great Destroyer were walking in darkness, and we know not on whom next he may lay his hand.

And now Pharaoh not only yields but makes a complete surrender. He sends in haste for Moses and Aaron, and not only allows them to go, but is eager that with bag and baggage they should every one of them be gone. And, poor man, he utters a touching prayer: "Bless me also!" Yes, I know that the blessing of the Almighty is with you, and will follow you. Don't leave your curse behind you; think of miserable me; don't let me be utterly ruined! The entreaty of Pharaoh that they would depart is echoed by all the Egyptian people. And now it was that the Israelites found them so willing to load them with their choicest ornaments. No price was too great to purchase exemption from further calamities; the Egyptians all felt like dead men.

The Passover was enjoined to be observed by the Israelites for ever in their generations. It continued all through their history a remarkable testimony both to the fact and likewise to the manner of their deliverance from Egypt. The same event was kept in remembrance by another ordinance—the redemption of the first-born. In connection with the proceedings of that night, every first-born, whether of man or beast, was consecrated to the Lord. Animals fit for sacrifice were sacrificed; other animals were redeemed. Subsequently, the tribe of Levi was substituted for the first-born son in every family. The practice of sacrificing the first-born of cattle, and of redeeming the first-born of men, gave rise to inquiries by children into the reason for these things. So also the paschal supper itself, and the practices connected with it, were directed to be carefully explained to the young. The domestic character of the ordinance, not observed in a great temple, but in ordinary dwelling-houses, brought it home, as it were, to every household. If the historical reality of the exodus were denied, these institutions would establish it on a firm foundation; such institutions, observed from the very beginning, are infallible proofs of the reality of the events out of which they sprang.

Soon after midnight, on the morning of the 15th Nisan, the whole host of Israel were in motion towards the place of rendezvous which had been appointed—Succoth. Succoth signifies "tents" or "booths" (see Gen. xxxiii. 17), and probably it denotes merely a place where caravans were accustomed to encamp. Thither, along various routes, not from Rameses only, but from other cities likewise, the columns of the children of Israel would converge. Their instructions everywhere were, that they were to eat the Passover with their sandals on their feet, and as soon as daylight permitted were to make the best of their way to Succoth. When all had arrived there, their future route was determined. And it was not to be by the nearest path. The route by which Jacob and his sons had come into Egypt would have taken them in a north-easterly direction from Rameses, skirting the sea-coast, and then passing through Shur and the land of the Philistines. But for good reasons God did not lead them by that path. He knew that a nation of slaves, as the Israelites really were, were unable to cope with the martial energy and courage of the Philistines, so that, to avoid the fighting for which they were not yet able, he caused them to travel by a more circuitous route, through the wilderness of Sinai.

What their precise route was has long been matter of much learned discussion. Again and again some new route has been propounded, and much ingenious discussion bestowed on it. Some think that the passage was effected close to Suez, where the gulf is so narrow and so shallow that but little miraculous power would have been needed; others place the line of passage opposite Ayin Mousa (the Wells of Moses), five or six miles to the south of Suez; and others at a point still more to the south. Dr. Brugsch, on the other hand, thinks that the sea crossed was not the Red Sea, but an arm of the Mediterranean much further to the north. He has bestowed extraordinary pains in the investigation of names in support of this hypothesis; but it has not been accepted. The old theory still holds the ground, that the passage of the sea occurred a little to the south of Suez. The difficulty in this case is that it is not a route that the Israelites would have taken, or that Moses would have taken on his own responsibility; but it was obviously chosen by divine direction, and for purposes in harmony with the divine plan which it pleased God to ordain.

Some have objected to the Bible account of the exodus that the number of the people was far beyond what it would have been possible for Moses to form into an orderly camp and to lead onwards without inextricable confusion. But the number of the males of each tribe in the desert, in the beginning of the second year, is given with such precision in Num. i., the total being 603,550, that the idea of an error of enumeration cannot well be entertained.* We must observe that the existence of an exact list of the males of every family and every tribe shows that, notwith-

* Rawlinson's "Moses," p. 120.

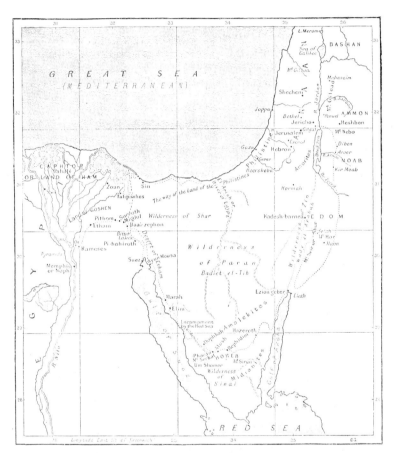

MAP OF EGYPT, SINAI, AND PALESTINE.

standing the rigours of their captivity, the people were thoroughly organized in Egypt. The institution of elders secured this organization, along with other results. Further, we must bear in mind what has been already adverted to—the remarkable love of order and power of organization that belonged to the heads of the nation, especially Abraham, Jacob, and Joseph, and (as we may believe) to many of their descendants likewise. And still further, we must remember that among Eastern peoples, especially of the Bedouin class, extensive migrations are of common occurrence, and the methods and machinery for accomplishing them are matters of quite ordinary knowledge. Dean Stanley adverts to an illustration in the history of the last century, which records the sudden departure, under cover of a single night, of a whole nomadic people — 400,000 Tartars — who withdrew themselves from Russia, and made their way over several thousand miles of steppe from the banks of the Volga to the confines of the Chinese Empire. "And the great caravans of pilgrims which even now traverse the East without confusion or disorder give something like a picture on a small scale of the movements of such a host as that led forth by Moses. They are marshalled and arranged by the caravan-leader ; each company knows its place ; they encamp and break up from their encampments silently and in an orderly way ; they have each their train of animals ; they traverse long distances in a fairly compact body ; once started, they pursue their way with a regularity and an absence of confusion that leave little to be desired ; and they usually accomplish. their journeys in the time prescribed, without serious loss, except perhaps of the animals."*

It is a remarkable proof of the deliberation and care with which all the details of the march were executed, that the bones of Joseph were not forgotten, nor the promise made to the dying patriarch. Had the departure been a helter-skelter rush, Joseph's bones would have had little chance to be remembered. It is expressly said that it was Moses, who was of the tribe of Levi, that took them (ch. xiii. 19), although we should suppose that the

* "Jewish Church."

custody of them was committed to Ephraim. But as we often
find that it is the busiest men who have leisure for the smallest
matters, so it is the most burdened men who are most thoughtful
about what seem to be trifles. The carrying away of Joseph's
bones was a beautiful act of faith, as it was also a very notable
proof that there was to be no return to Egypt—*vestigia nulla
retrorsum;* the enterprise would not end till the seven nations
were vanquished, and Israel got their own.

With reference to the places where the host of Israel is said
to have halted after leaving Succoth—Etham, in the edge of the
wilderness, Pi-hahiroth, Migdol, and Baal-zephon—it cannot be
said that the attempts to identify them have been very successful.
Most probably they were in the neighbourhood of Suez. The
sea which is mentioned here is almost universally believed to have
been the western arm or gulf of the Red Sea (see xiii. 18).
What is called the Red Sea fills a deep and rocky basin extending
fourteen hundred miles from Suez to the Strait of Babelmandeb,
without receiving, in its whole course, the waters of a single
river. It is called in Scripture Yam Suph (the Sea of Reeds or
Weeds), from the quantity of sea-weed found in it, often of a red
colour. Its present Arabic name is Bahr Souf. At its northern
boundary the sea divides into two gulfs, between which rise the
mountains of Sinai. The more easterly of the two, called the
Gulf of Akaba or Ailah, was known to the Greeks and Romans
as Ælanites, or the Elanitic Gulf, and is much the smaller. The
western arm is called the Gulf of Suez, anciently Heeropolites;
it is about one hundred and sixty miles in length, with a mean
breadth of thirty, but very much narrower at its northern
extremity. There is good reason to believe that at one time the
Gulf of Suez extended considerably further to the north than it
does now.

The Israelites, we are told, went out of Egypt " with an high
hand " (xiv. 8). They did not steal away, like runaway slaves,
but marched bravely in the face of day, with something of the air
of conquerors. The Egyptians were occupied the first day with
the burial of their dead, and the triumphant march of the depart-

ing Israelites must have been a striking contrast to their mournful mood and occupation. But no sooner was the burial of the dead over than the old spirit once more took possession of Pharaoh. An army was speedily got ready, admirably adapted for the pursuit of fugitives. It was an army of chariots, such as Egypt was famous for, and such as are constantly represented in the monuments. For, unlike other nations, the King of Egypt and the flower of his army are not represented as riding on horseback, but in small two-wheeled chariots, in which the warrior has scarcely more than standing room, and where, with the reins lashed round his waist, controlling the horses by the movement of his body, he is furnished with bow and arrows, or a javelin, and sometimes

EGYPTIAN CHARIOT.

with a weapon somewhat resembling a reaping-hook. Six hundred chosen chariots and all the other available chariots of Egypt were got ready for the pursuit; a most formidable force, capable of inflicting utter destruction on the undisciplined masses of Israel.

The course of the Israelites after leaving Rameses appears to have been south-easterly, but when they came to the sea they performed a movement so remarkable that we cannot suppose that Moses could have ordered it on his own responsibility. We read that they were ordered to "turn and encamp before Pi-hahiroth, between Migdol and the sea, over against Bàal-zephon." The effect of this movement, as Pharaoh who was now in pursuit of them quickly saw, was that "they were entangled in the land, the wilderness had shut them in." They seem to have run themselves into a kind of *cul-de-sac*—hemmed in between the sea, the mountains, and the wilderness, with no outlet in any direction except the entrance. Moses, who must have known the locality well, would never have selected this route. His object would have been to get them across into Sinai as quickly as possible, avoiding the sea altogether (as he probably had done himself when he fled from Egypt), and taking the northerly route, even though it should be necessary to make a detour southward on reaching Sinai. But the route actually taken could not have been better devised if the purpose had been to betray Israel into the hands of the Egyptians. The inference is unavoidable that they acted by divine direction. And the form in which that direction was given is remarkable :— "The Lord went before them by day in a pillar of a cloud, to lead them the way ; and by night in a pillar of fire, to give them light ; to go by day and night : he took not away the pillar of the cloud by day, nor the pillar of fire by night, from before the people." The divine purpose was to make their victory over Pharaoh so conspicuous and complete as to furnish overwhelming evidence of the presence and protection of their God ; thus to strike terror into the hearts of their other enemies, and to prepare the way for their unopposed entrance into their country—as certainly would have happened, had they not for their sins been doomed to wander forty years in the wilderness.

It is no great wonder that, when the Israelites looked behind at Pi-hahiroth and saw the chariots of Pharaoh dashing towards them, they fell into panic. Such a sight was fitted to cause a flutter even to the stoutest heart. But after all that they had witnessed we are hardly prepared for the burst of utter unbelief and the mean torrent of reproach flung out against Moses. Is there any pang of heart more hard to bear than, when one has been doing one's utmost in the cause of others, to be overwhelmed, the moment a disaster comes in sight, with stinging reproaches? What meanness to vent one's irritation on the man that has been acting so nobly ! As the responsible leader of the host,

Moses had need in the emergency of all that could contribute to a cool and wise decision; but these people, like so many others, did their best to disturb his judgment and weaken his hands. And then there was the meanness of eulogizing their wretched condition in Egypt as preferable to this. And the further meanness of fathering on Moses what had been done by God—abusing the instrument when they dared not abuse the author of their trouble.

What a contrast to this the bearing of Moses! How meekly he bears their reproaches, trying to pacify them as a mother would pacify a frightened child: "Fear ye not, stand still, and see the salvation of God, which he will show to you to-day: for the Egyptians whom ye have seen to-day, ye shall see them again no more for ever." To face an exasperated crowd is said to be one of the greatest trials of courage. Moses bore that test, and quieted the crowd. Was not the pillar of cloud in front of them? and did it not show that there was no real cause for apprehension on account of Pharaoh?

And yet Moses does not seem to have been perfectly calm. There was some unquelled anxiety of spirit that was always prompting him to prayer—perhaps silent, perhaps ejaculatory—imploring God to intervene. Our sympathies go with Moses; we are so sure that we should have felt the same. Yet anxiety was weakness—it was sin. "Wherefore criest thou unto me?" Why this secret anguish of soul? Watch the pillar of cloud—is it not moving forward? Why are you standing still? Is it not your duty to get the people to follow it? Speak to them; order an advance after the cloud. Say to them, "Go forward!" mind not difficulty; in the name of God, advance!

But how are they to advance with the sea in front of them? "Lift thou up thy rod, and stretch out thine hand over the sea, and divide it: and the children of Israel shall go on dry ground through the midst of the sea." So *this* is the wonderful plan of God, Moses might well think—exceeding everything which could have entered into his mind. Yes, his anxiety *was* weakness—it *was* sin. How able God is to do exceeding abundantly, above all that we are able to ask or think!

And not only does God provide an outlet for his people from the trap in which they seemed to lie waiting for the enemy, but the turn of the enemy comes to fall into the trap, with none to deliver him. "And I, behold, I will harden the hearts of the Egyptians, and they shall follow them : and I will get me honour upon Pharaoh, upon his chariots, and upon his horsemen. And the Egyptians shall know that I am the Lord, when I have gotten me honour upon Pharaoh, and upon his chariots, and upon his horsemen."

It has been maintained by some that the drying up of the sea was caused solely by the east wind which arose that night, not by any miraculous cause. But what can be more plain, on the very face of the narrative, than that whatever the wind may have done, there was a great miracle in the case? It is God's usual method to make the most of natural causes — to make the supernatural begin only where the natural ends. How could the crossing of the sea have been represented, as it always is, as an unprecedented marvel, if it had been wholly due to natural causes? And besides, this was not the only miracle. The pillar of cloud and flame, which had hitherto preceded the Israelites, now slowly changed its position to their rear, its dark side being turned towards the Egyptians, so as to hide the movements of the Israelites, and its bright side to the people, illuminating their strange path through the sea. With God thus for their "sun and shield," Israel advanced along the oozy channel, heartily ashamed of their unbelief and their unjust reproach against Moses, their bosoms heaving with the excitement of their wonderful deliverance, and their hearts full of trust and gratitude towards their leader on earth and their Leader in heaven.

This was their "baptism unto Moses in the cloud and in the sea"—not a water baptism, as some suppose, as if the cloud (which was a cloud of smoke) had dropped water on their heads, but a spiritual baptism, a new consecration, their initiation into a new life of trust and obedience and holy fear ; for "the people feared the Lord, and believed the Lord and his servant Moses." The significance of this statement can only be appreciated if we think how their feelings as to the God of their fathers had been dimmed and dulled, perhaps in some cases obliterated, by their long residence in Egypt. On that night they had got a new revelation of the God of salvation; henceforth they must know no other God but him.

As soon as the cloud was sufficiently removed to let them advance, the Egyptians had ventured after them into the sea. " In the morning watch the Lord looked unto the host of the Egyptians through the pillar of fire and the pillar of cloud, and troubled the host of the Egyptians, and took off their chariot wheels, that they drave them heavily ; " and not only the sea but "the earth swallowed them" (ch. xv. 12). They sank in the quick-sands even before the waters were recalled and made to cover them. No words can tell the terror or describe the horrors of that scene. It was still night, but the light of the moon high in the sky sufficed to reveal the completeness of the disaster. Every chariot that had ventured into the channel was caught in the embrace of the closing waters—the entire expedition became an utter wreck. Never was catastrophe so complete. Not so much as one of those who had entered the sea escaped. With the dawn of day, the ghastly faces of the men thrown up on the shore, or the broken wheels and planks of the chariots, were the only memorials of the mighty host. Whether Pharaoh himself was among the dead is not very clear. That he left Egypt with the expedition seems plain (xiv. 4), but it is a vague expression that is used to denote those that entered into the sea (ver. 23) ; and in the historical addendum to the song of Moses, it is said only that "the horse of Pharaoh went in with his chariots and with his horsemen." No light is thrown on the catastrophe by the monu-ments. It was not the humiliations but only the glories of Egypt that were pictured there. And there is some reason to think that the reign of Menephthah, after the catastrophe, was a long one, although his first-born died early.

When the passage was made, and the excitement of his people was somewhat quieted down, the first thing Moses did was to compose a song of triumph, and have it publicly sung and accompanied to music. One might have thought that with that family of two millions upon his hands, and all their pressing wants to provide for, Moses would have no time for composing songs or setting them to music. But he evidently felt this to be his first duty, even in his unexampled position. The spiritual must take precedence of the carnal. The people have for the moment got a right impression; their hearts are suitably affected toward God. But this may be only the morning cloud and the early dew. Let him take all suitable means to deepen and perpetuate it. The idea of a great national song occurred to him as suitable for this purpose. Probably he got the idea from Egyptian history or literature, for as yet nothing of the kind was known to the Hebrews.

In the song itself we have a proof of his remarkable gifts and culture. What might not Moses have done in the field of lyric poetry, if he had set himself to cultivate that gift, and made this a prominent object of his life? As it was, he limited himself to two great efforts—or, as we ought to put it, these two efforts were hallowed by divine inspiration—the one at the beginning and the other at the close of his public life. Both of them show a marvellous share of "the vision and the faculty divine," with a not less wonderful gift of expression—a capacity of song fitted not merely to express the feelings of the redeemed on earth, but also the redeemed in heaven.

If we study the song, we find it marked by many wonderful qualities.

1. It dwells on the completeness and glory of the deliverance, culminating in the utter annihilation of the enemy. The horse and his driver are thrown into the sea—drowned—swallowed—dashed in pieces—consumed as stubble : they sank as a stone, as lead in the mighty waters. And this complete overthrow is contrasted with the boasting spirit of the enemy, who said, " I will pursue, I will overtake, I will divide the spoil ; my lust shall be satisfied upon them ; I will draw my sword, my hand shall destroy them." Never did such pride go before destruction, or so haughty a spirit before a fall.

2. The deliverance is ascribed entirely to God :—" He hath

triumphed gloriously.......The Lord is my strength and my song, and he is become my salvation." "Thy right hand hath dashed in pieces the enemy." It is most striking that the name of Moses occurs nowhere in the song. Not the faintest desire is shown on his part for a single ray of the glory. The evidence that it was written by his own hand, that it is not the composition of some subsequent writer, is thus very striking. What subsequent writer would have dared to leave Moses so completely out, introducing the name of Miriam in connection with the song, but describing her as "the sister of Aaron"? But Moses himself had such a conception of the divine glory of this deliverance, that he would not so much as name himself. "Not unto us, O Lord, not unto us, but to thy name be the glory."

3. Unbounded admiration and delight are expressed towards this God :—"Who is like unto thee, O Lord, among the gods, glorious in holiness, fearful in praises, doing wonders?" It is strange that this should have ever been taken as a proof that at this time the unity of God was not fully recognized. The very purpose of the eulogy, and the very point of the question, is to signalize this God as immeasurably exalted above all that are called gods—so immeasurably exalted that the very idea of a comparison is ridiculous. And this infinite superiority is not merely the superiority of power, but of inward excellence, of holiness too. He is "glorious in holiness, doing wonders." And this makes it such a glorious privilege to be his, and such a blessed thing to claim him and cling to him as such :—"He is my God, and I will praise him ; my father's God, and I will exalt him."

4. The song pledges the singers to suitable steps for the continued and abiding worship of this God :—Not only will I sing now to the Lord, but I will prepare him an habitation ; I will not leave this great duty to contingencies or accidents, but establish it as a permanent institution, hallowed by all the memories of the past and all the hopes of the future.

5. Great satisfaction is expressed with the effects which this miracle was to produce on the nations :—The inhabitants of the Philistine plain, the dukes of Edom and Moab, the nations of

Canaan, would all be visited as by paralysis, " till thy people pass over, O Lord, till the people pass over, which thou hast purchased."

6. Confident assurance is expressed that God will complete all that he has promised ; that he will bring his people in, and plant them in the mountain of his inheritance, in the place that he has designed for his own dwelling, in the sanctuary which his hands have established.

7. And finally, Jehovah's everlasting reign is the subject of crowning satisfaction and delight :—" The Lord shall reign for ever and ever."

It may be useful to note these conspicuous features of the song ; but after doing so, we should read it again as it stands, to take into our minds in one great impression its stately march and noble rhythm, the glow of its enthusiasm, the firmness of its spirit of trust, and its marvellous fitness to rally and concentrate every right feeling in the hearts of the people, and direct them in one mighty current toward the production of an enduring piety. This is the aim of Moses. He understands the fickleness of man, and he recognizes the claims of God ; and he cannot let this splendid chance pass of pressing these claims in their most attractive aspect, and doing everything that he can to rouse in support of them the deepest feelings of the people. It is the grandest view of Moses we have yet got. We see the intensity of his nature ; we see the sublimity of his gifts and genius ; and we see the whole devoted not in the faintest degree to his own interest, but entirely to the good of his people and the honour of God.

The passage of the Red Sea was a unique event, even in the extraordinary history of Israel. It sank very deep into the soul of the nation ; and for ages after we can trace all manner of allusions to it, in the psalms and prophecies, in the gospels and epistles, and so late as the Apocalypse. Every great nation has some favourite exploit in its past history on which generation after generation dwells with thrilling interest and admiration. In Scottish history, the battle of Bannockburn, the struggles of the Reformers, the martyrdoms of the Covenanters ; in English, the destruction of the Spanish Armada ; the siege of Derry in Irish ;

the struggle of the seven provinces in the Netherlands against the tyranny of Philip; the feats of William Tell in Switzerland; the landing of the Pilgrim Fathers on Plymouth Rock, belong to the same category of immortal deeds—deeds that never lose their power to thrill the hearts and rouse the enthusiasm of succeeding generations. To this category, but excelling all of these in grandeur and glory, belonged the passage of the sea. No other display of God's power was so stupendous:—" Come and see the works of the Lord : he is terrible in his doing toward the children of men. He turned the sea into dry land : they went through the flood on foot : there did we rejoice in him." No other event furnished such a pledge of God's care for his own in days of darkness :—" Awake, awake, put on strength, O arm of the Lord ; awake, as in the days of old. Art thou not it that hath cut Rahab, and wounded the dragon? Art thou not it that hath dried the sea, the waters of the great deep ; and that hath made the depths of the sea a way for the ransomed to pass over?" No other event afforded such proof of God's power to still the war of moral elements, often so frightful :— " The floods have lifted up, O Lord, they lifted up their voice ; the floods lift up their waves. The Lord on high is mightier than the noise of many waters, yea, than the mighty waves of the sea."

Last of all, the passage of the sea is reproduced in a striking vision of the Apocalypse, where the seven angels are preparing to pour the seven last plagues on the worshippers of the beast. But before this is done, there is seen " a sea of glass mingled with fire ;" and standing thereon, " those who had gotten the victory over the beast, and over his image, and over his mark, and over the number of his name." " And they sing the song of Moses the servant of God, and the song of the Lamb, saying, Great and marvellous are thy works, Lord God Almighty ; just and true are thy ways, thou King of saints. Who shall not fear thee, O Lord, and glorify thy name? for thou only art holy : for all nations shall come and worship before thee ; for thy judgments are made manifest." The sea of glass is a sea smooth as glass, in opposition to a sea agitated by storms, indicating that the tempest is past, the victory has been gained, the state of repose has been reached which Israel found on the farther shore of the Red Sea. The glassy sea in the Apocalypse was "mingled with fire." When the pillar of fire darted its rays upon the water, the Red Sea must have seemed as if mingled with fire. Even in a state of calm this appearance of the sea may sometimes be seen. The setting sun falling upon it sometimes gives it the appearance of fire—a great molten mass of fire ; but, strange to say, not an image of terror, but an image of glory—a thing to gaze at, with exulting spirit, till the eye can gaze no longer—a scene the very recollection of which gladdens and elevates, even when you turn your back on it, and are immersed in the dark shades of night. Such was the scene beheld by the prophet when those who had gained the victory over the beast, represented by the rough physical might of Pharaoh, stood with their harps of gold, corresponding to Miriam's tabret, and sang the song of Moses and of the Lamb. The main thing implied in this vision was, that they stood in the serene attitude of triumph, conquerors over their foes, but kept humble by that fire-like glow, which indicated the gracious presence and help of God.

Thus we get a glimpse of a great truth—of the symbolic import of this Old Testament history, and its destined fulfilment on a wider scale and in a higher region. Not for Israel alone were these things done, or were these things written : they shadow forth truths of far deeper import, concerning that greater redemption which was achieved by a greater Servant of God ; and they are written for our admonition, upon whom the ends of the world are come.

## CHAPTER V.

### FIRST WEEKS IN THE WILDERNESS.

(Ex. xv. 23–xviii.)

THROUGH the hand of Moses, God has now received his bride from the tyrant that sought to keep her from her genuine Lover, and to degrade her to his own vile ends. The next step is to lead her to the marriage altar at Sinai, and there celebrate the glorious nuptials; thereafter to bring her home "to his own house, his own hearth, to the land flowing with milk and honey." But the bride, straight from her life of bondage, needs much to fit her for her new position. She knows but little of her divine Bridegroom, or of the order of his house; little of his character, his resources, his worthiness to be loved and trusted, or of his ability to raise her to a higher life, to endow her with a richer inheritance than any other lover can bestow. She is as yet unfit to take the vows of everlasting trust and obedience. The few weeks between the Red Sea and Sinai are to be spent in forming a better acquaintance with her future Husband; and Moses is to be her tutor. To him the task is committed of instructing her in her Husband's care and love, of training her to honour all his appointments, to rely on his never-ceasing interest and sympathy, and in the simplicity of perfect love and trust to give her whole heart to him.

The slave-life of Egypt had done great damage, both in what concerned matters of ordinary life and matters of religion. Slaves trained to obey in everything, never allowed to think or act for themselves, with all self-reliance and self-contrivance suppressed—

what can be expected of them but to despair when any difficulty presents itself, and to turn to their leader, growling at their distress, which they ascribe wholly to him, and demanding that he should free them from it? It was just to be expected that the Israelites should have no resource, no courage, no patience ; that they should turn upon Moses with the bitterest reproaches, and hurl all manner of invectives at his head. Evidently they had lost the trust characteristic of their fathers : they no longer saw Him who is invisible ; their vision could not penetrate beyond the immediate present. But this was not the fit temper for the bride of Heaven. The spouse of Jehovah must have confidence in her unseen Lord ; and in order to this, or rather as the result of it, she must acquire the kindred graces of courage, serenity in danger, and self-control under temptation. It is no easy task that is now committed to Moses. It was hard enough to deal with Pharaoh ; in some respects it is harder to deal with Israel. Pharaoh had simply to be subdued ; Israel has to be educated, inspired with a new spirit, taught a new life. If Moses at the burning bush shrank from the one task, it would have been no great wonder if, on the shore of the Red Sea, he had shivered at the other.

But there was a wonderful change on Moses since God had met him at the burning bush. His spiritual education had made marvellous progress. There was little to be seen now of the trembling shepherd that had pleaded so hard with the angel not to send him for the deliverance of his people. Nothing seemed now too great a task for his courage, or too great a trial for his faith. To undertake the care of these two or three millions of people in the desert, as has been well remarked, needed a greater effort of faith than to fling aside all the riches and glory of Egypt. To become responsible for the people was a great trial, as regarded material interests, but far greater as regarded the enterprise of taking possession of Canaan. Probably enough the host were not altogether destitute of food in the wilderness ; there is reason to believe that Sinai was more productive then than now. The people had their flocks and herds that would supply them with milk and butter, while trading companies were often traversing the desert who, in return for some of the Egyptian jewels, would give them food. But all this would have been far too little, without supernatural supplies. And besides this, there was the risk of *émeutes*, and rebellions, and outbreaks of sensuality and of idolatry, to say nothing of the attacks of enemies. Yet Moses went on in calm confidence, in sublime simplicity of faith, the same in foul weather as in fair, and never much disturbed save when the distrust of the people amounted to a renunciation of the covenant. We see now the purpose of the long training to which he had been subjected. First, the profound distrust of himself produced by his failure forty years before, and deepened during that long period into something like self-contempt ; then the equally profound faith in God, gendered by the long contest with Pharaoh, culminating in the profound conviction that wherever God had appeared to be defeated, he was only preparing a more glorious triumph. Between the Red Sea and Mount Sinai, Moses laboured incessantly to communicate his own faith to the people. If only they could be got into a right attitude to God, all would be well. They would enter into their marriage covenant there with the greatest cordiality ; and from Sinai they would go up to Canaan to take possession of the land flowing with milk and honey.

"It is not difficult," as we have remarked elsewhere, "to picture the situation of the Israelites on the morning after their miraculous passage of the sea. Here, at the water's edge, are groups of men and women watching the rolling tide as it casts heavily on the beach the ghastly bodies of the Egyptian warriors. Yonder, where the rock juts out into the water, are clusters of children, who have never before seen the sea, gathering the red sea-weed and the brilliant shells and corals, or watching the movements of the strange-looking creatures that roam among the pools. Away, dotted over the rocky heights, or in closer masses in the hollows between, are flocks of sheep, of goats, of oxen, and of camels, cropping up the spare herbage of the desert, or making eager journeys in quest of water. Conspicuous above the encampment is the strange column, that appears as a pillar of cloud by day and of fire by night, and becomes from this time the

Heaven-sent guide of the host through the wilderness. The whole multitude have that excited look which denotes the recent occurrence of some strange transaction. Everywhere their conversation bears on the great event of the night—intimate friends telling one another what they saw and how they felt, tasking their fancy to describe the coloured glow of the waves, 'as it were a sea of glass mingled with fire,' or the awful crash of the crystal waves as they clasped the Egyptians in their merciless embrace. An expression of freedom sits on every face. As yet they have not begun to think of the future." * The wonderful scenes through which they have passed absorb all their thoughts.

We have already referred generally to the character of the region, the peninsula of Sinai, into which the Israelites now entered (see page 310). We commonly speak of it as "the wilderness," but by this is not to be understood a mere expanse of sand. The larger and more northerly part of Sinai is a plateau of limestone hills, now called El Tih, about two thousand feet above the sea-level; while the southern part, occupying the wedge-shaped space between the two arms of the Red Sea, is occupied by a tangled mass of mountains, the tallest of which, Um Shomer, rises to a height of nine thousand three hundred feet. It was among these mountains that the nuptial ceremony took place, the law was given, and the covenant between God and Israel ratified. Between the mountains run narrow threads of valleys or *wâdys*, which in winter are traversed by streams, and on the sides of which a thin coating of vegetation relieves the bareness of the scene. "Almost every mountain nourishes some vegetation, and generally a vegetation peculiar to itself. Um Shomer is named from the fennel (*shomer*) which once undoubtedly characterized it; Ras Sufsâfeh, from the willows which still cling to its sides; Serbal, from the myrrh (*ser*) which creeps over its ledges to the very summit. The most probable origin even of the name Sinai is to be found in the saneh, or acacia, with which it once abounded. One wâdy is named Wâdy Abu-Hamad (the Father of Fig-trees), from its producing that fruit; another, Wâdy Sidri, from

---

* "Manual of Bible History," pp. 121, 122.

its bushes of wild thorn; another, Wâdy Sayal, from its acacias; another, Wâdy Tayibeh, from the 'goodly' water and vegetation which it contains." *

We have said that at one time the peninsula was more productive than now. The change, according to the report of a recent official survey, "is due to neglect. In former times it was more richly wooded; the wâdys were protected by walls stretching across, which served as dams to resist the force of the rushing waters; the mountains were terraced, and clothed with gardens and groves......The bad times of the Mohammedan rule came, which let in the Bedouin to waste and destroy. Then the protecting walls across the wâdys were broken down, the green terraces along their sides were destroyed, the trees were cut down or carried away by the winter torrents." † Even yet, however, there is some fertility in the peninsula. Rivulets fringed with verdure are still to be found among the southern mountains, some of which are perennial, with large tracts of vegetation around.

The journey from the Red Sea to what is called Mount Sinai occupied between two and three months, corresponding to our April, May, and June.

Five principal incidents occurred during this period—the sweetening of the waters of Marah; the giving of the manna; the procuring of water at Rephidim; the battle with the Amalekites; and the meeting with Jethro.

1. *Marah.*—Near the spot where the Israelites are usually supposed to have halted on crossing the Red Sea are certain springs, called Ayin Mousa (the Wells of Moses), where Robinson counted seven wells, other travellers making them seventeen. A few stunted palm-trees cluster round them, and a few tamarisks bear them company, "which they much need in this lonely spot, for the desert spreads all around, bleak and bare as the sea itself." Three days' march through the desert of Shur brought them to Marah, where the waters were bitter and undrinkable. This is thought to be a place now called Huwarah (destruction), twenty

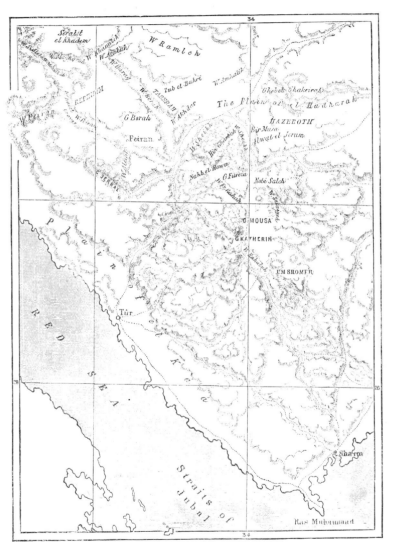

SOUTHERN PORTION OF THE PENINSULA OF SINAI.   *Page 360.*

or thirty miles from Ayin Mousa, with a few stunted palms around it, and still containing bitter water. " Should the thirsty traveller hasten forward now to drink of it, the Arabs will restrain him by the cry, 'Murrh, murrh!' (bitter, bitter)." By the time the Israelites reached this place, the supply of water they had brought with them in leathern bottles, replenished perhaps at Ayin Mousa, was probably spent, and the multitude were beginning to experience a sensation, peculiarly distressing when it comes to a height—thirst in the wilderness. No doubt it was very disappointing when at last they struck water to find it bitter. But there was a childish pettishness in their tone when they came murmuring to Moses, and asked him, "What shall we drink?" Moses was at a loss till he cried to the Lord, and was directed to a tree which restored to the waters their proper flavour. Travellers have inquired of the natives for any tree in the neighbourhood that possesses this property, but in vain. That such a tree may have existed at the time is quite possible, inasmuch as in various parts of the world natural means are found of correcting unpleasant water, as the early settlers in America infused into the water the branches of sassafras.*

God seemed to wish to teach the lesson that the antidote is commonly not far from the bane, the remedy is near the poison ; a lesson useful for all of us in reference to the common ills and sorrows of life, and culminating at Golgotha, where, at the very headquarters of death, we find the elixir of life.

At the scene of this their first trial, and immediately after their deliverance from it, Moses made a kind of rehearsal of what was afterwards to be more fully gone into—God's covenant with the nation. The healing of the waters was a type of a wider healing, or, better still, of divine preservation from all sickness. It was a sample of what God would do for them on a larger scale, if only they would accept his service. Moses takes every oppor tunity to lead them to decision—to induce them to make a clean breach with the religious rites they had seen in Egypt, and to accept, in its unreserved fulness, the revelation he was to make

* " Pictor. Comment.," quoted from Burder, " Oriental Literature," i. 146.

to them respecting the worship of God. And here he skilfully calls up some painful associations with Egypt in the form of "diseases," like the boils and blains with which they had recently been familiar there, from all which they would be kept intact if they should accept of God's covenant. Even the Israelites could appreciate the value of bodily health, and therefore the advantage of a God who, among his other attributes, revealed himself as the Healer; although as yet probably they were little able to understand how much higher a gift is imparted when this heavenly Healer cures the pride, the greed, the hardness of heart, the sensuality of the disordered spirit, and brings to it a health or wholeness corresponding to the purity of his own nature. In full accord with the spirit of the assurance given by Moses, the next halting-place was Elim, where there were twelve wells of water and threescore and ten palm-trees. It is believed to be the modern Wâdy Ghurundel, "a charming oasis," with palms, and the feathery tamarisk, and the gray foliage and bright blossoms of the acacia.

2. *Manna.*—It was not long ere another grievance had to be dealt with. Some six weeks after leaving Egypt, the people had advanced into the wilderness of Sin, between Elim and Sinai. No doubt it was a very desolate and repulsive region. At first, near Marah and Elim, their camp was pitched among the low limestone hills that spread over the northern part of the peninsula; but in the desert of Sin they were encamped in a flat, sandy plain. It was a great contrast to Egypt, with its numberless water-channels bringing the Nile water to every field and garden, brightening all with an abundant vegetation; the cattle grazing contentedly in the meadows; while the orchards were heavy with fruit, and the gardens swarmed with vegetables. Again the murmuring spirit found an outlet.

We ought to remember, as a slight palliation, that men will sometimes bear privations quietly for themselves which excite them more keenly on behalf of others. One may bear little food for oneself, but it is hard to bear it for starving children or a delicate wife. But nothing can excuse the savage tone of the complaint now hurled against Moses and Aaron. "Would to God we had died by the hand of the Lord in the land of Egypt, when we sat by the flesh pots, and when we did eat bread to the full; for ye have brought us forth into this wilderness, to kill this whole assembly with hunger." How irritating this complaint must have been to Moses, so soon after the experience of Marah, and the "statute and ordinance" enacted there! Had they any memory? had they any sense of gratitude? had they the smallest grain of faith? One should not have wondered at a smart chastisement for a speech that indicated such sinful distrust and base forgetfulness of mercies. But the people were as yet only at the beginning of their lesson, and much forbearance was shown till after they had formally accepted God's covenant. To meet their necessities, after a striking display of God's glory in the cloud, manna was sent them in the morning and quails at night. Here was variety, in addition to what might be furnished by the flocks and herds, in accordance with a well-known physical law that variety of food is wholesome for our frame.

It is not easy to throw light on the manna. If the amended rendering of verse 15 in the Revised Version be correct ("They said one to another, What is it? for they wist not what it was"), it was as strange to the Israelites as to us. Some have attempted to identify it with the gum distilled by the tamarisk and other odoriferous plants; but the conditions do not agree. The gum in question cannot be baked, it does not dissolve in the sun, and it is found during but a few months of the year. Called as it is by our Lord "bread from heaven," the manna is surely to be regarded as a supernatural provision.

In the manner in which the manna was sent, there was a provision for promoting orderly habits on the part of the people, and likewise an arrangement requiring them to show respect for the Sabbath. In the whole arrangement it was made apparent that the heavenly Bridegroom might be securely relied on to provide the necessaries of life for his bride. In this matter, as in similar cases, provision was made by Moses for perpetuating the impression produced by this heavenly gift: a pot of the manna was

WILDERNESS OF SIN.

Page 373.

directed to be laid up before the Lord, and to be kept for the instruction of future generations.

The reference to the Sabbath is interesting. It is couched in terms that imply that the institution was already known, although it had probably been allowed to fall into disuse. We have evidence that in Chaldæa the primitive Sabbath had not been forgotten, but there is not the same proof of its observance in Egypt. In Chaldæa there was a division of time into seven days, which were named after the sun and moon and the five planets.* There is every reason to believe, as we already observed, that Abraham and the patriarchs observed the seventh day. But in Egypt it had probably lost its sacred character, or at best preserved it but imperfectly. The arrangements connected with the manna not only provided for its being regularly observed, but stamped it conspicuously with the divine sanction. Hence the fourth commandment was not in the form of a new law but a reminiscence—" Remember the Sabbath day, to keep it holy."

3. *Rephidim.*—The host had now reached a new part of the peninsula—the region of lofty mountains, of sandstone, porphyry, and granite rocks, which gradually rise toward the south-west, culminating in the range of Horeb, and rising into the various peaks of which mention will afterwards be made. It appears that with each change of scene the complaining temper of the people burst out anew. Every traveller speaks of the impression of awe which these mountains produce ; desolation and majesty are their great characteristics. They proclaim the littleness of man and the majesty of God ; but in their bare dry slopes, their jagged ridges and empty ravines, there is little to call to mind God's goodness, tenderness, and bounty.

Writing of some of the rocky ravines up which travellers have to toil, a well-known lady traveller says :—" What a place was this for the Hebrew mothers with their sucking babes ! They who had lived on the banks of the never-failing Nile, and drunk their fill of its sweet waters, must have been aghast at the aspect of a scene like this, where the eye, wandering as it will, can see nothing

* Sayce's " Babylonian Literature," pp. 54, 55.

but bright and solemn rocks, and a sky without a cloud !......At every step we found the scriptural imagery rising up before our minds—the imagery of overshadowing rocks, sheltering wings, water-brooks, and rain filling the pools. Even we, with our comforts and our well-filled water-skins, relieved our mental oppression with imagery like this. The faith of Moses must have been strong to bear him up in such a scene ; and what must have been the clamour and despair of the slavish multitude, whose hope and courage had been extinguished by that bondage which yet left their domestic affections in all their strength ? " *

The want of water was again keenly felt, and the maddening sensation of thirst in the desert. But instead of being more reasonable, more patient, and more believing when this new want pressed on them, the people became more offensive. Though the manna was provided day by day, not by Moses but by the hand of God, they came to Moses at Rephidim to chide with him and to say, " Give us water to drink." And after the remonstrance of Moses they were even worse—they demanded why he had brought them out of Egypt to kill them and their cattle with thirst ; they were even ready to stone him, and in the extremity of their complaint questioned the very presence of God, and asked, " Is the Lord among us or not ? " The more that Moses had tried to teach them, the more vehement and even blasphemous had they become. It was one of the most trying moments of his life. Appealing to God, he was directed to go with some of the elders to the rock in Horeb, where God would be standing, and to strike the rock with the rod wherewith he smote the Nile. Why the supply of water was provided in this particular manner it is not very difficult to see. The manna fell at every man's door ; the water was provided up among the hills. They had refused to see God in the manna, impiously demanding, "Is God among us or not?" It would not have been fitting to provide the water in the same easy way. Something must be done to make it unmistakably clear that GOD WAS PRESENT—that the water was his gracious gift. The spot where the water was provided seems to have been at a considerable

* " Eastern Travel," by Harriet Martineau.

distance.  And when Moses and the elders reached it, God was standing on the rock—that is, there was a display of the divine glory, to denote the immediate presence of God, and to rebuke the unbelief of the people.  Nevertheless, the water does not actually come till Moses strikes the rock with his rod.  Human instrumentality is again employed, and honour is again put on Moses, and on the rod which had mastered the waters of the mighty Nile and changed them into blood.  The name of the place is called Massah and Meribah, "trial" and "chiding," to perpetuate the folly of the people and the grace of God.

The spot where this great miracle occurred has naturally been sought for with great interest.  Monkish tradition points to a rock in the valley, a large block of granite, a cube of some twenty feet, marked by a number of fissures at unequal distances from each other, such as might have been formed by water flowing from them. But there is no reason to suppose that this was really the Rock of Moses, though it bears his name, partly because it lies in the plain and not up among the hills, and partly because other stones in the neighbourhood show similar markings.  The conjecture of Dr. Wilson of Bombay has not a little to recommend it, that it was high up the mountain that the rock was smitten, and that from this elevated source the stream descended now through one valley, now through another, according to the situation of the camp. This seems to agree with the various allusions in Scripture to the phenomenon.  Moses speaks of "the brook that descended out of the mount" (Deut. ix. 21).  In the 78th Psalm we read, "He clave the rocks in the wilderness, and gave them drink as out of the great depths.  He brought streams also out of the rock, and caused waters to run down like rivers."  In the 105th Psalm : "He opened the rock, and the waters gushed out ; they ran in dry places as a river."  So also in a well-known passage (1 Cor. x. 4), St. Paul, expounding the spiritual significance of the stream, says, "They drank of that spiritual Rock that followed them ; and that Rock was Christ."  The fantastic notion of the Jewish rabbis that the rock itself followed the people is quite unnecessary.  It was "the waters" that "ran in dry places like a river."  The applica-

REPHIDIM.

*Page 378.*

tion to Christ is made on the ground that the whole economy had a typical character, spiritual things being habitually shadowed forth by material. The likeness of the stream to Christ is seen vividly in many particulars : the element was water, and the form of it a flowing stream—" He that drinketh of the water that I shall give him shall never thirst ; " its source was a smitten rock, and the most loved of all our hymns has sanctified the analogy, " Rock of ages, cleft for me ; " the region through which the stream flowed was the wilderness, which it cheered, refreshed, and fertilized ; and it was ever near to those who needed it—it followed them, thus affording a constant supply. The reference of the apostle is in the way of solemn warning : the Israelites abused their privilege, and so may we if we do not take heed to our ways.

4. *Amalek.*—Two of the greatest trials to a nation traversing the wilderness had now been effectually disposed of—hunger and thirst. There was yet a third—enemies. One enemy had been engulfed in the sea ; but what of enemies yet in their front, some of whom hated Israel because his forefather had been preferred to theirs, while others hated him because his acknowledged purpose was to take possession of their land. It was to inspire them with confidence in reference to all enemies that, at this early stage, they were brought into hostile contact with Amalek. If God's power should show itself in this encounter on the side of Israel, they knew that it would bear them to victory in all future wars.

Of the various tribes that had settlements in the peninsula, the two most conspicuous were the Amalekites and the Midianites, sometimes called Kenites. Some have derived the Amalekites from Amalek, a grandson of Esau ; but the name is older than even the age of Abraham (see Gen. xiv. 7), in whose time " the country of the Amalekites " denoted the region stretching south of the Dead Sea towards the peninsula of Sinai. These Amalekites were alarmed by the entrance of Israel into the peninsula, of which they had hitherto been virtually the masters, and they resolved to try to drive them out. The manner of their attack was mean and cowardly ; for they fell upon the rear of Israel, where the feeble and sick of the company were placed, incapable of resisting them, and no doubt they inflicted much suffering there (see Deut. xxv. 17, 18). In this attack the Amalekites were actuated not only by a very bitter feeling toward Israel, but also by a contemptuous spirit toward God. All that they had heard of God's marvellous protection had made no impression on them; they "feared not God" (Deut. xxv. 18), but flung him out of their calculation as a force not worth their notice. Their attack was as much the result of contempt for God as of hostility to Israel—something like the spirit which Milton ascribes to Satan in his endeavours to ruin the human race. After this dastardly attack the Amalekites probably retired to some strong position, intending to return as opportunity might offer. But Moses was resolved to bring matters to a speedier issue. Joshua, son of Nun, and grandson of Elishama, prince of the tribe of Ephraim (comp. Num. i. 10, and 1 Chron. vii. 26, 27), of whom we hear for the first time, but who had doubtless already shown himself suited for the task assigned to him, was instructed to choose a band for the purpose of attacking Amalek, which he did next day. It was not an easy service, for Amalek probably occupied one or more of the heights, and Joshua and his troop would have to attack them as best they might—here charging up the mountain side, yonder stealing up through a concealed ravine, and again hurling arrows, stones, and missiles at them from neighbouring heights, of which Israel may have taken possession. One commanding height was reserved for another purpose. God had been pre-eminently insulted by the Amalekites in this matter, and it was fitting to show, in an emphatic and conspicuous manner, the power of that God whom Amalek had defied. Moses, accompanied by Aaron and Hur, went to the top of the hill, with the rod of God in his hand, the symbol of Almighty power, and stretched it out where the conflict was raging. As long as he displayed his divine symbol Israel prevailed, at other times Amalek. The battle raged obstinately the whole day to the setting of the sun; and that touching symbol of friendly support was brought into play which has so often been applied in a spiritual sense—Aaron and Hur holding up the hands of Moses to enable him to continue to extend his rod. It would not have been effectual if either Aaron or Hur had held the rod. God designed that this should be reserved for Moses, in order that his honour might be vindicated from past affronts, and that he might have the more influence with the people when he came to transact with them respecting the divine covenant. It was not enough for Joshua to fight; He whom the rod symbolized must fight along with him. And thus in all ages has the lesson been enforced in spiritual warfare, that if the praying brigade are idle, the fighting brigade will make little progress. In the battle with the spiritual Amalek it is the same as it was then—if the divine Power be not constantly invoked, Amalek will prevail.

It was a heavy doom that was pronounced on Amalek: " I will utterly put out the remembrance of Amalek from under heaven." In pronouncing this doom, God exercised his own prerogative. It is not for us to determine when any community or individual has become so utterly wicked that no effort at reclamation shall be made ever after; God only can determine that. We are never to despair of any. Our business is to do good to all men as we have opportunity—specially to them that are of the household of faith. However reprobate one may seem, we know that many a brand has been plucked from the burning, and that a great principle in the kingdom of God lies in the words, "The last shall be first, and the first last."

Moses never loses an opportunity of pressing good lessons on his people. While the treachery of Amalek and his signal defeat was to be written for a memorial in a book, and rehearsed in the ears of Joshua, Moses himself builds an altar to the Lord, and calls it by the name of JEHOVAH-NISSI—" the Lord my banner." Thus the four great deliverances have each their memorial : the deliverance from Egypt is commemorated by the Passover and the song of Moses; the deliverance from hunger by the pot of manna laid up before the Lord; the deliverance from thirst by the stream that continued to follow them in the desert; and the deliverance from Amalek by the book and by the altar Jehovah-nissi. Moses knew well what poor memories his people had, when anything spiritual or unseen had to be remembered; every suitable device was resorted to to strengthen these memories, and keep them in mind of their Benefactor. But in spite of all, their history had to be summed up in the words—"They remembered not his hand, nor the day when he delivered them from the enemy " (Ps. lxxvii. 42).

5. *Jethro.*—The other conspicuous tribe in the desert is that with which we have already become acquainted—the Midianites, one of whom, daughter of the priest, Moses had married. Sometimes they, or a part of them, are called Kenites (Judg. i. 16; iv. 11, 17). In the days of Balaam the Kenites were evidently a powerful people (Num. xxiv. 21). Partly in consequence of the connection of Moses with the tribe, but partly also, as seems evident from the narrative, because they had faith in Israel as the people of God, they were actuated by a spirit the reverse of Amalek's, and were not indisposed to friendly relations.

All that God had done for Moses and for Israel had made a powerful impression on Jethro, his father-in-law. Whether this Jethro is the same as Reuel, the name formerly given to the priest of Midian (Ex. ii. 18), or whether Jethro was the son and successor of Reuel, but is called by a term which as some think may denote a father-in-law, a son-in-law, or a brother-in-law, according to the connection, is a question not easily determined, although the paternal spirit manifested by the man inclines us to the former supposition.

The parting of Jethro and Moses had been friendly, and their reunion is not less so. Jethro brings with him Zipporah, Moses' wife, and his two sons. One should have liked something to show that this was a happy family reunion. But in true Oriental style, nothing more is said of the wife; but a picture is drawn of a pleasant meeting and interesting conversation between Jethro and Moses. Traditionally, this meeting is said to have taken place in the Wâdy es Shu'eib, or Vale of Jethro. In the midst of a great wilderness of mountains lies a plain, Er Râhâh, a mile or two in width and length, and sprinkled with shrubs. In front of the plain rises a dark, solemn, frowning cliff, fifteen hundred feet in perpendicular height. At the side of this cliff runs a deep narrow valley about a mile long, between perpendicular rocks; and in the valley lies a garden of fruit-trees and cypresses. This is "the Vale of Jethro," now occupied by the convent of St. Catherine.

In one way, at all events, the valley agrees with the history— in its contrast to all that surrounds it. Up to this point, at least since Moses began his conflict with Pharaoh, the narrative has borne a character of surpassing grandeur. The events are all in the region of the marvellous, the sublime, the supernatural—corresponding with the scenery of the peninsula, and its high, solemn, magnificent mountains. Then after Moses and Jethro have had their quiet domestic interview, when the story goes on to the giving of the law, we are again morally in the same region of majesty and sublimity, and physically amid the grandeur of Mount Sinai. But between these sublime events there is thrown in this quiet domestic picture of Moses and Jethro ; and we turn aside to this secluded valley, with its fruit-trees and cypresses, to enjoy the scene. Very pleasant it is to read of the two friends asking each other of their welfare, and of Moses rehearsing in the language of common life all that the Lord had done to Pharaoh and the Egyptians, and telling how he had delivered them from all the troubles by the way. Very refreshing to him must have been the sympathy of Jethro, "rejoicing for all the goodness which the Lord had done to Israel." A deeper feeling would be gratified when Jethro avowed his conviction that the God of Israel was greater than all gods—thus, as we may believe, making him, if he had not already made him, the supreme object of his worship and trust. Then came the solemn act of united worship : Jethro, as priest, offers a burnt offering to the God of Israel, and Aaron, with all the elders of Israel, partakes of the sacrificial feast ; thus joining in the highest service in honour of the one supreme God who had revealed himself to Abraham, and who now, after a long interval of more than four hundred years, had shown himself so mindful of his promises. Very delightful to Moses it must have been to find Jethro so thoroughly at one with him—renouncing whatever was inconsistent with the pure worship of Israel's God, and thoroughly satisfied to do so. May not Zipporah have shared in the impression under which Jethro so plainly came, and may

THE VALE OF JETHRO.
(Convent of St. Catherine.)

Page 35.

not the rest of Moses' domestic life have been rendered happier by this fusion of interest and sympathy in the highest region of family life?

The real friendliness of Jethro was further evinced by his desire to relieve Moses of part of the burden that fell so heavily upon him. In Egypt, as we have seen, there had been a system of domestic government under " the elders," by whom the ordinary quarrels of the people had been settled, and possibly minor punishments inflicted. The excitement and novelty of the march through the wilderness had thrown that system out of gear, and Moses personally had undertaken for a time to arrange these matters, unable probably to trust the elders in the entirely changed circumstances of the case. Jethro was concerned to see him occupied thus from morning to night, and to see how thoughtless the people were about him, and he could not but think that he must break down very speedily. He proposed the very natural and judicious plan of a gradation of rulers, who, while Moses in fellowship with God should be the great ruler, would dispose of all the smaller cases, and leave only the most difficult for him to settle. It was probably in substance an extension of the old method of government by elders, but more thorough and complete. It was piously submitted to Moses, subject to the condition, "if God command thee," and it was very cordially accepted by him. It affords another proof of the orderly methods of Hebrew life, of the force and extent of regulation among the people, and of the absence of confusion and random habits.

At length Jethro's visit to Moses came to an end. " He went his way unto his own land;" but he went away in closer fellowship with the true God, and to reap his share of his promise, "I will bless them that bless thee."

# CHAPTER VI.

## THE GIVING OF THE LAW.

### (Ex. xix.-xxxi.)

IT might, perhaps, not unreasonably be thought that the spot where two or three millions of people saw a sight that thrilled every fibre of their being, and of which they must have spoken to their children and children's children in the tone of rapturous wonder, would never have been forgotten, but would be well marked and familiar to all future generations. Yet there is no place of historical eminence, with the exception, perhaps, of Calvary, the scene of our Lord's crucifixion, which it is so difficult to identify. And on fuller consideration this will not appear very strange. Sinai became to the Jews a place of dreary associations, if not evil omen. In the whole course of Old Testament history we hear of but one visit paid to it—that of the prophet Elijah ; and his visit was a freak of disgust, not an excursion of pleasure. Seventeen or eighteen centuries ran their course before pilgrimages to Sinai became common. When the monastic fever broke out in the early Christian Church, the desolate wilds of the peninsula attracted the attention of many, and at one time no fewer than six thousand monks had their abodes in its solitudes. By that time the old names had nearly all disappeared, and the pilgrims of those days did as travellers do now—they endeavoured to find out what places on the whole seemed to answer best to the incidents of the history as recorded in the Bible. In this they were so little successful that monkish tradition now counts for hardly anything in determining the sites of Sinaitic history.

We cannot discuss all the theories that have been held as to
the real Mount Sinai—the mountain on which the Lord descended,
and on which he gave the law to Moses. The names Sinai and
Horeb are no longer in use. The three tallest summits in the
peninsula are : Mount Serbal in the north-west, Mount St. Catherine in the east, and Um Shomer in the south-east—this last being
the tallest of the group. Each of these has been claimed as the
true Mount Sinai, but none of them quite fulfils the conditions of
the history. The traditional mountain is that which bears the
name of Jebel Mousa (the Mountain of Moses), near the Convent
of St. Catherine. The plain now called Er Râhâh, which lies at
the foot of Jebel Mousa (noticed in our last chapter as being near
the meeting-place of Jethro and Moses), is most frequently regarded as the place where the people were encamped : it is large
enough for a great encampment, and some of the mountain summits are visible from it. There is also a plain to the south of
Jebel Mousa large enough for the encampment, which some think
to have been the position of the Israelites. From this plain the
highest peak of Jebel Mousa can be seen, but not from Er Râhâh.
But there are other peaks of Jebel Mousa visible from Er Râhâh,
and on one of these, now called Ras es Sufsafeh, it is the opinion
of many of the best authorities that the Lord descended in fire
and proclaimed the law. This view was first propounded by the
eminent Biblical traveller Dr. Edward Robinson, and though not
accepted by Carl Ritter, it has been adopted by the conductors of
the Ordnance Survey of Sinai.* Right in front of the plain of
Er Râhâh rises an abrupt perpendicular cliff, twelve or fifteen
hundred feet high, which might well entitle it to be called " the
mount that might be touched." Higher up, the rocks, which are
of reddish granite, are split and twisted and torn into huge masses,
which make the ascent extremely difficult.

At the foot of this mountain the people might be seen assembled
on the third month after the departure from Egypt, for the purpose
of formally agreeing to the covenant of God. Here, probably, was

* Ordnance Survey of the Peninsula of Sinai, by Captains Wilson and Palmer,
under direction of Colonel Sir H. James, R.E., Director-General of the Ordnance Survey,
1869.

RAS ES SUFSAFEH (SINAI).

*Page 389.*

the spot where, as the prophet Habakkuk solemnly says : " His glory covered the heavens, and the earth was full of his praise. And his brightness was as the light ; he had horns coming out of his hand : and there was the hiding of his power.  He stood, and measured the earth : he beheld, and drove asunder the nations ; and the everlasting mountains were scattered, the perpetual hills did bow."

Before the law was actually given, three days were occupied in preparation.  It is important to consider what the object of this preparation was, and for this purpose to examine somewhat carefully the object of the whole transaction between God and Israel at Mount Sinai.  For what end did God make that clear, full, and awful proclamation of his law which took place on this mountain ?

Now, we must carefully observe that before one word of the law was proclaimed Israel was already in covenant with God. For Israel was not only his chosen people, but his redeemed people.  God in the exercise of his free grace had drawn near to Abraham and the fathers, and of his own accord, and apart from all merit on their part, had made very gracious promises to them and to their seed.  In fulfilment of these promises, he had already redeemed them from their bondage in Egypt, and he was pledged to bring them into a land flowing with milk and honey. They had already received many gifts as the fruit of God's free grace—such as this deliverance from Egypt, the miraculous guid-ance of the pillar, the manna, and the water ; and they had received these amid not a few tokens of unworthiness on their part, amid not a little complaining and rebellion of spirit.  To these gifts of his grace God makes express reference in the very first message he sent from the top of the mountain to the people : " Ye have seen what I did unto the Egyptians, and how I bare you on eagles' wings, and brought you unto myself."  And again, immedi-ately before the decalogue was announced : " I am the Lord thy God, that brought thee out of the land of Egypt, out of the house of bondage."

The law, therefore, was not the basis of God's covenant, for the covenant was in full play before the law. It was rather *the rule of His house*, the explanation of what he expected of his bride, when she came to dwell, as it were, in her Husband's home. Until she should hear the rule of the house fully announced, she was not required formally to accept the bridal covenant. She had indeed accepted it provisionally, as it were, when she was "baptized unto Moses in the cloud and in the sea;" but a *formal* acceptance was not demanded of her till she should hear the whole law proclaimed. A second time she accepted it by anticipation when she said to Moses, "All that the Lord hath spoken we will do" (ch. xix. 8).

But more than even this was judged necessary. Israel might nominally and legally be Jehovah's bride, but very poor and meagre would be her enjoyment of this position if she were but the legal wife. It was congeniality of soul between the divine Husband and his spouse that would bring out the full blessedness of the relation. It was union of hearts that would make the covenant a delight—that thorough harmony of will in all the matters of life that not only averts strife and collision, but at every point creates the sweet enjoyment of loving hearts joined in the same pursuit. From the nature of the case, the bride could have no voice in laying down the law of the house; that must be regulated by the eternal rectitudes, the everlasting order of the divine mind. The bride was now to hear the order of the house proclaimed; and on the cordiality with which she accepted it, and the faithfulness with which she observed it, her comfort in her future relation would depend. So also her divine Husband's satisfaction in her must be measured by the heartiness of her accord with him in carrying out his rules: if only she should show herself hearty in her allegiance, no blessing would be too great, and no honour too high, as the reward of her faithfulness.

But if this was God's purpose in proclaiming the law from Sinai, why did he do so in such a terrible manner? Why the thunders and lightnings and the voice of a tempest, which voice they that heard entreated that it should never again be heard any more? Was this the way to deal with a timid bride? And why has Mount Sinai become to us the very symbol of terror, so that it is with the force of a profound climax that it is set against Mount Zion, the type of all that is comforting and soothing? (Heb. xii. 18–21).

In reply to this we can only say that God desired to convey to Israel a profound sense of the majesty and inviolability of his law—to show them in a way they could appreciate that it was not a flexible rule, not a law to be trifled with, that its obligations were infinitely strong, and that the most tremendous penalties were involved in its violation. There was but one way in which this impression could be made effectively in the then condition of the people, and that was through the bodily senses. The thunder, the lightning, and the earthquake were object-lessons to convey the truth that God's will is the sovereign, indefeasible, everlasting rule for his creature man. The people were indeed in a terrible fright; they were too agitated to combine the two manifestations that had taken place—that of grace and love and mercy in the deliverance from Egypt, and in all the wilderness blessings, with that of indefeasible righteousness and overwhelming and irresistible power. Afterwards God treated his people as persons whose education was further advanced. In our time he teaches us the majesty of his law, not through the bodily senses, but by considerations addressed to the soul. He takes us to Mount Calvary, and in the death of his Son for sin shows us at once his righteousness and his love. And this twofold manifestation of divine attributes is made so simultaneously that we are not in danger, like the Israelites, of dividing the impression, of receiving only the half of it, since we see so clearly the combination of divine goodness and severity. In the person of the Son of God enduring the penalty of transgression, we are taught profoundly the majesty of the law that required such a sacrifice, while we see the infinite depth of the love that made the sacrifice in our room. The moral law as given at Sinai is still the rule of the Bridegroom's house, and the rule for us; but we are not called to gaze on that naked and unrelieved view of its demands that was presented to Israel.

The sky is now spanned by the rainbow of grace, and the voice of the thunder blends musically with the voice of a great multitude, and the voice of many waters, saying, " Alleluiah ! for the Lord God omnipotent reigneth. Let us be glad and rejoice, and give honour to him : for the marriage of the Lamb is come, and his wife hath made herself ready."

These explanations may give us a better conception of the part which Moses had to perform on this memorable occasion.

In the first place, the physical activity of a man of eighty, hale and hearty at that age though he was, was put to an extraordinary strain. No less than four times is he called up the mountain into God's presence, and sent back with messages to the people. First (ch. xix. 3), he goes up and gets a general message, expressing God's readiness to make his relation to the people a most honoured and happy one ; this message he comes down to deliver to them (ver. 7). The people, rashly no doubt, but at the moment sincerely, promise absolute obedience to God. Again he goes up and communicates this reply to the message ; but as if God meant to reprove their impulsiveness and to demand more consideration, he is sent back to call them to the three days' preparation—to tell them to wash their clothes and be ready against the third day. Then on the morning of the third day—the great day, when Mount Sinai was altogether on a smoke, like the smoke of a furnace, and was quaking greatly—Moses brought the people out of the camp to meet with God ; and the Lord descended on Mount Sinai, amid the sound of a trumpet that ever waxed louder and louder.

Was it to beseech a little abatement of the terrific scene that " Moses spake "? (ver. 19.) Anyhow, God answered him in articulate speech, came down on the top of the mount, and called up Moses thither.

But even now God was not prepared to begin his communication. Moses was charged to go down once more and warn the people, lest they should break through in some irreverent way and suffer the penalty of death. The priests also were to be warned once more, lest they too should be guilty of some presumptuous act. Moses ventured to say that there was no fear of any such thing, and that the people had been sufficiently warned (ver. 23). Perhaps he was impatient, eager for the great event of the day; but God was peremptory, and Moses had to make his third descent to warn the people. He did not know Israel so well as God did. Perhaps they might be disposed to gaze with undue curiosity, in hope of discovering some similitude by which God might be represented; they must be made to understand that when God was pleased to manifest himself, there must be the profoundest reverence and humility on the part of men.

It seems to have been about mid-day, or on the afternoon of this third day, that the divine voice was heard from the top of Sinai proclaiming the law of the ten commandments. What an impression it must have made! Even a human voice sounding out from the top of a mountain, in tones so loud and clear as to be heard in every valley for miles around, would have had an unprecedented effect. But when the voice was the voice of God; when all of solemnity and power that even God could breathe into it was heard in its tones; when the effect was heightened by the dark and solemn forms of the mountains around; when all the forces of the thunder, the lightning, and the earthquake were in play; and when a thousand thousand awe-struck faces on every side showed themselves paralyzed by terror,—it is no wonder that the multitude were overcome, and pleaded, as if for life itself, that the voice should not be spoken any more.

When the law of the ten commandments had been uttered, there were evidently renewed thunderings and lightnings and sound of trumpet, and it was then that the people in their terror entreated that God would not again speak to them with that awful voice, because they could not live under it, but that Moses should speak to them, for they could listen in safety to him.

What a tribute this was to Moses! What a different mood it showed from that of a few weeks before, when they had so bitterly reproached him, and had even threatened to stone him! Now, in the dread presence of God, they pay him the highest honour, as the only man among them who can stand before God and listen to

his voice. How entirely does the presence of God alter our estimate of men and things! Many a man who in health has railed
against God's servant, denounced him as righteous over-much, and
bitterly opposed all his doings and teachings, has been fain to send
for him as God drew near to him in the chill hour of death, and
entreat his counsels and his prayers. Not only does this show
faith in a good man's religion, but also in his Christian magnanimity, in his willingness to forgive and forget the past in view of
the awful condition of a trembling sinner about to be ushered
into the presence of a holy God.

Eager to serve his people, Moses drew near into the thick
darkness where God was. In his holy courage he now seemed
like a superior being. When all shrank in terror, he ventured
into the most holy presence, though the mountains skipped like
rams, and the little hills like lambs. What an education he had
gone through since he had stood trembling, about a year before, at
the burning bush! It was his mature faith, his ripe confidence in
God that now bore him up,—his conviction that while his law was
thus awful in its holiness, God himself was full of grace and
truth. All the scenes he had gone through had convinced him of
the fatherly character of God, and assured him that he desired
nothing but the welfare of Israel. It is this conviction of faith
that keeps him calm and self-possessed while all around him are in
wild excitement. But there is no presumption in his spirit; his
reverence and his obedience are alike most profound; amid all his
calmness the feeling of his heart is, "Who is like unto thee, O
Lord, among the gods?......glorious in holiness, fearful in praises,
doing wonders."

That part of the law of his house which God made known to
Moses when he drew near to the thick darkness where the Lord
was, was mainly a collection of social rules and ordinances which
he designed for the Jews, interspersed with words of kindness,
chief of which was the promise of his angel to go before them, to
keep them in his way and bring them into their country. It was
a sort of protocol or first draft of the rules under which they were
to live. Moses was sent down with it to lay before them, and it

met with their hearty concurrence ; they agreed to it at once. " All the words which the Lord hath said will we do " (ch. xxiv. 3). And this assent of theirs is solemnly ratified by Moses. God's words are written in a book, read over, and again agreed to. An altar is built, sacrifices are offered, blood is shed, the altar and the book are sprinkled with the blood—for even now it is clearly revealed that without blood there is no covenanting with God—and the people are called to witness that their acceptance of the covenant has been ratified by sanctions of the highest order. It is a beautiful sight, a whole people covenanting with God—one of the few pleasant scenes in this wilderness drama : transitory, it is true, and therefore superficial ; but it must have gladdened Moses, and so far it was pleasing to God.

Another summons into God's presence comes to Moses. He is to receive another instalment of the law. But why this piecemeal legislation ? Why does God not despatch the whole business at once and be done with it ? Doubtless for the purpose of making the greater impression on the people—for the purpose of detaining their minds on the solemn transaction, and making the image deeper and clearer on their memories for evermore.

This time Moses is instructed to take up with him Aaron, Nadab and Abihu his sons, and seventy of the elders of Israel. But they are not to go near God ; they are to worship afar off. It was God's purpose that the leading men of the people should see something of his glory, although it was reserved for Moses to get the near and most impressive view of it. About the middle of the mountain they saw a display of the glory of God ; but not the brightest part, only the pavement under his feet. Ornamental floors of tesselated pavement were common in Egypt ; the halls of the temples and palaces were laid with them, and one variety of the bricks at which the children of Israel had laboured might be the tiles used for such pavements. But how much more glorious than any floor of Egyptian temple the pavement underneath the feet of the Almighty ! The slabs were bright blue, like sapphire stones, and gloriously transparent, like the vault of heaven. If the pavement was so glorious, what must the throne be, and the canopy over God's head? They saw God; but he laid not his hand on them, he inflicted no hurt: for they had been sprinkled with blood, and their sins were blotted out. After the vision "they did eat and drink," partaking of a sacrificial feast, consisting of the flesh of the animals that had been slain in sacrifice. For true worship is not merely the expression of our needs; it is followed by the reception of God's blessings. It was a poor half of divine service the man performed who merely brought his animal and confessed his sins; and it is a poor half that those perform who merely confess and adore and entreat. No one should leave God's presence without spiritual eating and drinking—without appropriating and delighting in the blessings of divine forgiveness and love.

And now Moses is called up into the mountain to receive further communications from God. He is made to understand that the business to be transacted there will demand considerable time. He is not to be back soon. But Aaron and Hur are left to act in his absence in pressing business.

Moses is to receive from God tables of stone, and a law and commandments. It is one of the supreme moments of his life when he leaves his friends behind him and advances to meet God face to face. He has to wait six days before any communication is received; for God is never in haste, and the spirit of patient waiting is among the most needful of human graces. Forty days and nights are then spent on the mount, during which Moses receives a further instalment of the laws of Israel. The ordinances now communicated bore chiefly on the worship which the people were to render to God, and the form and construction of the various articles that were to be employed in that worship. Of all that was communicated on this subject, the most remarkable and characteristic related to a Tabernacle, which was to be the symbolical dwelling-place of Jehovah and the scene of his gracious manifestation. Under the economy of grace and blessing now inaugurated, the Bridegroom and the bride were not to dwell apart, but in such happy fellowship that each might be refreshed by the loving presence of the other. During the forty days there was much time for Moses to reflect on what was communicated to him, and we may easily understand what happy thoughts he would have in connection with this tabernacle, and what bright visions his fancy would paint of the future, when God's abiding presence would shed on his people such influences of grace and love. His only misgiving would be as to the capacity of his people to appreciate their privilege, and to cherish and delight in it with suitable emotion. It was not long ere a lurid light was thrown on this question, and the visions which he had been framing of coming bliss, like the tables of stone which he carried down from the mount, lay dashed in shivers on the ground.

# CHAPTER VII.

## THE GOLDEN CALF.

### (Ex. xxxii.-xxxiv.)

"O FOOLISH Galatians, who hath bewitched you, that ye should not obey the truth?" Would not this have been a suitable exclamation for Moses, changing only the name, when he came down from the mount and saw the golden calf? Of all sudden changes of mood and action by a multitude, was there ever one to compare to that which we encounter now? Moses left the whole nation covenanting, giving themselves to God with enthusiasm, the solemn mountains everywhere echoing the shout, "All that the Lord hath said will we do, and be obedient." Now they are worshipping a golden calf, made in imitation of the Egyptian Apis or Mnevis, as many of them, no doubt, more or less openly had worshipped in Egypt! Whatever we may say of the impulsiveness of the people, of their weariness of waiting for the return of Moses, of the desolate and uninteresting scenery of the wilderness, such a wheeling round as this from their former attitude is hard to be accounted for. We can but conclude that the idolatrous worship of Egypt had not only been very common, but had sunk very deep into their hearts, and that their professions on behalf of the God of their fathers were merely the result—the honest result, it may be—of the overwhelming emotions of the moment, not of any profound turning of heart and will to God. Whenever the bent bow returned to its natural position, whenever the excitement of marvel and miracle subsided, the natural proclivities of their hearts resumed their sway, and these were strong toward idolatrous worship.

There are four acts in the drama of the golden calf :—1. Its construction by Aaron. 2. God's conversation with Moses about it on the top of the mountain. 3. Its destruction and degradation as soon as Moses came down. 4. The return of Moses to the top of the mountain, and his memorable intercession for his guilty people.

1. The movement in favour of this piece of idolatry evidently began, not with Aaron, but with the people. And the feeling under which they acted was impatience—that miserable feeling that we think so little of and allow so often to get the better of us. It was a costly bit of temper to the Israelites. It nearly cost the whole nation its life ; and it did cost the death of three thousand, while it left on the national history a fearful stain that could never be wholly removed. And they were not content with renouncing God and deposing Moses from his leadership ; they must add a sneer at "this Moses, the man that brought us up out of the land of Egypt." On the whole they were not displeased to be rid of him. Poor fickle multitude ! So long as Moses is among them they dare not breathe their cherished wish ; but when he is out of sight, it comes out in its most naked and offensive form. What they really wished was to return to Egypt—"in their hearts," as Stephen puts it, "they turned back again into Egypt." If they were to return to Egypt they must propitiate the Egyptian gods and the Egyptian people. They had offended both, and would be punished by both ; but if they returned to Egypt doing honour to a golden calf, that would be highly pleasing to the Egyptians, and would show that after all—after the ten plagues, after the catastrophe at the Red Sea, after all the apparent victories of the God of Moses—the calf was still in the ascendant ! No doubt the more intelligent of them, like Aaron, might excuse themselves on the plea that the calf or ox was only a symbol of a divine quality, a symbol of strength, and that under this symbol they might still worship Jehovah, and adore him whose outstretched arm had been so conspicuous in their recent history. But all such refinements of sentiment have no practical effect in restraining a multitude from the grossness of idolatry. The Psalmist puts the matter very plainly : "They made a calf in Horeb, and worshipped

the molten image. Thus they changed their glory into the similitude of an ox that eateth grass. They forgat God their Saviour,
which had done great things in Egypt......Yea, they despised the
pleasant land ; they believed not his word " (Ps. cvi. 19–21, 24).
And how did Aaron, brother and viceroy of Moses, whom he
had left in charge of the people, fulfil his trust? We see from
the very way in which the people spoke to him that they felt they
had a weaker man to deal with than Moses. There was something
peremptory in their tone—" Up, make us a god which shall go
before us." They would never have spoken to Moses in this
fashion. But perhaps they expected difficulties and objections
from Aaron, and the peremptory tone was adopted to strangle
these in their very birth. Instead, however, of boldly resisting
and denouncing the proposal, Aaron seems to have thought he
might turn them from it in an indirect way. "If you are to have
a made god, it must be a very costly one. The form must be a
young ox, and the material gold. And you know there is but one
way of getting the gold. You must break off the golden ear-rings
which are in the ears of your wives, and of your sons, and of your
daughters, and bring them unto me." Did he reckon that this
proposal would bring them to their senses? Did he trust to the
strength of avarice and vanity, love of gold, and love of ornament,
to frustrate the proposal? If so, he reckoned without his host.
The idolatrous feeling was stronger than even avarice and vanity.
The ear-rings were brought to him with the utmost alacrity ; and
there was nothing for it now but to construct the god.

Why should they have got Aaron not merely to sanction their
idolatry, but to construct the calf? Very probably in Egypt he
had been accustomed to such work ; for he goes about the business in quite a workman-like manner. He first melts the material,
runs it into a mould having the figure of a calf, then with graving
tools completes it, and finally builds an altar before it. And if at
first he might have wished to quash the proposal, he seems now to
be quite cordial in the matter. "To-morrow," he says, "is a feast
to Jehovah." He did not mean to renounce the God of their
fathers, but to use this visible god as a medium of worship. The

proposal of a feast found great favour ; but it was carried out not with the solemnity of a Hebrew ordinance, but in the tumultuous fashion of a heathen festival. In the early morning "they offered burnt offerings and peace offerings ;" afterwards "they sat down to eat and drink, and rose up to play." Their sensual nature was excited, and the usual sensual revel ensued. There is no mention now of returning to Egypt; the thought may have been only in their hearts, and not yet shaped into definite form.

2. The second act of this drama is enacted on the top of the mountain. Our hearts bleed for Moses, called to endure such a terrible ordeal, doomed to find that the great object on which his heart had been so long set was utterly and, as it seemed, hopelessly frustrated, and that all the toil, and self-denial, and anxiety, and effort of the last few months was utterly lost. There are few trials more crushing to the heart of one trying to do good among his tempted fellows, than to see one who has been reclaimed from guilty ways after an untold expenditure of effort, anxiety, and prayer, fall back suddenly into the mire, and revel, apparently with as much gusto as ever, in the abominable pleasures of sin. Moses had left the people in the full swing of a joyous experience, covenanting heart and soul with God ; now he hears that in the interval they have swung completely round, and are actually worshipping a molten calf. And as if the anguish of his own heart were not burden enough, God seems to aggravate his distress by his manner of making known what has happened, as if he were to blame. " Go, get thee down," he says—leave my company ; "for thy people, which thou broughtest out of Egypt, have corrupted themselves." Why does God speak thus to Moses? Were they not much more God's people than his? Yet God seems to disown them, and to cast on Moses the whole odium of their wicked deed.

More than that. God seems to put on, in reference to the transaction, the spirit and feelings of men. He speaks to Moses about it as if he were the more collected, thoughtful, and wise of the two ; and, strange to say, he seems to ask leave of him to adopt the course which he is thinking of. " Let me alone ;" don't attempt to thwart me ; just let me give full effect to my feelings, that I may consume this people, " and I will make of thee a great nation."

But God has a purpose in this method of proceeding. He likes, when he is sure of a man, to place him in circumstances that will bring out the greatness of his faith and other noble qualities, and will show these noble qualities triumphing over every form of opposition. When he strained the sinew of Jacob's thigh, it was to draw out the intensity of his desire for his blessing. When Jesus made discouraging remarks to the Syrophenician mother, it was to show, through her manifest rising above them, what a triumphant faith she had. And now, when he taunts Moses with the rebellion of his people, and offers to make a great nation of him, it is to draw out—what he knows to be so deep and true— the intensity of Moses' love for his people, and his utter repugnance to the thought of being put in their room. If God thus suffers himself to appear to be outdone by his creature in generosity, we must remember that it is he that confers the grace by which his creature conquers; just as, in the struggle at Peniel, it was he that gave Jacob the strength by which he overcame.

When it comes to Moses to speak, he shows how well he understands the purpose of the taunt when Israel was spoken of as *his* people, and he as having led them out of Egypt. It is not necessary for him to reason against this; it is only necessary silently to correct the language—" Lord, why doth thy wrath wax hot against *thy* people, which *thou* hast brought forth out of the land of Egypt with great power, and with a mighty hand?" When it is his own children that have sinned, why should their own father be excited against them? The sin of a child does not cancel paternal responsibility, and does not quench paternal affection. And why should occasion be given to the Egyptians to put a false construction on the deliverance from Egypt, as if God had only enticed Israel into a trap where he could not but perish? Moreover, had not God pledged himself to Abraham, Isaac, and Jacob, swearing by himself that he would multiply their seed as the stars of heaven, and give them the land of Canaan for an ever- lasting inheritance? Moses says not a word of the offer of God to put him in the place of Abraham, and make of him a great nation. By this silence he showed how far ambition for himself or for his family was from his thoughts. No proposal could for a moment be thought of that interfered with God's promises to the fathers of the nation.

The whole demeanour of Moses brought out wonderfully his disinterested love for his people. The warm sense of brotherhood that brought him out, forty years before, from Pharaoh's palace; the intense attachment which bound his heart to them as really as a mother's heart is bound to an only son, or a nurse's heart to a favourite child; the holy interest he had in a people who in the fulness of the times were to be the kindred, according to the flesh, of the great Deliverer, would not let him think even for a moment of the substitution of his own family for them, or find one grain of sweetness in the prospect of his seed being glorified while they were consumed.

3. From the top of the mount we pass with Moses to the bottom. He carries with him two blocks of stone, probably the red granite of the district, on both sides of which the ten commandments had been engraven by the finger of God,—the most vital of the rules of the covenant to which the people had vowed obedience. At the spot where he had left him six weeks before he finds his faithful and patient Joshua—a model of obedience and faith, although one of those active spirits to whom so long waiting must have been most irksome. As they draw near a strange noise is heard; it seems to Joshua, with his military ear, like the noise of a battle. No; Moses knew better: it is a wild festive noise; and when he came closer, he saw by their licentious undress that the people were indulging in the vile revelry common in idolatrous festivals. His indignation rose to the highest pitch. He dashed the two tables of stone from his hands, shivering them on the rock. The covenant was at an end; memorials of it were worthless. It does not appear that Moses was rebuked for this outburst of feeling, nor, when he reviewed the matter forty years afterwards, did he seem to think he had done wrong. It was a burst of righteous, not selfish indignation. Thereafter he took the

calf, cast it into the furnace to destroy its shape, then ground it to powder, strawed the powder on the water, and, to throw ridicule on their idolatry, made the people drink of it. We are not to suppose that all this was done at once ; it must have occupied some time. In this, Moses trusted to the overawing influence of his personal indignation bringing the outrage home to the people, so that for the time resistance should be paralyzed. As in the case of our Lord purging the temple, moral courage was transformed into a great physical force, and with great success.

But marvellous though the first effect was, it did not extinguish the spirit of rebellion. Aaron had shown himself weak and foolish, and had at once succumbed to his brother ; but all were not as easily cowed as he. A large band of men seem to have stood out, as if determined to resist. Moses called for volunteers—" Who is on the Lord's side ? " His own tribe, Levi, presented itself cordially for service. The opponents seem to have taken possession of the gates of the camp, and the Levites were sent to attack them and slay them without mercy. It was a holy war ; for if these champions of idolatry had carried their point, the whole nation would have perished under the sweeping judgments of an offended God. In the onslaught three thousand Israelites fell ; a fearful number, well fitted to show what an awful sin had been committed, and to teach a lesson never to be forgotten—that if men will sow the wind, they must reap the whirlwind.

4. Once more Moses returns to the top of the mount, and again in the character of intercessor, to plead anew with God for forgiveness to his people. Already he had interceded for them, when at first God threatened to consume them and make a nation of him. At that time he was so far successful that God is said to have " repented of the evil which he thought to do to them," but not to have taken the people back into covenant. When Moses returns, he owns with his whole soul the greatness of the sin, but still implores forgiveness—implores it so vehemently that he would take it at any personal sacrifice, even if he should be blotted out of God's book. Only men of the spiritual patriotism of Moses and Paul (Rom. ix. 3) are capable of such a feeling—

of such a request; prepared to renounce their every interest in life, and their very hope for the future, if only it could be well with their countrymen.

In reply to this unprecedented appeal, God continued to deal with Moses after the manner of men, and allowed himself to be driven, as it were, from one concession to another. As to blotting him out of his book, that was impossible; only sinners would be blotted from his book. But God agreed to a second concession— that his angel should go before the people; an inferior angel, not himself, not "the angel of the covenant." He declines to show himself among them as he had shown himself before.

But notwithstanding the concession, even this was a grievous thing. When the people heard it—heard that though not guideless they were to be godless—they mourned and put off their ornaments. They had undergone another of their sudden changes—from idolatrous enthusiasm to godly concern. Moses now took a new line of action. He took what is called "the tent or tabernacle, and pitched it without the camp, far off from the congregation, and called it The Tabernacle of the Congregation." This cannot mean the tabernacle for which he received orders on the mount, for evidently it was not constructed till afterwards. Probably it was a tent that had been used for the more prominent and public acts of worship, and that had acquired pre-eminence and become known as "the tent" thereby. The Revised Version alters the rendering thus: "Now Moses used to take the tent and to pitch it without the camp, afar off from the camp, and he called it The tent of meeting." Moses now proceeded thither in order to transact with God; and the people, when they saw him going, as if pricked in their hearts, flocked to the tent, or followed him to it with their eyes and with their hearts. And as if in recognition of this better feeling, "the cloudy pillar descended, and stood at the door of the tabernacle." And all the people worshipped.

Encouraged by the presence of the symbol, Moses, now face to face with God, implores a further concession—implores the blessing of his own gracious presence among them. If he has·

found grace in his sight, if he is to lead up his people, how can he dispense with this? He entreats God to consider that the people he has charge of are still his people. And again Moses prevails. "My presence shall go with thee, and I will give thee rest." This is even more than was asked. Moses asked for the presence, and besides that he is promised rest. He will not always have the troubled, anxious time he dreads. He will have rest when he seeks it in the conscious guidance of God. Happy assurance! Life seems again worth living. Without God the enterprise would be all too dreary. It could not be thought of; it would be a *fiasco*—an utter failure. "If thy presence go not with me, carry us not up hence." Again he is assured of the divine presence, and God adds an encouraging word, "I know thee by name." Thou art my personal acquaintance, my friend. Whom should I be with, if not with thee?

Ah, then, pleads Moses, "I beseech thee, show me thy glory." In one sense a strange request. What had God been doing all these past months but showing him his glory? In the plagues of Egypt, in the division of the sea, in the pillar of cloud and fire, in the thunder of Sinai, what had they all been seeing but God's glory? Ah, but, Moses virtually pleads, if I have found grace in thy sight, if thou knowest me by name, there is an inner manifestation of thy glory that I may surely look for; there is a moral and spiritual glory, a subduing and transforming glory, which I am eager to see. The view which he desired seems to have been a compound one—something at once to impress the senses and instruct the soul. Perhaps Moses thought that they could not be separated. Was it not the yearning of the earnest heart for an incarnation, a near view and blessed experience of God—that yearning which was afterwards fulfilled when the Word became flesh and dwelt among us? What he knew of God already only begot the desire to know more. He longed for something that would give him an adequate impression of the Supreme, that would abide with him evermore, moulding and moving him by a divine influence, cheering him in times of depression, fitting him for his difficult office, enabling him to perform aright his mighty task towards the people committed to his care. He was not content with official fellowship with God. There were depths of spiritual beauty in the divine character which he longed to know, like the Psalmist afterwards—" One thing have I desired of the Lord, that will I seek after, that I may dwell in the house of the Lord all the days of my life, *to behold the beauty of the Lord,* and to inquire in his temple." The highest ambition of the spiritual heart is to get a near view of the divine excellence, and to be thrilled by the sight ; to come under its transforming influence, to be changed into the same image. So far as Moses was capable of receiving it, the desired vision was promised. But it was only a veiled view that he was capable of sustaining. Had he got more he would have been like that Puritan who, having prayed for a full view of God's love, was deprived for a time of his senses through the intensity of the impression. Only from a cleft of the rock Moses would be shown something of God's glory, and after all it would be but a back view ; he was incapable of bearing the full view of Him who dwelleth in the light that is inaccessible and full of glory.

All alone, on the top of the mount, with two tables of stone in his hands, which he had been instructed to take, that he might receive again the words of the holy law, Moses once more takes his place, and enters a cleft of the rock. The strange situation of the hearer, and the sublime platform of the Speaker, might have suggested an awful message. Instead of that, " The Lord passed by before him, and proclaimed, The Lord, The Lord God, merciful and gracious, long-suffering, and abundant in goodness and truth, keeping mercy for thousands, forgiving iniquity and transgression and sin, and that will by no means clear the guilty ; visiting the iniquity of the fathers upon the children, and upon the children's children, unto the third and to the fourth generation."

There evidently was a physical display, a brightness exceeding the brightness of the sun, showing how infinitely God was above all other gods—how he stood alone in his majesty and his power. But this was little compared to the glory of the moral and spiritual qualities revealed in the proclamation.

It is impossible rightly to apprehend the soothing power with which the enumeration of the divine attributes would fall on the ears of Moses, agitated as he had been by the thought of the people's guilt and the terrible retribution to which they had become liable. The fulness and richness of the language reminds one of the firmament studded with stars, or a royal crown thick with jewels. Moses now knew not only that the sin of his people was forgiven, but that it was forgiven because God's nature was one of infinite grace as well as infinite righteousness. How the two were to come together—how God, while infinitely righteous, could yet be infinitely forgiving—may have been hard to see, but it was not hard to believe; the ground of forgiveness was not yet made plain, but the reality of it was very certain, because he knew from his own proclamation that GOD IS LOVE.

Forty more days were spent by Moses on the mount. The law of the kingdom was again engraven by the divine finger on the tables of stone in token of a renewed covenant, and new ordinances and charges were given; but above everything else, the impression of God's goodness, as revealed in the proclamation, filled and cheered his heart. The light that brightened his face as he descended from the mountain was not only the reflection of the glory he had been beholding, but likewise the expression of his own gladness in bearing to his people such cheering news.

This shining of the face of Moses as he came down from the mount, and the veil which he had to put on after speaking with them, are the subject of special applications in the New Testament. (See 2 Cor. iii. 13–18.) But first, we must notice the translation of Ex. xxxiv. 33 in the Authorized Version—"And *till* Moses had done speaking with them, he put a vail on his face." The conjunction *till* is supplied by the translators; but the Revised Version gives *when* instead. While Moses was speaking with the people his face was not veiled; the shining of his countenance gave majesty and authority to his words; but when he ceased speaking he put on the veil. The explanation of the apostle is that the brightness was a symbol of the glory of the dispensation, while the veil by which it was concealed indicated that it was a

temporary glory. The economy was glorious; the relation of
God to Israel was glorious; the types and symbols by which
better things to come were shadowed forth were very glorious.
Moses was the representative of that economy, and the shining
lustre of his face represented its glory. But the face of Moses
did not shine always; at times it was covered with a veil, and
after a time the lustre passed away. In writing to the Corin-
thians the apostle makes a characteristic application of this. He
supposes the veil to cover, not the face of Moses, but the law
which he made known—not the revealer, but the object revealed.
In this way he explained the unbelief of the Jews. They read the
Old Testament through a veil, and in this way they missed Christ.
But under the gospel we read God's revelation with unveiled
face; we see the great object of divine revelation with open
face, not through types and symbols. And not only do we thus
get a clearer view, but we become the subjects of a more power-
fully transforming influence. "We all, with open face beholding
as in a glass the glory of the Lord, are changed into the same
image from glory to glory, even as by the Spirit of the Lord."

Thus concluded another very important chapter of the life of
Moses. His last chapter had been spent mainly in struggling
with Pharaoh, the greatest monarch of the world. Much though
he had shrunk from that conflict when it was proposed to him at
the burning bush, he had carried it out steadily and successfully.
The power of God had been with him, and his progress had been
from victory to victory, until he attained his crowning triumph.
But the chapter following was spent mainly in struggling with
the people, and with God on their behalf. This was an infinitely
more difficult and more painful operation. If sometimes he had
felt disposed to run away from the contest with Pharaoh, much
more would he have that feeling in the battle with Israel. It was
well for him that during this period he had to be in official communication with God; otherwise he might have sunk into despair,
and shrunk utterly from approaching him on behalf of a people so
utterly demoralized and disgraced. He was held to his task by

the very necessities of the case. Through this process he got himself steadied and qualified for that long and most trying piece of work which was before him—the management of the people for forty years in the wilderness. What a blessing it is that we do not see all that is before us until we are in some measure trained to bear it! Moses is now better acquainted with God and with the people. He has known the people at the worst, he has got through the most trying experiences he can ever have of them, and got larger and fuller promises of divine grace ; he is nearer to the great fountain of light, and more confident of gracious help.

Thus we see how Moses ultimately mounted so high. We are liable to forget that he was flesh and blood, and to think of him as a supernatural being, invested with extraordinary powers, that kept him from knowing anything of the troubles and infirmities of ordinary men. No doubt he had rare supernatural powers ; but he was a human being all the same, and it was through the process of earthly training that he became supremely fitted for his exalted mission. How seldom a man reaches his full stature in quiet times ! It is amid bitter experience of opposition and strain ; it is in having to contend with beasts at Ephesus, skirting ever and anon the gulf of despair, and being often thrown down and almost buried under avalanches of misfortune, yet never suffered to lose all hope, or to despair of God, but enabled to rise up again and take courage and renew the conflict ;—it is amid difficulties of this sort that men rise to their full stature and become giants. If Moses became one of the greatest of men, it was not merely because he was intrusted with an unwonted measure of supernatural power, but also because he was called to pass through the most trying apprenticeship that was ever assigned to mortal man, and, like his divine Antitype, was made perfect by suffering.

# CHAPTER VIII.

## THE LAWS OF MOSES.

### (Ex. xxxv.-xl.; Num.; Lev.)

THIS is no place for discussing the question, on which modern criticism has expended so much labour, as to the authorship of the books of Moses or of the Mosaic legislation. Whatever may be held as to the authorship of the books in their present form, the legislation from the beginning has been so constantly associated with Moses that it would be an act of unprecedented violence to dissever them.

But there is another question of more interest for us in this biography of Moses. In the process of communicating laws to the people, was he a mere passive instrument in the hands of God, simply communicating what God made known to him? or did God first influence him in such a way that his own mind reached the conclusions which are associated with him? Was Moses a mere amanuensis, or did he think out the laws and institutions for himself? Did they pass through the alembic of his own mind, just as in New Testament times the doctrines of grace, as revealed to St. Paul, were first worked into the texture of his own mind, and thereafter communicated to the Church, with the stamp of divine inspiration?

The question is not without difficulty, because on the one hand the communications to Moses bear so much of the form of verbal instructions that our natural impression is that he was only the recipient of them. What else, it may be asked, was going on all the time that he was with God on the mount? Was not God simply communicating to him what he afterwards imparted to the people? And in reference to certain definite operations, such as the construction of the tabernacle, was not the command given expressly, " See thou do all things according to the pattern shown to thee on the mount"?

On the other hand, the idea of Moses being merely a mechanical recipient of the revelations given to him is out of harmony with God's ordinary way of communicating his will. The prophets were not mere channels for conveying instruction, reproof, or consolation; their own souls were alive and aglow with their messages, and this gave to these messages a far greater effect. The cases are not quite parallel; the minute regulations of the Mosaic code place them in a different category. It is impossible to give an explicit deliverance on the question, and especially the details of the question; but at the least we must believe that there was an intelligent sympathy on the part of Moses with God in reference to the laws and ordinances which he got by revelation. There was such an understanding and appreciation of them that they came from him to the people with that weight which characterizes a message when the messenger's own mind and soul are alive to its significance and impressed by its importance.

The language of Scripture seems in many places to imply that personally, as well as officially, Moses, under divine inspiration, was identified with the legislation which bears his name. Our Lord recognizes him as exercising his will and judgment in some particulars; for when the question was put to him, " Why did Moses command to give a bill of divorcement?" he answered, " Moses, for your hardness of heart, suffered you to put away your wives; but from the beginning it was not so." All that was characteristic of the prophets must have been found in the greatest of the prophets. In what manner the mind of Moses conspired with the mind of God in all these enactments we are not able to explain. We believe it to have been such that Moses' knowledge of Egyptian and other institutions, and his judgment on the suitableness of some of these and the unsuitableness of others for the spiritual benefit of the people of Israel, might have been made

use of in constructing the system.    It is a great law of God's
kingdom that the supernatural begins where the natural ends.
The natural and the supernatural were both made use of in the
Hebrew economy ; but where the one ended and the other began
we are not able to tell.

It is useful to try to have a clear conception of the religious
condition of the Hebrew people as they followed Moses from
Egypt into the wilderness.    Our materials, however, are very
scanty.    Doubtless they retained the tradition handed down by the
fathers, Abraham, Isaac, and Jacob, and of the covenant which the
great Jehovah made with them.    They recognized him as the God
of their fathers, and probably kept up the forms of service which
Jacob and his sons had brought with them.    But along with this,
under the influence of that tendency which they always showed to
conform to the idolatrous rites of their neighbours, they doubtless
observed many of the religious practices of the Egyptians.    Amos
(v. 26) charges them with having in the wilderness " borne Siccuth
your king [*marg.*, the tabernacle of your king, or of Moloch] and
Chiun your images, the star of your god, which ye made to
yourselves " (Revised Version).    Stephen makes the same charge
against them : " Ye took up the tabernacle of Moloch, and the
star of the god Rephan, the figures which ye made to worship
them " (Revised Version).    The passage is obscure, but it shows
plainly that shrines and images of heathen gods were more or less
openly borne about in the wilderness.    Israel was to a large degree impregnated with Egyptian paganism, even when they were
" baptized unto Moses in the cloud and in the sea."

The Egyptian religion was by no means homogeneous ; it had
higher and lower elements.    It had its gods of various groups,
greater and less ; it had its worship of the heavenly bodies, pre-
eminently of the sun ; and with this it conjoined the worship of
nature—of hills, rivers, and trees, and even of certain animals.
The passage just quoted from Amos would seem to indicate that
star-worship was borrowed from the Egyptians ; but it was a
new, a lower, a more debasing form of worship—the worship of
animals—to which they mainly inclined.    It is hard for us to

understand wherein the fascination of this practice lay; perhaps it was in the excitement and sensual pleasures with which it was connected. We must remember that during all the time the Israelites were in Egypt they had had no new revelation that we know of—nothing to quicken into new activity the traditions of the past. A higher and better element of Egyptian religion was belief in a future state of rewards and punishments; death was but the door to immortality, and after death came the judgment.

The religious system of Moses no doubt borrowed a few features from Egypt, but in the main it was a protest against the Egyptian religion, and an emphatic assertion of its opposite in most things.

1. First it maintained strongly the unity and spirituality of God: "Hear, O Israel, the Lord our God is one Lord." It was he who had entered into covenant with the fathers, and who had redeemed them from the bondage of Egypt. Every conceivable perfection was found in him. And as he was the one only God, and the God of their fathers, infinitely holy and infinitely gracious, no sort of worship or sacrifice was to be offered to any other being, and no sort of image or idol was to be used in his service. Herein the law was inexorable. Deities greater or lesser, sun-gods, moon-gods, nature-gods of any kind, were never to be thought of; no more were teraphims, amulets, or images as helps to recall the object of worship. This was the feature where Judaism was absolutely intolerant; no relaxation or abatement could be endured in this.

2. Highest of all the requisites for God's service was a strict moral life, recognizing alike the claims of God and of man. As the decalogue was the part of the law of the house first proclaimed, and proclaimed under by far the most impressive conditions, so it was the part of the law that lay at the foundation of all the rest. Unless the bride should accept this condition with heart and soul, there could be no real congeniality between her and her divine Husband. Most carefully was that miserable defect of pagan religions guarded against — the severing of religion from the domain of moral life. Every department of human duty was hedged round by divine sanctions. And though the spirituality of

the commandments was not so fully set forth as it was afterwards in the Sermon on the Mount, yet it was made clear to the people that not the outer life only but the heart itself must come under their sway ; for the tenth commandment expressly forbade every covetous outgoing of the heart, and the whole decalogue rested on loving the Lord with all their heart, and their neighbour as themselves.

It was as illustrations of the ten commandments, and particularly of the second table of them, that many miscellaneous enactments were added bearing on the intercourse of man and man. Laws modifying slavery ; assigning penalties to certain forms of injustice, violence, and inhumanity ; requiring the considerate treatment of the poor, the stricken, the unfortunate ; prescribing certain becoming courtesies towards strangers, rulers, aged persons, and the like, filled out the bare outlines of the decalogue. We are struck with the apparent want of order in which such matters are introduced, and the repetitions that occur without apparent reason. But possibly they were rules laid down in connection with particular cases that had arisen requiring judgment. Certainly they do not form a cut-and-dried system, after the manner of modern systems or bodies of "rules and regulations." We are not entitled to judge of the work of so ancient a time and so peculiar a legislation by modern rules.

3. But the main provision of the Mosaic legislation was for WORSHIP.

(*a*) We note the provision for the *persons* that were to superintend the worship. The first-born had already been dedicated to God (Ex. xiii. 2, 12), but subsequently the tribe of Levi was substituted for them (Num. iii. 41). For the priesthood the family of Aaron was set apart, but with many ceremonies of blood-atonement and purification ; another proof that it was not merit but grace that regulated the appointment of those who were called to special honour—a truth already illustrated in the selection of Jacob and Judah as heirs of promise.

(*b*) The *place* of worship was the subject of very special enactment. There was to be an erection consecrated in a special sense to God, where manifestations of his presence would take place, and where the most solemn worship of the nation would be offered. It was to be in the form of a tent or tabernacle, suitable for the condition of things in the wilderness. This would be a pledge of God's presence, in accordance with his covenant, so long as the people should be faithful to his law.

(c) The *acts* of worship were likewise most carefully prescribed. And the main feature of the worship was to be sacrifices and offerings. From the days of Abraham, and even earlier, certain sacrifices had been offered to God, in accordance with his revealed will, and what were now enjoined were chiefly amplifications of the older rites. What the precise significance of sacrifice was, it is not easy to determine ; but the sacrifices were of various kinds, and answered different purposes. They seem to have belonged to three great classes. The *sin-offering* denoted propitiation : the hand of the offerer laid on the victim denoted the bringing of the offerer into fellowship with God ; and, in this case, the shedding of its blood, the sacrifice of its life, denoted that the animal's life had been substituted for the offerer's. The *burnt offering*, which had to be preceded by the sin-offering, denoted the entire consecration of the worshipper to God, in the spirit of Rom. xii. 1 : " Present your bodies a living sacrifice, holy and acceptable to God." The *meat-offering*, the peace-offering, and other offerings were tokens of thankfulness to God for his mercies, and were followed by the eating of the offering by the offerer, in token of that friendly fellowship with God of which sitting at one's table is the ordinary sign. A guilty being like man could not approach God on the footing of nature ; the shedding of blood showed that atonement was an indispensable requisite to acceptable worship.

4. Very elaborate were the enactments bearing on the *times* or *occasions* of worship. There was the weekly Sabbath with the other sabbatical institutions. But more frequent than even the Sabbath was the daily morning and evening sacrifice. Of the more prominent occasions for worship there were the three annual festivals—Passover, Tabernacles, and Pentecost, when, after being settled in Canaan, all the males had to go up to the

appointed place of service. There were other times of great solemnity and importance—pre-eminent among these the great day of Atonement.

The three great festivals were designed to exemplify the combination of *enjoyment* with the service of God. Divine service was not meant to be a gloomy experience—the experience of men forcing themselves against their will to do homage to a Being of whom they stood in awe—but the happy feelings of children rejoicing in the love and goodness of their Father, and enjoying life all the more that they could think of him as their Friend, and as bestowing his numberless gifts upon them in order that their lives might be the brighter and the better thereby.

Many of the subordinate arrangements of the law of Moses were designed to make the provision for the worship of God and the welfare of the people more complete. Among these were the strong enactments against superstition, especially in its most deadly form, sorcery or witchcraft; the many enactments for the purification of the person and of the dwelling; the institution of the order of Nazarites, as a standing warning against the danger of wine and strong drink; the marriage law, designed to give protection from unholy connections ruinous to family prosperity; and the provision of cities of refuge, as a protection to the involuntary manslayer.

The civil economy of the nation was not drawn out with the same fulness and explicitness as the ecclesiastical. We see, however, many remarkable provisions for social welfare—provisions which are in some respects in advance of our civilization at the present day. The fundamental principle on which the whole structure rested was that "righteousness exalteth a nation." But righteousness was not to be left without the help that comes from sound social provisions. When they were settled in the land, every citizen received a substantial interest in the welfare of the commonwealth by being made a sharer of its property; industry, forethought, and integrity were encouraged by ample and not distant rewards; the recklessness engendered by overtoil was checked by the interspersion of frequent holidays with the days of labour; instruction in God's law helped to check vice and pro-mote the order and well-being of the community; genial allevia-tions were provided against the grip of poverty, and by the jubilee law the certain prospect of regaining its position within fifty years at furthest was held out to every down-trodden family. Incidental though most of these provisions were, they tended more to advance the Hebrew people in civilization and general comfort than all the social constitutions could have done that have been elaborated during the last fifty years; and it is partly a result of this system that the Hebrew people have retained such wonderful vitality, and that the physical woes and wretchedness which disgrace so many of our so-called Christian cities are hardly known among them.

We have already adverted to the question whether the whole law recorded in the five books of Moses was issued in the wilder-ness, or whether part of it was the result of future developments. (*See Introduction.*) There are difficulties connected both with the older view and with the new theories of the higher criticism. But that the whole system of legislation was "the law of Moses," is the testimony of Scripture from beginning to end.

We proceed to notice the steps taken by Moses to carry into effect the method of worship which was the great object of the communications made to him by God on the mount.

Prominent among the objects to which his attention had been earnestly called were the erection of the tabernacle and the in-stitution of the priesthood. The whole system of divine worship centred in the tabernacle. It represented God dwelling in the midst of his people, and its place accordingly was in the centre of the encampment. The preparation of the tabernacle and its furniture was the great event of the months that elapsed between the giving of the law and the removal from Mount Sinai. The people had nothing else of a public kind to occupy their thoughts all this time. And Moses, under divine direction, took wise and useful measures for interesting them in the work, and for inducing them to become acquainted with every detail of the structure, and every part of the service that was to be rendered in connection with it.

In the first place, two of their own number were appointed to execute and superintend the work. These were Bezaleel, of the tribe of Judah, the grandson of Hur—perhaps the Hur who held up the hands of Moses in the battle with Amalek, respecting whom an old tradition, of which Scripture says nothing, affirms that he was killed by the people for resisting the resolution to make the golden calf. The other was Aholiab, the son of Ahisamach, of the tribe of Dan. Bezaleel was an inspired workman, in more than the sense in which men of mechanical genius excel their fellows in wisdom of conception, beauty of design, and cleverness of execution. The first sphere for his genius had probably been in Egypt, where there was ample scope for work in gold and in silver and in brass, and in the cutting of stones to set them, and in carving of wood to make any manner of cunning work. It was a happy thing for Bezaleel that in connection with the tabernacle his talents now found so much higher a sphere. Aholiab seems to have been equally distinguished for his abilities as a workman, but more perhaps in the department of the weaver and the embroiderer in blue, in scarlet, and in fine linen, of which many of the hangings and other parts of the furniture of the tabernacle were constructed. With these were associated every wise-hearted man, in whom the Lord put wisdom and understanding, and all who were willing to aid in the work.

In the next place, Moses invited the whole congregation to contribute to the erection. He knew how much more interest men have in a work to which they have given aid, and which thereby becomes in some degree their own. The response to this invitation was most remarkable. Besides the first great contribution, fresh supplies continued to pour in every morning. An order had at last to be issued forbidding all further contribution. There was more than enough even for the costly structure. And the supplies were as superior in quality as they were large in quantity. Gold and silver and brass, precious stones of every hue, the finest linens and the richest embroideries, were profusely given, exciting in the minds of the people a magnificent idea of the splendid product that would be constituted by the skilful combination of all these materials.

Moreover, the work was done in public. All saw what was going on, and enjoyed the marks of steady progress. And there was no time wasted. As the year drew to its close, the work drew to its completion. And as the first day of the first month of the second year was fixed for the setting up of the tabernacle, and the ordination of the priests who were to preside over it, the people, young and old, looked forward to a most interesting new-year's day.

The great alacrity with which this work went forward must have been most cheering to Moses. The hearts of the people were thoroughly in it, and their enthusiasm must have done much to obliterate the sad impression of the golden calf. God was manifestly fulfilling his promise to dwell among them, and giving them the best tokens of his presence. Winter had changed into glorious summer, and there seemed every hope of a prosperous future.

The tabernacle was a tent of two chambers—an inner and an outer. In the inner was placed the ark of the covenant, containing the tables of the law; above the ark was the mercy-seat, on which once a year the high priest sprinkled the blood of atonement; and over the mercy-seat knelt, face to face, two golden cherubim with outstretched wings, denoting that through the appointed propitiation the holy God now held blessed intercourse with his creatures. In the outer sanctuary or holy place, separated by a curtain or veil from the inner, stood various pieces of sacred furniture—the altar of incense, the table of show-bread, the golden candlestick; and here, day by day, the priests came to offer incense with the daily sacrifice. · In the court outside, at the door of the tabernacle, stood the altar of burnt offering, on which the daily sacrifices were presented in sight of the assembled people; also the laver of brass, containing water for the daily ablutions of the priests. The tabernacle was covered with curtains of rare and varied beauty. In the contrast between this simple structure and the highly elaborate stone temples of Egypt we see the divine mind pointing to simplicity and spirituality as the acceptable qualities of worship, while the costly and beautiful curtains seem to have been designed to symbolize that holy human nature in which God was to be revealed when the Word should become flesh and tabernacle with men.

When the sanctuary was completed, and the law of its offerings fully made known, it was opened, as we should say, for divine service, according to appointment, on the first day of the second year.

THE INSIDE OF THE TABERNACLE WITH ITS HOLY VESSELS.

| | |
|---|---|
| H. The most Holy Place. | H P. The Holy Place. |
| A. The Ark. | N. Altar of Incense. |
| G. The Cloud of Glory. | C. Golden Candlestick. |
| V. The Veil dividing the Holy Place from the most Holy. | T. Table of Show-bread. |
| | E. The Curtain at the entrance of the Tabernacle. |

First, the whole furniture of the tabernacle was duly taken in and arranged by Moses. Then the priests were solemnly inducted into their office. The priesthood had been assigned to Aaron and his sons, little worthy of the office though Aaron had shown himself in the matter of the golden calf. But the whole economy was founded on grace and forgiveness, and the fact that Aaron got this honour was a proof how thoroughly, on the intercession of Moses, God had forgiven him his sin. But the occasion was not without trial to Moses. The high priesthood and the priestly office generally were the highest honours of the nation. The high priest would virtually be the head of the community; and apart from his civil rank, his near intercourse with God on the most solemn occasions of the national life would

invest him with a rare spiritual pre-eminence. Why should not this honour have been conferred on Moses, and made hereditary in his family? Moses was a man with ordinary human feelings, and there is nothing men feel more keenly than being passed over in favour of others who have not a hundredth part their claim to an office. But it was not for Moses to make anything of himself, or to question the wisdom and the righteousness of the divine appointment. He enters into all the arrange-
ments for the induction
of the priests with his
usual cordiality; and
there is no exception in
this part of his work
to the great rule which
he constantly followed:
"Thus did Moses; ac-
cording to all that God
commanded him, so did
he."

The services con-
nected with the conse-
cration of the priests
occupied a whole week,
and it was not till the
eighth day that all the
sacrifices were offered,
the rites of purification
fully performed, and the

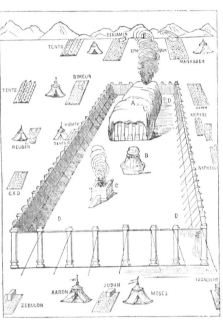

THE TABERNACLE WITH THE COURT AND CAMP.

| A. The Tabernacle. | C. Altar of Burnt Offering. |
| B. The Laver. | D. The Court. |
| E. The Cloud of Glory. | |

priests duly installed in their office. When all was done, Aaron the high priest, stretching his hand over the people, blessed them in the name of the Lord; then Moses and Aaron, the one the extraordinary and the other the ordinary high priest, went into the sanctuary to transact with God, and when they came out, both blessed the people. The very words of benediction are not recorded, but they must have corresponded in meaning to those beautiful words afterwards given by Moses as the permanent form of blessing : " The Lord bless thee, and keep thee ; the Lord make his face shine upon thee, and be gracious to thee ; the Lord lift up his countenance upon thee, and give thee peace " (Num. vi. 24–26). Then the divine glory shone out, and a tongue of fire leaped from the Holy of holies, wrapped itself round the burnt offering and the fat, and sent them in circling wreaths to heaven, in token of divine acceptance. A shout of joy revealed the gladness that filled the susceptible hearts of the people, and the prostrate attitude into which they fell showed that for the moment at least they were disposed to give the homage of boundless reverence to that great Being who had done such wonders among them.

The spectacle, indeed, so solemn and beautiful in itself, with so hearty and happy a people taking part in it, seemed to betoken a second Eden. But there is seldom in this world a paradise without a fall—seldom a scene of holy innocence that is not speedily marred by the footsteps of sin. A very serious offence was committed by Nadab and Abihu, two of the sons of Aaron. This consisted in offering incense on strange fire before the Lord. The appointed rule was that in offering incense fire was to be taken from the brazen altar. Nadab and Abihu seem to have thought that if they got fire anyhow it did not matter where. It seems to have been just a sin of carelessness ; but from some regulations given immediately after (Lev. x. 9), it appears to have been caused by drinking. We may perhaps deem capital punishment a severe retribution for such an offence. But of all persons the priests were bound to set the example of rigorous obedience to the very least of God's requirements. Nadab and Abihu not only neglected this, but, if they were drinking, showed contempt for the holy duties of their office. The men that went nearest into God's presence showed the least concern for his instructions. We must bear in mind, too, the typical character of the economy, and the importance that was thus attached even to the smallest requirements. If the tabernacle shadowed the incarnation, the sacrifices the atoning death of the Son of God, and the incense the acceptance of that atonement by God, any deviation from the appointed ritual was like a dislocation of the great divine propitiation that was to be revealed in the fulness of the times.

It must have been a dread spectacle when the divine flame darted like a serpent's fang into the bodies of Nadab and Abihu, and they fell down dead. Aaron, we have said, had been forgiven his offence in the matter of the golden calf; but it did not follow that no further chastisement would fall on him. The offences of good men are often chastised through their sons, and Nadab and Abihu were now the instruments of a sore chastisement to Aaron. The death of these young men was one of those public and striking expressions of the divine mind that constrain the suppression of one's private feelings. "Aaron held his peace." But all the more would his grief and distress work inwardly. It would be many a day before he would forget, when he went into the sanctuary, the awful scene he had there beheld; it was impossible indeed he could ever forget it altogether, impossible he could ever spend one day all the forty years that elapsed till he climbed the bleak cliffs of Mount Hor to die there without the image of that tragedy flitting across him and casting a tremulous chill on his heart.

And it seemed, on the afternoon of that very day, as if another tragedy of the same kind were about to befall. Another act of carelessness seemed to have been committed by the priests not eating part of the goat offered as a sin-offering. But Aaron had a reason for this. To eat the flesh of the sacrificial animals was a festive act, expressive of joy and peace. How could he and his surviving sons, broken-hearted by the tragedy of the morning, have taken part in an expression of joy?

## CHAPTER IX.

### THE JOURNEY NORTHWARD.

(Num. ix.-xii.)

ANOTHER week elapsed, and the second passover was observed. It must have been a happy time, recalling the great deliverance, and bringing up many an incident, both to Moses and the people, of that night much to be remembered. And as they had advanced into the wilderness after their first passover, so now after their second they prepare to leave it. It must have been with a delightful feeling of relief that on the twentieth day of the second month of the second year they witnessed the cloud ascending from the tabernacle, and proceeded on their journey. The cloud now became an active messenger from God, signifying by its movements by day, as well as its rest by night, that God was among them ; a ceaseless interest was imparted to the journey by its changes, whether in the morning Moses devoutly prayed, " Rise up, Lord, and let thine enemies be scattered," or at night, " Return, O Lord, to the many thousands of Israel." We cannot overestimate the satisfaction of Moses and other devout men as they thought how the outgoings of each morning and evening were thus made to rejoice, any more than we can exaggerate the peace in every age of those whose morning and evening prayers bring a corresponding blessing.

The order of march was very carefully arranged. First, the tribe of Judah, in token of regal pre-eminence, and associated with them the tribes of Issachar and Zebulun. Then the sons of Gershon and Merari, Levites carrying the pieces of the tabernacle. The tribe of Reuben came next, with Simeon and Gad, followed by the sons of Kohath, carrying the sanctuary. The other tribes followed in their appointed order. The first halting-place was three days' distance from Mount Sinai (Num. x. 33); but as the names that occur in Scripture are no longer in use, it is impossible for us to trace their route with certainty. The cloud rested in the wilderness of Paran, which we are told had been the dwelling-place of Ishmael (Gen. xxi. 21).

Before leaving the mount of the Lord, Moses has a brief conference with Hobab, his brother-in-law. We know of his conference a year before with Jethro. It would seem that Jethro had returned home thereafter, but that his son Hobab either remained or came afterwards to visit his friends. Moses gives him an affectionate request to accompany them—first, on the ground of the advantages which he would derive from them, and then of the benefit which they would derive from him. The faith of Moses draws a beautiful picture of their prospects : " We are journeying unto the place of which the Lord said, I will give it you : come thou with us, and we will do thee good : for the Lord hath spoken good concerning Israel." It would appear that friendly though Hobab was, his faith was not strong enough to accept of this glowing picture. Perhaps, however, he declined it because he was not of the chosen people; therefore he must return to his country and his family. Another appeal was made on the ground of the useful service he might render them ; knowing the country so well as he did, he might be to them instead of eyes. And the assurance was given him that in the ultimate settlement he would share with the chosen people. It was a good sign of Hobab's character that an appeal of this sort might reasonably be made to him. Whether or not he yielded to it we do not know, but it is certain that some of his people—" Kenites," as they were called—did go with Israel ; and a very favourable judgment is expressed of the Kenites as contrasted with the Amalekites—"for they showed kindness to the children of Israel when they came out of Egypt " (1 Sam. xv. 6). It was a proof that Moses now cherished an unflinching trust in the promises to Israel that he so earnestly begged Hobab to join them. Hobab could not have done so without present loss and inconvenience; but the end seemed to be near, and Moses believed thoroughly in the recompense of reward.

If Moses had good cause to be hopeful after the fine spirit of loyalty shown in connection with the offerings for the tabernacle, it was not long after the march was begun before his hopes were dashed by too palpable manifestations of the old spirit. "The people complained" (Num. xi. 1); not only showed a complaining temper, but began to quarrel with the whole plan of operations. Growls and grumbles in connection with the inconvenience of the journey through that most desolate region would not have been visited by serious punishment. "Advancing eastward," says a traveller, "we dive by a narrow cleft-like ravine into a dark mountain ridge, winding for six hours among naked rocks and beetling cliffs—one wild scene of stern desolation......Emerging from this long ravine, a broad sandy plain opens to view, and the country for many a long mile is dreary, desolate, featureless, and pathless." A whole host travelling through such a region must have had many hardships. Mothers rising from sick-beds, and with babes of a week old in their bosoms, riding roughly on the back of a camel; aged men and frail old women clambering over the rocky precipices, in momentary terror of a fall; adventurous boys scaling the rocks, and throwing their mothers into a fever of anxiety,—such things were trying to the temper, and no surprise need have been felt if they led to grumbling. But "the fire of the Lord" was not for such offenders; it was for men who, in a careless and perhaps contemptuous spirit, resisted God's appointments, and refused his worship. The name "Taberah" would not have been given to the place had there not been a serious crime to punish and a serious warning to administer to all who trifled with God's law.

Then came another outbreak of discontent, not so serious, but very ugly, and very discomposing to Moses. It began with the mixed multitude, of Egyptian or of mongrel origin, that accompanied the Israelites in their flight. They fell a-lusting. They had all the inconveniences of the wilderness, and none of its counterbalancing benefits. The Israelites would have scorned to be led by this rabble; but there is something in a grumbling spirit and in a lustful spirit that is very infectious and that travels fast. When a fire breaks out in a slum, it communicates itself with wonderful ease to the stately mansion that rises beside it. The people, entering generally into the feelings of the camp-followers, presented an absurd aspect, sighing for the cucumbers and the melons, the leeks and the onions and the garlic of Egypt till the tears rolled down their cheeks. We call it a childish ebullition when it had so poor a cause; but are the schemings and agonizings of men for this bit of worldly good or that, and their cursing and swearing, their howling and raging when they are disappointed, in any degree more reasonable?

The attention of Moses was soon called to the matter, and his anger was kindled greatly ; in fact, his temper seems to have lost its balance. Just because it was a trifle that the people were excited about, it was the more difficult to be calm. In presence of an overwhelming trial, good men compose themselves and restrain every impatient utterance; when it is but a trifling provocation, they are off their guard, and the Philistines fall upon them. When one absolutely fails in an undertaking, one may calmly resign oneself to the disappointment; but when one succeeds so far, and then, before the end, everything is frustrated by the provoking folly of others, it is hard to be composed. The labour of Tantalus is the hardest trial of all. In his heated state of temper, Moses addressed himself to God in the very same complaining spirit which had provoked him in the people. He even charged God foolishly. He reproached God with afflicting him in laying on him all the burden of the people ; he demanded whether he had brought them all into being to make him carry them like babies in his bosom ; he wished to know how he was to answer their demand for flesh, and concluded by begging that if this sort of provocation was to continue, God would put an end to an existence that was too miserable to be endured.

It has been remarked that men of well-defined character do occasionally act in a way that is not like themselves, not according to the general course of their life. This was true of Moses on the present occasion. He was not fair to God. He was not like himself. And this is probably the reason why God did not reprove him. He knew that in a very little while he would be sure to come to himself, and then he would be grieved for what he had said. His language was too vehement to bear his own scrutiny when he should have calmed down to his ordinary temper.

What God did was to promise another supply of quails, but he did not promise his blessing with them. And when they came, the people fell on them so ravenously, and stored them up so copiously all about the camp, that a pestilence was bred. "He gave them their request, but sent leanness to their souls."

And further, seeing that Moses was really overburdened, God bade him appoint seventy of the elders and bring them to the door of the tabernacle, promising to take of the Spirit that was upon him and put it upon them, so that they would help him in teaching God's will to the people, and trying to lead them in his ways. The divine injunction was at once complied with, and at the door of the tabernacle the seventy elders received a visible token of recognition. On being thus invested with the Spirit, "they prophesied"—prophesied, that is, in the sense of making known to the people and pressing upon them the will of God. Two of the seventy had not been at the door of the tabernacle when the Spirit was given, yet they prophesied as well as the rest. The irregularity attracted the attention of Joshua, Moses' aid-de-camp, who seemed disappointed that so many persons should now be sharing in the privileges of his master, and lodged his complaint with Moses accordingly. The incident would seem to be recorded solely for the purpose of giving emphasis to the noble sentiment of Moses, so full of self-repudiation, so emphatic for the good of others— "Would God that all the Lord's people were prophets, and that the Lord would put his Spirit upon them!" Certainly Moses was now himself again—caring nothing for himself, caring everything for the public good.

There seems to have been at this time a very epidemic of complaining. The next complaint came from persons that should have been the very last and slowest to complain—Miriam and Aaron. All that they were they owed to Moses, and yet they were jealous of him, and claimed to have as good a right to speak in God's name as their brother, who was younger than both. Probably the recent distribution of the Spirit among the seventy elders had led them to question Moses' right to his pre-eminent position, and to desire to bring him down. The occasion of their complaint could have been little more than a pretext. It was on account of the Ethiopian woman that Moses had married—not the woman herself, but her nationality : she was an Ethiopian, a Cushite. Some have thought that Moses had recently taken a second wife—possibly in Egypt. But there is no real ground for such a supposition. It is Zipporah that is meant by the Cushite woman. In our English Bible we find three districts whose inhabitants are called Ethiopians—one near the garden of Eden ; another in Arabia, close to the country of the Midianites ; and a third in Africa, to the south of Egypt. The Ethiopians in Arabia might in some degree have intermingled with the Midianites, and Zipporah may have had Ethiopian blood. The fact that Miriam's name is first in the narrative would seem to show that female jealousy was an impelling cause of the complaint. Certainly it was a noble testimony to Moses that they could find no other loose joint in his armour, nothing else on which they could raise a plausible complaint.

But what a strange plot for Miriam to be engaged in ! Who is this Moses she is now trying to lower? Go back, Miriam, over the long stretch of eighty years, and think what you were doing then. You have taken your place on the banks of the Nile, and young though you are, care sits on your fair brow, and your heart beats fast as you see that group approaching from the palace. Why is your eye fascinated to the spot where the reeds are thickest, and why would you rather have died than see cruel hands laid on the infant in that ark of bulrushes? And since that never-to-be-forgotten day has your young charge done anything to make you repent of your care? Has he not been the saviour of your nation, and gained for you and your brother a place in the world's history that would never otherwise have been yours? And there are you plotting to bring discredit upon him, and virtually to depose him from his seat of authority, doing when you are old what you never would have done when you were young—showing in old age a hardness and bitterness of heart that contrasts most painfully with the ingenuousness and tenderness of your early years !

Moses is speedily and completely vindicated, God dealing with the culprits in the door of the tabernacle, and inflicting on Miriam the punishment of leprosy. It was an awful disease—death in life ; for the leper was, as it were, a walking corpse, carrying death in his very vitals. But for Moses to see her a leper was to forgive her all. Not a trace of displeasure lingered in his bosom. No sense of gratified revenge dulled his heart to her awful condition. The cry to God, " Heal her now, O God, I beseech thee," bore up to heaven the very anguish and agony of his heart.

This is one of the incidents that had a speedy as well as happy ending—an end certainly for the disease of Miriam's body, and we may surely hope for the disorder of her heart too. After seven days' separation, according to the law for lepers, she was restored. We may hope that she now detected in her heart a weakness and a wickedness that she had not suspected, and that she tried to make up for her meanness and injustice by increased loyalty and affection to her brother in days to come.

# CHAPTER X.

## THE MISSION OF THE SPIES.

### (Num. xiii., xiv.)

THE Israelites had now traversed the peninsula of Sinai—
"the great and terrible wilderness"—by a north-easterly
route, and had arrived at Kadesh-barnea, on the borders of
Canaan, which is described (Deut. i. 19, 20) as "the mountain," or
elevated plateau, "of the Amorites, which the Lord our God doth
give us." The exact position of Kadesh-barnea is not known,
but our ablest authorities place it a little to the north-west of
Petra, the capital of Edom. If the host had been brave and
courageous, they would have been prepared to advance into the
country as soon as the guiding pillar should go before them. For
this, however, they were not prepared. It was proposed by them,
with the divine approval, to send twelve men into the country, to
examine its condition, and report on the best way of invading it,
and on the cities that should be taken. The twelve men were
accordingly appointed, a man for every tribe; and they took their
departure. Their road would probably lead them first past the
green slopes of Beersheba, and Isaac's wells; thereafter they
might rest under Abraham's oak at Hebron, and visit the cave
of Machpelah; passing the height of Moriah, they would come to
Bethel, so memorable in the history of Abraham and of Jacob;
the vale of Shechem would appear in all the glory of its green
fields and wooded hills, and they might sit down and drink of
Jacob's well; as they passed Dothan they would think of Joseph
moving along in boyish glee, so soon to be the victim of the

jealousy of his brethren ; further north, the glory of Lebanon would burst on them, with its cedar groves and snowy peaks, till they reached the town of Rehob, where they turned and retraced their steps.   On the way home they cut a bunch of grapes in the valley of Eshcol, near Hebron, still the head-quarters of the vine in Palestine, as a sample of the produce of the country, so heavy that it had to be carried on a pole between the shoulders of two of the men.   What has chiefly to be noticed in reference to this journey is that almost every place they came to was like a sermon, recalling God's dealings with their fathers and his promises that their seed should possess the land.   Only by a process of dogged resistance to the lessons that came perpetually before their eyes could they conclude that to invade the country was a hopeless undertaking.

Forty days were spent in this exploration of Palestine ; and the spies returned, reporting that it was a land that flowed with milk and honey—a great contrast to the sterility of the wilderness—but a land that ate up its inhabitants ; moreover, that the inhabitants were a strong people, their cities walled up to heaven ; and last, not least, that the race of giants, the children of Anak, were there.   Caleb, representative of the tribe of Judah, offered a strong resistance to this discouraging report, and was supported by Joshua, the representative of Ephraim ; men of faith, they looked beyond the seen and the carnal, and strove to assure the people of the divine help, and of the certainty of victory in the name of God.   But their representations were in vain.   The effect of the report was that all the congregation lifted up their voice and cried, and the people wept that night.   The "congregation" probably consisted of picked representatives who ought to have been strong in faith, giving glory to God.   Here, then, was the course which the excitement ran.   Ten of the twelve spies, "the cream of the cream," fell under the influence of panic ; the ten gave the panic to the hundreds of the congregation, and the hundreds gave it to the thousands of the people.   And as it passed from the one rank to the other it probably became worse.   Then came the old story—" All the children of Israel murmured against

Moses and against Aaron : and the whole congregation said unto them, Would God that we had died in the land of Egypt! or would God that we had died in this wilderness! And wherefore hath the Lord brought us unto this land, to fall by the sword, that our wives and our children should be a prey? And they said one to another, Let us make a captain, and let us return unto Egypt."

"Worse than ever!" might well have been the exclamation of Moses when he heard these words. All the promises to the fathers had gone for nothing; the plagues of Egypt, the doom of Pharaoh, the passage of the sea, had gone for nothing; the daily manna, the water from the rock, had made no real impression; the lightnings and the thunders and the earthquake and the very voice of God at Sinai had all been forgotten; their repentances, their promises, their enthusiasm over the tabernacle, had all been in vain; the spirit of distrust was rampant in their bosoms; they were denying God and repudiating his covenant; their cry was, Make us a captain, and let us return to Egypt. Often before it seemed as if Moses had drunk the bitterest possible cup of humiliation; but here is something worse than he has ever experienced—"in lowest depths he finds a lower still."

What does he do? "Moses and Aaron fell on their faces before all the congregation of the children of Israel." They are paralyzed, overwhelmed, prostrate before God. While they lie thus, brave Joshua and Caleb attempt the task of converting an excited and furious assembly, and inducing them to repose trust in God and go courageously forward. An appalling shout bursts out "Stone them!" like that which afterwards burst out in reference to Another—"Crucify him!" Possibly the furious proposal would have been carried into execution, had not the glory of God appeared in the tabernacle of the congregation. In God's visible presence sinners are appalled and stand still.

What followed was almost a repetition of the sequel to the golden calf. God is wearied and worn out with this unimpressible people. He is weary of showing signs that are only set at nought. It is no use continuing this hopeless struggle. "I will smite them with the pestilence, and disinherit them, and will make of thee a greater nation and mightier than they."

It is a word that recalls Moses to himself. He repeats the old remonstrance that the Egyptians and the heathen would have such a triumph, and would say such disparaging things about the power of God; and then he recalls the memorial which God had given him in the cleft of the rock in Sinai, and beseeches him to show himself what he then proclaimed—long-suffering and of great mercy, and to crown his other acts of forgiveness by forgiving this sin also. Not a word about the offer to make a great nation of Moses; that is simply and utterly out of the question, and never for a moment to be thought of.

And God, acting as before after the manner of men, suffers himself to be persuaded, and forgives the people. No slur shall be cast on the divine name. Not only Egypt and the nations of Canaan shall respect it, but " as surely as I live, all the earth shall be filled with the glory of the Lord." The people shall remain his people, but they shall be sorely chastised. Unbelieving and insulting to God as they had been, they shall never see the land of promise; their carcasses shall fall in the wilderness— every man of them from twenty years old and upwards shall perish amid its desolation. Only faithful Caleb and Joshua would be exceptions to this doom. As for the rest, they should wander forty years in the wilderness—a year for every day occupied by the spies in their work of exploration. And the ten spies that had brought the discouraging report should die immediately of a plague.

Like the ears in a corn-field when the wind changes, the people were turned right round by these expressions of the divine mind and purpose. And now they were as eager to go up against the people of the land as they had been the day before to return to Egypt. Even Moses could not restrain them. The absence of any signal from the cloud over the tabernacle could not restrain them. The assurance of Moses that they would be defeated and slain by the Amalekites and Canaanites could not restrain them. A message from the Lord forbidding their advance could not restrain them. Up they would go. But the Amalekites came down, and the Canaanites which dwelt in that hill, and discomfited them even unto Hormah. And though they returned and wept before the Lord, it was only to find him inexorable. In sadness, in self-reproach, in great humiliation, they abode in Kadesh many days.

These frequent outbreaks in the Israelites of the spirit of lowest distrust do come on us with surprise, and are almost beyond belief. But we must remember that for generations they had been a nation of slaves, and that for nearly a century the policy of their masters had been to crush the manhood out of them, to destroy all self-reliance and enterprise, and to lay such burdens on them as would utterly cow them, and reduce them to the helplessness of children. And very like children they were. Whatever view was pressed strongly on their attention, they yielded to that for the moment, heart and soul. When the spies pressed their view, the people could think of nothing else, and were in despair. When God appeared and reminded them of all his signs and wonders, that view filled their hearts for the moment, and they were so eager to fight that they could not be restrained. Such a people were not ripe for national life, or for the duty of witnessing for God in the midst of the heathen. They must become more steadfast to their convictions, less like reeds shaken by the wind, more like a rock immovable amid all the play and fury of the waves. A new generation must be brought forward. The generation that came out of Egypt had thus been weighed in the balances and found wanting. Men of firmer texture and robuster faith were needed to take possession of the land.

A question forces itself on our attention : Did God now sustain the same relation to the people as before? It is certain that circumcision was not practised in the wilderness, and it is more than doubtful whether the passover was again observed. It was not till the people took the decisive step of crossing the Jordan that the full measure of their covenant privileges was restored.

## CHAPTER XI.

### THE FORTY YEARS' WANDERING.

#### (NUM. xv.-xx. 13.)

FORTY years in the wilderness suggests the idea of a life so
monotonous, so wearisome, so lifeless, that we can hardly
imagine how it was spent.   As far as Moses was concerned,
his stated employment as leader and judge would demand much
of his time.  He would be eager, too, to instruct the people as
fully as possible in those laws which he had received from heaven
for their guidance.  The books had to be written that have been
of such value to all future ages.  It used to be thought that the
Book of Job was written by Moses, and that it was composed
during the residence in Sinai; but this belief is now generally
abandoned, and the book, though not the history it records, is
usually ascribed to the time of Solomon.  With one other composition ascribed to Moses we are familiar — the 90th Psalm.
We turn to it with renewed interest after surveying this period
of the history.  We can enter into the feelings of the man of
God, pathetically surveying the checkered scene of human life,
and feeling deeply that all its trials and sorrows and mockeries
were but the result of sin, of sins which God could not overlook,
whether open iniquities which he set before him, or secret sins
which he placed in the light of his countenance.  The deepest
thought in his mind was the absolute dependence of man on God.
What a grievous thing it was for man to forget this—to provoke
the only Being that could bless him, to rouse against him the
power of his wrath !  Yet how very graciously was God disposed

to Israel! He had been his dwelling-place, his home, his shelter, and his comfort in all generations. It was sin that made man acquainted with God's wrath; it was sin that shortened and embittered his days. What a blessing if God would return to him, and he would return to God! What a blessing if the period of spiritual desolation were to end, and they were speedily to be satisfied with the divine mercy! What a blessing if a time of gladness were to be vouchsafed in Canaan, which would swallow up the remembrance of these weary years in Sinai, and the long centuries of Egyptian oppression; and if God would grant to the people generally such a view of his glory as he gave to Moses in the cleft of the rock—a transfiguring and satisfying view, which would at once clothe them with God's own beauty, and establish upon them the works of their hands! For Moses knew well that happiness and holiness must go together, and he longed to see his people not merely sitting each under his vine and under his fig-tree, but spiritually blessed, their hearts full of God's love, and their lives bright with his beauty.

Unfortunately, any incidents that are recorded of the forty years are not very creditable. This may be accounted for on the ground that the ordinary and better life of the people flowed so quietly as to call for no record; whereas any serious interruption to this quiet flow that did call for notice was of an unfavourable character. It is only when the waters of a smooth-flowing river come into collision with some large stone or piece of rock that a commotion is caused which attracts attention. Happy, says the proverb, is the nation that has no annals. The forty years had hardly any annals. But some time in the course of them an insurrection occurred of a most serious character, which, both from its nature and its magnitude, must have been a source of great anxiety and distress to Moses.

This was the insurrection of Korah, Dathan, and Abiram. Korah was a member of the tribe of Levi, and was evidently the moving spirit of the rebellion. The ground of his discontent was pride. As a Levite, he had only some of the inferior offices of divine service to perform, while the high honours of the priesthood had been conferred by Moses on his brother Aaron and his family. With this arrangement Korah was mightily displeased. Why should a few men be called to the exclusive honours of the priesthood when the congregation were holy—every one of them? And why should Moses and Aaron take so much on themselves—dictating laws, instituting ordinances, requiring obedience, as if they had a monopoly of God's favour, whereas God was certainly among them all?

The rebellion which Korah thus raised was widespread. The tribe of Levi marched in company with that of Reuben, and several of the ringleaders were Reubenites. Dathan, Abiram, and On are especially mentioned ; but as On's name is dropped after the first mention, it is probable that he withdrew from the rest. Along with them were "two hundred and fifty princes of the assembly, famous in the congregation, men of renown." It would seem also that they were supported by the great mass of the congregation. "Korah gathered all the congregation against them unto the door of the tabernacle of the congregation." To all appearance the case was desperate. Other mutinies had been of the nature of heterogeneous *émeutes ;* this was a well-organized and well-led rebellion. At other times the cause of disturbance had been connected with food, or drink, or some other common interest ; now, as in the case of the golden calf, it bore upon a very vital matter of religion : it had for its object to overthrow the divine regulation which had conferred the priesthood on the house of Aaron alone, and it was thus directed against the authority of God—against the very indications of God's will which had been made by the symbol of his presence over the tabernacle and its services.

Perhaps the rebellion was the more serious that Aaron and his house had not commended themselves very highly in the office which they held. The character of Aaron appears to have been feeble—wanting in firmness and independence, easily influenced by others. At Sinai the people had prevailed on him, contrary to all propriety and decency, to construct the golden calf and set it up for worship. More recently, he had been induced to join Miriam in her unworthy assault on Moses in connection with the nationality of his wife. At the very outset, his two elder sons had been cut off for carelessness, if not immorality, in connection with divine service. It is not easy to uphold an office if the personal character of the occupant affords ground for attack. If Aaron and his family were personally weak, it was easy to place Moses in a bad light for appointing such men to the high office of the priesthood because they were his near relations. And as for Moses, noble and true-hearted though he was, a hero in faith, a lion in courage, a saint in self-denial and in unsparing devotion to the interests of the people, he seems to have wanted the charm of manner that readily wins hearts—the *bonhomie*, the geniality for which David was so remarkable, which "bowed the hearts of the people like one man." With all his excellence, Moses does not seem to have readily made friends. He lived apart, in almost cold isolation, doing his duty to the people right nobly, loving them with a love stronger than death, yet unable to let his feelings flow out freely, or play easily and warmly around them. And so in the hour of trial he finds himself comparatively alone, accompanied, indeed, by the elders (ver. 25), but with the congregation against him.

His course of action was just what it had been in like circumstances before. When Korah gave his challenge, "he fell upon his face"—his usual mode of expressing profound humiliation before God, and of appealing to him for aid. He was so confident that this was a quarrel in which God's honour was concerned, and in which God would openly vindicate his glory, that he dared to invite the rebels to a practical ordeal. Let Korah and all his company take censers next day, and put fire in them and incense, two hundred and fifty of them, and come before the Lord; the Lord would himself make it apparent which of them he chose, and to these the honours of the priesthood should belong. He boldly retorted their own charge, and affirmed that it was they that took too much upon them. As Levites, they had been placed in a position of eminence; but they were not content with that—they must have the priesthood also. When the Reubenite ringleaders,

Dathan and Abiram, were sent for, they contemptuously defied his authority, and refused to appear.

The presence and countenance of God were assured to Moses, and the divine indignation, ready to burst out when the whole congregation were seen gathered against Moses and Aaron, had to be deprecated in one of those acts of intercession into which Moses threw himself so nobly. The desire of Moses now was to sever the general congregation from the active promoters of the rebellion, that they might not be consumed in the divine judgment which he knew was impending. To his great relief, the mass of the congregation rose up and left the rebels. But there was no sign of yielding on the part of Korah and his company; they remained firm in their rebellion, even when the others had left. Moses solemnly foretells the coming judgment; and as soon as he has ceased speaking, a great fissure opens in the earth, in which Korah, Dathan, and Abiram, and all their company are engulfed, the chasm closing on them, and burying them alive in the presence of all the congregation. The two hundred and fifty men that had offered the incense were consumed by fire.

The effect was not what might have been looked for. Thinking, probably, that there would be no further judgment, but smarting under the death of so many princes—the flower of the flock, as probably they regarded them—the congregation brought a charge against Moses and Aaron of having "killed the people of God." Again the divine glory shone out in support of Moses and Aaron; again God threatened to consume the whole congregation, and a plague had actually begun its ravages among them, when Aaron, as instructed by Moses, took a censer and put fire therein from off the altar, and put incense on it—a hasty token of unworthiness, and of entreaty that the judgment might be turned away. The atonement thus symbolized prevailed; but before it was accepted, fourteen thousand seven hundred men had died of the plague. There was no further complaining by the congregation against Moses and Aaron that they had killed the people of the Lord.

But even now the embers of rebellion continued to burn, so

that some step of a calmer nature, free from the terrific excitement produced by the three terrible agents of destruction—earthquake, fire, and pestilence—was needed, to lodge in the minds of the people a clear and indefeasible conviction that it was by divine authority that the priesthood had been committed to Aaron and his family. Twelve representatives of the princes were appointed, who were to bring each a rod, to be laid up in the tabernacle of the testimony before the congregation. Each prince's name was to be written on his rod, and particularly the name of Aaron on his; and a divine notice was given that the rod of the man who had God's sanction as priest would blossom, and thus for ever terminate this contest. The rods were laid up as appointed; and next morning "the rod of Aaron for the house of Levi was budded, and bloomed blossoms, and yielded almonds." This rod was ordered to be kept for a token against the rebels. At last the desired effect was produced : the sense of danger took full possession of the people's hearts, and the dread of death made them cry out, " We perish." But there was little evidence of anything more than mere submission—no token of the filial spirit that mourns its guilt and grieves for having offended a father.

The forty years came at length to a close; and after all their wanderings the people again found themselves at Kadesh, the place from which the spies had gone to search out the land. It was a new generation that now gathered round the tabernacle. Gray hairs and bald heads were rare; the most of them were under fifty or sixty. Men that had seen God's wonders in Egypt were comparatively few,—men who would be listened to with wondering respect when they told their children of the passage of the sea. The links with the olden time were passing rapidly away; even in the family of Moses the grave had begun to claim its due. At Kadesh, Miriam died. The first chapter of her life was the best and brightest, claiming for her a respect and affection which we can hardly continue to cherish to the end. Her timbrel was put to a noble use when first the host set foot on the shores of Sinai, and all the women went out after her with timbrels and with dances. Why she is called "a prophetess" we cannot very clearly discover, unless it be that, being then in close connection and apparently in close sympathy with Moses, she did her best to spread and commend to her sisters the communications which he received from the Lord. Josephus makes her the wife of Hur, and grandmother of Aholiab, the constructer of the tabernacle. It is pleasant to think of her consecrating her musical gift to the service of God, leading her sisters in the song of praise, training the young to sing and play, helping to enliven the solitude of the desert, perhaps at times cheering Moses himself by song and timbrel when he needed refreshment and exhilaration. But the picture has a dark side too. Her railing against Moses on account of his wife was a very serious offence, which it is hard to reconcile with the idea of an otherwise godly character. But in the study of human life and even holy character we so often meet with serious blemishes side by side with remarkable excellence, that we must charitably hope that Miriam's life was on the whole a blessing, and that she found her place with those who by faith " obtained a good report."

It would appear that the stream that flowed from the rock at Rephidim did not follow the Israelites so far as Kadesh. When the people arrived there, there was again a scarcity of water, and, as of old, they gathered themselves against Moses and Aaron, and raised the childish and impious cry, " Would God that we had died when our brethren died before the Lord ! " There was something peculiarly offensive, insulting, to God as well as to Moses, in this reference to the rebellion of Korah. It is not easy to think of any combination of discontent and impiety more glaring than the form of their words expresses—" Would we had died with our brethren *before the Lord !* " Was it to sting Moses as sharply as possible that they thus ran their weapons against him into the quick, into the most susceptible fibres of his heart, declaring that death in that awful tragedy would have been better than the life they were then living? Whatever the intention of the wail, it certainly had the effect of deranging the temper of Moses, and inducing him to commit a serious offence.

It will be observed that God took the complaint of the people calmly, and thus set to Moses an example of forbearance which it might have been expected that he would follow.  Since God simply indicated to Moses the means of supplying the people's wants, might not he, with the same calmness, have proceeded to comply with the divine instructions ?  It is evident that Moses was in a state of hot excitement when he met the people.  " Hear now, ye rebels," he addresses them.  Was this a dignified way for the vice-gerent of God to summon their attention ?  Was it fitted to bring them into a right temper ?  Was it not adapted to irritate them into further resistance ?  " Must we fetch you water out of this rock ? "  Must *we ?*—is it Moses and Aaron that are to do this ? What has become of that beautiful spirit that in the song at the Red Sea did not even name the name of Moses, but gave all the glory to God ?  And why that expression *must ?*  Was not the request for water reasonable in itself, though the manner of pre-ferring it had been atrocious ?  Was not the gift of water involved indeed in God's covenant ?  Was it not what a kind father would be ready to provide of his own accord for his children, without complaining that they were subjecting him to an unreasonable necessity—putting him under the compulsion of a *must ?*  And why does Moses strike the rock, and strike it twice, when the divine command was to speak to it ?  Does he not believe that speaking will be enough ?  Is there not much carnal excitement expressed in this act of striking, repeated as men do repeat a stroke when their temper is ruffled, and they are under the in-fluence not of godly but of carnal feelings ?  It was a serious matter for Moses ; it brought on him God's rebuke, and it shut him out from the honour of leading his people into the land of promise.

This was the chastening of Moses ; and a most painful reproof it was.  For to enter into the land was the one earthly wish he cherished, and cherished with all his heart ; the one vision of delight that had flitted before his fancy all the forty years, and reconciled him to all his hardships and trials.  Hardly, indeed, on his own account would he have thought of a quiet, happy home in the land of promise, with no dark shadow of care falling on it—of a simple life, whose chief joy would be to sit in his tent door in quiet hours, and think of the labours that were now ended, the anxieties that were now for ever quelled. That pleasure he could have easily foregone ; perhaps he would have preferred to die in harness. But parents do long to see their children settled in life, and Moses must have longed for this on behalf of the children of Israel with quite a peculiar intensity of desire. And now it is abruptly intimated to him that of this last solace of his heart he is to be deprived. When he parts with his people, most of them will still be wanderers. He is not to see the crown put on the labour of his life, though he is so near it, after waiting such a time. His bones are not to be laid in the hallowed sepulchre of Machpelah, nor in any spot of the land which it had been the dream of his life for nearly a hundred years to visit, since ever he began to think in Pharaoh's palace of the promises to Israel. It does seem a hard and painful chastisement. Has he not on the whole served God right well? Was there no less crushing chastening that would have served the end?

It is hard to sympathize with God's decision in this case of Moses, till we carry our view forward fifteen hundred years, and call to mind how his desire to set foot in that land was not denied for ever ; how he did long after alight upon its surface, even on the Mount of Transfiguration, on a mission far higher than that of leader of Israel, and to prepare for a redemption infinitely more glorious than that which would have been crowned by the settlement of the tribes in Canaan.

There were two routes by which the Israelites might advance from Kadesh to the land of Israel. One was near, direct, and short ; the other long, roundabout, and dangerous. The former was the way by which the spies had advanced, straight along through Beersheba and Hebron, into the very heart of the country. The other led them across the territories of Edom into those of the Moabites, and thereafter into the Amorite kingdoms of Sihon and Og ; after encountering whom they would still have to cross the Jordan, and deal with the great bulk of the seven nations. One cannot but regard the selection of this second route as a punishment for the offence of which the people had just been guilty at Meribah. Their provocation of God there was very great, very insulting, and could hardly have been let pass finally without some token of displeasure. But this view is not incompatible with the supposition that something was to be gained ultimately by the *détour*. The host would in this way have the advantage of being led a little longer by Moses, and of encountering their foes at first under the influence of his calm courage and unfailing wisdom. The general under whom they had left Egypt, and by whom Pharaoh had been defeated, might well give them courage for their encounter with the Amorites. Joshua, too, might thus be trained for his work, and the people prepared to accept him cordially as the successor of Moses. Further, there was a consideration of a military or engineering kind to which some weight is due. The structure of the country is such that it would have been very difficult to subdue it by an enemy invading it from the south. So many ravines run across it that a defeated foe might simply retire from one ravine to another, getting additions at each new spot, and offering a fresh opposition to the invaders every few miles. By entering the country from the east, Joshua at once cut it in two, and was able in three pitched battles to dispose of all opposition. Moreover, had the Israelites gone straight from Kadesh to Beersheba, they would have had the Philistines on their left flank, and might have been exposed the whole time to attacks from them. The selection of the more difficult route was a chastisement in the first instance, but a blessing in the end.

# CHAPTER XII.

## CONQUEST OF THE EAST OF JORDAN.

### (NUM. xx. 14–xxxii.)

ARRIVED at the confines of Mount Seir or Idumæa, the country of the Edomites or descendants of Esau, Moses sent a most polite and brotherly request to the king for leave to pass through his borders. Referring to their common origin as children of brothers, and appealing to his compassion in connection with their long sufferings in Egypt, he bound himself and his people simply to pass along the highway, not touching the produce of their fields or vineyards, not even using their wells. The highway which they were not to leave was a great caravan route (as we have already seen) from Syria on the north to Egypt, India, and other countries on the south. When the king refused this request with a threat of violence, Moses, thinking he had been misunderstood, made it plainer that water or any other commodity they might require would be duly paid for; but only with the result that the king came out with a great force against him.

Edom being the brother of Israel, and not being included among the doomed nations, Moses was not allowed to oppose force to force, and had no alternative but to conduct his people outside his borders. Notwithstanding the reconciliation of Jacob and Esau, and their last meeting at their father's tomb, the descendants of Esau continued for many centuries to cherish the bitterest hatred to Israel, and their long-continued animosity was crowned at the siege of Jerusalem under Nebuchadnezzar, when their voice was lifted up with insulting cruelty, "Rase it, rase it, even to the foundations thereof." It was an important lesson in self-control that Moses taught his people when he proposed that they should march through Idumæa without touching a single grape, or drinking a cup of water, except for payment; and the circumstance deserves to be borne in mind in connection with the slaughter of the Canaanites, so often represented as one of those horrid massacres which one barbarous nation inflicts on another. We see that Moses trained his people to great self-restraint; and even the

MOUNT HOR.

destruction of the Canaanites was gone about, not with the ferocity of a massacre, but with the calmness of a judicial execution.

Going round the southern border of the territories of Edom, they came to Mount Hor. Hor is a huge, bleak mountain, as desolate as Sinai, without grass or tree or shrub, hewn and riven by frightful chasms. The view from its summit is very bleak. It was here that it was appointed to Aaron to pay the penalty he had incurred by his conduct at Meribah. But there was such a mingling of mercy with judgment in his chastisement that what might have been the death of a criminal was transformed into the translation of a saint. It must have been a touching sight when Aaron, in the holy robes of the high priest, left the tabernacle and the camp, never to return. We seem to see him toiling up the rugged cliffs of Mount Hor, with failing energies, never in this life to revive, leaning on the kindly arm of his brother and of his son, pausing from time to time to recover breath, till at last the top is reached. The holy robes are solemnly stripped off him by Moses, and put on Eleazar, his son, and then death comes silently, and Aaron passes away.

Whatever impression Aaron may have made on us in his life, we are profoundly touched with the circumstances of his death. We are touched with the calm, unresisting spirit of submission in which, Isaac-like, he receives the intimation that he is to die, and ascends the mountain to encounter the last enemy. Without anything of the grandeur of his brother's character, often yielding weakly to temptation, and acting the coward when he should have proved the hero, we cannot but think that the high office which he held must have given him some true and exalted thoughts of God and truth and duty. Could it be that all the solemn mysteries he had celebrated had never given forth one ray of gospel light to him ; that all the blood he had poured out on the altar had failed to present the image of a nobler victim; that from the altar, and the ark, and the unuttered mysteries within the veil, no voice of peace ever came to cheer his own soul? We cling to the belief that he was forgiven and accepted ; and that with all his shortcomings he found the privileges of that holy band with whom he is connected in the psalm : "Moses and Aaron among his priests, and Samuel among them that call upon his name ; they called upon the Lord, and he answered them. He spake unto them in the cloudy pillar : they kept his testimonies, and the ordinance that he gave them" (Ps. xcix. 6, 7).

The Edomites were not the only hostile people in those parts ; the Canaanites, under king Arad, expecting that the Israelites would advance by the way which the spies had taken, came from that quarter and attacked them, at first successfully, taking a number of prisoners. Israel, no doubt under the guidance of Moses, cast themselves on the Lord. It is refreshing to find them for once not grumbling, but laying hold of their great Arm of strength. Most encouraging was the result. Arad was utterly defeated, and his cities destroyed ; and thus the first instalment of punishment was inflicted on the seven nations,—the first-fruits of the great harvest of retribution that was yet to follow.

To get round Edom they had to go back to the edge of the Red Sea, to the angle of the Elanitic or eastern gulf, then advance on the eastern side of Mount Seir, through the Wady el Araba—described as a weary waste, sand-hills upon sand-hills, tufted with broom and other bushes, affording good pasturage, but still a howling wilderness. From the excellent spirit they had shown at Hormah they swung round now to the opposite extreme, speaking bitterly, as of old, against Moses and against the Lord, and charging them, as usual, with bringing them to die in the wilderness. One cannot but be amazed at the disrespectful manner in which they allowed themselves to speak of God : they seem at times to have thought of him as one of themselves, or as one of the gods of the heathen. We are reminded of the charge brought against them in the prophet Amos, as rehearsed by Stephen in his speech to the Sanhedrim, " Yea, ye took up the tabernacle of Moloch, and the star of your god Remphan, figures which ye made to worship them." Their ideas of God were often not higher than those of the heathen ; hence the revolting charges which they hurled against him, and the insulting language in which they spoke.

For a chastisement of this disrespectful and unbelieving outburst, a visitation of fiery serpents was sent, which caused the death of many. Then came humiliation, confession, and the request that Moses would pray for them. Relief came in a singular way. Moses was directed to make a serpent of brass and raise it aloft on a pole, and whoever looked on this serpent was to be cured.

It is not said whether the serpents that bit the people were called " fiery " on account of their red appearance, or, what is more likely, on account of the inflammation and burning pain

inflicted by their bites. Many authors testify to the multitude
of serpents in that part of Arabia. Herodotus, whose account is
mingled with fable, describes them as winged, and some of the old
commentators and painters used to represent them accordingly.
The notion is a simple monstrosity. Herodotus does not say that
he saw any such winged serpents, but he does say that he beheld
the skeletons of an immense number of serpents in heaps of various sizes. One might suppose that the serpent of brass, placed on
the top of the pole, was in some danger of being treated as an idol,
especially by a people whose tendencies were so strong in that
direction. And, indeed, in the days of Hezekiah this proved true,
so that it became necessary to destroy it; it was then called
Nehushtan—a piece of brass. But no encouragement was given
to idolatry; the Israelites were not called to adore it, or to make
any offering to it, but simply to look on it. One should suppose it
must have been plain to the poorest capacity that the serpent was
nothing but a channel through which God was pleased to work,
and some would likewise apprehend this lesson—how God can
turn that which comes first as a means of destruction into a channel of benediction. We cannot say whether any would be able to
apprehend the very blessed spiritual lesson which our Lord indicated in words that have proved a blessing to myriads : "As
Moses lifted up the serpent in the wilderness, so must the Son of
man be lifted up : that whosoever believeth in him should not
perish, but have everlasting life."

Getting round Mount Seir, they reached the land of Moab.
They seem to have met with no obstruction till they came to the
brook Arnon, a border of Sihon, king of the Amorites. In fact
the opposition of the Edomites seems to have been disarmed by the
meek submission of the Israelites to the long journey round Mount
Seir; for in Deuteronomy (i. 28, 29) they, with the Moabites, are
described as having at last virtually given them what they had
asked—that is, they relented a little when they saw the needless
toil and suffering which their stern refusal had caused to the host.

When they reached the Arnon, a message was sent to king
Sihon of similar tenor to that which had been sent to the king of

Edom, and it received a similar answer. The Amorites were among the doomed nations, therefore they were not to be spared. A pitched battle was fought at Jahaz : a great victory was won by the Israelites, and the whole country lying between the Arnon and the Jabbok taken possession of. Advancing northwards, still on the east side of the Jordan, they next encountered Og, king of Bashan, a man of gigantic stature and terrible appearance. He, too, was entirely subdued and his force destroyed. And now there remained no foe to dispute their possession of the whole region that came to be known as Eastern Palestine, extending from the river Arnon on the south to the range of Anti-Lebanon on the north.

The Amorites were a very powerful tribe of the Canaanites, who had become highly renowned in war, and at a former time had dispossessed the earlier inhabitants of those parts, and seized their lands. They had also seized part of the land of the Moabites and Ammonites. They were spared by God for a time, because their iniquity had not become full when the promise of the land was first made to the fathers. When subdued by the Israelites, they were only repaid in their own coin ; nor would they even then have been dispossessed on the east of the river but for the violence with which they met the peaceful request of Israel. Their country was rich and fertile, eminently adapted for pasturing cattle. The territories of Og, king of Bashan, were of the like character. Bashan was remarkable for the number of its fortified cities : the region of Argob alone contained "threescore cities, fenced with high walls, gates, and bars, besides unwalled towns a great many." A recent traveller confirms this statement, having tested lists of more than a hundred ruined cities and villages, and found them correct if not complete. It used to be thought that many of these ruins, presenting massive walls and colossal stone doors of black basalt, were the remains of Og's cities ; but this view has been questioned by more recent travellers.

Many proofs are given of the fertility and beauty of Bashan. On the sides of the range of mountains now called Jebel Haurân, as well as in other places, the oak forests rose for which

Bashan was famous. The region Haurân has been called "the granary of Damascus." Gilead was another part of the dominions of Sihon and Og, each owning a part. We need not wonder that the dormant love of beautiful scenery, waking up to sudden strength after the dreary scenery of the desert in the susceptible bosoms of the Israelites, and the calmer spirit that could appreciate the value of so fertile fields, made some of them desirous to settle in Bashan. Even the aged Moses felt his enthusiasm stirred by the prospect. The rich glow of poetical feeling that beautifies his farewell song and prophecy is at least in perfect keeping with the interesting scenery amidst which it was composed. It was from Bashan that he borrowed his images when he pictured Israel " riding on the high places of the earth," even " the high hill of Bashan ; " " eating the increase of the fields " of the Haurân ; " sucking honey out of the rock, and oil out of the flinty rock "— the black, iron-like basalt of the Lejah ; " butter of kine, and milk of sheep, with fat of lambs, and rams of the breed of Bashan, and goats, with the fat of kidneys of wheat " (Deut. xxxii. 13, 14).*

There was one very sacred spot in this territory to which it is probable that Moses came. The river Jabbok was the northern boundary of Sihon's kingdom, and on its banks was Peniel, where Jacob wrestled with the angel and had his name changed to Israel. It was something to have been at that one memorable spot in the history of the fathers. And was not that blessing which Jacob had sought so earnestly now about to be given in a higher sense ? Jacob had sought that his brother Esau might not hinder him advancing into the country, and had prevailed. God had brought him thus far in spite of all obstruction. Would he not now fulfil his promise more conspicuously and completely ?

After the conquest of Bashan, the host turned southwards, and entered the land of Moab as it extended from the Arnon along the eastern shore of the Dead Sea. A range of mountains east of that sea, called the Mountains of Abarim, is often described by travellers as " the dark wall of Moab," in consequence of the precipitous side which it presents to the west, and the dark colour of

---

* " Manual of Bible History," pp. 150, 151.

the rock. A level tract opposite Jericho bore the name of "The Plains of Moab." When the Israelites arrived here after the conquest of Sihon and Og, the Moabites became alarmed, though without cause, lest they should be dispossessed too. Their king, Balak, entered into an alliance with some Midianite tribes in his neighbourhood; and having observed that the Israelites were greatly helped through divine influences, he sent for a celebrated Chaldæan sorcerer, Balaam, whose curses and blessings were reputed to carry an extraordinary effect, in the hope of overcoming one spiritual force by another.

The record of Balaam's proceedings presents a strange combination of faith and superstition. Believing in one supreme God, he yet thought, or professed to think, that he might be induced, by cabalistic ceremonies and devices, to change his favour for Israel into opposition. The result was that even Balaam found God far too powerful for him : he saw that Israel was hedged about by a protecting power that insured for him a glorious future; and instead of pronouncing on him his intended curse, he could not but break out into beautiful benedictions and prophecies. But what Balaam could not do directly, he had cunning and cleverness enough to accomplish by a foul stratagem. His impelling motive was greed—a foul craving for the rewards offered by the king of Moab. He got many of the Israelites induced to accept invitations to the idolatrous feasts of Moab, and to plunge into the vile sensuality associated with the worship of Baal-peor. For this the Israelites were punished with a plague, while an expedition was afterwards directed against the Midianites, who seem to have been more guilty than the Moabites in ensnaring Israel. Balaam himself was slain in this expedition.

Moses does not appear to have had any personal intercourse with Balaam ; yet the mere contact of the two men was deeply interesting. Both were men of great genius and learning—the one brought up in Egypt, the other in Chaldæa. They were kingly men, men of power and commanding influence, the first men in their respective spheres. Both had a knowledge of the true God, and a profound sense of his greatness ; and both were constrained.

but the one unwillingly, the other willingly, to obey his behests. Both underwent the temptation of the riches and honours of the world; but the one renounced them, the other fell before them. They fought the same battle; the one triumphed gloriously, the other was basely defeated. The one is an example, the other a beacon. The one exemplifies the power of faith, the other the power of lust. Both were profoundly convinced of the happiness of God's people; but the one only admired them from a distance, the other threw in his lot with them. In them we see two men cast in the Creator's noblest mould, starting together in the race of life. The same temptation comes to both : the one seeks the divine help, and rises to the highest level of excellence and usefulness; the other quenches the Spirit, sows to the flesh, and disappears in the vilest pit of shame and degradation.

The tribes of Reuben and Gad and half the tribe of Manasseh were allowed by Moses to settle in the country east of the Jordan. But this was not an unmingled blessing. The deep Jordan valley separated them physically from Western Palestine, where the nation had its headquarters, where the national religious services were established, and where the best and highest influences prevailed. They were more exposed to enemies than the tribes on the west, and, in point of fact, they were reduced to captivity before the rest. The spirit of Lot in some degree dictated their choice—regard to temporal advantages above spiritual blessings; reversing the order of the precept afterwards given by our Lord, which all Scripture and all history attest—" Seek ye first the kingdom of God, and his righteousness; and all these things shall be added unto you."

# CHAPTER XIII.

## THE FAREWELL WORDS OF MOSES.

### (Deut. i.-xxxiii.)

ONCE again, after the memorable defeat of Sihon and Og,
Moses makes a humble appeal for the remission of the
sentence that excluded him from the land of promise (Deut. iii.
23). But he who had so often succeeded when appealing for
others has no success when appealing for himself. There are few
even of the best of men whose ardour would not have been chilled
by such refusal, and who would not have felt disposed to withdraw somewhat from an enterprise which had brought them such
a reproof. It is a fine testimony to the nobility of Moses that,
so far from yielding by one iota to this feeling, his interest in
his people and his efforts to serve them became only the more
intense when he knew conclusively that, owing to his offence at
Meribah, his days were numbered, and he could not enter the
land.

In four different forms he tries to leave on their minds the
impression which would be most salutary for them. First, by a
rehearsal and, as some would say, "improvement" of their history
while under his charge, constituting the chief part of Deuteronomy; second, by an alternative prophecy, portraying the consequences of disobedience on the one hand, and fidelity on the
other; third, by a song adapted to be committed to memory
and sung, like that which was composed at the Red Sea; and
finally, by a blessing foreshadowing the course of each tribe's
history, with suggestions, implied rather than expressed, of the

bearing which would be becoming for them in the circumstances of each tribe. Evidently Moses had a remarkable impression of what his people were capable of becoming. He knew how nations become great, and he saw the extraordinary chances for Israel. A nation that had had such fathers, and such a history, and such divine discipline, and such laws and institutions, and such promises and hopes, was capable of rising to the very summit of national greatness, if only they did not trifle with their position and throw away their unrivalled advantages. With heart and soul, Moses pleaded with them to mark well the true cause of greatness, honour, and usefulness, and never, on any pretext, deviate by a hairbreadth from the blessed career which was thus possible for them.

1. The last gathering of the people to hear his farewell words must have been profoundly affecting. "The host of Israel was far too large to be within reach of his voice; but the elders and princes would probably assemble and listen to him from day to day, each perhaps repeating to his own people what he had heard from the lips of their inspired teacher. With what veneration must they have gazed on him! That was the head that had been laid by the loving hands of Jochebed in the ark of bulrushes in the far-distant days of the persecuting Pharaoh. That was the man who had been called to choose between the attractions of Egypt on the one hand and the claims of God's service on the other, and had so nobly chosen to suffer affliction with the people of God. These were the very eyes that under the shadow of Horeb had looked on the angel in the burning bush. That was the hand that had been stretched out over Egypt, and had overwhelmed it with plagues. That was the face that had shone with the reflection of the divine glory on the mount. That was the much-tried man that had been so often and so unjustly accused, that had borne his many trials so meekly, that had guided his people so faithfully and advised them so wisely, and had refused honours for himself because he loved them so well. And now they were listening for the last time to his voice! Never were a people so favourably

placed for receiving a lasting impression, and no address could have been more suitable." *

What he felt so deeply was, that his people were face to face with privileges of stupendous importance, yet that they were ignorant of their value, and in imminent danger, through sheer carelessness, of losing all the good that lay within their grasp. It was the feeling intensified which presses on all Christian ministers, parents, and teachers, as they think of their youthful charge, so liable, in the frivolity of inexperience, to fling from them the only influences that can secure for them a happy, useful, and honourable life. In his people, foolish and wayward though they had shown themselves in the wilderness, he seemed to see the germ of that remarkable character which has distinguished the Hebrew race for more than three thousand years, and which has been all the more conspicuous since their downfall and dispersion ; because no one could have thought that under the cloud their energies would blossom out so vigorously, not only in commerce, but in literature, in science, in art, in philosophy—in all those departments to which they have contributed so many illustrious men. Every effort of which he was capable he put forth to rouse them to the grandeur of the occasion, and induce them to improve it. It was one of those times when an ordinary man would have felt the insufficiency of any words he could use to express his feelings, and covet the tongue of the impassioned orator, that with a rushing stream of persuasion he might set forth the truth and bear down opposition. Moved by the Holy Ghost, Moses attained a still higher elevation.

At the beginning he recalled to them what they owed to the God of their fathers in their recent history, and to the very impressive way in which he had interposed for them. It was well for him that he could appeal to so many well-known facts, which had only to be placed in their right setting to form an overwhelming argument. The escape from Egypt, the humiliation of Pharaoh, the passage of the sea, the manna, the water, the visible tokens of the divine presence in the wilderness—did they not

* " Manual of Bible History," pp. 156, 157.

bear irresistible testimony to the reality of God's interest in them and to the value of his favour? Although Moses does not pass by the rebellions and other discreditable proceedings of the people, he does not make these prominent in his rehearsal. He does not name the golden calf, nor the rebellion of Korah, nor the graves of lust. He does not wish to depress but to raise their spirits. He gives prominence to the numberless acts of divine grace in the history, and introduces what was unfavourable on their part only to magnify the divine forbearance and goodness. The one thought he is eager to leave with them is the singular graciousness and mighty power of their God. To keep his friendship is the one great interest of the nation. All pains are to be taken to honour his will, to observe his ordinances, to instruct the rising generation in his law, and emphatically to shun idolatry—all participation in heathen services and tampering with heathen rites. Most emphatic stress is laid on their having been chosen by God from among other nations, and brought into covenant with him, not because they were better or greater, but simply because God loved them. And no less stress is laid on the fact of their having been redeemed from the bondage of Egypt. If there be anything fitted to draw the heart of a slave to another, it is that he was redeemed by him from bondage. Moses felt that their having been thus redeemed was a crowning argument to secure their loyalty; just as the apostle Peter, while urging a like loyalty on Christians, presses the corresponding argument: "Forasmuch as ye know that ye were not redeemed with corruptible things, as silver and gold, from your vain conversation received by tradition from your fathers; but with the precious blood of Christ."

While pressing this consideration as of supreme importance, Moses at the same time takes the opportunity to urge a number of precepts bearing more on the concerns of daily life (Deut. xii.–xxv.). What is prominent in these is their humanity. The main object of these laws is to make life more humane, more brotherly, more civilized. It is interesting to mark how much Moses was concerned about this aspect of the character of his people. He did not desire a one-sided development, where, as in so many cases,

there should be a hot zeal for religion without the tempering and
sweetening influence of a genial humanity. How far advanced
Moses was in this view we are only now beginning to see. We
have long been accustomed to mark in some ancient religions a
divorce between religion and morality, which, instead of a blessing, made them a curse; and we readily recognize as one of the
most essential features of true religion that it should be based on
righteousness, and should be in the closest connection with all
the moralities. But the alliance of religion with humanity is
an interest of more recent date. And while philanthropy and
efforts for social amelioration are felt to be so important aims and
adjuncts of true religion; while the charity of 1 Cor. xiii. is recognized as the sweetest flower and the richest fruit of spiritual
Christianity; while the place of courtesy is acknowledged among
the Christian graces; and while the averting of pain and the
conferring of pleasure are looked on as virtues essential to the
spirit of Christ, it is interesting to turn to the words of Moses
in Deuteronomy and find him enjoining regulations on behalf of
the stranger, the widow, and the fatherless; protecting slaves and
debtors from being utterly crushed; denouncing those who cause
the blind to wander from the way; securing the freedom of the
dam when a nest of eggs or young birds is taken; modifying the
harsh usages of war; protecting the trees when a city is under
siege; giving the traveller leave to pluck a few grapes from the
vineyard, or a few ears of corn from the field; enjoining a brotherly
feeling even toward the Edomite; or turning the religious festivals
into seasons of pleasant recreation and social fellowship. We see
what a large view he took of what conduced both to individual
and national well-being: with all his earnestness in pressing a
right condition Godwards, he sees how much life is sweetened and
religion glorified by regard to the humanities and amenities which
are often thought of so little even by devout men.

When he had finished the rehearsal of past mercies, and
pressed his solemn charge to faithfulness, Moses enjoined two
ceremonies on the people, to be gone through as soon as they
crossed the Jordan and got possession of their new inheritance.

Large stones were to be taken and covered with plaster, and on these all the words of the law were to be written very plainly. Then they were to halt for a time at the spot where Abraham had his first encampment, and where Jacob likewise halted after leaving Padan-aram. On either side of the green valley of Shechem rise the mountains of Ebal and Gerizim. The memorial stones were to be set up on Mount Ebal, and an altar built to the Lord. The blessings of obedience and the curses of disobedience were to be read out by the Levites. Half the tribes were to stand on Mount Gerizim to echo the blessings, and half on Mount Ebal to echo the curses. But the tribes that were to echo the blessings were more numerous and far more distinguished than those that were to echo the curses. It seemed to be indicated by this arrangement that on the whole the blessing would preponderate over the curse, much in the same way as in Rom. v. 20 it is said that "where sin abounded, grace did much more abound."

The blessings and the curses were solemnly set forth by Moses. It was not till the days of Joshua that the appointed ceremony was carried into effect. In Joshua, Moses had a successor animated by his own zeal for the law and the covenant, whose exhortations were the echoes of his own, and who was under the same overwhelming sense of the blessedness of God's favour and the awfulness of his curse.

2. The proclamation by Moses of the blessings that would follow obedience and the curses that would follow disobedience to the Lord's covenant was a remarkable document. A special interest belongs to the denunciatory part, because it is the part that in these latter days has been remarkably fulfilled. It may be well said that never did seer or prophet foretell such a career for any people as that which Moses now foreshadowed. Such a combination of calamities as they were to suffer from the elements, from ferocious enemies, from disease, disappointment, and vexation ; such bewilderment and broken-heartedness and madness as were to fall on them under the pressure of their intolerable grievances, had never been foretold of any people. Hundreds of years in advance, the siege of

Jerusalem by the Romans is portrayed as vividly as if the writer had been a witness of the event, while the strange modern history of the Jews—their being scattered among all people from the one end of the earth even to the other ; their finding no rest, but instead a trembling heart and failing of eyes and sorrow of mind ; their saying in the morning, Would God it were evening! and in the evening, Would God it were morning!—all this is portrayed in a way that can find fulfilment in the history of no other people, while it is eminently true of the Jews. Even those who make Deuteronomy hundreds of years later than Moses must admit that never was there a strange prophecy so remarkably fulfilled as this was in the strange history of the Jews.

3. Viewed as a poem, the SONG of Moses is full of charms. Like St. Paul, he combined many opposite qualities : he was a great legislator, a great leader, a great administrator, intensely taken up with the *real*, yet able at suitable times to spread his wings and soar into the region of the ideal, and bring down from it garlands of surpassing beauty. The notion that because Moses had so much of plodding, prosaic work he was incapable of writing such a song, and that therefore its authorship must be ascribed to another, is surely untrue to human nature. Manifoldness of gifts is often the characteristic of our greatest men ; and if it be said that the fire of poetry burns only in youth, and its visions come not to the aged, we have, to refute the assertion, the case of our greatest poets of the age—Longfellow, Browning, Whittier, and Tennyson.

This parting song of Moses was written by God's express command ; but it had a mournful purpose—it was to be a solemn protest rather than a song of triumph, a testimony against Israel, a witness on God's part, taken before earth and heaven, that he had nourished and brought up children, while they had rebelled against him. It is a lay of Paradise Lost. It tells the story of a gracious God, great, holy, and unblamable, and of his readiness to bless Israel beyond all people. It proceeds on the ground that this God could do nothing wrong ; whatever, therefore, Israel came to suffer was due wholly to himself. For, first of all, God chose him; he found him in the wilderness and called him; he trained him there—"as an eagle stirreth up her nest, fluttereth over her young, spreadeth abroad her wings, taketh them, beareth them on her wings; so the Lord did lead him." He settled him in a land flowing with milk and honey, of which already the tract east of Jordan was a sample. "He made him ride on the high places of the earth, that he might eat the increase of the fields; and he made him to suck honey out of the rock, and oil out of the flinty rock; butter of kine, and milk of sheep, with fat of lambs, and rams of the breed of Bashan, and goats, with the fat of kidneys of wheat; and he did drink the pure blood of the grape."

God was the source of all this bliss. It was he that chose, he that called, he that trained, he that brought Israel into his inheritance. His care began in the wilderness; but by his love God could transform the wilderness as really as the sun can transform the dullest scene. There is no magic in nature like the magic of the sunbeam. It can make the grass to sparkle after rain with pearls and diamonds; it can convert the column of smoke into transparent wreaths, pure-looking as the sky toward which they go; it can light up the murky cloud with gold and glory worthy of the gates of heaven. God's presence had in this way made the wilderness glorious. And that divine presence which had blessed the desert was equally needed in the paradise to which the desert led.

But into this paradise the serpent, as usual, is seen crawling and persuading the people that God was not essential to their happiness, and that they would do better to conjoin with his service the worship of other gods. "Jeshurun waxed fat and kicked." Moses is now writing as a prophet. Prosperity has spoiled the Jewish people and made them fancy themselves independent. And God now leaves them to themselves. All kinds of sorrows are multiplied. The sword without and terror within; the teeth of beasts with the poison of serpents; grapes of gall and clusters of bitterness; the poison of dragons and the venom of asps—under such figures the calamities are shadowed forth with which the people are to be so long familiar. But the song does not close without a glimpse of a better time coming. When the worst comes to the worst, when their power is gone and there is none shut up or left, God will renew his dealings with them ; he will bid them say what good they have got of all their vanities, and will anew reveal himself as their Rock and their Defence.

And here we have a glimpse of Paradise Regained. And it is a glimpse that not only reveals Israel as again in the enjoyment of prosperity and blessing, but calls on the nations of the world to share the joy of God's people. For at last the blessed word is fulfilled—"In thee and in thy seed shall all the families of the earth be blessed." When the prodigal son returns, the whole household is called to eat and drink and be merry. The casting away of them was the reconciling of the world, but now the receiving of them is as life from the dead. This last revelation must have been eminently comforting to Moses. The immediate future of his people was anything but pleasing, and it must have cut him to the very quick to think that in spite of everything that had been done for them they would fall away. Yet in the meanwhile others might get the blessing which they refused ; and in the end of the day both Jew and Gentile would rejoice together ; the ransomed of the Lord of all nations and tribes and tongues would return and come to Zion with songs and everlasting joy upon their heads ; they would obtain joy and gladness, and sorrow and sighing would flee away.

4. The closing BLESSING is not so depressed as the song. Partly it is prophetic, but partly it expresses the desires of the prophet's heart. It is constructed on a principle of selection rather than exhaustion. And the selection embraces the more interesting and hopeful features of the character and destiny of the tribes. One tribe is excluded altogether, and of the rest some are dwelt on with a fulness and cordiality indicating that Moses had a special interest in them. For though the blessing was inspired, inspiration did not exclude the thoughts and feelings of the writer's mind, but purified and consecrated them. Doubtless Moses had his preferences, and it is not difficult to see that his own tribe, that of Levi, was very dear to him.

If Levi was to have no share of the soil of Canaan, he was to have a better heritage. " Let thy Thummim and thy Urim," Moses prayed, " be with thy holy one"—that is, with thine anointed high priest, with him who bears on his mitre the inscription, " Holiness to the Lord." The prayer is hardly less significant that the Thummim and the Urim are a mystery to us. We know only that they were instruments through which God revealed his will, so that the prayer is virtually this : Let Levi ever be in fellowship with thee, ever know thy will, see light in thy light, dwell in the secret place of the Most High. The zeal of the tribe for the honour of God, shown at times of general declension, was very refreshing to Moses, whose heart was so often wrung with the fickleness and waywardness of the people. Their office, as representing God, was as high as man could hold— to teach his law to the people ; and as representing man, to offer sacrifice and incense to the Lord. No wonder that Moses looked on this tribe with peculiar affection, or that he most earnestly invoked God's blessing not only on Levi's substance but on the work of his hands, and that he sought for him the high protection of God from his enemies, that his ministry of blessing might never become corrupt, and might never fail from among his people. Judah also engages peculiar attention. It has been remarked as strange that this chapter contains no prediction of Messiah, the Prophet that was to arise like unto Moses. Perhaps the nearest to a Messianic passage is the blessing on Judah. Judah was to be a praying tribe—" Hear, Lord, the voice of Judah." He was to be a useful tribe to others—" Bring him to his people." His work was to be difficult—" Let his hands be sufficient for him ;" and his enemies were to be dangerous and strong—" Be thou an help to him from his enemies." If the song contains nothing more Messianic than this, it is a proof of its early date ; later times were full of more specific Messianic expectations, and some such passage would surely have been found here.

The blessing of Benjamin was manifestly prophetic. It looked forward to the selection of Jerusalem, within that tribe, as the dwelling-place of God. Many a man " beloved of the Lord " would dwell in Benjamin's lot—David and Nathan and Gad; Solomon, Jehoshaphat, Hezekiah; Isaiah, Ezra, Nehemiah—an exceeding great multitude which no man could number. But a higher glory awaited Benjamin—"The Lord shall cover him all the day long, and he shall dwell between his shoulders." Allusion is made to the temple at Jerusalem, which was in Benjamin's lot, and the Shekinah; possibly also to the "Word made flesh," the promised Seed, much of whose life would be connected with Jerusalem.

The blessing of Joseph is the longest of any, and the language is the most poetical and beautiful. A large part of it bears on his temporal prosperity. Yet the very glow of the passage seems to show us how much more rich even temporal prosperity becomes under the dew of the divine blessing. It is easy to understand the figure "the precious fruits brought forth by the sun," if figure it can be called; but what are we to make of "the precious things put forth by the moon"? The vulgar ideas of lunar influence pointed to harm instead of good, so that we seem to have no alternative but to refer the words to the monthly succession of vegetable products; each new moon, as it were, when it is seen in the heavens, bringing with it a new supply of vegetables and fruits and flowers; the new moon never coming alone, but introducing a company of vegetable friends, exceedingly needful and welcome, to the human family—like the tree of life in the apocalyptic vision, "that bare twelve manner of fruits, and yielded her fruit every month: and the leaves of the tree were for the healing of the nations." The most remarkable clause in the blessing of Joseph is that which invokes on him the good will of Him that dwelt in the bush. Moses must have been long accustomed to connect Joseph with that wonder. No doubt he thought of the career of Joseph as a remarkable fulfilment of the emblem, as exemplifying, more than the history of any other of the fathers, preservation amid agencies of destruction. Preserved from a miserable death in the pit, preserved morally in Egypt from the subtle temptations of lust, delivered from the dungeon after long years of confinement, preserved from Egyptian idolatry, preserved in his belief in the promises, preserved in his attachment to his people and in the hope of their possessing the land, of which that coffin among them was a remarkable token,—had he not personally experienced, in a very marvellous manner, what was meant by "the good will of him that dwelt in the bush"? And what better wish could be breathed for his tribe than that they too might enjoy that blessing? so that, come what might, they would be delivered from evil as their father had been, and would know the Lord God as a sun and shield, who would give grace and glory.

The remaining tribes have their appropriate words of benediction. But a closing burst of strength and beauty, at the thought of the singular blessedness of Israel, is reserved to crown the song. Never was such a gratulation addressed to any people. God is presented in his incomparable excellence, in his everlasting duration, and in his unbounded power; and this is the God of Jeshurun! His arms are the everlasting arms, and they are under Israel; he is their refuge and their strength, the shield of their help and the sword of their excellency; no enemy shall stand before them, no blessing shall be wanting to them, heaven and earth shall vie with each other in bringing them God's bounties. More appropriate or more stirring words could not have been spoken.

And these were the last words of Moses to his people.

# CHAPTER XIV.

## THE DEATH OF MOSES.

### (DEUT. xxxiv.)

IT were hard to say whether the birth, the life, or the death of Moses was the most striking. There was something singularly romantic and more than romantic in the first, something singularly grand in the second, and something awfully solemn and mysterious in the last. It would hardly have been fitting had he died a common death; and it would be difficult to conceive any form of departure more appropriate than that, after gazing from Mount Pisgah, and filling and feasting his eyes with the land, north and south and east and west, these eyes should close on all earthly scenes, and, apparently without any struggle, his spirit should pass away.

The great legislator of Israel, the father of the nation in the highest sense, surveying the land from the top of Pisgah, is one of those scenes that take hold of the mind of the painter, and indeed of every one possessed of any measure of imagination.

The name Pisgah seems to have fallen out of use; but the other names, Nebo or Neba, and Zophim, have enabled geographers, with considerable certainty, to identify the spot from which Moses had his view. The land of Moab is an elevated plateau, and the ridge of Nebo runs out from the plateau to the west, presenting a flat top with a ruined cairn. Major Conder, taking his survey on a dull autumn day, did not find the view very striking,* but believed that in the bright air and fresh vegetation

* Conder's " Heth and Moab."

of spring it would have appeared very different to Moses. Neither was he able to see some of the distant places specified in Deuteronomy; not on account of the state of the atmosphere, but because intervening mountain ranges intercepted the view. Either the sight of Moses was supernaturally extended, or a slight change ought to be made in the translation of Deut. xxxiv. 1–3, the word "towards" being substituted for "unto"—"The Lord showed him all the land of Gilead towards Dan, and all Naphtali, and the land of Ephraim, and Manasseh, and all the land of Judah, towards the utmost sea, and the south, and the plain of the valley of Jericho, the city of palm trees, unto Zoar." Whatever drawbacks to his satisfaction there may have been, it must have been eminently gratifying to him to obtain that view. It was all that God had promised to him, but not all that he had promised to Israel. But the God that had kept the one promise would keep the other; and why should Moses not be called to live by faith? Why should he not be required, like his people, to believe in the unseen; to believe that in a little while they would be dwelling happily in Canaan? Full of thrilling memories of the past, and of bright though not uncheckered hopes for the future, we can conceive Moses breathing out his soul in the words of the *Nunc Dimittis*—"Now, Lord, lettest thou thy servant depart in peace: for mine eyes have seen thy salvation."

"God," we are told, "buried Moses in a valley in the land of Moab, over against Beth-peor: but no man knoweth of his sepulchre unto this day." In the New Testament we read that there was a dispute between Michael the archangel and the devil over the body of Moses. Some have thought that God's reason for concealing the place of Moses' burial was lest the Jews should make it a scene of idolatrous worship, and that the devil sought to possess the body that he might tempt them to do so. But the Jews were never disposed to make tombs the seats of idolatrous worship; such a thing was never attempted at Machpelah. Contact with a tomb caused ceremonial uncleanness; and even if they had been disposed to pay divine honours to Moses, they would not have gone to the land of Moab to do so. We must leave the remarkable incident of Michael and the devil among the mysteries that surround the death and burial of Moses. Unlike Aaron when he ascended Mount Hor to die, Moses went up Pisgah alone. No bodily ailment that we know of prevailed over him whose eye was not yet dim, nor his bodily strength abated. No human eye witnessed his death, no human hand closed his eyes. No solemn procession followed his remains to the tomb, like that which had gone up from Egypt to bury Jacob. He died, as he had emphatically lived, with God, and God buried him. All that remained for the children of Israel was to weep for their great leader thirty days in the plains of Moab. He had named his son Gershom; "for he said, I have been a stranger in a strange land." This indeed was the epitome of his life : Egypt gave him birth ; in the desert he spent his life ; Moab gave him a tomb.

Nor did Moses continue to live on in his family. Neither Gershom nor Eliezer is heard of in the history. His descendants sank into obscurity, like the earthly relatives of our Lord. They were not even priests—only Levites. In what corner of the land they had their lot assigned them we are not even told. It would even seem that one of his grandchildren degenerated into idolatry, though this is not apparent from the Authorized Version of the Scriptures. But in the Revised Version we read, with reference to the colony of Danites that settled in Dan, that "Jonathan, the son of Gershom, the son of Moses,* he and his sons were priests to the tribe of the Danites until the day of the captivity of the land" (Judg. xviii. 30). Moses was as unambitious for his family as for himself; when the land was divided, no pre-eminent lots were reserved for them, as for Caleb and Joshua : and he had none of that disguised worldliness that professes to gather for the children what it would be ashamed to hoard for itself. It had been his one ambition to be the servant of the Lord and of the Lord's people. The greatest lesson that he had taught was, that in all respects God was worthy to

---

* In the Authorized Version, and in the margin of the Revised, it is "Jonathan, the son of Gershom, the son of Manasseh." In the Hebrew the difference between Moses and Manasseh is denoted by a single letter, and it is surmised that some copyist made the change out of respect for the memory of Moses.

be trusted. Levi had no inheritance in the land—the Lord was his inheritance; and if his sons were faithful to their Master, the Lord would provide. All that he had to leave them was a great name and a noble example.

The character of Moses unfolds itself so clearly and so fully in his history, that a formal summing up of it is hardly necessary. The faith in the God of Abraham, Isaac, and Jacob by which at the first he threw up his connection with the splendid court of Egypt remained through life his great guiding force. Sometimes it was weak, unable to rise at once to the vast heights to which it was called, and sometimes it was overborne by impetuosity of temper; but these were mere temporary shortcomings, hardly detracting from the magnificent consistency that marked his life. For no man can point to anything in the life of Moses that seriously compromised his profession, or that would have justified a charge of insincerity. He thoroughly believed in the unseen, and this faith was the strongest thing in him. He endured as seeing Him who is invisible. He had respect to the recompense of reward. God's approval was all that he cared for, and the whole tenor of his life witnessed to this fact. As God revealed himself to him more fully than to any before him, he honoured him even beyond the measure of his fathers. No such instance of distrust is recorded against him as against Abraham and Isaac. In the supremest moments of the national history he showed unswerving trust in Jehovah. All through his life God stood before him, glorious in holiness, fearful in praises—a God to be supremely honoured, loved, trusted, and obeyed.

In relation to his people his great characteristic was unselfish devotion to their welfare. Not only as his own countrymen, but as God's people, he lived wholly for them. No burden was too heavy, no work too laborious, no sacrifice too vast, no suffering too acute to be borne for them. For their sake he renounced all the riches of Egypt. In their interest he bore his dreary forty years in the wilderness of Midian. On their account he exposed himself to the perilous conflict with Pharaoh, and to the endless anxieties, worries, and toils of the desert. When they were guilty of fearful sin, he fell before God and threw his whole soul into his intercessions for them. Twice over he repudiated as too fearful to be thought of the proposal of God to cast away Israel and make his family the chosen nation. No man of them could charge him with any injustice—not an ox or an ass belonging to them had he ever coveted. To serve them faithfully, in accordance with the will of God, was the one end of his life. He was "faithful as a servant in all his house,"—setting God ever before them as the one only Lord; bestowing the utmost pains alike on the interests of divine service, of human justice, of social comfort, of individual welfare, and of national prosperity; labouring unweariedly as lawgiver, judge, leader, teacher, warrior, and intercessor; and at the close of his life bringing out those marvellous gifts that might have given him the highest rank as a poet, to clothe their duty and their privilege in robes of beauty that would never fade.

When he is called the "meekest" of men, an English word is used that hardly corresponds to his character as we see it. There was a hasty element in his temper and in his tongue that brought him once or twice into serious trouble. It was his impulsive temper that caused him to slay the Egyptian that was bastinadoing the Hebrew, and obliged him to fly to the desert. In the same spirit he dashed to the ground the two tables of stone when he came down from the mount. Perhaps the same quality was at work when he urged the tribe of Levi to fall with deadly impetuosity upon those who had been guilty in the matter of the golden calf. Certainly it was this impetuosity that made him sin at Meribah, and drew down on him his painful chastisement. What other manifestations of this weakness may have taken place we do not know. It is possible that the possession of so much power had an unfavourable effect on Moses, and that the spirit he showed at Meribah had been gaining on him in the latter part of his life. The unbecoming outbreak on that occasion may have been the climax of what had been growing into a habit; for with all his excellence, Moses was not proof against the subtle influence of supreme power. But his meekness or patience was marvellously shown in his bearing under his own trials. How quietly he seems to have left the court of Pharaoh! How uncomplainingly he fled from Egypt, not even denouncing the babbler that made known what he had done when trying to serve his countrymen! How contented he was all these years of servitude in Midian! The harsh taunt of his wife, with reference to his son, he bore calmly. It was not he that complained that his labours as judge in all matters of dispute were wearing him out. When Miriam drew down on herself the punishment of leprosy, he prayed for her. He kept up no grudge against Aaron for his unworthy participation in that unbecoming business. And as to the people, whose constant grumblings troubled his life, and were often as insulting in form as they were unjust in substance, his spirit to them was ever forbearing, exemplifying a love which many waters could not quench, which floods of provocation could not drown.

If we ask, What were Moses' views of the Messiah, and how far was he under the practical influence of these? it is only indirectly that we find materials to answer. But, beyond doubt, he was an heir of the faith of Abraham, who had desired to see Christ's day, and seeing it, was glad. He knew of Jacob's prophecy of Shiloh, and understood why the peoples would be gathered to him. Very clearly, too, did he foretell how God would raise up to his people, of their brethren, a Prophet like unto him, to whom they were to listen in everything that he should say to them. And we cannot doubt that to the coming Deliverer he looked for all that he personally needed as a sinner before the holy God. But to what extent he apprehended the symbolical meaning even of his own sacrifices and ceremonies, it seems vain for us to inquire. On that whole subject, not with reference to Moses alone, but the whole Old Testament church, a cloud rests which we cannot penetrate. We see how near many came to God, and how closely they walked with him; the precise way in which they came to conscious peace with him, and to the possession of his image, we cannot explain.

Personally, as we have already remarked, Moses does not seem to have drawn people very near to him, or inspired them with warm personal love. Nor was it during his lifetime that he acquired the exalted place which he afterwards held in the estimation of his countrymen. Stephen couples him with other dishonoured prophets, and speaks of him as one whom his countrymen refused at the beginning, and whom they would not obey, but thrust from them, even after the great deliverance. The generation had to die out with whose personal provocations and sins Moses came into collision, before his greatness was recognized. It was only when he came to be viewed by men who had not been implicated in the rebellious and provoking ways in which the fathers had indulged, and which he had been obliged to rebuke sternly, that he gained his proper place. Then it came to be universally acknowledged that "there arose not a prophet since in Israel like unto Moses, whom the Lord knew face to face, in all the signs and the wonders which the Lord sent him to do in the land of Egypt to Pharaoh, and to all his servants, and to all his land, and in all that mighty hand, and in all the great terror which Moses showed in the sight of all Israel."

At first it might be supposed that the case of Moses stood alone, in his being allowed to come so near to the accomplishment of the great purpose of his life, yet not to see it. But such cases have not been uncommon. Huss and Jerome in Bohemia, Wyclif in England, and Hamilton and Wishart in Scotland, were not permitted to see the final fruit of their life-long labours and sacrifices. God often teaches us that he is not dependent on any single man, however great and good; he has many a labourer in reserve whom he may call at the fitting time into his vineyard. Our great lesson is to be content to do as servants the piece of work allotted to us, leaving it to him to realize the consummation in accordance with the rule of his kingdom: "One soweth, and another reapeth."

# INDEX.

AARON goes in search of Moses, 316; meets him at Mount Sinai, 325; with Moses meets elders of Israel, 327; with Hur holds up hands of Moses, 381; with Abihu and Nadab goes up the mount, 396; with Hur left in charge of the people, 397; makes the golden calf, 401; consecrated to high priesthood, 422; his sons condemned to death, 424; with Miriam complains of Moses, 430; rebellion of Korah against, 440; makes atonement thereafter, 442; his rod blossoming, 443; his death on Mount Hor, 450.

Abarim, mountains of, 454.

Abel, biographical fragment concerning, xvi.

Abel-Mizraim, city of Canaan, 281.

Abib and Nisan, first ecclesiastical month, 348.

Abihu, Aaron's son, offence of, 424.

Abimelech, king of Gerar, 139, 184.

Abiram, conspirator with Korah, 439.

Abram, or Abraham, the first detailed biography, xii; his call, 1; his forefathers and occupation, 2; chronology of his life, 3; traditions of, 16, 20; conversion from polytheism, 16; intensity of his convictions, 18, 22; a witness, not a preacher, 20, 21; migration from Ur, 25; at Damascus, 36; first sight of Canaan, 37; Messianic hope, 41; in Egypt, 55; separation from Lot, 68; at Hebron, 71; rescues Lot from Chedorlaomer, 78; meets Melchizedek, 80; has a remarkable vision, 88; God's covenant with him, 91, 110; Hagar and Ishmael, 98; change of name, 111; visit of three angels to, 117; intercession for Sodom, 124; with Abimelech, king of Gerar, 139; commanded to offer up Isaac, 148; death of Sarah, purchase of Machpelah, 157; sends for wife to Isaac, 164; children by Keturah, 175; death, 176; character, 177.

Accadian people, the, 6.

Adam and Eve, biographical fragment on, xiv; their character, xiv; great lesson of their history, xv.

Ahuzzath, officer of king Abimelech, 188.

Akharru (Phœnicians), 46.

Amalekites (in Sinai), 380.

Amorites, the, 44, 453.

Amos, the prophet (idolatry in Sinai), 414.

Amu, ancient inhabitants of Syria, 46.

Angel of the Lord, the, 102.

Angel wrestles with Jacob, 219.

Angels visit Abram, 117; Sodom, 126.

Apepi, king of Egypt, 272.

Apis, sacred bull of Egypt, 299, 399.

Arad, king of the Canaanites, 450.

Archangel, Michael the, 470.

Arnon, river east of Jordan, 452.

Ashtoreth, Canaanite goddess, 47, 75.

Ass, the wild, 104.

Augustine, St., on the existence of God, 21, note; on Abraham's offering of Isaac, 151, note.

Ayin Mousa (in Sinai), 370.

BAAL, Canaanite god, 47.

Baba, Egyptian story of, 254.

Babel, Tower of, 14; topographical details concerning, xxvi; purpose of, xxvii; Chaldæan legends, 14.

Baker, Sir Samuel, quoted, 336.

Balaam, 455.

Balak, king of Moab, 455.

Baptism unto Moses, 359.

Bashan, country of Og, 453.

Beauplan, old traveller, quoted, 342.

Beer-lahai-roi, well of, 106.

Beersheba, well of, 141, 148, 187, 267, 433.

Beetles, plague of, 337.

Benjamin, birth of, 233; sent to Egypt, 258; his blessing by Moses, 466.

Benjamin of Tudela, visit to Machpelah, 159.

Bethel, Abraham at, 51, 64; Jacob at, 205, 232.

Beth-peor, 455, 470.

Bethuel, father of Rebekah, 168.

Bezaleel and the tabernacle, 420.

Biography, prominence of, in Bible, ix; our Lord's allusions to, xi.

Biographical fragments in the pre-Abrahamic narrative, xiii.

Birs Nimrod, or Borsippa, 29.

## 1981-82 TITLES

## TITLES CURRENTLY AVAILABLE